POLITICAL PARTIES AND THE STATE

PRINCETON STUDIES IN AMERICAN POLITICS:
HISTORICAL, INTERNATIONAL, AND
COMPARATIVE PERSPECTIVES

SERIES EDITORS

IRA KATZNELSON, MARTIN SHEFTER, THEDA SKOCPOL

Labor Visions and State Power: The Origins of Business Unionism in the United States
by Victoria C. Hattam

The Lincoln Persuasion: Remaking American Liberalism
by J. David Greenstone

Politics and Industrialization: Early Railroads in the United States and Prussia
by Colleen A. Dunlavy

Political Parties and the State: The American Historical Experience
by Martin Shefter

POLITICAL PARTIES
AND THE STATE

THE AMERICAN HISTORICAL
EXPERIENCE

Martin Shefter

PRINCETON UNIVERSITY PRESS   PRINCETON, NEW JERSEY

Copyright © 1994 by Princeton University Press
Published by Princeton University Press, 41 William Street,
Princeton, New Jersey 08540
In the United Kingdom: Princeton University Press,
Chichester, West Sussex
All Rights Reserved

Library of Congress Cataloging-in-Publication Data
Shefter, Martin, 1943–
Political parties and the state : the American historical
experience / Martin Shefter.
p.   cm. — (Princeton studies in American politics)
Includes index.
ISBN 0-691-03284-X (cl.)
0-691-00044-1 (pbk)
1. Political parties—United States—History.
2. Politics, Practical—United States—History.
3. United States—Politics and government.
I. Title.   II. Series.
JK2261.S45   1994
324.273′09—dc20   93-25806   CIP

This book has been composed in Bitstream Caledonia

Princeton University Press books are printed
on acid-free paper and meet the guidelines for
permanence and durability of the Committee
on Production Guidelines for Book Longevity
of the Council on Library Resources

Printed in the United States of America

1   3   5   7   9   10   8   6   4   2

1   3   5   7   9   10   8   6   4   2
(Pbk.)

Contents

List of Tables and Figures

TABLES

FIGURES

Preface

THIS BOOK analyzes the conditions under which political parties emerge, and the forces that influence the strength and character of party organizations. It focuses upon political parties in the United States, although to clarify the distinctiveness of American parties, the first and second chapters analyze the emergence of political parties in other nations.

Although I am a political scientist, much of the analysis in this book is historical. The explanation for my adopting this approach is both biographical and intellectual.

As a graduate student I worked closely with James Q. Wilson, who with his teacher Edward C. Banfield had just published a major work, *City Politics*. "Banfield and Wilson" became central to my intellectual development, and I undertook to define myself as a scholar in relationship to their ideas.

The core argument in *City Politics* is that the central division in the politics of American cities is between urban political machines and the forces of municipal reform. Political machines tend to prevail in cities whose population is composed predominantly of working-class Catholic ethnic groups (of Irish, Italian, and Polish descent), whereas municipal reform generally prevails in localities dominated by the Anglo-American middle and upper classes. Banfield and Wilson explain this association by arguing that machine politics—the exchange of patronage and individual favors for political support—accords with the "private-regarding" political ethos of immigrants from Catholic Europe, whereas reform politics—with its appeals to collective interests—accords with the "public-regarding" political ethos of Anglo-Americans and members of the middle class who have assimilated their culture.

This analysis is fundamentally sociological in character: to explain the basic nature of a city's politics, Banfield and Wilson looked to the social structure and cultural heritage of the city's population. But in seeking to understand the sources of machine politics, I turned away from sociology and toward history. I undertook to explore the origins of political machines and to "bring the state back in" to the analysis.[1] In their theory of machine politics, Banfield and Wilson focused on understanding the demands of voters—explaining the conditions under which citizens will demand individual favors or patronage in exchange for their votes—but it seemed to me that forces on the "supply side" of the political market were also relevant to determining when such exchanges will take place; that is, party politicians must be able to extract patronage from the state if patronage-based political machines are to emerge. Thus I argue that the relationship between political parties and public bureaucracies is of crucial importance in shaping the behavior of politicians. The relative timing of democratization and bureaucratization has crucially influenced the character of political parties both in Europe and America.

The effort to answer questions posed by the work of my teachers is thus a major explanation for the historical focus of the essays in this volume. This book also reflects the intellectual influence of scholars who are personal friends. I shared an interest in history with a number of friends and colleagues from graduate school and my first academic job: Peter Gourevitch, Robert Jervis, Stephen Krasner, James Kurth, and Peter Lange. The scholarship of Samuel P. Huntington and Barrington Moore bolstered our belief that historical analysis was important in political science. In addition, the scholarship of Theda Skocpol reinforced my conviction that it was necessary to "bring the state back in" to political analysis. This focus is reflected in Chapters 2 and 3 of this book. Another friend and colleague, Ira Katznelson, invited me to prepare a paper on working class formation in late nineteenth-century America for a conference he organized and a book he co-edited.[2] This paper appears as Chapter 4 below. Finally, Chapters 6 and 7 reflect the influence of Benjamin Ginsberg's work on political parties as institutions of political control.[3]

I recently was seriously injured in an accident, and the friends to whom this book is dedicated helped me to regain my footing as a scholar by reading and commenting on my recent writings. Ben Ginsberg, Ira Katznelson, and Theda Skocpol aided me most extensively with this book. I also wish to acknowledge my indebtedness to other good friends who provided support: Amy Bridges, Martha Derthick, Milt Esman, Ken Finegold, Peter Katzenstein, Isaac Kramnick, Ted Lowi, Jenny Mansbridge, Walter Mebane, Gil Merom, Elaine Swift, Sid Tarrow, Richard Valelly, David Vogel, and Jim Wilson. In addition, I would like to thank Walter Dean Burnham and Margaret Weir, who read this manuscript, for their generous comments and valuable suggestions.

Much of this book was initially published elsewhere. I acknowledge permission to republish the following material:

Chapter 2. "Party and Patronage: Germany, England, and Italy." *Politics & Society* 7 (1977): 403–52.

Chapter 3. "Party, Bureaucracy, and Political Change in the United States." *Sage Electoral Studies Yearbook* 4 (1978): 211–66.

Chapter 4. "Trade Unions and Political Machines: The Organization and Disorganization of the American Working Class in the Late Nineteenth Century." In *Working-Class Formation: Nineteenth Century Patterns in Western Europe and the United States*, ed. Ira Katznelson and Aristide Zolberg, 197–276. Princeton, N.J.: Princeton University Press, 1986.

Chapter 5. "Regional Receptivity to Reform: The Legacy of the Progressive Era." *Political Science Quarterly* 98 (Fall 1983): 459–83.

Chapter 6. "Political Incorporation and the Extrusion of the Left: Party Politics and Social Forces in New York City." *Studies in American Political Development* 1 (1986): 50–90.

Chapter 7. "New York City's Fiscal Crisis: The Politics of Inflation and Retrenchment." *The Public Interest* no. 48 (Summer 1977): 98–127 (© 1977 by National Affairs, Inc.); Martin Shefter, *Political Crisis/Fiscal Crisis: The Collapse and Revival of New York City* (New York: Columbia University Press, 1992), xi–xxvi.

POLITICAL PARTIES AND THE STATE

CHAPTER 1

Political Parties and States

THIS BOOK addresses three questions: Under what conditions will strong, disciplined party organizations emerge and dominate politics in a nation or a city? What influences the character of a nation's parties—for example, the extent to which they are programmatic or patronage-oriented? Finally, under what conditions will the political parties that dominate politics in a nation or a city be subject to attack or otherwise decline? Although this book analyzes the rise, character, and decline of political parties in a number of settings, it focuses upon American politics. The chapters below consider urban political machines to exemplify strong party organizations in the United States.

The essays in this volume embody a definite view about how to go about answering the questions they address. This analytical perspective has been labelled the "new institutionalism" by James March and Johan Olsen. Theda Skocpol has called it a "polity-centered" or "state-centered" approach to political analysis.[1]

STATE-CENTERED ANALYSIS

A central premise of the essays in this book is that to explain many significant political phenomena—such as the conditions leading to the emergence of strong political parties—it is less important to chart the views of mass publics than to understand how the strategic behavior of leaders is shaped by and in turn shapes political institutions.

Today, there is some tension between scholars who analyze the strategic choices of politicians and those who study the historical development of political institutions. The essays in this volume seek to overcome this tension.[2] These essays presuppose that it is useful to locate strategic considerations in a macro-historical context. The chapters below seek to understand how a particular political institution—the political party—has been organized and reorganized by leaders pursuing their strategic interests.

A number of the essays in this volume were written in response to the behavioral movement in political science. During the two or three decades following World War II, students of political behavior characteristically dismissed institutions as "merely formal" features of the political system. For example, political sociologists and psychologists observed that the Weimar

Republic's political institutions were formally democratic but, in the absence of broad popular support for democratic institutions in Germany, history's most brutal dictatorship was able to gain power in the 1930s. They argued that a realistic understanding of the rise of Nazism would pay less attention to the "mere" form of Weimar Germany's political institutions than to more fundamental features of the nation's life, such as the prevalence of authoritarian attitudes among Germans.[3]

It certainly is true that political institutions and practices will not be stable if large numbers of citizens regard them as profoundly illegitimate and act on those beliefs. But there are at least three reasons why less attention should be devoted to charting the distribution of mass opinion than to analyzing how institutions affect the interests and behavior of political leaders. First, it cannot be assumed that popular attitudes toward politics are autonomous and that they assume their character apart from the activities of political leaders.[4] To the contrary, it often is the case that members of the public will manifest no opinion on particular political questions until their leaders act. Publics take their cues from leaders and often come to believe that whatever those leaders do is appropriate.

Second, politicians are important actors in their own right.[5] Even in democratic political systems, politicians are not merely the agents or representatives of others. They have interests and views of their own. Not the least of their goals is retaining and expanding their power in the face of efforts by domestic rivals and foreign opponents to contain their influence or to drive them from power. Politicians who occupy distinctive niches in political institutions generally have an incentive to work on behalf of their goals and are in a position to do so effectively. By contrast, as Mancur Olson has argued, the members of large, inchoate groups characteristically do not have an incentive to expend resources in pursuit of collective purposes, even for goals that most group members share.[6]

Third, and finally, political institutions command resources that are often adequate to carry the day.[7] States expend vast sums—for example, the current annual expenditures of the United States federal government are roughly $1.5 trillion—and they can deploy coercive force to accomplish the purposes of their leaders. Although private individuals and groups may influence the policies of the government, few are able to prevail in outright opposition to the state.

THE EMERGENCE OF POLITICAL PARTIES

A state-centered analysis is useful for understanding the conditions under which strong political parties will develop.[8] In analyzing these conditions it is necessary to distinguish between two classes of political parties—"externally mobilized" and "internally mobilized" parties.

Externally mobilized parties are established by leaders who do *not* occupy positions of power in the prevailing regime and who seek to bludgeon their way into the political system by mobilizing and organizing a mass constituency. Many European socialist parties and Third World nationalist parties fall into this category.

Internally mobilized parties are founded by politicians who *do* occupy leadership positions in the prevailing regime and who undertake to mobilize and organize a popular following behind themselves. The leaders of internally mobilized parties undertake such mobilization either because they seek to secure their hold over the government in the face of a challenge by an externally mobilized party or because a major cleavage develops within the nation's governing class and each side seeks to overwhelm its opponents by appealing for popular support. The major political parties in American history and most conservative and centrist parties in Europe were founded in these circumstances.[9]

Externally Mobilized Parties

There are a number of strategies that outsiders can pursue to gain entry into a political system: the wealthy can bribe public officials; soldiers can stage military coups; students and intellectuals can propagandize and agitate; workers and peasants can stage general strikes and jacqueries. The lower classes also can demonstrate to win the right to vote and engage in bloc voting after they succeed in obtaining the suffrage.

The fewer resources any group of outsiders commands, the more it will have to rely on the weight of numbers to achieve its political demands. Hence popular forces depend upon mobilizing and organizing as large a proportion of their potential supporters as possible to make their weight felt. This would explain why the mass parties of Europe were organized "from the Left," as Maurice Duverger observes.[10] Parties that sought to win political or social rights for workers or peasants had to aggregate the resources of large numbers of people and rely upon mass actions—such as general strikes—to achieve their demands.

A second condition influencing the strength of externally mobilized parties is the amount of resistance the party must overcome to win a measure of power. The more determined the incumbent leaders are to exclude outsiders, the fewer the allies inside the regime that the outsiders enjoy, and the more powerful the regime an externally mobilized party confronts, the stronger and more broadly based the party of outsiders must be if it is to succeed in forcing its way into the political system.

The German Social Democratic party of the late nineteenth century is a case in point. The Social Democrats found it necessary to construct a strong party organization because they faced substantial resistance and could count upon the support of few allies in their effort to secure representation for the German working class. The black civil rights movement in the United States in the 1950s and 1960s is a contrasting case. Blacks were excluded from the political system in the southern states much as workers and peasants who failed to meet property requirements were excluded from the *regimes censitaires* of pre–World War I Europe. To dramatize their demands for political rights, black leaders organized civil rights groups, staged demonstrations, and often were compelled to endure violence. Civil rights demonstrations did not seek to impose sanctions directly upon their targets, however. Rather, demonstrations for voting rights and other civil liberties were staged to appeal for the support of the federal government and those northern whites who were potential allies of the movement. Because blacks were able to engage such support, they did not have to rely solely upon their own resources to finance their activities; nor were they compelled to organize a separate political party to gain a voice in Congress and the executive branch of the federal government. But for the very reason that blacks could draw upon the resources and support of powerful allies, the civil rights groups and the splinter parties they did establish proved to be short-lived and rather weak as organizations.[11]

Internally Mobilized Parties

Elites who occupy positions of authority within a regime, like outsiders who are seeking to gain entry into that regime, will construct a strong, broadly based party organization only if it is necessary for them to do so in order to gain, retain, or exercise power. As was indicated earlier, incumbent elites might find it necessary to appeal for popular support to sustain their position if they are challenged by an externally mobilized party or if a deep cleavage develops within the governing class and one side undertakes to mobilize outside supporters in an effort to overwhelm the other. In both these instances, however, incumbents may respond to threats without embarking on an all-out campaign of mass mobilization and organization. In particular, they may seek to smooth over incipient conflicts so as to forestall the emergence of an ever-widening spiral of mobilization and countermobilization, organization and counterorganization. Alternately, incumbent elites may seek to repress their rivals. The best way to understand the conditions that lead incumbent elites to pursue a full-scale strategy of mass-mobilization and party building is to turn this question on its head and ask what would prevent them from relying on one of these alternative courses of action.

In the sections below I will argue that the leaders of both externally mobilized and internally mobilized parties will organize an extensive popular following only if they must overcome substantial opposition to gain or retain power and they lack other means of accomplishing their ends.

MOBILIZATION VERSUS DEMOBILIZATION

Incumbent elites can avoid the necessity of constructing a strong and broadly based party organization either by colluding with their opponents or by repressing them.

Collusion

By coming to terms with their opponents, elites can interrupt the chain of events which, if allowed to proceed, leads internally mobilized parties to bring ever larger numbers of voters into the political arena. That chain proceeds as follows: a sharp cleavage on a question of major importance divides the political class. The losers in this conflict, in an effort to reverse the outcome, undertake to mobilize popular support for their cause, thereby threatening to swamp their opponents at the polls or to make it difficult for them to govern in the face of popular turbulence. To meet this threat politicians on the other side seek to establish a mass base for themselves. In this way, both sides come to construct broadly based party organizations. Under appropriate conditions, however, this process of competitive mobilization and party building can be aborted.

The conditions that provide party leaders with an incentive to collude with one another to contain the process of popular mobilization are similar to those that encourage business firms to restrict price competition and nation-states to restrict military competition: each side recognizes that it cannot destroy the other and fears that unrestrained competition will lead to their mutual destruction, or at least will impose intolerable costs on both.[12] In the case of political parties, total victory is out of the question when each party enjoys a solid base of support within some segment of the electorate. Party leaders will regard the effort to rally additional voters to their side as terribly dangerous if they fear that the entry of new groups into the electorate will lead the existing parties to be swamped by the new voters or if they fear that pursuing such a strategy will lead them to lose control over their own party.

Incumbent politicians are unlikely to enter into a process of competitive mobilization if the deepest line of cleavage in the political system runs along geographic (rather than class or sectoral) lines, and the nation's institutions allocate seats in the legislature to geographically defined constituencies. If each party controls a local bastion—be it a set of cities, provinces, or regions—it has little incentive to maximize the turnout of voters within its domain because it will not thereby increase its representation in the legislature. And if each party sees little hope of winning votes in the opposition's bastion, it will have no incentive to attempt to undercut its rival by invading its enemy's domain.

This state of affairs existed in the United States, roughly speaking, between 1896 and 1932. During this period the South was solidly Democratic, and the Republicans enjoyed firm majorities in many (though not all) northern states. Therefore the Republicans abandoned the effort to win any congressional seats, electoral votes, or control of state governments in the South, and the Democrats made only token efforts to compete in several northern states. For this reason, among others, electoral mobilization in the United States during the early decades of the twentieth century declined quite dramatically from the level it had achieved from 1840 to 1896.[13]

Political leaders will abstain from pursuing a strategy of mobilization and party building not only if the lines of cleavage within the political system fail to encourage such a course of action, but also if they fear that the entry of new voters into the political system will lead to their mutual destruction. It was such a (well-grounded) fear among the political classes of the nations of southern Europe—Italy, Spain, and Portugal—at the turn of the twentieth century that goes a long way to explaining why, despite the existence of nominally democratic institutions, political leaders colluded with one another to restrict the mobilization of new voters into the electoral arena. Consequently, mass-based party organizations failed to emerge in these nations prior to World War I.

The regimes governing the nations of southern Europe in the late nineteenth century were grounded upon coalitions of landowners and industrialists. The policies they pursued were beneficial to these coalition members and provided precious few benefits to anyone else.[14] Regimes pursuing policies that served the interests of such a narrow segment of the population would have found it difficult to survive in the presence of party competition. Moreover, active competition for the votes of the peasantry had the potential of undermining the harsh system of labor control upon which the landowners of these nations depended. Therefore, rather than engaging in a strategy of competitive mobilization and party building, the leaders of southern European parties developed procedures for alternating in power and inducing deputies who nominally belonged to the opposition to vote for the government of the day.[15]

Finally, if incumbent politicians are to contain the process of popular mobilization, they must have some means of maintaining themselves in power short of building a mass-based party organization. Moreover, the participation of groups that are excluded from the regime must in some way be limited or deflected. Again, the political systems of southern Europe at the turn of the twentieth century can be cited as examples. Italy, Spain, and Portugal adopted the institutions of the Napoleonic state. The government of the day was able to use the prefectorial system to "make" elections. The benign side of this system involved funneling patronage through public institutions to local landlords or creditors, who would redistribute it to their clients. On the other side, however, local bosses or *caciques* could with utter impunity rely upon violence to deal with the recalcitrant because the judicial system was entirely under the control of the central government and closed its eyes to such election practices. This system of electoral management was so reliable that Spain's official government gazette was able to report accurately the results of elections before they were actually held![16] These narrowly based regimes could survive, however, only so long as the politically excluded groups did not join in a concerted attack upon them. When the regimes' opponents did join forces, the systems collapsed and order was restored only after authoritarian dictators seized power.

In short, even in nations with nominally democratic institutions, incumbent political leaders can remain in power without building mass-based party organizations if (a) the lines of cleavage within the political class are not of such a character to induce them to embark upon a strategy of mobilization; (b) the leaders of the existing parties have reason to fear that the entry of new groups into the political system will lead to their mutual destruction; (c) politicians are able to rely on institutions other than parties to win elections; and (d) the politically excluded groups are divided or can be intimidated.

Coercion

The most obvious way for an incumbent elite to respond to challenges to its position is, of course, to repress its opponents. The authoritarian dictatorships that emerged in Italy, Spain, and Portugal between the two world wars, for example, relied upon force to maintain themselves in power.

For a number of reasons, however, elites may not be able to use coercion to defeat the opposition or they may find it to be more in their interest to embark upon a strategy of countermobilization than to use repression to deal with their rivals. First, the elites in question may not command a repressive apparatus sufficient to crush their opponents. The military forces these elites control may simply not be strong enough relative to the forces at the disposal of their rivals to enable them to intimidate the opposition. For example, one reason that the Federalist administration of President John Adams did not attempt to use force against the Republican opposition that Jefferson and Madison were organizing—the response Alexander Hamilton, in particular, advocated—was that the United States Army of the 1790s was not more powerful than the militia the Republican stronghold of Virginia could easily raise.[17] Alternately, incumbent elites may find themselves unable to crush their opponents because, were they to attempt to put down the opposition of the day, they could not count upon the loyalty of the repressive apparatus they nominally command.[18]

A second major reason why incumbent elites may pursue a strategy of countermobilization rather than repression in dealing with their opponents is that international considerations may preclude their pursuing the harsher course of action.[19] These considerations go a long way toward explaining why, despite the fragility of democratic traditions in Germany, Italy, and Japan, the conservatives who came to power in these countries in the late 1940s sought to outmobilize, rather than to repress, the major working class parties that contested their rule. The United States, which occupied these nations with its army and later was the military protector and creditor of these regimes, simply would not have tolerated any other policy. Or, to phrase this more precisely, these regimes resorted to only those repressive measures—outlawing the Communist party in Germany and Japan, and undertaking to split the labor movement and to expel the peasants from illegally occupied land in Italy—that the United States and the other Allied powers would tolerate.

The third and perhaps most important reason why incumbent elites may pursue a strategy of countermobilization rather than repression in dealing with their opponents is that they require the cooperation of these opponents to accomplish their own goals, especially to contend with threats from abroad. A nation seeking to mobilize the manpower, money, and industrial production that modern warfare requires cannot risk conscription riots, labor unrest, and tax strikes. These forms of resistance are less likely to occur the more firmly the population is attached to the regime that is calling upon them to make sacrifices. It was for this reason that the final wave of popular enfranchisements occurred in European nations, as they were plunging into World War I, during the war, and in the war's immediate aftermath.[20]

MOBILIZATION, ORGANIZATION, AND PARTY BUILDING

Politicians will have an incentive to embark upon a strategy of mass mobilization, organization, and party building if a serious cleavage opens up within the political class that divides it along functional or sectoral lines, and that leaders cannot readily compromise or smooth over. The challenge of an externally mobilized party that politicizes issues of religion, culture, or social class also can lead incumbent elites to respond with a strategy of countermobilization. The last three decades of the nineteenth century and the first decade of the twentieth century witnessed a burst of competitive party building in Europe because precisely such cleavages were generated by the growth of international trade during that era, which encouraged the extension of state power into new realms of life and into the peripheral regions.[21]

Political leaders will respond to these challenges by pursuing a strategy of mobilization and countermobilization only if they are confident that they will not be displaced and that the political and economic power of the classes with which they are allied will not be completely destroyed in the process. There are a number of circumstances under which such assurances can be provided. Incumbent officials may agree to restrict the authority of elected politicians so that they and their elite allies will not be displaced from key government positions. For example, as noted in Chapter 2, a proposal for civil service reform in Great Britain had been roundly defeated in 1854, but another proposal was passed without arousing any opposition whatever immediately upon the heels of the suffrage extension of 1867. The insulation of the civil service from the influence of party politics assured Britain's traditional governing classes that lower middle class and working-class politicians would not be able to use patronage to build an independent base for themselves, and that the grip of the aristocracy and the upper middle classes upon positions of leadership in the Liberal and Conservative parties, the cabinet, and the higher civil service would not be loosened.[22] Alternately, party leaders may strive to exclude potentially threatening issues from the arena of electoral politics. The very politicians who were responsible for building the world's first mass-based party organizations—the leaders of the Democratic and Whig parties in the United States—attempted in a variety of ways over a twenty-year period to exclude the question of slavery from the national political arena, an issue they correctly perceived would shatter their parties.[23]

Another precondition for incumbent leaders' pursuing a strategy of party building and political mobilization is that no single public or private institution so completely overshadows all others in civil society that politicians are able to maintain themselves in power simply by allying themselves with it. In that event they would have no incentive to undertake the hard work involved in building a structurally autonomous party organization. This is one reason why political struggles took the form of competitive party building more often in nations that industrialized early than in late industrializers or nations at the periphery of the world economy.[24] The economies of late industrializers and peripheral nations are commonly dominated by a few large corporations, banking combines, or the state itself. Where this is so, politicians are likely to be able to withstand challenges by drawing on the material and organizational resources of these corporations. Where this alternative is not available, the only way politicians may be able to link themselves to a popular base and mobilize electoral support is to build an organization for this very purpose—that is, a mass-based party organization.

Finally, incumbent political leaders are likely to respond to challenges to their rule by building strong, broadly based party organizations only if they are not in a position to rely upon intimidation to deal with their opponents. This will be true if a regime requires the active loyalty, rather than merely the sullen acquiescence, of its citizenry in order to accomplish the goals of its rulers. Such was the case in northern Europe in the late nineteenth and early twentieth centuries, where the integrity of international boundaries was far from assured, and where political leaders sought to foster rapid industrialization. Statesmen were prepared to take a "leap in the dark," as Benjamin Disraeli put it—to deal with their opponents by seeking to out-mobilize them, rather than through repression—because this was a more effective means of political stabilization than a strategy of demobilization. The very process of channeling political participation through party organizations and the institutions of representative government contains it and reduces the probability that it will take violent forms and be directed against the regime itself.[25]

CHALLENGES TO PARTY GOVERNMENT

The circumstances of a party's origins can have enduring consequences for the strength of the organization it constructs and the breadth of its popular base. If the leaders of a regime gain or retain power by constructing a broadly based party organization, the party they build is likely to play a major role in the nation's politics thereafter for several reasons. The party organization leaders construct to meet early challenges to their rule will be on hand to meet the problems they subsequently confront in governing the regime they now control. Moreover, to the extent that rulers were able to maintain themselves in power by relying upon a party organization, they will have an incentive to use their authority to further strengthen the party. Finally, the mobilization of the masses into politics permanently changes the perceptions, expectations, and norms of political actors—the very language of politics.

But history does not come to an end when the masses appear on the political stage. The ties binding voters to the party that brought them or their ancestors into the political system can be shattered if that party proves to be incapable of protecting their way of life in the wake of a major depression, a period of hyperinflation, or the social dislocation of wartime mobilization and postwar demobilization. Millenarian expectations arising from religious revivals or foreign revolutions can also lead to changes in mass political behavior.[26]

Elites may also abandon the political parties with which they once had been allied, and come to advocate changes in political arrangements they once had supported or at least tolerated. For example, businessmen who had been allied with a political machine may desert it if in an effort to retain mass support it lives beyond its means and accumulates a large public deficit. Urban machines that behave this way may ultimately be unable to borrow funds to finance their deficits, and national political parties that live beyond their means can generate severe balance-of-payments difficulties, rampant inflation, and serious social turmoil.

As such fiscal and economic crises erupt, the business interests that once had supported the party in question are likely to abandon it, and to insist that a program of retrenchment and "reform" be adopted. Such events encouraged businessmen, higher civil servants, and army officers to support military coups against civilian regimes in Latin America in the 1970s.[27] Similar developments led to the formation of business-dominated reform movements in American cities from the mid-nineteenth to the mid-twentieth century.

Finally, mass-based party organizations may be subject to external challenges they are unable to withstand or to internal strains that seriously undermine their strength. Among these challenges are the emergence of new forms of organization and new media of communication that enable politicians to mobilize popular followings apart from older political structures. The rise of television, the emergence of professional campaign firms, and the development of computer-based mass-mailing operations have enabled candidates for elective office in the United States to appeal to voters apart from, and in opposition to, old-line party organizations.[28] Finally, mass-based party organizations may be seriously weakened from within, so to speak, if they are unable to maintain control over their cadres. This is an especially severe problem for parties that attract cadres by holding out to them the prospect of obtaining positions or promotions in the civil service, for this system can be undermined if the civil servants form labor unions to protect their interests against the politicians who helped them get their jobs in the first place.

Developments that loosen the ties binding voters, elites, and cadres to old parties provide political entrepreneurs with the opportunity to piece together a new governing coalition. Any effort by such entrepreneurs to bring about major political changes, however, is likely to precipitate political struggles. The higher the stakes in such struggles, the more likely it is that each side will pull out the stops and attempt to rally all the allies it can find to support its cause—including allies who exercise control over the means of production, administration, and, in the extreme case, violence. As groups that normally remain on the sidelines are drawn into the struggle, and as conflicts spill outside normal institutional channels, the political situation becomes increasingly unstable and its outcome difficult to predict. Nonetheless, it remains true that the better organized and the more broadly based were the parties constructed by politicians prior to the current challenge, the stouter the defense they will be able to mount on behalf of existing institutional arrangement. This is because a well-organized and broadly based party is less likely than a weaker one to suffer massive defections and to collapse in the face of the various challenges mentioned above. Consequently, the leaders of such a party will be able to retain a base of support for resisting the political forces that rally against them.

In sum, the party organizations that are constructed when a mass electorate is first mobilized into politics are not immune to subsequent challenge or change. Subsequent developments may lead to the emergence of political forces that conclude that their interests can best be served not by working through the existing party system but by attacking that system broadside. Self-styled reformers may seek to restructure or destroy the existing parties or to alter the relationship between the parties and other public institutions.

Parties that mobilized a very broad popular base and constructed a strong organization early in the democratic era are in the best position to withstand such challenges. But there are challenges that even strong parties cannot withstand without suffering defections. The outcome of a full-scale battle may be uncertain and the fight itself may impose costs on both sides. For this reason party leaders have an incentive to come to terms with their opponents. Such deals are arranged by granting influence over a portion of the state apparatus to the forces that challenge the old parties. By this means the structure of party politics may be preserved, while the domain of the party system is diminished. In the United States during the twentieth century, this process has occurred in several guises: reforming the civil service and creating independent agencies not directly subject to the control of elected officials; forging a bipartisan consensus in the realm of foreign policy and vesting control over foreign policy in the hands of officials nominally divorced from party politics; and defending various political claims as rights that are constitutionally guaranteed and judicially protected. It is precisely such processes that have contributed to the decay of political parties and the demobilization of the electorate in the United States.

POLITICAL PARTIES AND THE AMERICAN STATE

The chapters below further discuss the issues addressed in this introduction. Chapter 2 argues that the role patronage plays in party politics is a function of the relative timing of democratization and bureaucratization. Where the creation of a mass electorate preceded the establishment of civil service examinations or other formal procedures to govern recruitment into the bureaucracy, politicians were able to gain access to patronage for party building. The party organizations they constructed acquired a widespread popular base and the political capacity to successfully raid the bureaucracy for patronage, even after formal procedures governing civil service recruitment and promotion were enacted.

On the other hand, where formal civil service recruitment procedures were enacted, and a political constituency committed to their defense emerged, prior to the development of mass-based political parties it was likely that this "constituency for bureaucratic autonomy" would be able to prevent party politicians from raiding the bureaucracy. In such circumstances, politicians were compelled to build mass-based party organizations that did not depend upon patronage. Commanding such organizations, party politicians did not thereafter have an overriding incentive to extract patronage from the bureaucracy.[29]

Chapter 3 discusses how the relationship between political parties and public bureaucracies has changed over time in U.S. national politics. This chapter also analyzes the implications of these changes for the structure of political parties in the United States and the character of the American regime.[30]

Chapters 4 through 7 discuss American urban political machines and the "reform movements" that opposed these party organizations. From the middle of the nineteenth century to the middle of the twentieth, political machines were the characteristic institution of urban politics in the United States. The machines that dominated politics in major American cities— such as the Tammany machine in New York, the Kelly-Cermak and Daley machines in Chicago, the Crump machine in Memphis—were the strongest party organizations in the history of the United States.

How can one account for the emergence of party organizations in American cities in the late nineteenth century that were patronage-oriented and so powerful? Although American political machines had an electoral base among the lower classes, they were not founded by political outsiders. These party organizations were founded prior to the enactment of civil service reforms. Enjoying a measure of support among established political forces, they were able to acquire access to government patronage.

Established elites constructed strong party organizations to shape the governance of rapidly developing cities. As noted in Chapter 4, party leaders in New York and elsewhere learned through experience that local officials would exploit opportunities to grow rich from corruption in growing cities so long as party organizations were weak and undisciplined. Spectacular episodes of corruption, such as New York's Tweed Ring scandals in the 1870s, encouraged local newspapers, clergymen, leaders of the business community, and other forces of respectability to enter the political arena and attempt to "throw the rascals out." To avoid such reform crusades and preserve their alliances with elites, party leaders had an incentive to establish a measure of discipline within urban party organizations. This encouraged

American urban politicians to strengthen patronage-oriented political machines at the same time that their working-class supporters were engaged in the organization of relatively class-conscious trade unions. The emergence of political machines in American cities in the late nineteenth century thus is not explained by the narrow loyalties of the urban electorate.[31]

Party leaders established disciplined organizations so that they would be able to compel national, as well as local, officials elected on the party's ticket to behave in ways that would enable the party to retain elite support. For example, as noted in Chapter 5, Republican and Democratic machine politicians in the Northeast and Midwest in the late nineteenth century were able to win support among bankers, manufacturers, commercial elites, and other elements of the business community by virtue of their parties' stance on the monetary, tariff, and trade policies of the national government.

Businessmen in the West were less likely than their counterparts in the states east of the Mississippi River to support the local organizations of the Republican and Democratic parties, because in this region the issues dividing the national parties were not central concerns of the upper classes. The profitability of firms in the sparsely settled West was more influenced by their access to rail transportation and the railroad rates they had to pay than by the monetary and tariff policies of the federal government. Thus during the Progressive era opponents of the major party organizations were able to acquire more extensive support in the West than in the Northeast. This explains variations in "regional receptivity to reform."[32]

Political parties are mechanisms of political control as well as instruments of popular representation. Through parties, political elites can establish a popular base for themselves and they may be able to overwhelm more radical, and potentially disruptive, political movements. Chapter 6 describes how New York City's major party organizations were able to "extrude" from the city's political system radicals who attempted to speak for several of the city's ethnic and racial groups following the Second World War.[33]

Reform movements are an important feature of American politics. What is noteworthy about these movements is that they sought to eliminate more than patronage from electoral politics. Reformers also undertook to destroy the party organizations that were the major institutions through which the working classes participated in American politics. The ideologies of reform movements in the United States were never explicitly antidemocratic. But attacks upon party government by self-styled "reformers" often reduced the influence that the masses were able to exercise in American politics.

Chapter 7 analyzes one of the most striking recent examples of this—the reorganization of New York City's government and politics following the municipal fiscal crisis of 1975.[34] The 1960s had witnessed a substantial mobilization of popular forces in New York City—especially racial minorities and unionized municipal employees—and a significant increase in the flow of public benefits to these newly mobilized groups. The cost of these benefits exceeded the city's revenues. To finance its expenditures the municipal government found it necessary to borrow increasing sums. By 1975, participants in the municipal credit markets came to fear that New York might be unable to repay the money it was borrowing and the market for the city's paper dried up. This threatened disaster because New York had to be able to borrow to pay its bills.

To prevent the collapse of New York City's government, New York State intervened. The state government removed ultimate control over municipal finances from elected city officials, substantially limiting democratic self-government in New York City. In the 1977 municipal election, Edward Koch ran for mayor as a reformer, denouncing the incumbent mayor and other machine politicians for driving the city to ruin. After taking office, Mayor Koch attacked municipal labor leaders and black political activists ("poverty pimps," he termed them), reversing the political mobilization of the 1960s, or at least sharply limiting its effect. The aftermath of New York's 1975 fiscal crisis illustrates how an attack upon machine politics—municipal political "reform"—can come at the expense of popular political forces. This analysis of the political aftermath of New York's 1975 fiscal crisis—a recent example of the collapse of the politics of popular mobilization and organization—brings the book to a close.

Taken together, the essays in this volume indicate that political parties are not simply devices for transmitting to leaders whatever views happen to prevail in the electorate. Rather, parties are institutions constructed by political elites to mobilize popular followings. This book analyzes the conditions leading elites to engage in mass mobilization and organization, the forces shaping the character of the parties they construct, and the consequences of their pursuing a strategy of party building.

An important consequence of party building is enhancing the stability and authority of the political system. By organizing and expanding political participation, parties extend the popular base of regimes and contribute thereby to political stability. Regimes characterized by extensive popular mobilization and organization generally are more powerful than regimes in which political parties are weak.[35]

For this reason, the decay of political party organizations in the United States over the past several decades is a matter of concern. As Benjamin Ginsberg and I argue in *Politics by Other Means*, American political elites in recent years have developed and increasingly employed weapons of "institutional combat," such as the revelation of wrongdoing by the opposition, and the investigation and prosecution of opposition politicians for their alleged misdeeds.[36] The use of such weapons enables politicians to prevail over their opponents without winning the loyalty of a larger number of voters. American politicians thus no longer have as powerful an incentive as formerly to engage in popular mobilization. The recent decay of political parties in the United States, along with the development of weapons of political struggle that neither require nor encourage popular political mobilization, helps to explain the declining authority of the contemporary American state.

Part I

PARTY AND PATRONAGE
IN EUROPE AND AMERICA

CHAPTER 2

Patronage and Its Opponents:
A Theory and Some European Cases

POLITICAL PARTIES AND PATRONAGE: A THEORY

A political party may employ one of two basic strategies in its efforts to attract voters, contributors, and activists to support its candidates. It may distribute divisible benefits—patronage of various sorts—to the individuals who support the party. Alternatively, it may distribute collective benefits or appeal to a collective interest in an effort to elicit contributions of money, labor, or votes from its supporters.[1]

Under what conditions are parties likely to pursue one or the other of these strategies? Over the past twenty or thirty years a number of social scientists have addressed themselves to this question, and though they have proposed many different answers to it, something of a scholarly consensus has emerged with respect to where the answer is to be found. The theories of political patronage enjoying the greatest currency today are fundamentally sociological in approach. They seek to account for variations among nations in the role patronage plays in political parties by searching for variations in social structure or political culture that can be correlated with differences in party behavior. And they all tend to explain any correlations they find in a similar way—by arguing that voters who have the social characteristic in question are especially likely to demand patronage in exchange for their votes. Thus scholars in recent years have variously argued that machine politics will prevail where the bulk of the electorate is in a transitional stage of social modernization, in societies that have cognatic kinship structures, among groups that have a private-regarding or individualist political ethos, in cities whose electorate is ethnically heterogeneous, among social classes whose orientations are more parochial than cosmopolitan, and so forth.[2]

These theories of patronage are deficient in a number of respects. In the first place, they are overly narrow in focus: they fail to recognize that the issue of patronage has a bearing upon the interests of groups besides ordinary voters and party politicians, and that these groups may be in a position to influence, or place constraints upon, the strategies parties adopt. In particular, the question whether political parties will be able to raid the bureaucracy in search of patronage raises several of the same issues that were

involved in the struggles that occurred in many nations during the predemocratic era over the creation of a modern bureaucracy and a "reformed" civil
service—conflicts that often took place before mass electorates and party
politicians appeared on the scene. Furthermore, sociological theories of patronage are deficient to the extent that they are ahistorical. They generally
fail to recognize that the interests various groups acquire and the alliances
they form during conflicts over patronage in the predemocratic era can per-
sist into the era of mass suffrage, and that the outcome of these earlier struggles can have enduring consequences for the strength of the contending
forces in later struggles over party patronage. These consequences can endure, moreover, in the face of social changes of the sort—modernization,
industrialization, assimilation, acculturation—that according to sociological
theories of patronage lead to the rise or decline of patronage politics.

In this chapter I seek to construct a theory of patronage that avoids these
shortcomings. I begin this task in the section below by presenting some
evidence that casts doubt upon the explanatory power of sociological theories of patronage. I then discuss some important conditions that influence
whether political parties are likely to rely upon a patronage strategy—
conditions that do not receive sufficient attention among current theories—
and propose an alternative theory that takes these forces into account. The
middle sections provide evidence for this theory by showing how it is able
to account for the role patronage plays in the party politics of Germany,
Great Britain, and Italy—nations that illustrate three of the major historical
alternatives specified by the theory I propose. The concluding section indicates how the theory outlined here can be reconciled with two cases, France
and the United States, that on their face appear to contradict it.

The Neoclassical Theory of Patronage

It is possible to discern some common themes within the recent scholarly
literature on patronage, themes that distinguish these writings from those of
an earlier generation of scholars and that warrant one's speaking of a new
scholarly consensus with regard to how patronage and machine politics are
to be understood. In the first place, these writings rely upon a common
model of party behavior, one rather similar to the model of the firm in neoclassical economic theory. Political parties in open electoral systems, it is
argued, are unable to use coercion to remain in power; rather they must
respond to the demands of voters in order to win popular support, just as—
or so the argument goes—business firms operating in free markets are compelled to respond to the tastes and preferences of consumers if they are to
sell their products and reap a profit. In the second place, as noted above,
these writings all assume that the demands and preferences of voters are

TABLE 2.1
Party Character and Social Base

Party Inducements	Social Base	
	Migrants, Uprooted Peasants	*Middle Class, Industrial Working Class*
Individual (patronage)	Philippines: Nacionalistas Ghana: Convention People's Party Chicago, Philadelphia: Democratic Machine Indiana, Ohio: Democratic Party	France: Radical Party New York, Pennsylvania: Republican Party Nassau County: Republican Machine Italy: Christian Democrats
Collective (public policies, ideology)	Bologna: Communist Party Republican Spain: Socialist Party, Anarchosyndicalists Michigan, Wisconsin: Democratic Party	United States: Progressives Britain: Labour, Conservatives Germany: Social Democrats, Christian Democrats

determined by their social background and cultural heritage. And though their explanations as to why this is so differ widely, they generally agree that immigrants, displaced peasants, and the poor are especially likely to demand patronage in exchange for their votes, and that voters who belong to the middle class and to the industrial working class are more likely to respond favorably to parties that offer collective or programmatic benefits. From these common premises a common conclusion follows: political parties are most likely to be patronage oriented when they rely upon the support of voters of the former type, and they are most likely to stage collective or ideological appeals when they rely upon the support of voters of the latter type. This argument, implicit in the writings of James C. Scott, Edward Banfield and James Q. Wilson, Leon Epstein, and numerous other political scientists, can be termed the neoclassical theory of political patronage.[3]

Table 2.1 enables us to subject this theory to a rough test by classifying parties according to the two attributes suggested by the neoclassical theory: whether they distribute individual or collective benefits to their supporters and whether they rely upon the votes of urban migrants and uprooted peasants, on one hand, or the middle class and industrial working class, on the other. The political parties listed in this table are cited merely as examples, but they do suggest that with little difficulty one can locate cases that are not consistent with the neoclassical theory, namely those grouped in the lower left and in the upper right.

Consider first the parties listed in the lower left: each of these is an ideological or issue-oriented party or relies heavily upon solidaristic appeals, yet each of these parties has a social base rather similar to that of the patronage-oriented parties listed in the upper left. During the decades following World War II in Bologna, for example, the Communist party (PCI) relied heavily upon votes of recent migrants from the surrounding countryside, and since it controlled the local government, it was in a position to raid the public treasury in a quest for patronage. Nonetheless the PCI did not degenerate into a patronage machine, and the city of Bologna was administered with less corruption and petty favoritism than comparable Italian cities that were governed by the Christian Democrats.[4] More generally, as both Michael Paul Rogin and Sidney Tarrow have noted, in the industrializing cities of Europe in the late nineteenth century, socialist parties had a popular base quite similar to that of the political machines governing the industrializing cities of the United States at the same time: uprooted peasants who migrated to the cities of Europe—to Rome and Berlin—were mobilized by parties that preached revolution and class solidarity, while their cousins who migrated to the cities of the United States—to Chicago and Philadelphia—were mobilized by conservative patronage machines.[5] Similarly, in rural Europe earlier in this century one could find political parties that mobilized peasants *against* traditional patron-client structures, as well as parties that dealt with peasants *through* such structures: Republican Spain provides examples of each.[6] Finally, to cite some examples from recent American politics, as David Mayhew observes, the states of the lower Midwest (e.g., Illinois, Ohio) were governed by patronage-oriented "traditional party organizations," while parties in the upper Midwest (e.g., Michigan, Wisconsin) relied on "purposive incentives," although both relied upon the support of working-class voters of immigrant stock.[7]

In a similar vein, it is possible to cite many examples of patronage-oriented parties that rely heavily upon the support of the middle classes, parties that would be located at the upper right of the table. A clear-cut case is the French Radical party of the Third and Fourth Republics—the classic middle-class party of small town notable and Parisian *ministrables*.[8] Political parties in the United States from their beginnings have fallen into this same mold. The spoils system of the Jacksonian Democrats was perfected before poverty-stricken peasants from Ireland and from southern and eastern Europe became a major element in the American population, when the United States was still predominantly a country of relatively prosperous Protestant gentry and yeomanry. Patronage continues to this day to play an important role in the party politics of most states of the Northeast and lower Midwest, including those parties (e.g., the Republican parties in Pennsylvania, Ohio, and New York) that draw much of their support from the middle classes. (Indeed, throughout most of this century one of the strongest county party organizations in New York State has been the Republican machine of heavily middle class Nassau County.)[9] Finally, one might cite the case of the Christian Democratic party in contemporary Italy, whose orientations toward patronage are attributed by Luigi Graziano and Alessandro Pizzorno to its efforts to win support within the middle classes.[10]

Taken together these examples suggest that the behavior of political parties is not strictly determined by the composition of their popular base: parties have managed to win the support of migrants and peasants in transitional societies both by working through "vertical" patron-client networks and by organizing them into "horizontal" associations; parties have been able to mobilize the middle and working classes in more modern social settings both by distributing patronage to individual members of those classes and by appealing to broader class and occupational loyalties among them.

Constructing an Alternative Explanation

If the neoclassical theory is not fully satisfactory, how can a superior theory be constructed? In order to begin this task it is useful to return to the model of the political party with which we began, a model that conceives of political parties seeking votes in open electoral systems as analogous to business firms seeking customers in a free market. This analogy is a helpful one, but in arguing that a political party will be compelled to respond to the preferences of potential supporters if it is to receive their votes, the political scientists cited above introduce a questionable assumption. They assume that the political preferences of voters exist prior to, and apart from, the alternatives that are presented to them in the electoral arena. This assumption is the political equivalent of the notion of the autonomy of preferences (or exogenous preferences) in neoclassical economic theory—a notion that has been subject to telling criticism by economists, and that, as the examples cited above suggest, is equally dubious in the political realm.[11] Evidently the political behavior of voters in both "transitional" and "modern" settings is far more variable and malleable than neoclassical theorists assume. Political parties have found it possible to elicit support from voters in each of these settings by staging both individualistic and collective appeals.

If the strategies parties adopt are not totally constrained by the characteristics of the voters whose support they seek, one must turn elsewhere to account for their behavior. Again, the analogy to the business firm is helpful. To the extent that the behavior of a firm is not determined by the (autonomous) preferences of its customers, the chief executive of that firm, in deciding which products to produce and which marketing strategies to pursue, can respond to other considerations.[12] The classic example, of course, is the commitment of the Big Three automotive companies during the decades following World War II to the set of policies—the manufacture of large cars, the proliferation of models, annual restyling—that so outraged their critics and that eventually made them vulnerable to foreign competition. In order to explain the behavior of General Motors, Ford, and Chrysler, one must take into account three factors. First, there are the tastes and preferences of consumers: the American public was indeed prepared to buy such automobiles. But the production and marketing decisions of the auto manufacturers cannot be attributed solely to consumer demand. The automobile companies, after all, advertised extensively to cultivate and to reinforce this demand, and once foreign manufacturers began selling smaller and less stylish cars in the United States it was evident that a market existed for such automobiles, one that the Big Three were rather slow to cultivate. Second, at any moment it was simply more feasible for the American auto manufacturers to supply the market with large cars than small ones. The resources available to them—their physical plant, their technologies, the skills of their employees, and their very organizational structure—all were geared to the production and marketing of large, stylish automobiles. Third, and most important of all, the production of large, stylish automobiles best enabled the top automotive executives to deal with their several "constituencies"— constituencies other than their customers, namely, their managers, creditors, shareholders, labor unions, subsidiaries, suppliers, and potential (American) competitors—in that the strategy they pursued enabled gross revenues, profits, wages, and entry costs to be maintained at a high level.[13]

By the same token, at any moment there are three considerations that enter into the decisions party leaders make concerning whether to adopt or eschew a patronage strategy. First, there are the orientations and preferences of the voters to whom the party is appealing for support. Second, there are the resources available to the party. Third, there are the interests of the activists who staff the party apparatus and of the elites (if any) with whom the party is allied or who are capable of levying sanctions against it. If a party is to rely upon a patronage appeal, for example, the voters whose support it is seeking must value the particularistic benefits it distributes; the party must enjoy access to a pool of resources from which such benefits can be generated; and the party leadership must calculate that, considering the reactions of elites as well as voters, the gains to be realized exceed the losses the party might incur, including the opportunities it forgoes, if it uses these resources in this way.

VOTER DEMANDS

Now, as I already have suggested, the first of these factors—the orientations of the voters to whom the party is appealing for support—cannot be considered apart from, and prior to, the techniques parties actually have employed to win support among the voters in question. Except under one unusual set of circumstances, which need not be discussed at any length here,[14] the social composition of the electorate does not uniquely determine party behavior. Rather, as I shall argue below, the way the members of a social group will react to electoral appeals of various sorts is a function of how that group initially was mobilized into the electorate. Thus the analysis here must begin by considering the factors, apart from voter preferences, that influence the strategic choices parties make.

THE SUPPLY OF PATRONAGE

The next of the above-mentioned factors cannot be laid aside quite so quickly. Clearly, a party must enjoy access to a pool of resources out of which patronage can be generated if it is to distribute patronage to its supporters. Now at first glance it would appear that there are two conditions under which a party will *not* enjoy such access: (1) if the leaders of the party themselves neither occupy public office nor are allied with elites who control some source of patronage; or (2) if governmental agencies are protected by civil service statutes and other general laws that specify how public benefits and burdens are to be distributed and that thereby prevent politicians from intervening in the administrative process on a case-by-case basis. The first of these conditions is, indeed, sufficient to explain why parties founded by outsiders—by leaders who do not occupy positions within the preexisting regime—are compelled to rely upon ideological and solidary incentives *before* coming to power; it can explain why, for example, the major working-class parties of Europe relied upon inducements of this character in their early years. This condition itself, however, cannot explain why parties such as Labour in Great Britain, the Social Democrats (SPD) in Germany, or the Communists in Italy continued to eschew patronage appeals *after* they came to power, after they obtained access to the resources of the state. I will argue shortly that the circumstances of a party's origins—whether or not it enjoyed access to patronage at the time it first undertook to mobilize a popular base—can crucially influence the party's subsequent behavior, but in order to construct such an argument it is necessary to proceed further down our list of explanations.

The second condition under which it would appear that parties will not enjoy access to patronage—if governmental agencies are protected by civil service laws—is suggested by Leon Epstein in *Political Parties in Western Democracies*.[15] Epstein argues that patronage plays a lesser role in the party politics of European nations than it does in the United States because political parties emerged in Europe after the adoption of civil service laws, while they emerged in the United States prior to the enactment of such laws. For this reason, Epstein suggests, politicians in Europe did not enjoy access to patronage during the era of party building, whereas their counterparts in the United States did enjoy such access and acquired a stake in the patronage system, a stake they were willing to defend by fighting rearguard actions after civil service laws were adopted. I shall argue below that the relative timing of these two events may be of crucial importance, but in order to see that Epstein's formulation is not entirely satisfactory, one need only note that many of the most prominent patronage-oriented parties in the world today were founded or acquired mass constituencies after the adoption of civil service laws. One thinks, for example, of the Christian Democrats in postwar Italy, the Cermak-Kelly machine in Chicago, and, if one's universe of cases is broadened, the machine parties that emerged in newly independent Third World nations in the 1950s and early 1960s.

The mere enactment of a civil service statute is not sufficient to stanch the flow of patronage because such laws are not self-enforcing. Rather, if a civil service system (or any administrative arrangement providing for the allocation of public benefits and burdens according to general rules) is to resist the depredations of patronage-seeking politicians, the administrators or public officials who would defend it must be backed by a constituency that has a stake in the system and that is sufficiently powerful to prevail over competing forces. Only if it fears arousing the opposition of such a constituency will a governing party be constrained to forgo the immediate gains it would realize by directing bureaucrats to reward the party's friends and to punish its enemies. The groups that oppose the patronage system, that insist that public benefits and burdens be allocated according to a set of general, universalistic rules and procedures, and that seek to defend the autonomy of the bureaucracy from politicians who seek to intervene before it on a case-by-case basis, might be termed a "constituency for universalism" or a "constituency for bureaucratic autonomy."

Who comprises such a constituency? Its members wish, of course, to overcome what they regard as the evils of patronage politics, and patronage politics, as Carl Landé notes, undermines the regulatory and extractive capacities of the state.[16] Constituencies for bureaucratic autonomy characteristically are organized by leaders who wish to strengthen the state in these respects. But these leaders generally must enter into coalitions with other forces if they are to have any chance of overcoming those who benefit from the patronage system. At the same time, general rules allocating public benefits and burdens are by definition neutral between individuals, but they need not be neutral between social groups. Leaders of a constituency for bureaucratic autonomy thus can broaden their basis of support by entering into a coalition with groups that seek through general rules to obtain privileged access to public offices and benefits.

ELITES AND CADRES

The concept of a constituency for bureaucratic autonomy leads us to the third consideration I mentioned above. A party, I noted, will be compelled to eschew a patronage strategy if the losses it would incur by using the resources of the state to generate patronage exceed the benefits it would realize by so doing, and it will have an incentive to adopt a patronage strategy if the benefits of so doing exceed the costs. A party will be driven in one direction or the other depending upon which group it can least afford to alienate—the opponents of the patronage system (the constituency for bureaucratic autonomy) or its defenders. The latter grouping, to maintain terminological balance, can be labeled a "constituency for patronage," and its leading members, as Epstein notes, are the politicians—ward bosses, notables, *caciques*, and *askari*—who are dependent upon the continued flow of patronage to keep a hold on their clients and followers. There are many resources that these two groupings may be able to mobilize to back up their claims—wealth, notability, expertise, the capacity to disrupt or overthrow the government—but in an electoral setting the balance can be tipped decisively to one side or the other if one side is backed by a mass base; and the more extensive and the more highly organized that popular base, the more decisive will be the advantage enjoyed by that side. If the patronage-oriented politicians within the party enjoy such support—as they do, for example, in Chicago's Democratic party today—then "reform" will be the cause of only narrowly based elites, and the party would ignore the claims of the constituency for patronage at the peril of losing its base of popular support. If, to the contrary, the claimants for patronage within a party do not enjoy such backing, then the party leadership can heed the demands of a constituency for bureaucratic autonomy without fear that it thereby is courting disaster at the polls.

Whether a party will or will not be crucially dependent upon the distribution of patronage to maintain its hold upon its supporters is a function, in turn, of how the leadership of that party initially established a linkage with a popular base. If, for reasons I will discuss shortly, the party was not in a position to distribute particularistic benefits when it first undertook to mobilize mass support, its leaders will have been compelled to rely upon or to establish a network of mass organizations—labor unions, peasant leagues, churches, party sections—that did not need to be fueled by patronage. A party linked to a mass constituency through such an organizational structure will not, once it comes to power, be compelled to raid the public treasury in order to maintain its hold upon its supporters. On the other hand, a party that undertook to win popular support by distributing particularistic benefits through local notables or politicians will not have established such an organizational structure to bind voters directly to the party, and consequently such a party will only be able to maintain itself in office by heeding the demands of the patronage-seeking politicians who are affiliated with it.

A "Critical Experience" Theory

My argument is this. Once a party does come to power, its tendency to adopt or eschew a patronage strategy is a function of the third of the above-mentioned considerations: whether it will gain more than it will lose if it intervenes within the administrative process on a partisan, case-by-case basis. Whether gains will exceed losses, or losses will exceed gains, depends upon the relative strengths of the elites and party cadres who have a stake in the patronage system, on one hand, and the elites and cadres whose interests are served by more universalistic systems of public administration, on the other hand. And the influence that these two constituencies will have in the inner councils of the party is a function, in turn, of how the party first undertook to mobilize popular support. In other words, the way in which a party initially acquires a popular base is a character-forming or "critical" experience, in the sense in which that term is used by Philip Selznick and Ira Katznelson.[17] Political parties, as Samuel Huntington notes, are "formed by the organized linking of political faction to social force,"[18] and the way that linkage initially is established influences the character of the organization the party builds, what it subsequently must do to hold on to its social base, and consequently the bargaining strength within the party of practitioners of patronage politics and of their opponents.

Under what conditions will the founders of a political party use or not use patronage to establish a linkage with a mass base, that is, to acquire popular support? In order to answer this question, it is useful to recall a distinction that can be found in the literature on the origins of political parties, a distinction to which I have already alluded. Political parties, as Duverger and Huntington have both observed, emerge in one of two circumstances.[19] Parties have been founded by elites who occupy positions within the prevailing regime and who undertake to mobilize a popular following behind themselves in an effort either to gain control of the government or to secure their hold over it. Such parties might be termed "internally mobilized" parties. The Democratic-Republicans and the Federalists in the United States and the Liberals and Conservatives in Great Britain fall under this heading. Political parties also have been established by outsiders who did not hold positions within the prevailing regime and who organize a mass following either in an effort to gain entry into the political system for themselves and their supporters or in an effort to overthrow that system. Such parties might be termed "externally mobilized" parties. Socialist parties in Europe and nationalist parties in the Third World fall into this category.

Because they are established by outsiders, political parties in this second category—externally mobilized parties—do not enjoy access to state patronage at the time of their founding and perforce are compelled to rely upon other means to acquire a following. The situation with regard to internally mobilized parties is more complex. Parties founded by elites that occupy positions within the prevailing regime will be in a position to use the resources of the state to acquire a mass base and will have every incentive to make use of that advantage unless the party undertakes to mobilize a popular following after a constituency for bureaucratic autonomy has coalesced and become entrenched. The sequence in which these two events occur—the formation of a constituency for bureaucratic autonomy and the mobilization of a mass electorate—thus has enduring consequences for internally mobilized parties.

One can identify two different constituencies for bureaucratic autonomy that historically have emerged in nations governed by internally mobilized parties—two different coalitions of elite groups that historically have sought to abolish patronage in the public service, to establish civil service systems based upon purportedly merit-related standards of entry and promotion, and to defend thereafter the integrity of such systems.[20] The first of these, which might be termed the "absolutist coalition," was led by monarchs who during the seventeenth and eighteenth centuries sought to increase the extractive and regulatory capacities of their regimes and to create an army so that they would be better able to meet foreign military and economic competition and to bring their opponents at home to heel. This entailed creating a modern, centralized, bureaucratic state to replace the decentralized, patrimonial *standestaat* of the earlier era. The way modernizing monarchs proceeded toward this end varied from place to place, but generally speaking they won crucial political support for this program by filling positions in the reformed administrative system with members of the haute bourgeoisie and the aristocracy, that is, by creating a new administrative elite that was drawn in part and had links to older elite groups. These groups continued in the democratic era to serve as the constituency for the reformed state apparatus. The second coalition might be termed the "progressive coalition" because the role played by absolute monarchs in the first coalition was played in the second by a rationalizing middle class whose ideology was Benthamite in England, Positivist on the continent, and Progressive in the United States. Although the leading elements of the first and second coalitions differed, their remaining members were drawn from similar groups. In order for a rationalizing bourgeoisie to bring about administrative reforms and thereafter to be successful in providing political backing for a reformed civil service, it had to draw support from elements of the groups—be they aristocrats, patricians, or less exalted public servants—that held positions under the earlier regime.

The upshot of this analysis is that the circumstances under which a party first mobilizes a mass following has enduring implications for its subsequent behavior. To summarize: externally mobilized parties will tend to eschew the use of patronage (a tendency that will be stronger the greater the resistance the party must overcome in order to gain power) regardless of the social composition of their electoral base. Internally mobilized parties will tend to be patronage oriented unless they operate in a setting where either an absolutist or a progressive coalition became entrenched prior to the mobilization of the masses into politics. The circumstances of a party's origins influence its subsequent behavior regardless of the social characteristics of the voters upon whose support the party relies, because the formative experiences of a party have implications for the three factors that, as I noted earlier, determine whether a party will adopt or eschew a patronage strategy: (1) the demands and expectations of the party's rank-and-file supporters; (2) the material and organizational resources available to the party; and (3) the orientations of the party's leadership and its cadres and the interests of the elites who are allied with the party or who are capable of sanctioning it.

EXTERNALLY MOBILIZED PARTIES

The relationship between party origins and subsequent behavior is quite straightforward in the case of externally mobilized parties: the more "external" the circumstances of the party's origins—the fewer the allies it had within the preexisting regime, the greater the social and ideological distance between the party's founders and that regime, the greater the resistance the party is compelled to overcome in order to gain power—the less likely it is that the party will decay into a patronage machine after it does come to power. This relationship is clear-cut because the birth pangs of such a party, if they are severe, can permanently shape its character.

Consider the extreme case: parties whose founders have no significant allies among power holders or other elites. The leaders of such a party will not enjoy access to governmental or other sources of patronage and will find it necessary to rely upon other appeals to mobilize their supporters; it is precisely under these conditions, of course, that Puritanism emerged as the ideology of a politically excluded gentry (and Calvinism as the ideology of a politically excluded provincial nobility) in the seventeenth century, that liberalism emerged as the ideology of a politically excluded bourgeoisie in the eighteenth century, that socialism emerged as the ideology of a politically excluded working class in the nineteenth century, and that anarchism emerged as the ideology of a politically excluded peasantry in the twentieth century.[21] The fewer the allies such a party enjoys within the preexisting regime, moreover, the more strongly is that regime likely to resist the party's claims, to the point of seeking to repress it. In this situation, rank-and-file members of the party will be compelled to endure considerable sacrifices in order to affiliate with the party; the party will find it necessary to construct a strong organization to link its members and leaders to one another; and, most important of all, the party will be compelled to mobilize an extensive base in order to attain power.

These early experiences have enduring implications for the party's standing along each of the three above-mentioned dimensions. First, voters who undertook major sacrifices to affiliate with a party prior to its coming to power are not likely to demand particularistic payoffs as a condition for their continued support after the party comes to power. Nor, once such voters are brought into the electorate, will they be available for bribery by machine politicians from other parties, for, as Seymour Martin Lipset and Stein Rokkan have observed, the party that first brings a social group into the political system retains a privileged hold upon the members of that group for decades, and even generations, thereafter.[22] Finally, if the party mobilized an extensive mass base prior to coming to power, it will not, in order to stay in office, find it necessary subsequently to seek additional support among groups of voters that did not share the experience of affiliating with the party when it was an opposition force, and whose devotion to the party, therefore, is not quite so strong. As for the second of the above-mentioned considerations—the material and organizational resources available to the party leadership—party leaders who construct a strong organization prior to gaining access to patronage (an organization that necessarily will be grounded upon ideological and solidary inducements) will not subsequently find it necessary to fuel that organization with patronage in order to keep it running and to maintain a linkage with their subordinates and followers. Moreover, a leader who commands such a strong party organization will not find it necessary to tolerate corruption and empire building on the part of his subordinates; he will be in a secure enough position to discipline and even to fire officials who use public authority to build personal political followings.[23] Third, and finally, the leaders and cadres of such a party themselves will comprise a constituency for universalism, and the party will not be beholden to any constituency for patronage. The leaders and cadres of an externally mobilized party, as I have suggested, are likely to be committed to an ideology—a vision of society—and once they come to power, they are not going to be willing to fritter away in patronage the authority they now have to remold society, at least not if it was only with great difficulty that they got hold of that authority. And if these leaders acquired a mass following prior to gaining access to the resources of the state, and if the party did not rely upon the support of local elites and notables in order to acquire that following, it will not subsequently be dependent upon the support of patronage-oriented politicians in order to retain its popular base.

This set of considerations can explain why the European socialist parties listed in Table 2.1—parties that acquired mass followings before they gained access to patronage—did not decay into political machines after winning control of municipal, or eventually national, governments. And this has been true of these parties regardless of the social composition of their electoral base, even when their supporters were drawn from groups (uprooted peasants, recent urban migrants, Catholics, Latins) whose members in their private and social lives are said to have narrow, family-centered loyalties.

At the other extreme are those parties that did not find it necessary to overcome substantial resistance from the powers-that-be as a condition of coming to power, a category that includes the nationalist parties that took control of most Third World nations in the immediate post-independence period. These parties were not compelled to mobilize a substantial mass following or to build a strong party organization before they were handed the keys to the public treasury. Consequently, when they *for the first time* did find it necessary to mobilize popular support—in elections that were sponsored by the colonial power or that were held after independence was granted—these parties were an element of the prevailing regime and did enjoy access to the public bureaucracy. Having no alternative means of reaching into the countryside (or even the shantytowns around the capital city) it is not surprising that they would attempt to acquire a following by making use of the patronage at their disposal. In other words, at the moment when they first undertook to acquire a mass base, these parties for all intents and purposes stood in the same relationship to potential supporters as do internally mobilized parties. It is this consideration that explains why students of political development have found patronage to be so prevalent in the party politics of Third World countries, including those countries (the Philippines, Ghana) listed in the upper left of Table 2.1.[24] (By contrast, those Third World parties that were compelled to fight their way to power, for example, Tunisia's Neo-Destour, are less patronage oriented, even when they rely upon peasants or migrants for much of their popular support.)[25]

INTERNALLY MOBILIZED PARTIES

In a similar vein, the way in which an internally mobilized party initially establishes a linkage with its popular base has important consequences for its subsequent character. In order to specify the nature of this relationship one must divide the universe of internally mobilized parties into two subcategories: parties that undertake to acquire a popular following after the formation of an absolutist or a progressive coalition, and parties that mobilize a mass base before a constituency for bureaucratic autonomy of one or the other of these types coalesces. Parties in the former subcategory will tend thereafter to eschew patronage appeals, whereas parties in the latter subcategory will tend thereafter to be patronage oriented. The relationship between party origins and subsequent behavior, however, is somewhat looser in the case of internally mobilized parties than it is with externally mobilized parties, because the implications of the early experiences of the former for the subsequent orientations of the party's rank-and-file supporters and the subsequent character of the party's organizational structure are not quite so strong as they are with parties whose formative years were marked by the stuff out of which enduring loyalties and strong institutions are made: the shared experience of intense struggle and conflict. The formative experiences of an internally mobilized party do, however, strongly influence whether the party in subsequent years will be more beholden to a constituency for bureaucratic autonomy or a constituency for patronage, and for this reason in particular internally mobilized parties falling into the first subcategory are less likely to be patronage oriented than those falling into the latter subcategory. In the remainder of this chapter I will seek to substantiate this proposition.

To anticipate, I shall argue that in nations where either an absolutist or a progressive coalition emerged prior to the mobilization of the masses into politics, internally mobilized parties will not have been in a position to use patronage in order to establish a linkage with a mass base but rather will have been compelled to rely upon other appeals (e.g., to patriotic or religious sentiment) and other forms of organization (e.g., churches, interest groupings). Because the party did not acquire a popular following by distributing patronage through a network of local politicians it will not thereafter be crucially dependent upon the support of such patronage-seeking politicians. And the very emergence of an absolutist or progressive coalition in the nation in question means that the agrarian and/or urban upper classes with whom internally mobilized parties are allied will have a stake in the rules and procedures that guarantee these groups control over the reformed bureaucracy and privileged access to positions within it. For these reasons the party leadership will have every incentive to avoid the use of patronage: they are allied with a constituency for bureaucratic autonomy and are not dependent upon the support of a constituency for patronage. These considerations explain why the European conservative parties listed in the table— Germany's Christian Democratic Union/Christian Socialist Union and Britain's Conservatives—today eschew the use of patronage (an absolutist coalition emerged in Germany and a progressive coalition in England before the creation of a mass electorate). More generally, I suspect (though I am not certain) that these considerations explain why patronage plays the smallest role today in the party politics of those European nations that, in Immanuel Wallerstein's terminology, were governed by the "strong core states" of the sixteenth-century world-system.[26] (I am prepared to argue, but will not do so here, that this consideration explains why patronage plays a relatively small role in the politics of cities in the South and West in the United States and why it plays a relatively small role in state politics in the American upper Midwest and trans-Mississippi West, even when the parties in question rely upon the votes of working-class immigrant voters.)[27]

On the other hand, in nations where neither an absolutist nor a progressive coalition emerged prior to the extension of the franchise, internally mobilized parties will enjoy access to patronage at the moment when they first undertake to acquire a popular following, and, for the very reason that they are not confronted with a constituency for bureaucratic autonomy, they will have no incentive to avoid taking advantage of that access. Rather, they have every incentive to acquire popular support by distributing patronage to notables and politicians who have local followings. Such a strategy both follows the line of least resistance—it can be accomplished far more rapidly and with far less difficulty than building a party organization from scratch—and has the advantage of enabling the elites who are affiliated with the party to secure their hold over their clients and even to increase their power locally. These politicians and notables will become dependent upon the continued flow of patronage to maintain their power locally and within the party—they will develop into a constituency for patronage—and because the party is linked to its popular base through these politicians, the party will be dependent upon this constituency to maintain itself in power. A party whose political fate is so tied to the patronage system—one that requires patronage to hold its organization together and to maintain the support of its voters and its cadres—will not be in a position to respond favorably to a constituency for bureaucratic autonomy *if and when such a constituency does subsequently emerge*. These considerations, I would argue, explain the patronage orientation of the governing parties in southern Europe (the most notable being Italy's Christian Democrats) and they explain the significant role that patronage plays in the party politics of those states of the American East and lower Midwest (New York, Pennsylvania, Illinois) listed in the above table, and in the major cities in these states (New York City, Philadelphia, Chicago). In each of these cases, moreover, patronage plays a role in binding elements of the middle class, as well as other voters, to the party in question.

In the remainder of this chapter I will provide evidence for this argument concerning internally mobilized parties by analyzing three cases. The first, Germany, is a case where an absolutist coalition emerged prior to the creation of a mass electorate; the second, England, is a case where the formation of a progressive coalition preceded the full mobilization of the masses into politics; and the final one, Italy, is a case where neither of these coalitions emerged prior to the creation of a mass electorate. The order in which these events occurred, I shall argue, can explain the greater or lesser role that patronage plays in party politics in each of these nations today.

GERMANY

Germany stands as perhaps the paradigm case of a nation in which an absolutist constituency for bureaucratic autonomy coalesced and became entrenched in the predemocratic era, and it illustrates quite clearly the consequences of this development for the subsequent evolution of party politics. In the sections below I will discuss the emergence of an absolutist coalition in Brandenburg-Prussia during the seventeenth and eighteenth centuries, and I will argue that the ability of this coalition to survive the changes of regime Germany experienced subsequently, and to defend the autonomy of the bureaucracy, has been responsible for the limited role that patronage has played in the political parties of the Second Empire, the Weimar Republic, and the Federal Republic—including those parties that have relied upon the support of voters who supposedly are most responsive to patronage appeals.

The Emergence of an Absolutist Coalition

The attack upon a decentralized administrative structure staffed by aristocratic patronage dates in Germany from the aftermath of the Thirty Years War. Germany was devastated in that war and the Hohenzollern rulers of Brandenburg-Prussia, especially Frederick William (1640–88), King Frederick William I (1713–40), and King Frederick II (1740–86), attempted to recoup by creating a powerful standing army, an army that would defend the integrity of the Hohenzollern domains and lift Prussia into the ranks of the Great Powers.[28] The Great Elector recognized, however, that the Estates of the Realm, which dominated the existing governmental structure, would refuse to tax themselves in order to finance a large standing army, especially one under the control of the king. Consequently, he created an administrative apparatus that would enable him to bypass the estates, to extend his control over his domains, and to generate the revenues necessary to finance his army.

In recruiting officials to serve in this bureaucracy the Hohenzollerns attempted to accomplish a number of things. First, they sought to find royal servants who would be personally loyal to the king and who would support the crown rather than the estates in the struggle for control over Prussia. Second, they wanted their officials to be competent, to be adept at performing the tasks they would be assigned. And finally, in making appointments the Hohenzollerns sought to build a social base for their regime, to induce acquiescence among those whose support was necessary if their venture was to succeed. These goals had conflicting implications for the recruitment process. The best way to ensure that civil servants would be loyal to the crown would be to appoint commoners and foreigners to the bureaucracy, for they would be utterly beholden to the king for whatever status and power they enjoyed; the preservation of their status would be contingent upon the triumph of the crown in its struggle with the estates; and they had fewer ties to the estates than did officials who were aristocratic by birth.[29] An effort to maximize the competence of the bureaucracy had roughly similar implications, both because such an effort implies that one not give favor to candidates by virtue of their birth and because most university graduates in Prussia were of bourgeois, rather than noble, birth.[30] On the other hand, the necessity the Hohenzollerns faced of maintaining support for their regime and for their efforts at state-building had different implications for the recruitment process. The aristocracy was the class the monarchy could least afford to alienate, because it possessed the means to forcibly resist anything it regarded as tyrannical and because it was the class from which the officer corps of the Prussian army was to be drawn. For these reasons the kings of Prussia had an incentive to appoint Junkers to positions in the state bureaucracy.[31]

The Hohenzollerns pursued these several goals by recruiting civil servants from both the bourgeoisie and the aristocracy. The relative standing of these two classes within the bureaucracy fluctuated as political conditions changed.[32] In particular, Napoleon's victory over Prussia at the battle of Jena in 1806 discredited the army and the aristocracy and enabled a group of reformers led by Stein and Hardenburg and backed by the middle classes to come to power.[33] The reformers of the Stein/Hardenburg era insisted that national regeneration could be achieved only if greater weight were accorded to the claims of talent and education than to those of birth. A system of examinations for entry into the bureaucracy was devised to determine whether candidates for civil service appointments possessed these traits, examinations that required young men who wished to pursue a career in the bureaucracy to acquire a classical and legal education. Such an education could be obtained only by attending a classical gymnasium and then a university. This requirement limited careers in the upper civil service to the wealthy, but it did not discriminate between those whose family wealth came from land and those whose wealth came from commerce. The ideology of talent and education, of *Bildung*, and the civil service examination system through which it was institutionalized, thus enabled the bourgeoisie to solidify its claim upon positions within the bureaucracy. It enabled burghers to do so, however, without utterly alienating the aristocracy, for the civil service examination system accorded the aristocracy representation within the bureaucracy far out of proportion to their numbers, and the ideology of *Bildung* provided a justification for the disproportionate power that, after Jena, they sorely needed. The civil service examination system and the ideology of *Bildung* served a final purpose, a purpose that helps explain the political utility of these practices and principles to the groups that defended them. As Hans Rosenberg notes, these procedures and principles enhanced the autonomy and power of the bureaucracy, and hence that value of bureaucratic positions to those who could obtain them, because it gave the civil service control over its own recruitment and thereby prevented outsiders from influencing the bureaucracy through the hiring, firing, and promotion of civil servants.[34]

It was through these processes, then, that the Junkers and elements of the upper middle class obtained privileged access to positions in the bureaucracy and acquired a stake both in the regulations that gave them that access and in protecting the autonomy of that bureaucracy against "outside interference." In other words, these groups became a constituency for bureaucratic autonomy.

The Second Empire

This absolutist coalition retained its stake in the civil service under the Second Empire, as parliamentarians and party politicians became the major "outsiders" against whom the autonomy of the bureaucracy had to be defended. Otto von Bismarck, the most talented representative of Prussian Junkerdom and the architect of German unification, was flexible in a number of respects, but he was intransigent on this point. Bismarck was prepared to make various concessions as circumstances dictated to industrialists, Catholics, and even the working class. But he was not prepared to concede to any of these groups, or to the politicians who spoke for them, the slightest control over the army or the civil bureaucracy.[35] The constitution of the Second Empire provided that the chancellor and the cabinet were to be responsible to the Kaiser alone, and correlatively, that the Reichstag would have no control over the ministry and the bureaucracy.

Practice did not deviate from constitutional precept during the Second Empire. Parliamentary politicians were scarcely accorded any access to the very top level of government, let alone to the intermediate and lower levels of the bureaucracy: the majority of all cabinet ministers were recruited from the civil bureaucracy and the army rather than from the Reichstag. Large numbers of bureaucrats obtained seats in the parliament, while it was not possible for parliamentary and party politicians to obtain positions for themselves or their supporters within the bureaucracy.[36] Under the Second Empire, then, Germany was ruled by what Otto Kircheimer has termed a "military-bureaucratic complex," and the social groups linked to this complex would not countenance any interference in what they regarded as their private preserve from the politicians who were their agents in the electoral and parliamentary arenas, let alone from politicians who belonged to opposition parties.[37] The parties allied with the Junkers and/or the upper middle class and enjoying the closest ties to the government—the German Conservative party, the Reichspartei or Free Conservatives, the National Liberals—for this reason made no effort to use what power the Reichstag did possess under the constitution—its budgetary and legislative powers—to extend parliamentary and party control over the bureaucracy. Rather than attempting to use patronage to appeal to the working classes and the peasantry, the Conservatives instead sought to win such support by allying first with

Adolf Stoecker's anti-Semitic Christian Social movement and then with the Farmer's League.[38] As for the nonregime parties of the Second Empire—the Social Democrats, the Catholic Center, and the Progressives—they simply were not in a position to raid the bureaucracy and obtain patronage even if their leaders had cared to do so.

Weimar

Germany's defeat in the First World War led to the collapse of the monarchy and to the destruction of the institutions that had denied political parties any influence over the bureaucracy and that had prevented the members of all but the highest social classes from gaining entry into the upper reaches of civil service. During the early months of the revolution of 1918 the political parties sought to take full advantage of this new situation: they attempted to penetrate and gain control over the administrative apparatus of the old regime and to use whatever influence they managed to obtain within it to strengthen their organizations.[39] The revolution of 1918, however, was aborted. In order to crush a wave of left-wing insurrectionary activity, the early socialist governments of Weimar found it necessary to turn to military units from the old regime, and in order to carry on routine tasks of administration, the government was compelled to rely upon the administrative apparatus and the bureaucrats it had inherited from the Reich. The military-bureaucratic complex that had governed the empire thus was able to survive into the new era. And because the German revolution was unfinished—because the economic and the political bases of the Junkers and of the upper bourgeoisie had not been destroyed—the class coalition that defended the autonomy of this complex continued to be a potent political force during the Weimar period.

The desire of the Republican parties to make peace with these political forces was sufficiently strong that they did not attempt to change in any fundamental way the structure, recruitment procedures, and social composition of the civil service.[40] Indeed, in Ralf Dahrendorf's judgment, the influence of administrative officials relative to other political actors was greater in the Weimar period than it had been under the previous regime.[41] Unregenerate opponents of the Republic were so firmly entrenched in Weimar's administrative apparatus that adventurers such as Adolf Hitler were able to conspire against the regime, as in the Munich Beer Hall Putsch, without being seriously punished by the Weimar judiciary.[42]

The survival of Germany's absolutist coalition into the Republican era had a number of important and ultimately fatal consequences for political life in Weimar, two of which are of concern to us here. In the first place, this constituency for bureaucratic autonomy was allied with parties of the Right—especially with the German National People's party (DNVP) and the German People's party—and it thereby exercised an internal constraint upon whatever tendency these parties might have had to raid the bureaucracy in search of patronage. This constraint was particularly notable with respect to the DNVP, which sought to mobilize support among the peasantry and which therefore might have been expected to rely upon a patronage strategy, but which relied instead upon nationalist and anti-Semitic appeals.[43] It was, rather, the Center party, which did not have ties to the absolutist coalition, that appears to have been the most inclined of the parties of the Weimar period to use its positions within the government to influence bureaucratic appointments, in an effort to increase the representation of Catholics in the bureaucracy. This endeavor, however, met with only limited success.[44]

The survival of Germany's absolutist coalition into the Republican era exercised an external constraint upon all of Weimar's parties as well as an internal constraint upon the parties with which it was allied. Republican politicians dared not overturn practices and procedures that protected the autonomy of the bureaucracy and that gave the upper classes privileged access to high positions in it for fear that if they attempted to do so, the social groups that were linked to the bureaucracy would turn openly against the Republic. For this reason the parties of the Weimar coalition—the Socialists, the Democrats, and the Centrists—decided against purging the bureaucracy of anti-Republican elements in the wake of the Kapp Putsch in 1920.[45] It is true that after the assassination of Walter Rathenau in 1922, a law was passed that increased the number of administrative positions subject to political appointment, and the Republican parties sought to "democratize" the civil service by appointing their adherents to these positions, but these parties hesitated to take full advantage of the opportunities provided by the 1922 law for fear of provoking the regime's opponents.[46] The proof of how discreet the Weimar parties had been came after the Nazi seizure of power. The Nazis in April 1933 promulgated the Law on the Reestablishment of the Career Civil Service, which provided for the removal from the bureaucracy of Jews, Communists, and "party-made" officials, that is, officials who had been brought into the civil service since 1918 without filling the normal requirements of the positions they held. But very few civil servants turned out to be liable for dismissal under the terms of this law.[47]

The existence of these severe internal and external constraints upon the freedom of action of political parties in Weimar Germany can explain why these parties were not, in the judgment of contemporaneous political scientists, especially patronage-oriented.[48]

The Third Reich

The Nazi revolution did not destroy the autonomy of the German civil service or sever the links between the bureaucracy and its traditional social base any more than had the revolution of 1918. Indeed, to the extent that the Nazis did purge from the bureaucracy elements that had entered it since 1918, the initial consequence of Hitler's coming to power was more restorative than revolutionary. However, after the limited purges of 1933, Nazism exerted surprisingly little impact upon the civil service, as David Schoenbaum's study indicates.[49]

The civil service was so successful in maintaining its autonomy because the vast majority of all civil servants inherited by the Third Reich conscientiously served the new regime and were loyal to it. The regime thus had little incentive to disrupt established bureaucratic routines or to insist that party considerations be accorded priority over technical proficiency in the appointment process. For this reason, as Schoenbaum notes, "despite the ostensible merger of State and Party, the outstanding loser in the struggle for survival was the Party. Advantages to Alte Kampfer [Nazis who had joined the Party before 1933] were kept to a minimum; direct party interference in the traditional civil service sectors was eliminated almost immediately. The files of the Ministry of the Interior could be read as a series of jurisdictional conflicts in which, almost without exception, the civil service won and the Party lost."[50]

Because the Third Reich had pretty much left the German civil service alone and did not substantially alter its social composition, the heirs of Germany's absolutist coalition were able to defend the autonomy of the bureaucracy when an open political system was restored in the Federal Republic after the Second World War.

The Federal Republic

The civil service of the Federal Republic is the lineal descendent of the bureaucracy that served earlier German regimes—the Third Reich, the Weimar Republic, the Wilhelmian Reich, and ultimately, Hohenzollern Prussia—both in law and in fact. As for juridical continuity, a federal law of May 1951 passed pursuant to Article 131 of the Bonn constitution granted all regular civil servants, including those dismissed after 1945 for their Nazi connections and those expelled by the East German regime, a right to reinstatement by the Federal Republic.[51] And more than ten years after the collapse of the Nazi regime, 60 percent of the individuals who occupied top civil service positions in the Federal Republic had held comparable positions in the administrative structure of the Third Reich.[52] In fact, the proportion of civil servants who survived the regime change in 1945 was identical to the proportion who survived the transitions from the Wilhelmian Reich to Weimar in 1918 and from Weimar to the Third Reich in 1933.

I stated above that the constituency for bureaucratic autonomy in the Federal Republic today is the *heir* of Germany's absolutist coalition, rather than *identical* to the coalition that defended bureaucratic autonomy in earlier regimes, because I would not deny that German society has changed in many important respects in the past several decades. The combined impact of industrialization, war-time decimation, and postwar partition destroyed the Junkers as a social class. But the two centuries of bureaucratic absolutism that preceded (and brought on) many of these changes have had their effect. The creation of an absolutist coalition implied not only the militarization of the Prussian aristocracy but also the "feudalization" of the Prussian bourgeoisie—the emergence of a *bourgeoisie d'état* that aspired to assimilate into the aristocracy, that adopted its etatist values, and that has carried on this tradition even though the class that had previously exercised moral hegemony over them has passed from the scene. It is this class (and those who now aspire to enter it), with its orientation to public careers, its high level of corporate consciousness, and its conviction that it stands "above politics," that has defended the autonomy of the civil service in the Federal Republic.[53]

This constituency for bureaucratic autonomy has been an enormously powerful force in German politics. The ability of the civil service to survive the collapse of the Third Reich and the Allied military occupation with only minimal changes in personnel and structure is a reflection of that political strength.[54] Upon assuming control of Germany the occupation authorities, especially the Americans, intended to bring about the "denazification" and the "democratization" of the civil service; that is, they intended to purge and to reorganize the bureaucracy. The responsibility for carrying out these reforms, however, was left to the German authorities, and politicians in postwar Germany found it politically impossible to resist the pressure of defenders of the bureaucratic status quo. The Deutscher Beamtenbund (DBB), the major spokesmen for the higher civil servants, was particularly insistent in demanding that the "vested rights" of the Beamte be honored. One measure of its success is that only one thousand of the fifty-three thousand civil servants who were initially removed in denazification proceedings were in the end permanently excluded from the bureaucracy, and ultimately the Federal Republic passed the law of May 1951, which I described above. The power of Germany's constituency for bureaucratic autonomy is such that, as Taylor Cole has observed, the civil service was the public institution in Germany that passed through the occupation with the fewest changes.[55]

The political power of Germany's constituency for bureaucratic autonomy

in the postwar era rested upon a number of foundations. First, as the Socialists learned in 1918, as the American, British, and French occupation forces rediscovered in 1945, and as politicians in Germany have recognized to this day, any regime that is not prepared to countenance a
sustained period of disruption must delegate the task of administering the
routine functions of government to the civil servants it inherits from the
previous regime. The critical position that it occupies gives Germany's traditional bureaucratic elite enormous bargaining power.[56] Second, civil servants in Germany are well organized and rely upon pressure-group activity
to assert their claims and to defend their position in the politics of the Federal Republic.[57] Third, the civil service is closely linked with other institutions in German society, most notably with the legal profession and the
universities.[58]

A fourth and final practice that strengthens the defenders of bureaucratic
autonomy in Germany is one that might be termed "reverse colonization."
Political parties are prevented by law from placing their agents in the career
civil service; career civil servants, however, have colonized the parties and
the public institutions—especially the Bundestag, the Bundesrat, and the
Landtag—of the Federal Republic. This practice has its roots in the nineteenth century, and the DBB fought hard during the occupation, ultimately
with success, against the Allies' proposal that a law be passed, akin to America's Hatch Act, that would severely restrict the political activities of civil
servants. The DBB recognized that the practice of reverse colonization enabled the civil service to gain representation for its corporate interests in the
inner councils of the Federal Republic.[59]

Because the defenders of bureaucratic autonomy have links to so many
important institutions in German society, any party that expects to govern
the nation finds it necessary to come to terms with this constituency—
unless, as was true of the SED in the East, it was prepared to sponsor a social revolution. This is doubly true of a party such as the Christian Democratic Union (CDU) that is allied with the social groups that are advantaged
by the traditional recruitment procedures of the German civil service. The
relationship between these groups and the CDU goes a long way to explaining its behavior toward civil service reform and toward patronage in the
postwar era.

The stance of the CDU toward the civil-service reform proposals of the
Allies was, as Karl Hochswender puts it, "moderately conservative."[60] Ade-
nauer and the other top leaders of the party rejected the idea of totally
overhauling the civil service and insisted that the public personnel system
of the Federal Republic be built upon the German Career Officials Act of
1937. As leaders of the ruling party in the Republic, they were, however,
interested in increasing the control that supervisors were able to exercise
over their subordinates within the bureaucracy and in increasing the techni-

cal proficiency of the civil service. Hence they supported reforms that would enable supervisors to demote and deny regular salary increments to officials who failed to perform their duties satisfactorily and that would provide "open competition" for civil service positions, that is, would permit individuals who were not career officials to compete for appointments in the upper reaches of the civil service. These proposals, however, encountered enormous resistance among spokesmen for the Beamte with the CDU, especially among the CDU members of the Bundestag's Civil Service Committee. The committee defeated the first, and the provision for open competition was able to pass only when some CDU members broke with a majority of their colleagues and voted with the SPD delegation in favor of it.

The CDU's alliance with Germany's constituency for bureaucratic autonomy also can account for the fairly limited role that patronage played within the party during the years it dominated the government of the Federal Republic. The CDU during this period was not totally indifferent to the identity of upper level bureaucrats, but as Hochswender notes (citing Theodor Eschenburg's study of the scope of patronage in the politics of the Federal Republic), the concern of the CDU leaders in these matters was limited to two issues.[61] First, in order to hold together the coalition governments that they led, the leadership of the CDU took care to see that the individuals appointed to upper level positions within the bureaucracy—the "politische Beamte"—as well as those appointed to the cabinet itself reflect the political composition of the government. Thus ambassadorships were allocated among the CDU's coalition partners. Second, as a quasi-confessional party, the CDU pays heed to the religious affiliations of civil servants, especially those in sensitive positions. Thus the position of chief of the Cultural Division of the Foreign Ministry is reserved for a Catholic while the chief of the Cultural Division of the Ministry of the Interior invariably is a Protestant, and religious elements within the CDU have argued that in Catholic areas chief gynecologists in public hospitals and teachers in public schools should be Catholics. These appear to be the only arenas, however, in which the defenders of the traditional recruitment practices of the German civil service have been compelled to make concessions to partisan and electoral pressures.

GREAT BRITAIN

An attack upon the patronage system may be spearheaded by a rationalizing bourgeoisie as well as by the forces of absolutism, and a coalition between such a grouping and older political and social elites—a progressive coalition—may thereafter serve as a nation's constituency for bureaucratic autonomy. Parties will eschew patronage strategies in political systems where such a coalition emerges prior to the mobilization of a mass electorate. Great Britain was the first country where this occurred, and thus I will illustrate this proposition by discussing the British case.

The Emergence of a Progressive Coalition

For reasons that need not be discussed here, a centralized bureaucratic state, headed by an absolute monarch and supported by a class of officials drawn from the aristocracy and haute bourgeoisie, was not established in England in the seventeenth century as it was in many nations on the continent.[62] The English Civil War prevented such a development and confirmed that public administration would remain decentralized in Great Britain in the era prior to the extension of the franchise. The major offices of domestic administration—most importantly, the justices of the peace—and the major programs of domestic policy—the maintenance of public order, the administration of local justice, and poor relief—were controlled by local gentry and their dependents. Those public functions administered centrally were controlled by a parliament that itself was a "committee of landlords."[63] And appointments to these administrative positions were made in a manner calculated to cement the parliamentary majority of the incumbent ministry: the eighteenth century was the classic era of patronage in British politics.[64] The governing classes of England, then, were not tied to a bureaucratic regime. In the absence of any such constituency for bureaucratic autonomy, party politics, or at least the politics of parliamentary parties,[65] was patronage-ridden.

The leadership in the fight against the patronage system was assumed by elements of Britain's professional upper middle classes, by a group that can appropriately be labeled a "rationalizing bourgeoisie." Those who sought to reform the home civil service by ending patronage appointments and by introducing competitive examinations were part of a more general movement to rationalize and renovate the major public and quasi-public institutions in Britain—the universities, secondary schools, the administration of India, municipal administration, the system of poor relief, and so on. Within this broader group, however, one can distinguish two subgroups. The first of these was oriented toward the concerns of the older, more established segment of Britain's middle classes. They sought to rationalize the nation's traditional institutions—the ancient universities, the elite secondary schools, the imperial administration—so that these institutions would be more attuned to the interests of England's liberally educated professional elite.[66] Part and parcel of this effort was the proposal, embodied in the Northcote-Trevelyan Report of 1854, that admission into the highest grade of the civil service be determined by an examination geared to a literary education such as could be obtained only at Oxford or Cambridge. This proposal would have limited access to upper-level positions in the civil service to the classes that sent their sons to these two universities, namely the aristocracy, the gentry, and established members of the liberal professions.

The second group of reformers was oriented more toward the concerns of the emerging entrepreneurial class. They attempted to rationalize the way in which the government dealt with the industrial sector of society. In particular, the leaders of this second stream pressed the government to assume the burdens of establishing the social preconditions for industrialization and of dealing with the externalities of industrialization. Men such as Edwin Chadwick and John Stuart Mill sought to socialize the costs both of educating, disciplining, and maintaining the health of the industrial labor force and of dealing with the "human exhaust of capitalism," the poor, the criminal, the dispossessed.[67]

The second group of reformers, like the first, sought to change the way in which civil servants were recruited, but since the goals they sought to accomplish differed, their proposals differed accordingly. Edwin Chadwick, John Stuart Mill, and the Administrative Reform Association (which was organized by a group of businessmen) proposed that civil service examinations be instituted that would favor individuals who possessed technical skills, not those who were liberally educated.[68] An examination system of this character they argued would increase the technical proficiency of governmental agencies, and it would loosen the grip of the upper classes upon the civil service, a grip that the Trevelyan-Northcote proposals would tighten.

The Trevelyan-Northcote proposals of 1854 were defeated because they failed to win the support of the entrepreneurial classes and the aristocracy. When a plan was fashioned in 1870 that was backed by these two classes, civil service reform was adopted with absolutely no controversy. The 1870 reform plan divided the civil service into three grades—administrative, executive, and clerical. Examinations for the administrative class were to be keyed to a liberal education, while examination for the executive class were to be keyed to an "English education," that is, an education in the English language and in modern subjects, as opposed to one in ancient languages and classical texts. In other words, the 1870 program embodied the proposals both of the reformers who were oriented toward the established professional class and those who were oriented toward the entrepreneurial class, and consequently both segments of the bourgeoisie could unite behind it. As for the landed classes, their support for civil service reform in 1870 can be attributed to the suffrage extension of 1867.[69] Once the franchise had been extended to householders and rent payers, the aristocracy and gentry no longer could assume that the patronage system would continue to provide them with preferential access to the civil service; its tendency, rather, would be to open public employment to the most numerous class of voters, to democratize the civil service. The reform of 1870, however, by restricting appointments in the administrative class to those with a liberal education, would preserve the preferential access to the higher civil service traditionally enjoyed by the landed classes, for they could afford to give their sons such an impractical education. To be sure, an examination system for entry into higher civil service would exclude the indolent, and it would reward only those members of the aristocracy who had acquired habits of concentrated work and who had attached themselves to the service ideal. But under the prodding of schoolmasters such as Thomas Arnold and Oxbridge dons such as Benjamin Jowett, the British aristocracy in the nineteenth century did make these adjustments to bourgeois values and did adopt the ideology of service, an ideology that justified their retaining their privileges and power in the industrial era.[70] These concessions staved off far greater losses.

The Party Response: The Conservatives

Patronage in the civil service was finally restricted in Britain, and a system of competitive examinations was instituted, when a reform plan was fashioned that could be supported by the landed and entrepreneurial classes as well as by professional elites. As such a constituency for bureaucratic autonomy emerged, the parties that depended upon the support of these classes were compelled to adjust their behavior accordingly. This adjustment was bound up with the response of these parties to the suffrage extensions and kindred reforms[71] that occurred at the same time—a conjunction of events that, as I have already suggested, was not in the least coincidental. The major parties in Britain did not adjust to these reforms without internal conflicts and difficulties. But they responded far more smoothly, and far more completely, than has been the case in nations where a constituency for bureaucratic autonomy only coalesced after the masses had been fully mobilized into the political system. In the paragraphs below I will provide evidence for my argument by discussing the case of the Conservative party.

As late as 1868, the Conservatives in most constituencies did not command a party apparatus that had an existence apart from the patron-client chains that linked Tory squires to their tenants and dependents.[72] Elections in the countryside were managed by landlords, and in the borough constituencies they were run by those figures from the underside of Victorian politics: wire-pullers, publicans, official treaters, paid messengers. The central affairs of the party were administered by the whips—the chief whip was simultaneously patronage secretary of the Treasury—and by a principal agent, who was the party leader's personal attorney, and who was happy to involve himself in party business because it brought a large number of lucrative election cases to his law firm. The principal agent and the whips put candidates who were looking for constituencies and constituencies that were looking for candidates in contact with each another; they raised money from the party's *grands seigneurs* and funneled it into constituencies; and they distributed patronage, both civil and ecclesiastical, to the party's supporters.[73]

A movement to create a different kind of party organization was initiated in the late 1860s and early 1870s and is closely associated with the career of John E. Gorst.[74] Gorst chaired the meeting in 1868 that established the National Union of Conservative and Constitutional Associations, an organization whose founders recognized that the future of Conservatism lay in mass party organization. In 1870 Gorst was appointed principal agent of the Conservative party by Disraeli, and he immediately set about to accomplish this goal by contacting prominent Conservatives in each constituency and encouraging them to organize a Conservative committee and to select local candidates. This nascent mass party organization ran the Conservative campaign in the election of 1874 and in large measure was responsible for the Conservative victory that year.

After the 1874 victory, however, serious tensions arose between the leaders and cadres associated with this new party apparatus, on one hand, and the party's Old Guard, those elements of the party whom Gorst termed "the old identity," on the other hand.[75] Gorst complained that once the party got into office, the leaders of the "old identity," the whips, undermined the new structure by intervening in local constituencies apart from the network of Conservative committees and associations whose creation Gorst had supported: the whips backed candidates without consulting the local Conservative leadership; they distributed patronage to their local friends and allies; they financed corrupt electoral practices. This demoralized the cadres who had been attracted into party work in the early 1870s, and the structure Gorst had built up began to crumble. Gorst complained bitterly to Disraeli that the practice of "managing elections at the Treasury" would be fatal to the party, but to no avail.[76] He resigned as principal agent in 1877.

Unable to reform traditional party practices from within, Gorst joined an attack upon them from without.[77] In the late 1870s the aggrieved party cadres began voicing their complaints at the annual meetings of the National Union. The conflicts between the proponents of the new and the old styles of party politics reached its peak after the Conservatives were defeated in the election of 1880. Lord Randolph Churchill and his allies in the so-called Fourth party—one of whom was Gorst—took up the complaints of the dissidents, gained control of the National Union, and attempted to use it as a springboard for vaulting Churchill into the leadership of the party. The Fourth party episode ended in a compromise, "a sudden reconciliation which," according to E. J. Feuchtwanger, "never has been quite satisfactorily explained."[78] In a broader perspective, however, this reconciliation is not difficult to understand: it was but another episode in the establishment of a modus vivendi between Britain's landed and urban upper classes—an earlier episode of which was the civil service reform of 1870—another step toward the formation of a coalition that it was very much in the interests of each side to enter.

The top leaders of the Conservative party, Lord Salisbury and Sir Stafford Northcote, were compelled by the Conservative defeat in the election of 1880 to recognize that they could not afford to alienate the opponents of the patronage system within the party. These opponents—chiefly, but not entirely, drawn from the provincial bourgeoisie—for their own reasons were extremely anxious to come to terms with the groups that comprised the traditional base of the Conservative party. As James Cornford notes, the major reason why the cadres of the provincial Conservative and Constitutional associations were willing to undertake the burdens of party work was that it gave them the opportunity to interact with the Tory aristocracy and gentry as collaborators in a common endeavor.[79] That incentive would only continue to be available if the two sides could come to terms with one another.

In the course of the 1880s an accommodation was hammered out with which both sides could live. The traditional governing classes maintained their privileged access to the cabinet.[80] Moreover, as both R. T. McKenzie and Samuel Beer stress, control over public policy continued to be vested in the government and the parliamentary party: in the realm of public policy making, conservative governments do not profess to listen to the constituency party.[81]

On the other side, a uniform network of Conservative associations was extended throughout the country, the control of these associations over the conduct of elections was acknowledged, and the executive committee of the National Union was reorganized so that it could serve as the spokesmen for the cadres who manned these associations in the inner councils of the party.[82] The Corrupt Practices Act of 1883 outlawed many of the traditional techniques the whips had employed to influence local elections, and the Reform Act of 1884 reapportioned the shires and boroughs in which yet older forms of electoral control were practiced. Most relevant of all to us here, in the 1880s the Conservatives came increasingly to respect the autonomy and integrity of the civil service. Harold Hanham reports that in the 1870s virtually all high level appointments that Disraeli made in the Treasury were handed out as partisan rewards; by contrast appointments to these positions were granted in two-thirds of all cases as promotions to civil servants from within the Treasury by both Conservative and Liberal governments in the 1880s.[83] As the political costs of violating the autonomy of the bureaucracy increased, both of Britain's major parties turned increasingly instead to the distribution of honorific positions, especially positions as magistrates, to their major local supporters.[84] In the 1880s the Conservatives began to grant titles of nobility to merchants and manufacturers who made substantial contributions to the central party fund or who played major roles in the Conservative party organization, a practice that quite literally led to the fusion of Britain's aristocracy and bourgeoisie.[85] By these means the Conservatives could reward party luminaries without meddling in the allocation of civil service positions and thereby alienating the constituency for bureaucratic autonomy upon whose support the party was becoming increasingly dependent.

This set of accommodations proved to be remarkably stable. The pattern of party organization established by the Conservatives in 1885 has endured, as McKenzie notes, down to the present day.[86] After a discrete and conflict-ridden transitional period, then, the Conservative party in Great Britain abandoned the practice of patronage politics. The constituency for bureaucratic autonomy, within the party was able to prevail, and older practices were abandoned leaving surprisingly few residues, because it was supported by a large popular following. One strongly suspects that had universal suffrage been adopted in England prior to the formation of a constituency for bureaucratic autonomy, the outcome of the struggle between the practitioners and opponents of patronage politics would have been quite different. In that event Britain would have recapitulated the experience of the United States during the Jacksonian Era. The wire-pullers within the Conservative party would then have been free to use patronage to acquire a genuinely mass following and their bargaining power vis-à-vis Salisbury and Northcote would have been as great as the leverage of the Fourth party and the National Union proved to be.

The imaginative exercise, however, requires one to introduce so many counterfactual assumptions that it is not fruitful to pursue it further. In order to understand the conditions that enable patronage to survive into the contemporary period, it is more useful to analyze a case where the creation of a mass electorate did antedate the formation of a constituency for bureaucratic autonomy. Italy is such a case.

ITALY

The "Blocco Storico"

Neither a progressive nor an absolutist coalition assumed control of the newly unified nation of Italy during the predemocratic era. It is not difficult to account for the absence of the former. Italy was simply too backward economically to follow the British path during the nineteenth century. It requires a somewhat lengthier explanation to account for the failure of Italy to follow the German precedent. On the surface, at least, there were some striking similarities between the Italy and Germany of, say, 1850. Both nations were politically fragmented; in both nations there was one state (Prussia in the case of Germany, Piedmont in the case of Italy) in which centralized bureaucratic institutions had taken root in the early modern period; and in both cases the process of unification involved the extension of that state's institutions over the rest of the nation. There were, however, some crucial differences between the two cases. In Germany prior to unification the region that was economically and socially most backward (East Elbia) was governed by the state whose institutions were extended over the newly unified nation. This meant, as I have argued above, that the most important segment of Germany's landed classes had been integrated into, and had acquired a stake in the integrity of, the nation's administrative apparatus. In Italy the region that in the mid-nineteenth century was economically and socially most backward (the Mezzogiorno) was governed not by the state that led the drive for unification, but rather by a regime (the Kingdom of the Two Sicilies) that was destroyed in the process. For this reason the landed classes of the south (which in the 1860s included members of the middle class who had seized land from the aristocracy, the Church, and the peasantry)[87] had no stake in the integrity of the bureaucracy that now governed them.

There was a second and related difference between the German and Italian cases. The forces of Prussian absolutism had to make very few concessions in order to absorb the other German states into the empire and to control the newly unified state thereafter. Under the constitution of the empire, Prussia dominated the upper house of the imperial legislature, the king of Prussia became the emperor of Germany, and the chancellor, the cabinet, and the bureaucracy were responsible to the emperor rather than the Reichstag. In this way the forces of Prussian absolutism were able to maintain their control over the entire executive apparatus. In order to build a majority in the Reichstag, one of the few major concessions Bismarck and his successors as chancellor had to make was to approve a tariff on industrial goods. This concession won them the support of the Rhenish industrialists and cemented the famous "coalition of iron and rye."[88] The forces of Piedmontese absolutism, by contrast, lost control of the government and bureaucracy of the new state fifteen years after the proclamation of the Kingdom of Italy.

Nonetheless the interests of northern elites were more than adequately served by the new regime, and a strong basis existed for a coalition between them and the gentry of the south—the coalition Antonio Gramsci termed the *blocco storico*.[89] What these elites wanted above all was to defend themselves against their Republican opponents and to control the new nation's economic policies. The southern gentry sought protection for their landholdings against the threat of peasant insurrection, and in light of the depressed state of the southern economy, they also welcomed any employment opportunities the new regime could provide. The "programs" of the northern and southern elites were fully compatible, and served as the basis for the alliance between them. The central government policed the south, putting down "brigandage" and "banditry," and it provided the gentry, who dominated southern representation in the legislature, with patronage, which they could use to maintain their control over their inferiors. In return for this assistance the southern gentry rallied to the government, and its deputies supported ministries whose commercial, financial, and industrial policies were oriented chiefly to the interests of northern capital. This logrolling arrangement underlay and was implemented through the practice of *trasformismo*, the process by which deputies who were elected as opponents of the government were "transformed" into its allies once they were granted patronage. The institution of *trasformismo* was perfected by the Liberal government of Depretis, which came to power in 1876 and was kept in office with the votes of southern deputies. Upon assuming office, Depretis removed those prefects whose loyalty he could not count upon and replaced them with individuals whom he could trust to use their power to sustain the government. The techniques perfected by Depretis were used by the governments that ruled Italy for the next forty years.[90]

Party and Patronage: The Christian Democrats

A constituency for bureaucratic autonomy did not emerge in Italy prior to the democratic era; to the contrary, the nation was governed by a coalition— the *blocco storico*—that depended upon patronage in order to hold itself together. This coalition has remained the dominant political configuration in Italy to the present day, and terms of trade outlined above have remained the fundamental basis of accommodation between the two major partners in this coalition.[91] This does not mean, however, that the structure of recent Italian politics is identical to what it was in the era of Depretis, Crispi, and Giolitti. With the introduction of universal suffrage in 1913 and with the removal by the Church of its ban upon the participation of Catholics in Italian politics, two new actors moved onto the political stage: the working classes, organized chiefly through the Socialist and then the Communist parties, and the Catholics, organized chiefly through the Popular party and then the Christian Democrats. Italy's older political classes attempted initially to exclude these new actors from effective power; the ultimate consequence of this endeavor was Fascism.[92] After the collapse of Fascism, however, Italy's landed and industrial elites found it necessary to throw their support behind the Church and to work through the Christian Democratic party in order to continue to exclude from power the groups that constituted the greater threat to their hegemony. The fears of northern industrialists and southern landowners in the troubled years of the 1940s, then, were the same as the fears of their predecessors in the troubled years of the 1860s—revolution in the north and peasant insurrection in the south.[93]

The solutions adopted in the 1860s and 1940s were fundamentally similar—an alliance among the upper and middle classes of the two regions. Although the Christian Democrats (DC) in this sense served the same function for these classes as did the parties of the Liberal era, it was more than simply one of these old parties in new dress, more than simply the Sinistra in a cassock and clerical collar. La Democrazia Christiana, after all, was the successor to Don Luigi Sturzo's progressive Partito Popolare; it was allied with the Catholic trade-union movement in the north and it supported land reform in the south; and if it were to govern a nation whose electorate new exceeded twenty-five million, and do so without the votes of deputies from the working-class parties, it would need to establish a broad base of popular support.[94] To acquire such support the DC mobilizes its constituency not through the old clientele structure but rather through an extensive network of party sections and affiliated organizations—a youth movement, a women's movement, an organization of farmers, and a trade union federation.[95] Although the mechanism through which the DC appeals to its supporters is that of a modern mass party, the substance of its appeal, at least in the south, is the traditional one of Italian politics. The DC has taken advantage of its control over the bureaucracy to place hordes of well-paid ushers and janitors on the public payroll.[96] It provides subsidies to marginal business, to firms that could not survive in the absence of state support and whose owners and employees therefore become dependent upon the party for their continued prosperity and employment.[97] Christian Democratic deputies and party functionaries, rather than lawyers and landowners, now write letters of recommendation on behalf of candidates for admission to state schools. Sidney Tarrow summarizes this development by speaking of a movement from "clientelismo of the notable to clientelismo of the bureaucracy" and "from vertical to horizontal clienteles."[98]

But how was this development possible? Why did the northern industrialists, who through the Confindustria financed the DC in the postwar period, tolerate the patronage, the corruption, the governmental inefficiency that was implicit in this method of operation? A possible answer to these questions is suggested by P. A. Allum.[99] Allum notes that the Italian economic miracle of the postwar era was grounded upon two things: the ability of Italian industry to pay low wages in the period before 1963 and the monetary and credit policies embodied in the "Einaudi line." Neither of these policies demanded much in the way of efficiency or effectiveness from the bureaucracy or were adversely affected by the patronage practices of the DC. The exclusion of the working-class parties from the government was a requisite for the first of these, and this was accomplished in 1948, partly in response to American pressure. The monetary and credit policies of Einaudi were administered through the Bank of Italy, an august institution outside the pale of the DC's patronage.

During the fifteen-year period following the Second World War, then, the industrialists who were allied with the DC and who might have been expected to object strongly to the party's patronage practices and to have fought for administrative reforms and greater governmental efficiency—who might have been expected, in other words, to lead a progressive coalition—did not have a strong incentive to do so. For this reason the DC was able to develop along the lines indicated above without fear of alienating this important set of allies. In the early 1960s, however, this state of affairs began to change. The extraordinary rate of economic growth that Italy had enjoyed as a result of the government's monetary policies and industry's ability to pay low wages slowed considerably by 1963.[100] Labor became more restive and less compliant than it had been previously, and the leaders of Italy's largest firms, who could afford to do so, were prepared to make economic concessions and to press for governmental reforms. Increasingly, the incompetence of Italy's patronage-ridden bureaucracy, and the cost of sustaining that huge bureaucracy, has come to be regarded as a major source of the "Italian crisis" and its reform has come to be regarded as a prerequisite for pulling the nation out of that crisis.[101]

By the time these tendencies began to manifest themselves, however, the constituency for patronage within the DC had become sufficiently powerful to block any would-be reformers. The very freedom the party enjoyed in the postwar period to use patronage to mobilize popular support enabled the practitioners of patronage politics within the party to build a mass base for themselves. For this reason, Raphael Zariski notes, the DC has become more factionalized the longer it has remained in office.[102] And the patronage-oriented factions within the party are not prepared to see reforms implemented that would deprive them of the fruits of power. As Sidney Tarrow observes, "Because state agencies have been used by party and factional groupings to service their electorates, no government has been able to undertake a reform of the state without threatening their political livelihood."[103] Were a DC government to propose reforms that alienated this constituency for patronage, it would risk splitting the party and losing much of its mass base.

The success of the DC's constituency for patronage contrasts markedly with the failure, described above, of its counterpart within the British Conservative party. In order to find parallels to the DC one must, rather, turn to other parties that mobilized and organized an extensive popular following before the opponents of the patronage system coalesced. The American party system provides many parallel cases, and the factional struggles within the Christian Democratic party resemble in substance and outcome nothing so much as the conflicts between regular and reform factions within the Democratic parties of Illinois or New York.

CONCLUSION

By way of conclusion I will briefly discuss two cases, France and the United States, which would appear to stand as counterexamples to the argument presented in this chapter, and suggest how their deviations from the patterns outlined above can be explained.

Over the course of the past two centuries France appears to have deviated in both possible directions from the patterns outlined above. An absolutist coalition emerged in the seventeenth and eighteenth centuries in France, well before the creation of a mass electorate, and yet patronage came to play a major role in the parliamentary and party politics of France during the second half of the nineteenth century and the first half of the twentieth.[104] Another change of direction occurred after the Second World War. Patronage played a less prominent role in the political life of the Fourth Republic than it had in the Third, and it has moved yet further into the background in the Fifth Republic.[105] As for the United States, the creation of a mass electorate in the Jacksonian period preceded by half a century the emergence of America's constituency for bureaucratic autonomy during the Progressive era, and yet the Progressives triumphed and managed to put an end to the practice of patronage politics in many states and cities in the United States. How can these cases be reconciled with the argument spelled out above?

In arguing that internally mobilized parties will avoid the use of patronage in nations where either an absolutist or a progressive coalition emerged prior to the mobilization of the masses into politics, and that such parties will be patronage oriented where the mobilization of the masses into politics antedated the formation of either one of these coalitions, I do not mean to suggest that the order in which these two events occurs utterly predetermines the subsequent character of a nation's party politics. My claim, rather, is more modest: the relative timing of these two developments weights the dice toward one outcome or the other. The "expected" outcome can be reversed, but any effort to reverse it engenders a crisis of the regime and requires the total reorientation of the nation's politics—perhaps even a revolution—to succeed. If and when such a crisis occurs, the challengers to the old order and the defenders of that order mobilize their forces, and the outcome of the struggle depends upon the breadth of the popular support and the character of the institutional backing enjoyed by each side. Germany, as I argued at some length above, experienced a number of such crises—for example, in 1848 and 1918—but the forces of absolutism were able to prevail in each instance. In France and the United States the challengers to the preexisting regime fared somewhat better.

France

It should be noted, however, that it required a series of revolutions and the topplings of a succession of regimes—three monarchies, two empires, and four republics—to bring about the changes in France mentioned above, and even then it is possible to see the residues of Bourbon absolutism in the France of today. The Revolution of 1789 neither destroyed the centralized state that Louis XIV created, as Tocqueville long ago argued, nor did it dislodge the forces of absolutism from positions in that structure, as the career of the most prominent representative of those forces, Tallyrand, illustrates; Napoleon, rather, built upon the foundations laid by the Bourbons.[106] It was only after the Revolution of 1830 that the old families of the *noblesse de robe* were driven from the prefectoral corps,[107] but even the revolutions of 1830 and 1848, the rise and fall of the Second Empire, and the creation of the Third Republic together were not sufficient to destroy the absolutist coalition or to drive its members entirely from the citadels of power in France. As Theodore Zeldin notes in his study of politics in the Third Republic, Republican *parliamentary* politicians did indeed regard themselves as opponents of the state and of the classes who were identified with it, and these politicians used the institutions of the Republic, namely, the Chamber of Deputies, to gain control over and to colonize those governmental agencies (Interior, Ponts et Chaussées, Education, or more generally, the field administration of the state) that most closely concerned the classes they represented, the provincial middle classes.[108]

Republican *ministerial* politicians, however—that small group (e.g., Sarraut, Briand, Freycinet) which monopolized cabinet positions in the Republic—found the overhead agencies of the central administration (especially the Conseil d'Etat and the Inspection des Finances) so useful for assuring their control over the regime that they did not undermine them.[109] There was a tacit arrangement between the government and the old forces of absolutism to exclude parliamentary politicians from influence over these agencies, as well as over the foreign, colonial, and military services, and recruitment into them was restricted to young men who had passed through the Ecole Libre des Sciences Politiques.[110] This institution and these departments remained the preserve of the absolutist coalition and were hotbeds of anti-Republican sentiment, as the events of 1940 were to demonstrate. In other words, under the Third Republic the state in France was divided along functional lines, and each half was grounded upon a different social base. The patronage system of the Third Republic fed upon that half of the state from which the absolutist coalition had been driven by the revolutions of the nineteenth century.

With the creation of the Fourth Republic the defenders of bureaucratic autonomy were able to erect a more extensive barrier between the bureaucracy and party politicians than had existed under the Third Republic by entering into an alliance with lower-level officials—an arrangement negotiated by a top Gaullist politician, Michel Debré, and the leader of the French Communist party, Maurice Thorez![111] As the base of support for a politically autonomous bureaucracy was extended this way, party politicians in the Fourth Republic found it more difficult to acquire patronage than had their counterparts in the Third Republic. And the weakening of parliament in the Fifth Republic has made it more difficult for them still.

I recount this history in order to underline two points. First, I would call attention to the severity of the political disruptions that were required to bring about changes in the role that patronage played in French politics and the magnitude of the realignments in the entire structure of national politics that these changes entailed. Second, I would note that despite this succession of revolutions and changes of regime, the constituency for bureaucratic autonomy that coalesced in the predemocratic era in France was able at all times to retain at least a foothold in the state administration and to emerge triumphant again in the contemporary period after it broadened its base of support.

The United States

If in France under the Third Republic the state was divided along functional lines between a constituency for bureaucratic autonomy and a constituency for patronage, in the United States in the twentieth century it has been divided along geographic lines: the practitioners of patronage politics have been able to hold their own in most states to the east of the Mississippi and their opponents have had the upper hand in most states to the west. The situation in the eastern states accords with the predictions of the theory outlined above: the enactment of white manhood suffrage in the United States antedated the formation of a constituency for bureaucratic autonomy (the former occurred in the Age of Jackson, the latter in the Progressive era); the major parties in the United States thus were free to use patronage when they undertook to mobilize mass support; consequently, the forces that had a stake in the patronage system enjoyed broad popular backing; and thus these forces were able to offer substantial resistance to the constituency for bureaucratic autonomy that coalesced under the banner of progressivism in the early decades of the twentieth century. By contrast, the opponents of the patronage system enjoyed considerable success in the western states, and this appears to contradict the theory outlined above.

This variation in the character of present-day party politics among the major regions of the United States can, however, be explained in terms consistent with the analysis offered in this chapter. The sources of this difference do not lie in the composition of the electorate, as Mayhew and Wolfiinger have argued.[112] Nor does it lie in differences in the social composition of the forces that led the attack upon the patronage system. The leadership of America's constituency for bureaucratic autonomy is drawn from roughly similar groups in all regions of the nation—from the professional upper middle classes and from those elements of the local notability and business community that do not enjoy privileged access to the locally dominant party—and it resembles in broad outline the social composition of the progressive coalition in Great Britain—if one considers the descendants of the New England patriciate to be the American equivalent of the English aristocracy.[113] The source of this variation lies, rather, along the other dimension I have emphasized: the extent to which party politicians had mobilized a broad popular base prior to the emergence of a constituency for bureaucratic autonomy.[114] Party organizations in all regions of the United States in the nineteenth century were patronage oriented, but in the states of America's "periphery" these organizations were less tightly organized and less broadly based than the political machines that governed the older states of the northeastern "metropole": the politicians who were the agents of "foreign corporations" (most commonly railroads) in the "colonial" regions of the United States, by virtue of the vast magnitude of the resources at their disposal relative to those possessed by other political actors, were able to dominate state politics without mobilizing widespread popular support. William Herren's Southern Pacific machine in California, for example, was not a mass party in the same sense as was the Democratic machine in New York.[115] The Progressives in the western states, I would hypothesize, were able to ride to power by winning support among the voters who had *not* been mobilized by the preexisting party system. What I am suggesting, in other words, is that although manhood suffrage existed throughout the United States at the time the forces of progressivism coalesced, the electorate in the peripheral regions of the United States had not been fully mobilized by a well-organized mass party, and consequently the constituency for patronage in these states was not so broadly based as it was in the states of the Northeast. This can explain why the Progressives in the West were able quite convincingly to picture themselves as spokesmen for "the people" against "the interests," whereas in the East the electorate was more inclined to regard reform as the cause of a narrow elite and to view machine politicians as representatives of the popular cause.[116] For an analysis of these conflicts see chapter 5 below.

CHAPTER 3

Party, Bureaucracy, and Political Change in the United States

INTRODUCTION

Over the past 200 years, a half dozen party systems have emerged, developed, and decayed in the United States. These successive systems have been distinguished from one another by the issues dividing the major parties, the proportion of the vote each party normally received, and the social composition of each party's electoral base. Equally important, changes have occurred from one party system to the next in the strength of political parties relative to other public institutions in the United States.[1]

Among the most important institutional changes that have accompanied the emergence of new party systems in the United States have been shifts in the power of political parties relative to public bureaucracies. The relationship between these two institutions is of great significance for a number of reasons. First, it has major consequences for the structure of political parties and for the electoral strategies they are able to pursue. If political parties are the stronger institution, they will be in a position to extract patronage from the bureaucracy and to distribute it to the cadres who conduct their campaigns and the voters who support their candidates; if parties are weaker than bureaucracies, they must find some alternative means of mobilizing popular support.[2] Second and more generally, the strength of parties relative to bureaucracies has an important bearing upon the character of the political system as a whole, as Figure 3.1 indicates.

Figure 3.1 is a simple typology of the relationships that may exist between the power of parties and bureaucracies. Where parties are strong and the bureaucracy is weak (cell I), parties will be in a position to dominate both the electoral and administrative arenas, and, as just noted, to use their power to generate patronage.[3] Such political systems can be said to be governed by "political machines." Where parties and bureaucracies are both strong (cell II), each institution will be able to dominate its respective arena, to exert some discipline over its members, and to protect its boundaries from lateral penetration. In this situation, parties will not find it possible to obtain patronage from the bureaucracy for distribution to voters, but will be in a position to deliver on whatever promises they make concerning the general policies they intend to enact. Borrowing a term that was popular a genera-

POLITICAL PARTIES

		STRONG	WEAK
BUREAUCRACY	**STRONG**	II "Responsible" Party	III "Irresponsible" Party / Bureaucratic State
	WEAK	I Political Machine	IV Regime of Notables Corporatist State Machine of Incumbents

FIGURE 3.1 Party and Bureaucratic Power

tion ago, one can label these "responsible parties." Where the bureaucracy is strong and parties are weak (cell III), executive agencies may be able to resist not only lateral penetration, but also control from above. In this situation, parties will be able neither to extract patronage from the bureaucracy nor to deliver on any promises they may make concerning the implementation of public policy; all they can do is offer voters empty rhetoric or appeal to their supporters' racial, ethnic, or national sentiments. These can be called "irresponsible parties" and a regime governed in this way can be termed "bureaucratic state."

The final category (cell IV) is the most complex. If both parties and bureaucracies are institutionally weak, the locus of power depends upon which particular political actors, organizations, or institutions dominate in their stead. Where local dignitaries dominate the electoral arena and use their influence to extract patronage from the bureaucracy for distribution to their personal clients, one may speak of a "regime of notables." Where interest groups have influence over the bureaucracy and are able to help candidates win elections to public office, one may speak of a "corporatist state." Finally, where professional politicians secure elective office by constructing personal campaign organizations and remain in power by intervening before the bureaucracy on behalf of their constituents, one may speak of a "machine of incumbents."

Since the emergence of the first American party system in the 1790s, the power of party relative to bureaucracy in the United States has changed dramatically a number of times, and the American political system could aptly be characterized, at least in part, in each of these ways. In this chapter, I seek to account for these patterns of institutional development, transformation, and decay.

My argument, briefly stated, is that changes in relative power of party and bureaucracy in the United States are intimately related to the process of critical realignment in American politics. Critical elections bring to power new political coalitions, some or all of whose members wish to use public authority for new purposes. By altering the relationship between, and the internal structure of, party and bureaucracy, elements of the new majority coalition seek to undermine the position of politicians who held power during the earlier party system, to seize control over the government, and to turn it to the purposes they want it to serve. Or to phrase this in somewhat greater detail, by restructuring the party and the bureaucracy, various contenders for power seek to create an institutional order that will enable them to (1) defeat their opponents in the other party, or in other factions of their own party; (2) subject voters to their discipline; (3) control the use of public authority; and (4) have the structural and technical capacity to perform those functions that the group in question wants the government to serve. Whether reformers in the wake of any given critical election will seek to strengthen or weaken the party as an institution, and to defend or to undermine the autonomy of the bureaucracy, depends primarily upon the structure of the antecedent regime and the nature of the resources the reformers command.

In the sections below, I will indicate how the major changes that have occurred from one party system to the next in the structure of, and relationship between, party and bureaucracy in the United States can be understood in these terms.

THE REGIME OF NOTABLES:
THE FEDERALISTS AND JEFFERSONIANS

The first political parties in the United States—the Federalists and the Jeffersonian Republicans—were coalitions of notables. During the period extending from the emergence of the two parties in the 1790s through their collapse in the 1820s, the level of political participation in most areas of the country was low, party organizations were weak or nonexistent, elective offices were monopolized by local notables, and these officials appointed their associates and clients to positions in the bureaucracy.[4] There were, however, some differences between what the Federalists and the Jeffersonians sought to accomplish, the opposition they had to overcome to do so, and the resources they commanded, and these shaped their orientations toward party and bureaucracy.

The Federalists spoke for a rather narrow segment of the American upper class. The central policies of the Washington and Adams administrations (Hamilton's financial program, the pro-British tilt in foreign relations, and policies with respect to public lands and Indian removal that retarded settlement of the West) served the interests of the nation's mercantile elite, a sector of the economy that had commercial ties with Britain and little geographic presence apart from the coastal regions of New England and the Middle States. Because this sector encompassed such a small proportion of the nation's population (at most 10 percent), the ideology the party professed and the political techniques upon which it relied were necessarily antidemocratic.[5]

Though there were some important exceptions, the Federalists, as Ellis observes, "publicly denied the ability of the people to govern themselves, stressed the need for elitist guidance, and never were able to successfully practice the art of popular politics."[6] Washington, in his farewell address, formulated the classic conservative critique of party, and one element among the Federalists was prepared to use the army, rather than to engage in countermobilization, in order to cope with the Republican opposition. Similarly, the bureaucratic appointment practices of the Federalists were narrowly elitist in their orientation. In selecting individuals to serve in the departments and agencies of his administration, President Washington chose men who in his words were "esteemed and honored by their neighbors," that is, local notables who "placed at the disposal of the [new government] a system of social relations in which they were already superiors, independently of their official tenure."[7] As opposition to Federalist policies congealed, the Washington and Adams administrations, if anything, narrowed their political base, and their patronage practices became more restrictive: they appointed only those notables who supported the administration in its conflicts with the Republicans.[8] This culminated in Adams's midnight appointments. By packing the federal bureaucracy and judiciary with Federalists, Adams sought to ensure that these institutions would remain bastions of Federalism despite the party's repudiation by the majority of the electorate in 1800.

The majority that supported the Republicans in the critical election of 1800 was composed of two major groups. The first were subsistence farmers who opposed the administration both because they stood outside the market economy and, therefore, could only be injured by Federalist economic policies, and because they were radically democratic in ideology. This group formed the radical wing of the Republican Party. The second was composed of commercial farmers who would profit from trading in a larger market than Britain alone provided. This group, the Republican moderates, was led by planters such as Jefferson and Madison, who, because they opposed Federalist policies on behalf of the nation's agricultural majority, were democratic in ideology and were able to successfully play the game of popular politics.

Although radical and moderate Republicans shared an antipathy to the mercantile, pro-British, and antidemocratic orientations of the Federalists, the economic and political orders they favored were not in the least similar. The moderates, unlike the radicals, wanted to build a commercial society and to have the government foster economic development through internal improvements and the chartering of banks. (The Republican moderates differed from the Hamiltonians to the extent that they wanted to develop the economy on an agricultural base and by strengthening the national market, rather than on a mercantile base and by tying the American economy to the British market.) And in the realm of politics, the moderates, unlike the radicals, regarded as dangerous all forms of political activity conducted apart from the established institutions and leaders of society; they were aghast at the Whiskey Rebellion, uncomfortable with the Democratic-Republican societies, and opposed to constitutional reforms that would radically democratize and decentralize the government.

To implement their program, the moderate Republicans sought to drive from the political arena extremists of both the right and the left—the High Federalists and the Old Republicans—and to construct a coalition of moderates from both parties who favored a republican polity, a market economy, and an ordered society. Jeffersonian practices with respect to party and patronage can be understood in light of this goal as well as the resources the Republican moderates were able to command, and the opposition they had to overcome to achieve it. When the Federalists, during the Adams administration, were preparing to use the army to crush opposition (or so it appeared), Madison and Jefferson were willing to ally with the radicals and to mobilize mass support—a strategy that involved creating the Republican Party.[9] After gaining power, however, the moderates slowly turned away from their alliance with the radicals and sought to conciliate the moderate Federalists. The Republican Party was permitted to decay once its function of defeating the "monarchists" had been fulfilled. As Richard Hofstadter has documented, Jefferson, Madison, and Monroe did not regard the Republican Party as a permanent institution, but rather as a temporary expedient to rout the enemies of republicanism and, thereby, to establish the preconditions for a partyless regime.[10]

In a similar vein, Jefferson refused, in the face of substantial pressure, to purge all Federalists from the bureaucracy and judiciary, for fear of alienating those he wished to conciliate. He sought to give the Republicans proportional representation in, rather than total dominance over, the bureaucracy. During his first two years in office, Jefferson replaced somewhat over half the officials appointed by his predecessors—186 of 316 presidential appointees—and then he stopped. In selecting officials to be removed, Jefferson sought in particular to frustrate Adams's effort to turn the judiciary and bureaucracy into a Federalist power base. He refused to recognize the commissions of the midnight appointees, removed Federalist marshals and district attorneys to ensure that Republicans would enjoy access to the federal courts, and fired field administrators who used their positions in ways which helped the Federalists and injured the Republicans. Jefferson appointed only Republicans to the vacancies thus created, but not just any

Republicans. In choosing whom to appoint, Jefferson canvassed the Republican notability in the locality in question, and individuals who wished to secure appointments from him submitted petitions and letters attesting to their good character and their acceptability to the respectable men of the community.[11]

The Jeffersonians, then, were very much a party of notables. Where they differed from the Federalists was that their regime was grounded upon a much larger segment of the nation's upper class and that, in order to defeat their opponents, they were prepared to appeal mass support—a strategy that led them to build the world's first modern party organization.[12] Once their position was secured, however, the Jeffersonians mobilized their followers and recruited public officials through the informal community networks commanded by members of the patriciate and gentry who were loyal to the administration, rather than through a well-organized party structure.[13] This system enabled the classes for which they spoke to gain privileged access to public benefits and to use public authority to discipline the groups that were excluded from the Jeffersonian regime. (During the Jeffersonian era, for example, public lands were sold only in large lots to commercial farmers, and federal marshals appointed by Republican presidents evicted subsistence farmers who were squatting on the public domain.) And because the Jeffersonian notability was rather well educated (it is not coincidental that Jefferson founded a university), the state they staffed in this way was quite competent to administer the mildly mercantilist policies the regime pursued.[14]

PARTY, PATRONAGE, AND POLITICAL MACHINES: THE JACKSONIANS

The system led by the Jeffersonians was overthrown following the election of 1828 by the Jacksonians. The politicians of the Jacksonian Era initiated a process that, in a different context, has been termed "the emancipation of the state from civil society."[15] They established a party system and a system of public administration that were independent of the informal social hierarchies upon which the Jeffersonians had relied. They did this by creating mass-based party organizations, reorganizing the bureaucracy, and perfecting the spoils system.

The Jeffersonian political economy had excluded, or at least disadvantaged, a rather heterogeneous collection of social groups. Chief among these were businessmen seeking to break into the existing order of limited mercantile privilege (the classic example is Wall Street's opposition to the Philadelphia-based Second Bank of the United States); farmers who faced competition in the local markets they once had monopolized from grain transported on government-subsidized canals; master mechanics being squeezed out by merchant-capitalists who were able to obtain credit from publicly chartered banks; and marginal farmers and laborers hurt by the price inflation caused, at least in their view, by the issue of currency by those banks.[16] The members of religious and ethnic minorities who were discriminated against by legislation enacted at the behest of more established groups also had reason to be dissatisfied with the prevailing regime.

This heterogeneous collection of social groups was available for mobilization by anti-administration politicians and by political movements which argued that the common source of all their problems was a regime which granted favors to those who occupied privileged political positions and which, in the process, intervened so actively in society that it upset the natural order of things. The Jacksonians proposed a dual remedy for these problems: open up the political system to the people; and limit the powers of government. They sought to implement this program by appealing for popular support apart from established leadership channels.[17] The reforms they sponsored in the electoral and administrative arenas were part and parcel of this effort to overthrow the notables' regime.

The Jacksonians sponsored a number of reforms in the procedures governing the conduct of elections and the recruitment of public officials that made it difficult for local notables to dominate these processes. Under the old regime, restrictions on the franchise, large election districts, the absence of a "top of the ticket" as a focus for popular enthusiasm (presidential electors and governors often were appointed by state legislatures), and, of course, the absence of an organized opposition, together limited the size of the active electorate. The restricted scope of the political universe in conjunction with viva voce voting enabled the leading men of the county to send one of their number to the state legislature. And because state legislatures or their appointees (governors, councils of appointment) commonly selected the heads of state executive departments, judges, and county officials, it was only necessary for the notability to dominate state legislative elections in order to dominate the entire governmental apparatus. The electoral reforms of the Jacksonian Era—white manhood suffrage; the paper ballot; small polling districts; direct election of governors, presidential electors, heads of state executive departments, and local government officials; and short terms of office—swamped the older, elite-dominated mechanisms of election management and political recruitment.[18]

After coming to power by overwhelming their opponents in the electoral arena, the Jacksonians sought to extend their sway over the bureaucracy. The doctrine of rotation-in-office, as is well known, legitimized this effort to expel their predecessors from positions in the bureaucracy. Somewhat less well known are the other moves the Jacksonians made in their effort to sever the ties between the notability and the bureaucracy and to extend their own control over it. In point of fact, the Jacksonians were responsible for the first major episode of administrative reform in American history. Though they were not at all self-conscious about what they were doing, they sought to transform the federal bureaucracy from a structure that operated according to the principles of personal organization into one that operated according to the principles of formal organization. Jacksonian officials such as Amos Kendall drafted administrative reorganization plans that specified the responsibilities attached to positions within the bureaucracy (rather than to the persons occupying these roles); established bureaus organized along functional lines within the executive departments; assigned officials to perform staff (as distinguished from line) responsibilities; created elaborate systems of inspection, reporting, and accounting to monitor departmental field offices; promulgated codes of official ethics; and insisted that officials distinguish sharply between their private funds and public accounts. Matthew Crenson,[19] who describes these reforms in an important book, argues, mistakenly in my view, that the Jacksonians established formal bureaucratic structures because rapid social change in the early nineteenth century had undermined traditional social institutions—the bar, the business community, the local community—and made it impossible to rely on them any longer to enforce standards of probity and good behavior upon bureaucrats.[20] I would argue, rather, that the Jacksonians established formal bureaucratic procedures instead of relying on these informal institutions to control the behavior of subordinate officials because these institutions (which continued to flourish well beyond the 1820s and 1830s) were controlled in the main by their political enemies. By removing the bureaucrats appointed by their predecessors, the Jacksonians sought to sever the ties between the bureaucracy and these traditional social structures; and by reorganizing the bureaucracy, they sought to subject it to the control of the officeholders whom they had elected, the institutions (especially the party organizations) they commanded, and the social groups for whom they spoke. In other words, the bureaucratic reforms the Jacksonians sponsored served to "emancipate" the output institutions of the state from the informal social hierarchies that an established class of notables controlled, just as the electoral and party reforms they sponsored served to emancipate the input institutions of the state from this segment of civil society.

The electoral and administrative reforms of the Jacksonian Era, then, were part and parcel of the realignment process: they were efforts by a new majority to drive from power the elites who had dominated the earlier regime. As such, they could be supported by all, or at least most, elements of the new majority coalition. Once enacted, however, these reforms had consequences for the distribution of power *within* the majority party. The expansion of the number of public offices subject to popular election, and the shortening of the terms of public officials, made legislators, executives, and

judges dependent upon the politicians who organized the enlarged electorates of the period, and turned party management into, if not a full-time
profession, then at least a vocation that demanded far more time and attention for its successful performance than had been devoted to it by the gentlemen dilettantes of the earlier regime. At the same time the expulsion of the
notables from institutions of policy making and administration, and the sub-
jection of these institutions to party influence, gave middle-class lawyers,
editors, and businessmen an incentive to devote themselves to the tasks of
party management, because these developments made it possible for such
men-on-the-make to live off politics by serving as agents for private interests
in their dealings with government (the Jacksonian period saw the rise of the
lobby), by moving into and out of public office, and by making personal
contacts and obtaining public contracts (e.g., printing contracts) that were
useful in their private careers. The Jacksonian reforms, then, placed at the
very center of the political system a group of middle-class professional or
semiprofessional politicians.[21]

The leadership of this group did not go unchallenged. The Jackson coalition, as mentioned above, was extremely heterogeneous. It included elements of the business community and the middle class that wanted, as Carl
Degler terms it, to "liberate the expanding American economy from the
fetters of a dying mercantilist approach to business enterprise,"[22] by permit-
ting anyone to obtain a bank or corporate charter (free banking and general
incorporation), and by expanding the supply of money and credit. It also
included marginal farmers, mechanics, and laborers who wanted to contract
the money supply, who regarded all banks and corporations as chartered
monopolies, and who supported other policies equally antipathetic to the
interests of the first group, such as the ten-hour day and the right to strike.
Many of the spokesmen for this position, especially in the larger cities, were
affiliated with the fledgling trade unions of the Jacksonian Era, organizations
that were seeking to establish their political hegemony over the working
classes. At different times these leaders worked through third parties—
organizing the workingmen's parties of the period—or through the Democratic party—forming its radical wing. To the extent that these leaders mobilized their supporters through craft organizations, their challenge to the
professional party politicians of the period was as backward looking as that
of the early Whig party; it harked back to eighteenth century patterns of
working-class political activity.[23]

The middle-class professional politicians in the Democratic party responded to this challenge in a number of ways. They came out in support of
some of the policies advocated by the radicals. Such concessions, however,
alienated the party's wealthier supporters.[24] It was possible, however, to
appeal to the rank-and-file members of the radical factions without splitting
the Jacksonian movement along class lines by pursuing two alternative strat-

egies. Democratic politicians appealed to working-class voters by stressing the party's stance on religious and cultural issues—its defense of immigrants and Catholics against the attacks of nativists and evangelical Protestants.[25] And Democratic politicians attempted to steal away the supporters of the radicals by pursuing a strategy of counterorganization. Whereas the radicals sought to organize their followers along craft lines or, more exactly, to politicize preexisting labor organizations, professional politicians organized their followers along residential lines (in ward and town committees) and politicized preexisting recreational organizations, such as volunteer fire brigades and militia companies.[26]

The control that politicians established over the organs of administration and policy making in the United States during the Jacksonian Era contributed to the success of this strategy of party building. The access they acquired to the bureaucracy enabled them to distribute patronage to the cadres who staffed the party apparatus, as well as to gang leaders, fire captains, and saloon keepers who enjoyed followings among the working classes.[27] Party politicians thereby provided these leaders with a stake in the success of the party organization and with an incentive to bring their followers into its camp. And the influence they enjoyed within city councils and state legislatures enabled party politicians to obtain public subsidies for militia and fire companies and for sectarian charitable institutions with similar consequences.

The party organizations that Jacksonian politicians built, and the bureaucratic reforms they simultaneously sponsored, then, were the means by which a particular political class squeezed out its competitors and came to power in the United States. The construction of a mass-based, geographically organized, and patronage-fueled party apparatus enabled professional politicians who were drawn from, or had ties to the middle class, to establish their hegemony over the working class and to triumph over leaders who depended on two older structures and traditions of political organization— namely, the elite networks of the notables and the autonomous craft organizations of the mechanics. And the building of this apparatus was linked to the bureaucratic reforms of the Jacksonian Era. The cadres who worked for the party organization were compensated for their labors with appointments to positions in the bureaucracy. And the activities of the organization were financed by political assessments levied on the salaries of civil servants.

In the dozen years between 1828 and 1840, the political forces that opposed President Jackson underwent a similar transformation. As had been true of the Jacksonians before them, they were transformed from a diffuse political movement, important elements of which were committed to earlier modes of political organization, into a political party that (a) was mass-based, autonomously organized, and patronage-fueled; (b) appealed to its supporters by focusing as much on ethnocultural concerns as on economic issues; and (c) was led by a corps of semiprofessional politicians drawn chiefly (though not exclusively) from the middle class. This metamorphosis was especially striking in the case of the Whigs because the very animus which had led to the party's formation had been its founders' opposition to the mode of political organization that the Jacksonians employed and the pattern of political activity in which they engaged, namely appeals to a mass public apart from established social hierarchies.[28] However, the imperatives of electoral law and political competition, and the availability of state patronage, enabled the William Sewards and Thurlow Weeds to seize the leadership of the anti-administration forces and to subject the old notability to their discipline, just as these imperatives and resources had enabled the Van Burens and Marcys to squeeze out competitors for leadership of the Jackson movement.

In a meaningful sense, then, a new political class came to power in the United States as the second party system emerged. The leaders of the Democratic and Whig parties resembled each other—in terms of their origins and career patterns, the organizations they constructed and the political techniques they employed, and the relations they established with the bureaucracy—more than either resembled the notability that ruled the nation prior to the Jacksonian realignment.[29] There was, moreover, a community of interest within this political class that united it across party lines. As Martin Van Buren recognized, such a leadership group could best maintain control over its followers if an opposition party existed.[30] The general acceptance by 1840 of the "idea of a party system," to use Richard Hofstadter's phrase, was the ideological expression of the hegemony of this political class, just as the general triumph of the party organizations these politicians constructed over alternative political formations was the institutional expression of its hegemony.

In sum, the electoral and administrative reforms of the Jacksonians emerged out of the efforts of a middle-class leadership group to overturn a previously dominant class of notables by pursuing a strategy of mass mobilization. The party organizations Jacksonian politicians constructed enabled them both to overwhelm these notables and to exert discipline over their political allies. The bureaucratic reforms they sponsored—the spoils system and administrative reorganization—enabled them to drive their opponents from the bureaucracy and to subject it to their own control. The Jacksonians were free to use bureaucratic appointments as a reward for party service to the extent that they wanted the state to perform only a limited range of functions—chiefly, delivering the mails, distributing public lands, collecting tariff revenues, and driving the Indians further west—and these did not require most civil servants to have skills and training beyond those that ordinary citizens possessed, as President Jackson himself observed in his first inaugural address.[31]

THE ATTACK UPON PATRONAGE AND
PARTY ORGANIZATION: THE MUGWUMPS

The dozen years that followed the realignment of 1860 were a turning point in American politics: they belonged both to an earlier era and to a later one. Upon coming to power, the Republicans, as had the Jacksonians before them, sought to extend their control over the entire governmental apparatus, and to use the patronage they extracted from the bureaucracy for the purposes of party building. Within a decade, however, an important group of Republicans launched an attack upon the party organization and spoils system, and formulated what would prove to be one of the modern alternatives to that system.

The Republicans who came to power in 1860 were a heterogeneous collection of radicals who wanted to abolish slavery, farmers who supported homestead legislation, manufacturers and workers who wanted tariff protection, and voters who had toyed with nativism in the mid-1850s. They were bound together by the ideology of free labor and by the conviction that the construction of a society organized around this principle was threatened by the "slavepower," which sought to control the western territories and the national government in order to build a society based upon entirely different principles.[32] During the 1860s the Republican Party was beset by factionalism; the issues that divided the party's radical, moderate, and conservative factions, however, did not center around questions of patronage and party organization. Thus, upon entering the White House, President Lincoln conducted the most thorough purge of the bureaucracy in the nation's history, and he used the patronage thereby generated to build a party committed to the unionist cause.[33] This endeavor was supported by radicals, moderates, and conservatives alike.

The very vigor with which the Republicans generated and used patronage for the purposes of party building in the 1860s, however, had consequences for the character of the party and for the distribution of power within it by the 1870s. It transformed the Republicans from a political movement into a political party and advantaged the party's professional politicians. As Morton Keller notes:

> Party leaders and political organizations hardly were unknown in . . . the 1860s. Nevertheless during the 1870s the character of American politics sharply changed. The passionate, ideologically charged political ambiance of the Reconstruction years gave way to a politics that rested on the perpetuation of party organization rather than the fostering of public policy. . . . These shifts of tone were accompanied by changes of party leadership. In state after state men who placed greater weight on organization than ideology came into or retained power.[34]

The leaders who were squeezed out by these developments—journalists, ideologues, clergymen, and professional men—came to regard the political practices that were responsible for their undoing (to which they formerly had not objected) as profoundly illegitimate. These Republicans (who were known at various times as Liberals, Independents, or Mugwumps) were distressed not simply because they had lost influence within the movement they had helped to found, but also because they disagreed with many of the policies enacted by the politicians who belonged to the party's dominant factions, the Stalwarts and the Half Breeds. The leading Liberals and Mugwumps were ardent advocates of hard money, strong proponents of free trade, and hard liners on labor issues.[35] Also as labor conflicts grew more intense in their own communities during the 1870s, they increasingly came to regard as dangerous to property and good order the effort to build a Republican Party in the South on the basis of black votes and in opposition to local elites.[36] The Stalwarts and the Half Breeds, on the other hand, as professional politicians, sought to fashion compromises on at least the first three of these issues (they did disagree on the southern question), compromises with which all elements of the party could live, and which would alienate the fewest voters. The Mugwumps labeled such behavior unprincipled.

The Liberals and Mugwumps were the leading advocates of civil service reform in the United States in the 1870s and 1880s: it was they who placed this reform on the political agenda. And, as they themselves explained, their chief motive for so doing was their desire to purify American politics.[37] They argued that if bureaucratic positions were distributed not as a reward for party service, but rather according to merit as indicated by performance on an open, competitive examination, political competition no longer would center around a struggle for the spoils of office; rather, it would involve the clash of principles. Politicians no longer would be able to entrench themselves in power through what amounted to a system of organized bribery; they would instead have to pay heed to public opinion. Or, to translate this into slightly different language: the party organizations that sustained the incumbent leadership would crumble if deprived of access to patronage, and the politicians affiliated with them would be replaced by the journalists, patricians, and professional men who were opinion leaders in their communities.

In addition to attacking the patronage system, the Mugwump reformers opposed the highly disciplined, "militaristic" pattern of party organization that developed during the 1870s and 1880s.[38] In contrast to the Progressives of the early twentieth century, however, they were not opponents of party per se; they were advocates not of *nonpartisanship*, but rather of *bipartisanship* and political *independence*.[39] Indeed, on the individual level, the defining characteristic of an Independent or Mugwump was his willingness to support whichever party nominated the best man. On the organizational level, as well, the Mugwumps sought to break the monopoly that party organizations had on the political loyalties and activities of citizens. They founded one of the first interest groups in American political history, the National Civil Service Reform League, an organization that worked outside party channels to secure the enactment of the policy it advocated, and which was prepared to endorse candidates regardless of party who pledged to vote correctly on this single issue. Finally, on the institutional level, the Mugwumps advocated bipartisan representation on commissions and boards as a solution to the problems of corruption and misgovernment.

The structure of political competition in the United States during the period of the "third party system" makes intelligible both the orientation of the Mugwumps toward political parties and their ability to secure enactment of the Pendleton Act. During the third party system, the division between the two major parties was the closest it has ever been in American history. The Democrats and Republicans, moreover, were evenly balanced on the state level, as well as nationally, in at least the larger states of the Union. This enabled the Mugwumps to play balance-of-power politics quite successfully, especially so after the last southern states were "redeemed" in 1877. The Republicans won the White House in 1876, after losing the popular vote, only because they secured a majority on the commission that certified disputed electoral votes; the switch of fewer than 2,000 votes in New York would have reversed the Republican victory in the 1880 presidential election; and in the elections of 1882, the Republicans suffered serious losses, especially in the states where the Mugwumps were strongest. By supporting the Pendleton Act in the short congressional session of 1882–83, the Republicans hoped to keep the Mugwumps from deserting the party in 1884. Moreover, they calculated that if the Democrats did win the presidency, the incumbent Republican president could take advantage of the new procedures by freezing Republican patronage appointees into the classified service before the new president was inaugurated.[40]

Although the Mugwumps managed in this way to secure enactment of the Pendleton Act, civil service reform did not alter the structure of party politics in the United States in the direction the reformers desired, at least not during the nineteenth century. During the twenty years following the passage of the Pendleton Act, the federal bureaucracy grew more rapidly than did the number of positions in the classified civil service, and most of the positions that were placed in the classified service were technical in character, and hence not especially useful for patronage purposes.[41] Moreover, civil service reform made little headway in the nineteenth century on the state level, the genuine locus of power in the decentralized party system. Only two states (New York and Massachusetts) adopted civil service statutes in the nineteenth century, and the merit systems in these states were quickly emasculated.[42] Consequently, the parties had no less federal or state patronage available to them in 1900 than they had had in 1883. Indeed, the very reason the parties were prepared to live with civil service reform was that it imposed no present costs on them, while it enabled the government to respond to technological change and defused the opposition of some disgruntled elites. In other words, it permitted the parties to maintain their positions as the central institutions of the American political system through the end of the nineteenth century.

In sum, the movement for party and bureaucratic reform in the third-party system was spearheaded by a political class *manqué* that attacked the patronage system in an effort to deprive the politicians in the dominant party factions of the resources they used to fuel their organizations. Because the major parties were well organized, broadly based, and evenly matched, the reformers pursued their goals by playing balance-of-power politics. Given these structural characteristics of the third party system, all alternative strategies—outmobilizing the dominant party factions, converting their supporters, or demobilizing them—would have been far more difficult, even impossible, to pursue. But for the very reason that the reformers did not acquire for themselves a broader mass base than the factions they opposed, they were not strong enough to defend the entire governmental apparatus against the patronage-seeking politicians who sought to extract resources from it. Only after the realignment of 1896 transformed the structure of party politics in the United States were the opponents of the patronage system able to enjoy greater success.

TOWARD A BUREAUCRATIC STATE?
THE PROGRESSIVES

In the history of American politics two periods stand out for their institutional creativity—the Jacksonian and Progressive eras. The Jacksonians sponsored a set of institutional reforms that, as noted above, created a party-centered political system in the United States. Following the realignment of 1896, the Progressives launched an attack upon the institutions of Jacksonian democracy and sought to establish in their stead an executive-centered political system.

There is a direct relationship between the realignment of 1896 and the emergence of the Progressive movement. Prior to 1896 the American political system was characterized by high levels of party competition both nationally and in most of the larger states of the Union. The 1896 realignment created a party system that was both regionally based and highly unbalanced. Consequently, in its wake, the great majority of states, and the national government as well, came to be governed by one-party regimes.[43]

This development provided a windfall for the incumbent leadership of whichever was now the dominant party in these one-party states. Moreover, since party politicians in turn-of-the-century America characteristically furthered their careers and strengthened their factions by drawing upon the resources of a major corporation or servicing a major economic interest within their state or city (e.g., the Southern Pacific Railroad in California, the Louisville & Nashville in Kentucky, traction and elevated railway companies in New York City), these developments provided a windfall for the sector of the business community that happened to be allied with the incumbent leadership of the locally dominant party.[44]

What is a windfall for one set of political leaders and economic interests can be a disaster for other leaders and competing interests. The emergence of one-party regimes after the election of 1896 rendered the minority party useless as a vehicle through which individuals and groups without preferential access to the dominant party could challenge those with it; it was now impossible for them to pursue a balance-of-power strategy akin to the one the Mugwumps had employed. The political actors who found it impossible to advance their interests *within* the party system were joined together by the Progressives in an attack *upon* the party system.

The Progressive movement, far more than the supposedly boss-dominated party machines it attacked, was closely associated with the careers of individual politicians, such as Robert La Follette of Wisconsin, Hiram Johnson of California, Albert Cummins of Iowa, William U'Ren of Oregon, and Theodore Roosevelt in national politics. These political entrepreneurs commonly had found their personal careers frustrated by the leadership of the dominant party or had been recruited into politics entirely outside party channels.[45] They drew their political following from among those groups that did not enjoy privileged access to the locally dominant party—among shippers in states where the party was tied to a railroad, among firms that sold in national markets in cities where the machine was tied to businesses that sold in local markets, among the native middle classes where the party drew support from the ethnic working classes.[46] The ideology that bound the movement together was formulated by a class of intellectuals and professionals who argued that a government that was dominated by a party machine, and that consequently enacted only those policies which served the interests that were tied to the machine, was both corrupt and irrational. Not only did such a government benefit some groups at the expense of others, it also failed to intervene in the economy and in society when such intervention would serve the long-run interests of all groups.[47] In lieu of such a regime, the Progressives proposed to create a set of institutions that would respond directly to the voice of the people, rather than filtering it through party, and that would pay heed to the dictates of science.[48]

Once the ideology and the institutional reforms of the Progressives had been developed in this core setting—in one-party states and cities—they were picked up by politicians and businessmen who found them useful in their struggles against incumbent party leaders in other cities and states, and in national politics. (Significantly, many Progressive reforms were labeled by their state or city of origin: the "Oregon idea," the "Des Moines plan.") The diffusion of the Progressive program was so rapid and widespread because the reformers established a network of organizations, such as the National Municipal League, and publications, such as the *National Municipal Review*, for this very purpose, and they were linked to others (namely, professional associations and national magazines) in whose interest it was to advance the cause. In all settings, however, the central thrust of Progressivism was an attack upon the political party—which since the Jacksonian period had been the central institution of American government—and an effort to create an executive establishment to supplant the party in this pivotal position in the American political system.

For each of the major institutional reforms of the Jacksonian era, the Progressives sponsored an equal and opposite reform. The Jacksonians had increased the number of executive offices subject to popular election; the Progressives sought to reduce that number and to create the position of chief executive through such reforms as the short ballot and the strong mayor plan of municipal government. The most extreme version of this strand of reformism—the city manager plan of government—removed even the position of chief executive from direct popular election. The Jacksonians extended the franchise; the Progressives contracted it through registration, literacy, and citizenship requirements.[49] The Jacksonians established party conventions to nominate candidates for elective office; the Progressives replaced them with primary elections. The Jacksonians created a hierarchical structure of party committees to manage the electorate; the Progressives sought to destroy these party organizations or at least to render their tasks more difficult through such reforms as nonpartisan municipal government, and the separation of local, state, and national elections. Finally, the Jacksonians established a party press and accorded influence to the political editor; the Progressive movement was linked with the emergence of a self-consciously independent press (magazines as well as newspapers) and with muckraking journalists.

The bureaucratic reforms of the Progressives were part and parcel of this more general program of institutional destruction and creation. Civil service reform was the Progressives' effort to destroy the spoils system of the Jacksonians. The Jacksonians had subordinated the bureaucracy as an institution to the political party. By appointing individuals to public jobs in exchange for party service, they were violating the institutional integrity of the bureaucracy for the purposes of strengthening the party. A major reason why the Progressives advocated the creation of an autonomous mechanism and set of procedures for recruiting personnel into the bureaucracy—namely, a civil service commission that would appoint candidates to positions on the basis of their performance on competitive examinations—was to deprive incumbent party leaders of access to the bureaucracy. Deprived of access to the resources necessary for their maintenance, the locally dominant party organization would crumble, and the field would be clear for the reformers to assume power by relying on the organizations and institutions that *they* controlled—the nonpartisan press, chambers of commerce, civic associations, and so forth. To this extent, the Progressive attack upon patronage resembled the one launched by the Mugwump reformers a generation earlier.

In addition, however, there was an affirmative component to the bureaucratic reforms of the Progressives, a component that had not been present in the earlier Mugwump movement for good government. The Progressives sought not simply to destroy the political party, or even to reduce radically the role it played in American government; they sought to create in its stead an administrative arm of government that would be subject to the authority of a chief executive. Toward this end, administrators and professors who were affiliated with the Progressive movement formulated the principles and practices of what came to be called "personnel administration": position-classification plans, career and salary plans, uniform promotion regulations, retirement and pension plans, efficiency reports, and so forth.[50] They also formulated the doctrines and techniques of what came to be known as "administrative management." The Committee on Department Methods (the Keep Commission) appointed by President Roosevelt in 1905 was the first task force or agency in American history commissioned by a president to inquire into, and recommend improvements in, federal administrative practices.[51] In Herbert Emmerich's words, it "stimulated management improvements in bureau after bureau in such varied fields as accounting and costing, archives and records administration, simplification of paper work, use of office machinery, personnel administration, procurement and supply, and contracting procedures."[52] Roosevelt also was the first president to request from Congress authority to reorganize administrative agencies by executive order. And the Commission on Economy and Efficiency (the Taft Commission), appointed by his successor, recommended among other things the creation of a central budget bureau to prepare an executive budget and of a central personnel bureau to develop efficiency records, position classifications, and rules governing the discipline of civil servants that would extend over all federal administrative agencies and employees.[53] On the city and state levels, the Progressives sponsored a parallel series of reforms in an effort to create a unified executive branch out of the dozens of commissions and departments that floated somewhere between the city council and the mayor or the state legislature and the governor.[54]

These reforms, when fully implemented, were to have major consequences for the political influence of various groups in American society, for the relative power of the nation's governmental institutions, and for the role it was able to play both in the domestic and international arenas. These consequences were closely intertwined, and can scarcely be discussed apart from one another. Consider first their political implications. An executive establishment that stood outside the domain of partisan conflict would be in a position to exercise stewardship over the economy as a whole, and would also be in a position to advance the national interest (as that interest was understood by whomever controlled the executive) in the international economy and state system. An executive with such responsibilities would be compelled to pay heed to various interests as much in proportion to their importance in their economy as in proportion to their weight in the electorate.[55] Such a view of presidential responsibilities was expressed by Theodore Roosevelt in his well-known stewardship theory of the presidency. And significantly, it was during the administrations of Roosevelt and his two successors, and with their full cooperation, that the first institutions of functional (or corporatist) representation developed in the United States.[56] In a similar vein, it was during their administrations that universities, professional associations, and Wall Street law firms and investment banks took their place beside the party as a channel for recruitment into the executive branch, and that the in-and-outer (e.g., Clifford Pinchot, Henry Stimson, James Garfield, Felix Frankfurter) made his appearance beside the patronage appointee in high level government positions.[57] The construction of an executive branch, then, was the work of men who commanded the great national institutions that were coming to play an increasingly important role in the American economy and society, and it provided a channel through which these men could influence public policy. Or to phrase this in slightly different terms, it was during the Progressive era that the executive acquired a constituency among the nation's "cosmopolitan" elite (which, as Samuel P. Huntington notes, was to sustain it for the next fifty years), and correlatively, that the Congress became the refuge of the nation's "parochial" elites.[58]

The administrative reforms of the Progressives increased the control that the president, and the groups that enjoyed access to the presidency, were able to exercise over the administrative apparatus of government, at the expense of the institutions and groups that competed with them for influence over it—the Congress, the political party, and most importantly, the bureaucrats themselves. Administrative reform involved the imposition of uniform procedures upon the bureaucracy—procedures, as mentioned above, governing accounting, records keeping, employee evaluation, promotions, salary scales, and so on. What these reforms meant concretely was that agency heads, chief clerks, and lower level bureaucrats no longer would have as much control as they formerly had over how their office accounts would be kept, which records would be retained, how the work of their subordinates was to be evaluated, who would be promoted, and over the salaries that individual bureaucrats would receive. At the same time, Presidents Roosevelt and Taft promulgated a series of executive orders—the most famous of which were Teddy Roosevelt's "gag orders"—that sought to restrict the lobbying and campaign activities of civil servants, as well as some more conventional union activities, that is, which sought to limit the ability of bureaucrats to win salary increases by working through the Congress, political parties, or labor unions, rather than by conforming to the uniform rules and standards the administrative reformers were seeking to impose on them.[59]

Finally, the administrative reforms of the Progressives increased the technical competence and the organizational coherence of the bureaucracy, and thereby endowed the government with the capacity to intervene far more actively in the economy and society. The Progressives, to be sure, were not New Dealers, and there were substantial disagreements among them (especially between the western insurgents who rallied behind La Follette and the easterners who looked to Teddy Roosevelt for leadership) concerning the policies the government should pursue. Nonetheless public officials who were commonly identified as Progressive generally sought to extend the sway of governmental regulations over the economy and to implement "reforms" in the areas of public health, education, welfare, morals, and in the management of the public domain.

In conclusion, Progressivism was a movement of political leaders and groups who did not enjoy privileged access to the one-party regimes that emerged in the wake of the 1896 realignment. As had been true of the Mugwumps before them, the Progressives attacked the patronage system and political machines in an effort to dry up the resources and destroy the organizations that incumbent politicians used to maintain themselves in power. There were important differences between the Progressives and Mugwumps, however, which enabled the later movement to be more successful than the earlier one. The Mugwumps had been closely associated with one segment of the nation's upper class—the mercantile and financial elite of the Northeast—and their reformism was in part an attack upon the politicians who played a mediating role in conflicts between this elite and other sectoral and sectional interests over monetary and trade policy.[60] The Progressives, by contrast, did not play the role of intransigent ideologues in such intraclass conflicts. To the contrary, by attempting to create an executive branch that was insulated from partisan influences and the vagaries of electoral competition, they were seeking to establish a governmental institution that would be in a position to take account of all major interests within the economy, and that could supplant the party as the central mediating institution of American government. In addition, the advisory commissions and legislative reference bureaus and municipal research bureaus the Progressives established provided the professional and managerial classes with channels of access to the government; and the civil service reforms they sponsored advantaged the middle class in the competition for positions on the public payroll. Taken together, the managerial and personnel reforms of the Progressives endowed the government with the capacity to administer the regulatory and social overhead programs whose enactment was supported by many of the nation's major business leaders, as well as by groups further down the social scale.[61] In other words, it was the political genius of the Progressives to discover how some of the economic and regional cleavages that had divided the American upper classes in the nineteenth century could be overcome, and how some popular backing could be acquired for an attack upon entrenched political machines.

The Progressive attack upon existing party and bureaucratic institutions, however, encountered substantial resistance. On the national level, the defenders of existing administrative arrangements, by working through the Congress, were able to defeat, or at least to delay, enactment of the major reform proposals of the Keep and Taft commissions. On the state and local levels, the Progressives enjoyed considerable success in those states and cities, chiefly in the West, where the locally dominant parties did not rest on a broad and well-organized popular base. Where the incumbent leadership had mobilized such support during the previous party system, however, it was able to survive the challenge of the Progressives with only temporary losses.[62]

TOWARD A RESPONSIBLE PARTY SYSTEM?
THE NEW DEAL

The second major wave of party and bureaucratic reforms in this century occurred in the aftermath of the New Deal realignment. On the national level, Franklin D. Roosevelt, in 1937, asked Congress to enact the most comprehensive package of administrative reforms since the proposals of the Taft Commission in 1912. And on the state level, as James Sundquist has noted, struggles between reform Democrats and the regular or machine faction of the party erupted in dozens of states as "aftershocks" of the New Deal realignment.[63] Moreover, the number of states adopting merit civil service systems shot up dramatically following the realignment. In the decade and a half following 1933, eleven states enacted civil service statutes, whereas in the decade and a half years preceding the realignment only one state had done so.[64]

The relationship between the New Deal realignment and the party and bureaucratic reform movements that followed it is broadly similar to that between the realignment of 1896 and the reform struggles of the Progressive Era. In both cases, reform movements were spearheaded by elements of the new majority party who wanted to turn the government to new purposes, and who sought, by attacking the patronage system and reorganizing the bureaucracy, both to undermine the politicians who opposed them and to extend their own control over institutions of government. There were, however, some important differences between the New Dealers and Progressives. Most importantly, New Deal liberals were prepared to pursue a strategy of mass mobilization and popular organization in order to overwhelm their rivals. In addition, on questions of political and administrative organization, Roosevelt, as the conventional wisdom asserts, was a thorough pragmatist. He was, for example, quite willing to collaborate with machine politicians who supported his administration. These considerations—the quest for power and control, the strategy of mass organization, and political opportunism—explain variations through time and across space in the party and administrative reforms the New Dealers pursued.

On the national level, administrative and political reform was of little concern to Roosevelt during the period of the "first" New Deal. To the contrary, positions in sixty of the sixty-five new administrative agencies created during the president's first two years in office were exempted from the classified civil service, and many of these new agencies were located outside the departmental structure of the executive branch.[65] The president's associates frankly admitted that administrative reorganization was too touchy a problem to tackle prior to Roosevelt's reelection, for, as they correctly predicted, it would generate furious opposition on the part of the interests threatened by it.[66] Roosevelt only appointed a commission to study executive reorganization in 1936, and he only submitted a reorganization bill to Congress in January 1937, after he had won his second term.[67]

Chronologically and politically, Roosevelt's administrative reforms belonged to the second phase of the New Deal—the phase extending from the Wagner Act and Social Security Act of 1935, through the court packing and reorganization bills of 1937, to the congressional purge of 1938—and were part and parcel of an effort to institutionalize both the programs of the New Deal and the power of the New Dealers. The Reorganization Act would institutionalize the *programs* of Roosevelt's first term by creating two new cabinet departments to administer the public welfare and the public works programs that had been enacted from 1933 to 1936, and by granting the president the authority to integrate other New Deal programs into the existing departmental structure. As the conservative opponents of the reorganization bill well recognized, these provisions would transform programs that had been enacted as emergency measures into permanent features of the American governmental system.[68]

The reforms of 1935–38 would institutionalize the power of the New Dealers by establishing a set of institutions that would link the administration to a mass constituency and would enable it to assert its control over the entire governmental structure; that is, these reforms would perform for the administration precisely those functions served by the party organization in cities and states governed by centralized political machines.[69] The first of these purposes was served by the National Labor Relations Act, which established procedures for organizing the industrial working class into unions that, as could be anticipated, were to become staunch supporters of the administration responsible for their creation; and also by the Social Security Act, which established a bureaucracy to provide benefits of the poor and working class in times of need—assistance that formerly had been provided, if at all, only by political machines.[70] Significantly, under amendments to the Social Security Act enacted in 1939, the Social Security Board required states to establish merit systems covering the employees who administered the program on the state and local level, a requirement which was policed by a Division of State Merit Systems and which led to the creation of the first civil service systems in most states of the union.[71] In this way, the framers of the act sought to ensure that locally dominant political forces would not gain control of the administration of the program and be strengthened by it. Rather, they wanted the flow of these new benefits to be controlled from the center, and the political advantages of the program to accrue to the administration that had enacted it.

The second of the above-mentioned purposes—the creation of a set of institutions that would enable the administration to extend its control over the entire administrative apparatus—was served by the Executive Reorganization Act of 1937. The Reorganization Act would expand the White House staff; extend the merit system and replace the Civil Service Commission with a single personnel director appointed by the president; transfer the preauditing function from the Comptroller-General (and the Congress) to the Budget Bureau (and the President); create a central planning agency in the Executive Office; and place all administrative agencies, including the independent regulatory commissions, under one of the cabinet departments.[72] Together these reforms would endow the administration with the institutional capacity to control the initiation, coordination, and implementation of public policy—a capacity whose only precedent in the political experience of the United States, again, was the control exercised by the party apparatus in cities ruled by centralized machines.

On the state and local levels, the New Deal realignment generated major struggles for control over the Democratic party between political forces committed to the programs of the national administration and the party's incumbent leadership. These aftershocks of the New Deal realignment occurred in some states while Roosevelt was still in the White House, while in others they did not erupt until fifteen or twenty years after his death.[73] The timing and the character of these struggles for power depended upon the stance the incumbent Democratic leadership took with respect to the national administration and the techniques it employed to maintain itself in power. Where incumbent machine politicians supported the New Deal (e.g., Chicago, Pittsburgh) Roosevelt was perfectly willing to use the patronage generated by New Deal programs to strengthen local party machines.[74] Where the incumbent Democratic leadership was hostile to the national administration and commanded a broadly based, patronage-oriented party machine (e.g., Tammany Hall in New York City), the liberals organized through third-party organizations or reform clubs (e.g., the American Labor Party and later the Democratic reform movement in New York). In these cities, the conflict between insurgents and incumbents resembled the battles between reformers and political machines during the Progressive era: the insurgents attacked the patronage system in an effort to dry up the resources upon which their opponents relied; they challenged the legitimacy of the party organizations their opponents led, accusing them of "bossism"; and they sought to demobilize their opponents' followers more than to bring new groups into the electorate.[75] Finally, where the incumbent Democratic leadership was hostile or indifferent to the New Deal and did not command a mass-based party organization (e.g., Michigan, Minnesota), the liberals were able with little difficulty to take over the Democratic caucus structure by allying with labor unions and farm organizations that had benefited from New Deal programs. In these states, factional struggles within the Democratic party took the form of a straight ideological conflict between liberals and conservatives; the issues of "bossism" and corruption did not occupy center stage.[76] Indeed, for the very reason that in these states liberals in the New Deal era (unlike the Progressives thirty or forty years earlier) were able to gain power *through* the existing party system and party structures, they were not (again in contrast to the Progressives) opponents of party per se. To the contrary, they became advocates of party government, by "responsible," issue-oriented parties.[77]

In states and cities, then, attacks upon the patronage system and efforts to construct issue-oriented party organizations in the wake of the 1932 realignment were led by New Deal liberals who sought in these ways to undermine the incumbent party leaders who opposed them and to gain power locally. In addition to these short-run political considerations, there were several long-run considerations that led the middle-class liberals who played such a prominent role in the New Deal coalition to favor bureaucratic and party reform. New Deal liberals wanted the government to play a rather active role in society, and a "modern personnel system" (competitive examinations, educational requirements, in-service training) was more likely than a patronage system to produce civil servants who had the technical proficiency to perform the tasks they wanted the government to perform. It also should be noted, however, that these recruitment procedures would skew the distribution of public jobs to the advantage of the upwardly mobile semiprofessionals—teachers and social workers, for example—who were an important element of the liberal constituency. And these personnel practices were a means of ensuring that the civil servants who administered New Deal programs at the grass roots would be socialized into the values and doctrines of the professionals who had initially drafted them, rather than the values of old-line politicians or "parochial" elites in local communities throughout the nation. Moreover, the greater the scale of government, the more compelling are arguments for administrative "coordination" and "rationalization," and the administrative reorganizations proposed by bureaucratic reformers during the New Deal era would, indeed, achieve gains in these respects. It must also be noted, however, that these reforms would transfer the tasks of coordination (and the power that inevitably flows to whomever coordinates the work of others) from politicians and political brokers to professional public administrators.

In addition, the long-run political interests of middle-class liberals would be served if America's decentralized, patronage-oriented party organizations were replaced by more disciplined, issue-oriented parties. Candidates who appeal for votes by promising to enact new programs, and incumbents who campaign for reelection by pointing to the new policies they have enacted, have need for the advice of professionals, technocrats, and administrators who are the most fertile source of ideas for new public policies. Presidential or mayoral "task forces" (the President's Committee on Income Security, which drafted the Social Security Act, was one of the earliest examples) accord far more influence to these groups than had the traditional mechanisms of policy formation in the United States, which were centered in legislatures and staffed by politicians. And to the extent that liberals were confident that the policies they favored enjoyed the support of a majority of the national electorate, they lamented the absence in the United States of a "responsible party system"—one that would enable a president elected by that majority and by virtue of his supporting those policies to extend his sway over the Congress.

In politics, the pursuit of short-run gains commonly prevails over long-run strategic considerations. Although the long-run interests of middle-class liberals would be served by the implementation of a full-scale program of bureaucratic and party reform, skilled political brokers during the postwar decades were able to integrate them into regimes that gave them something of what they wanted, but not everything. Mayors such as Richard Lee in New Haven, Robert Wagner in New York, and Richard Daley in Chicago were able to construct remarkably stable political coalitions, and to win reelection for term after term in the 1950s and early 1960s, by dividing the municipal government into "islands of functional power" and granting the party organization access to the patronage of only certain municipal departments; at the same time, agencies and programs that were of greatest interest to would-be reformers (urban renewal, education, social welfare) were placed under the control of professionals, civil servants, civic leaders, and the downtown business community.[78] It is little wonder that the three seminal studies of urban politics published in 1960 and 1961—books by Robert Dahl,[79] Edward Banfield,[80] and Wallace Sayre and Herbert Kaufman[81]— found the pluralist framework so useful! In the mid-1960s, however, these coalitions fell apart.

THE NEW POLITICS MOVEMENT

The third major movement for party and bureaucratic reform in this century, the New Politics movement, emerged during the 1960s and has had repercussions down to the present day.[82] Like its predecessors, the New Politics movement has sought in a number of fundamental ways to reform the procedures governing the selection of candidates for elective office and the recruitment of administrative officials; to alter the structure of authority within parties and bureaucracies; and to bring about changes in the way elected officials, bureaucrats, and private interests deal with one another. In contrast to the party and bureaucratic reform movements that preceded it, however, the New Politics movement did not emerge in the wake of a critical election. Nonetheless, I would argue that the reform movement of the 1960s can be understood in terms similar to those I have used to analyze earlier movements for party and bureaucratic reform. The difference between the New Politics movement and its predecessors with respect to the timing of its emergence is a function of the distinctive character of the post-New Deal party system—one in which the role of political parties and elections was rather circumscribed. This will become clear, I trust, as I describe the way the New Politics movement unfolded in the 1960s.

The reform movement of the 1960s was initially triggered by the Democratic victory in the 1960 presidential election. The election of 1960 was *not* a realigning election. The coalition that placed John Kennedy in the White House was very much in the New Deal mold; he was supported disproportionately by union members, city dwellers, Catholics, blacks, and southerners.[83] In organizational terms the Democratic party of 1960 also conformed to the pattern that had been established under Roosevelt: its cadres were an amalgam of old-line politicians, union leaders, and upper middle class liberal activists.

The influence of this last group was greater at the peak of the political system than at its base. If for no other reason than to retain the loyalty of this element of their constituency, Presidents Kennedy and Johnson were constantly in the market for "program material," proposals for new programs and policies. As a number of scholars have noted, the major urban programs of the New Frontier and Great Society were drafted not in response to demands from their presumed beneficiaries—black slum dwellers—but rather on the initiative of presidentially appointed task forces.[84] The members of these task forces were in the main "professional reformers"—academics, foundation officials, senior civil servants, representatives of professional associations, and so forth.[85]

On the local level, the picture was quite different. As mentioned above, in most large cities after World War II, a rather stable accommodation had been achieved among the major contenders for local power—party politicians, businessmen, union leaders, newspaper publishers, middle-income homeowners, the ethnic working classes. Writing at that time, Robert Salisbury described this pattern of accommodation as "the new convergence of power,"[86] and roughly speaking these forces converged around a program of urban renewal in the Central Business District for the business community and construction unions, low taxes for homeowners, and secure jobs in the municipal civil service for the lower middle class and upwardly mobile members of the working class. Upper middle class professionals had some influence over municipal agencies, but this was sharply constrained by the desire of mayors to keep taxes low, and of the municipal civil service to control its own work routines and to determine the standards that would govern the hiring, promotion, and firing of public employees.[87]

Upper middle class liberals sought to use their access to the Kennedy and Johnson administrations to circumvent these local accommodations and to extend their influence over the agencies of municipal government. The presidential task forces that drafted New Frontier and Great Society legislation argued that municipal bureaucracies did not command the resources, the talent, or the initiative that was necessary to solve the "urban crisis." To deal with this problem, they proposed to extend federal grants-in-aid to local governments to support "innovative" programs. To obtain these grants, cities found it necessary either to establish independent agencies under the control of the local counterparts of the officials in Washington who dispensed this money, or to have existing municipal departments contract with consulting firms or hire administrators who shared the outlook and knew the vocabulary of the dispensers of the federal grants. The "grantsmen," who were most successful in obtaining federal funds, naturally were those whose educational backgrounds, social origins, and institutional affiliations were similar to the federal grant givers, and who proposed to spend federal monies for purposes their Washington counterparts favored. In other words, the grant-in-aid programs of the Kennedy and Johnson administrations were the means by which upper middle class professionals—and their political allies—used their access to the White House to extend their control over the policies, programs, and hiring practices of municipal agencies.[88]

Blacks were useful allies in the endeavor. The attack upon municipal bureaucracies was justified, in part, by the assertion that they were "insensitive" and "unresponsive" to the needs of the black community. Blacks had strong reasons to join this attack because the mechanisms of community participation that were attached to Great Society programs provided them with channels through which they both could influence the way municipal departments distributed their benefits and could obtain access to the patronage that was directly controlled by federally funded community action agencies, model cities boards, neighborhood service centers, and community development corporations. These mechanisms of community participation furthermore legitimized federal intervention in local affairs apart from elected local governments, and they provided an institutional framework through which blacks could be organized to provide local political support for these programs.

The attack upon municipal bureaucracies conducted through the Great Society programs of the 1960s, then, was an effort by one segment of the old New Deal coalition—upper middle class liberals and blacks—to extend its control over the institutions of local government at the expense of other segments of that coalition. It was through this struggle for power at the periphery of the political system that the elements of the upper middle class were to rally behind the New Politics movement—the "new class" or the "conscience constituency"—first became aware of themselves as a distinctive political force.[89]

The second phase of the New Politics movement was triggered by President Johnson's escalation of the war in Vietnam. Vietnam turned upper middle class liberal Democrats against their party's national leadership, and at that point the struggle for influence at the periphery of the political system became an all-out battle for control at the center. The New Politics movement sponsored a series of party and bureaucratic reforms that were part and parcel of this effort to undermine the power of its erstwhile allies, and to construct a regime that the social forces for which it spoke could dominate.

The party reforms sponsored by the New Politics movement following the defeat of the antiwar candidates at the 1968 Democratic National Convention were the most comprehensive since those of the Progressive Era. Chief among them were rules requiring that delegations to future national conventions be composed of blacks, women, and youths in a "reasonable relationship to their presence in the population of the State"; encouraging states to select convention delegations through primary elections or open caucus procedures; and discouraging the slatemaking efforts of party organizations.[90] Organizations such as Common Cause also sponsored a number of reforms in the area of campaign finance: public subsidies to candidates, limitations on individual contributions, public disclosure of the names of contributors. Through these reforms the New Politics movement weakened the position of its major competitors for influence within the Democratic Party—big city party organizations, labor unions, business—and enhanced the importance of middle-class issue-oriented activists, and the influence of three of the major movements with which it was allied, namely, the civil rights movement, the women's movement, and the youth movement.

In addition to reforming the parties, the New Politics movement also sought to bring about changes in the structure of the federal bureaucracy and the conduct of administrative agencies. Indeed, as James Q. Wilson has noted, the "bureaucracy problem," which since the New Deal had been a concern of the Right, in the 1960s became a concern of the Left.[91] Practices that formerly had been the subject only of academic analysis became matters for journalistic exposure—the interchange of personnel between administrative agencies and the industries they regulated; the cocoon of minimum rates, entry restrictions, public subsidies, and tax benefits that had been placed around one sector of the economy after another since the New Deal; the mutually beneficial relationships that had developed between executive agencies, congressional committees, and private interests. Common Cause, the Nader organization, and various groups in the consumer and environmental movement attempted to put an end to these practices by sponsoring sunshine laws, inserting strict standards in regulatory statutes, subjecting administrative agencies to close judicial supervision, and by providing for "consumer" or "public" representation in the administrative process.

Finally, the New Politics movement launched a full-scale attack upon the national security establishment as well as upon agencies in the domestic sector. As in that sector, practices that previously had aroused little journalistic attention or public opposition now were labeled as improper: the Pentagon's tolerance of cost overruns in weapons procurement contracts, the public-relations campaigns and lobbying efforts of the Pentagon, the hiring of retired military officers by defense contractors, the failure of Congress to monitor the activities of the CIA and other intelligence agencies. The New Politics movement sought to subject the "military-industrial complex" to stricter external control, and more generally to reduce its size (by "reordering national priorities") and limit the role it had come to play in the nation's life during the Cold War years.

By attacking these practices, the New Politics movement was attempting to disrupt the structure of accommodations through which the New Deal coalition had come to terms with the major established social forces in American society in the 1940s.[92] This grand coalition was initially forged by Roosevelt in order to mobilize the entire nation behind the effort to win World War II.[93] Roosevelt's part of the bargain was to transform himself from Dr. New Deal into Dr. Win-the-War. After Germany and Japan had been defeated, however, the wartime coalition was subject to enormous strains: conservative, isolationist midwesterners fought bitterly with moderate, internationalist easterners for control of the Republican party; and the

New Deal coalition split into a left wing, center, and a right wing faction (i.e., Progressives, Fair Dealers, and Dixiecrats). In order to cope with the Soviet threat to American interests in Europe in the late 1940s, Truman, with the support of liberal and moderate internationalists in both parties, sought to reconstitute the bipartisan coalition. By the early 1950s, the moderates had emerged on top in both parties and a bipartisan consensus on national security issues came to prevail in American politics, but only after major concessions were made to the conservatives (left wingers were purged from the bureaucracy and the labor unions, the Democrats abandoned their efforts to revive the New Deal, the civil rights issue was dropped) and, of greatest relevance here, after NSC-68 was implemented and a massive and permanent military establishment was created. The creation of this military apparatus, and the development of all the practices to which the New Politics movement later objected, made it possible to give all the major actors in American politics a stake in the nation's national security policies, and therefore in its postwar regime. Elected officials were given access to a huge pork barrel, which incumbents could use to enhance their political security.[94] National defense made it politically possible for public expenditures to be maintained at a level that kept unemployment reasonably low, wages reasonably high, and labor reasonably happy. And through the procurement of weapons and supplies, those elements of the American business community that had been most strongly identified with the isolationist wing of the Republican Party—namely, midwestern industrialists as opposed to eastern financial and commercial interests—were reconciled to internationalism and big government.[95] In other words, the attack the New Politics movement launched against the military-industrial complex in the late 1960s was the institutional variant of its challenge in the ideological realm to the Cold War consensus on foreign policy: by attacking the military-industrial complex, the New Politics movement was seeking to undermine the agencies and the organizational patterns through which the grand coalition behind that consensus had become institutionalized.

In the area of domestic policy, a rather similar pattern of accommodations between the New Deal coalition and its erstwhile opponents emerged during the postwar period, and the persistent charge made by the New Politics movement, that agencies in the domestic sector were serving "private interests" rather than the "public interest," can be understood as an effort to disrupt these accommodations. The regulatory and expenditure programs enacted by Democratic congressional majorities during the postwar decades, as studies by economists and political scientists have repeatedly demonstrated, generally redistributed income to the more established or wealthier members of each of the major segments of American society and each of the major sectors of the American economy.[96] On the local level, federal redevelopment and highway programs financed the grand political coalitions that enabled Democratic mayors to secure reelection term after term. On the national level, their effect was quite similar. As David Mayhew's study of roll-call voting in the postwar congresses indicates, what distinguished Democrats from Republicans was their willingness to enter into logrolling arrangements to pass legislation of this character across a broad range of issue areas.[97] This enabled the Democrats to become a permanent majority party (indeed, the regime party) during the postwar era. In recent decades, congressmen from both parties have secured reelection by entering into logrolling deals, negotiated by the Democratic congressional leadership, to pass legislation that serves the major producer interests in their constituencies, and by interceding before executive agencies to obtain "particularized" benefits for individual firms and voters in their districts.[98] It is, of course, precisely this pattern of political behavior—logrolling; alliances between congressional committees, executive agencies, and producer interests; the receipt of campaign contributions for favors rendered—that the New Politics movement considered to be antithetical to the "public interest." By attacking these arrangements and the agencies implicated in them, the New Politics movement was seeking to undermine the practices and institutions that sustained its opponents in power.

If the political accommodations and the institutional arrangements underlying America's postwar regime can account for the *targets* the New Politics movement chose to attack, the composition of the coalition the movement assembled can account in large measure for the *content* of the administrative reforms it proposed. A comparison between the New Politics movement and the reform movements that immediately preceded it is instructive in this regard, because the administrative arrangements the movement endorsed were substantially different from those advocated by Progressive and New Deal administrative reformers. First, the New Politics movement severely criticized the public personnel system established at the behest of earlier administrative reformers, one built around competitive examinations and a career civil service. As an alternative to the former the movement advocated various mechanisms of affirmative action and community control. And as an alternative to the latter, the movement advocated that the performance of many public tasks be delegated to nongovernmental institutions whose employees are not career civil servants. Second, the New Politics movement challenged what has been *the* central tenet of administrative reorganization throughout this century: unity of command. It opposed presidential efforts to centralize control over the bureaucracy, and supported efforts to extend the influence of Congress, the judiciary, and the press.[99]

These differences between the bureaucratic reforms advocated by the New Politics movement and those endorsed by earlier administrative reformers are to be explained to a considerable degree by differences in the social and institutional bases of these movements. In contrast to the Progressives and New Dealers, who drew mass support from a middle class and upwardly mobile working class whose members could expect to secure civil service jobs through competitive examinations, the New Politics movement sought to win support of blacks, who were excluded from public jobs by such examinations, and from members of the upper middle class who had little interest in moving slowly up the ladder in career civil service systems. The black members of this coalition would benefit in obvious ways, however, from the explicit racial criteria in affirmative action programs, and from the implicit ones in community control plans. And upper-class members of this coalition would benefit quite directly if public responsibilities were delegated, and public monies allocated, to the institutions with which they were affiliated—alternative schools, consulting firms, legal services clinics, public interest law firms, and so forth.

In a similar vein, bureaucratic reformers who were associated with the Progressive and New Deal movements sought to increase the administrative powers of chief executives because both movements (by pursuing rather different strategies, to be sure) reasonably could hope to elect presidents, governors, and mayors. The New Politics movement, by contrast, rarely could command a majority of votes in general elections, and it was either unwilling or unable to do what was necessary to acquire additional support—as the drubbing the McGovernites received in the 1972 presidential election indicates, and as the extremely low rates of turnout in antipoverty elections also suggest. (Indeed, the very demand for guaranteed representation through racial or sexual quotas is an indication that the movement was not prepared to secure representation by seeking to win more votes than its rivals.) Because the movement rarely was able to elect chief executives, it opposed reforms—such as those proposed by the Ash Council in 1970, or the ones President Nixon sought to implement by fiat in 1973—that would increase their administrative powers. To the contrary, the New Politics movement sought to reduce the powers of the presidency, and to increase the influence within the administrative process of the institutions with which the movement was allied or to which it enjoyed access. Thus, the movement has sought to subject the bureaucracy to increased public scrutiny, and to influence its behavior through "investigative reporting" and Naderite exposés, because it was closely associated with an important element of the national press.[100] Civil rights, environmental, and consumer groups attempted to subject the bureaucracy to tighter supervision by the courts because they commanded considerable legal talent, and because the federal judiciary (in *its* search for a constituency) in recent years loosened requirements for standing, considerably narrowed the scope of the doctrine of political questions, and enriched the range of remedies it was prepared to consider in class-action suits.[101] And after decades of seeking to limit the powers of Congress, liberals sought to expand Congress's powers over the administration—especially in the areas of budgeting and impoundments, investigations and executive privilege—because in the 1970s and 1980s increasing numbers of senators and representatives associated themselves with the issues and political orientations of the New Politics movement.[102]

Finally, the New Politics movement sought to deal with the problem of administrative clientelism—the "capture" of regulatory and administrative agencies by producer interests—not by increasing the president's authority over "the headless fourth branch of government," which was the solution proposed by New Deal administrative reformers, but rather by establishing various mechanisms to represent the "consumer interest" or the "public interest" in the administrative process. In practice this meant they attempted to secure appointments to administrative positions for representatives of public interest groups, and they sought to create new administrative agencies (e.g., a Consumer Protection Agency) that would serve as official spokesmen for their groups. That is, unable to defeat in the electoral arena the productive coalition which served as the constituency for America's postwar regime, they sought to deal the social forces for which they spoke into the pluralist game.

In conclusion, then, there are certain broad similarities between the recent movement for party and bureaucratic reform and the movements that immediately preceded it. Like its predecessors, the New Politics movement was led by a coalition of groups (the upper middle classes and their black allies) within the majority party (the Democrats) that sought to extend its influence over the institutions of local and national government at the expense of the political forces (producer interests, including organized labor) that previously had been dominant. And the reforms the New Politics movement advocated, like those sponsored by its predecessors, would deprive the previously dominant political forces of some of the resources (e.g., the military pork barrel) that had sustained their power; would enhance the influence of the organizations (e.g., public interest groups) the reformers established and the institutions (e.g., the press) with which they were allied; and would provide these organizations and the social groups for whom the reformers spoke with privileged access to public authority (e.g., through consumer representation) and to public resources (e.g., through the "social" pork barrel).[103]

The distinctive characteristics of the recent wave of reformism can be understood in light of the distinctive characteristics of America's postwar, pluralist regime. As mentioned at the beginning of this section, the New Politics movement, unlike other movements discussed in this chapter, did not erupt in the wake of a realignment in the party system. It did not conform to this pattern because political parties have played a far less significant role in American government and politics in recent decades than at any time since the Jacksonian Era.[104] This in part was a tribute to the success of earlier bureaucratic reform movements, which had succeeded in creating an executive establishment largely insulated from the influence of party politics and directly linked to other major national institutions. This transformation in the institutional substructure of American politics explains how upper middle class liberals, who were affiliated with some of these institutions, could seek to use the national government to extend their influence over local bureaucracies in the early 1960s, even though they had little in the way of a local electoral base. And it explains how a full-scale struggle for control of the federal government could erupt in the mid-1960s when a number of national institutions, beginning with universities and the press, turned against the war in Vietnam, and sought to drive from power the incumbent leadership of the Democratic party, and to contain the power of the national security establishment. The party and bureaucratic reform movements of recent years, as I have argued, emerged from, and were part and parcel of, these struggles for power.[105]

CONCLUSION

As the analysis above indicates, the relationship between political parties and public bureaucracies in the United States, and the structure of these two institutions, has changed substantially a number of times over the past two centuries. The explanation most commonly offered for these institutional developments is that they are responses to changes in American society: shifts in the percentage of the population engaged in agriculture, industry, and the professions; the influx of European immigrants and then their assimilation into the middle class; the increasing scale and complexity of the tasks government must perform, and so forth. It would be foolish to deny that social changes such as these have played a role in the institutional transformations described in this essay. But they constitute at most half the story. For, as I have argued, changes in the structure of party and bureaucracy, and in the relationship between these institutions, have had major implications for the distribution of power in the United States. And the groups sponsoring institutional reforms, as well as those who resist them, have not been unaware of these implications.

There is no need to repeat here what I have argued above. Suffice it to say that my central theme has been that efforts to reform the structure of party and bureaucracy have been part and parcel of the struggle for power in American politics. These reform movements cluster in the wake of realigning elections, as elements of the new majority party seek, in the first place, to deprive the politicians who had played a major role in the earlier party system of access to the resources upon which they had relied to maintain themselves in power, and in the second place, to build an institutional order that they (the reformers) can dominate.

In other words, the emergence, development, and decay of the successive American party systems has involved not only fluctuations in the relative strength of the two major parties, but also in the relationship between political parties and other institutions: as one party system is succeeded by another, changes occur both in the balance of power *within* the party system, and in the balance of power between parties and other public institutions. And this finding leads to the following general conclusion: *In American politics, institutional conflicts are the functional equivalent of party conflicts.*

In asserting this proposition, I mean not only that controversies over the structure of institutions and conflicts between institutions are an integral part of the cycle of party realignment in the United States, but also that the outcome of these controversies and the very way they are resolved have their equivalents in the way governmental authority is allocated through a party system. Political institutions, as I have stressed in this essay, inevitably favor some interests over others: they elevate one set of spokesmen for a social group in preference to competing leaders; they skew the distribution of public benefits to the advantage of some segments of the population and the disadvantage of others; they give some interests preferential access to public authority at the expense of competing interests. This means that efforts to alter the relative power of different institutions (such as parties and bureaucracies), or to reform their structure so they will embody a new set of interests, can have consequences for the distribution of political power and public benefits as great as those occurring when one party trounces its rivals in the electoral arena.

Reform movements, however, rarely enjoy victories of this magnitude: institutional reformers generally are compelled to enter into compromises with their opponents, or at least to resign themselves to less than a total victory. For example, the Mugwumps succeeded in placing certain federal agencies under the jurisdiction of the Civil Service Commission, while others continued to serve as sources of party patronage; the Progressives triumphed in some states, but failed completely in others; during the post–New Deal period middle-class liberals enjoyed a measure of influence over certain municipal agencies in most large cities, while others remained under the control of old-line politicians; and, most recently, the New Politics movement has enjoyed remarkable success in opening up some federal agencies (e.g., the FCC) to the influence of public interest groups, while others (e.g., the Agriculture Department) continue to operate much as before. Or to describe these outcomes in more general terms, in the aftermath of critical elections and of the institutional conflicts that follow them, the governmental structure of the United States has been divided along functional (and/or geographic) lines, different government agencies (and/or state and local governments) have been parceled out to various contenders for power, and a coalition regime has been established. The process through which this has occurred in the United States is different in form, but not entirely different in substance or outcome, from the bargaining process that occurs in fragmented multiparty systems, where *after* elections have been conducted, the political parties and political factions jockey for advantage, seek to gain control of important government ministries, and ultimately resolve their differences by forming a coalition government. Thus, not only are institutional conflicts an integral part of the cycle of party realignment in the United States, but the process through which they are resolved and the regime that is established in their wake is equivalent to the way public authority is allocated through party systems that, on their face, do not resemble the American.

This last observation indicates that institutional conflicts can serve not only as a continuation of party warfare by other means, but also as a substitute for it. Groups unable to gain political power by seizing control of a political party or by constructing a new one, and using it to overwhelm the incumbents at the polls (a strategy of *mobilization*), can adopt two alternative strategies. They can pursue a strategy of *demobilization*: sponsoring electoral reforms that effectively disfranchise the voters who are likely to support their opponents, or sponsoring bureaucratic reforms that deprive the incumbents of the resources they use to link themselves to a mass base. Alternatively, they can pursue a strategy of *circumvention*: outflanking incumbent politicians by establishing executive agencies that stand outside the domain of electoral and party politics, and that provide the reformers with privileged access. The conflicts generated by mobilizing strategies are conducted within the party and electoral system; those generated by demobilizing or flanking strategies take the form of institutional conflicts— either disputes over the proper structure of institutions or conflicts between political institutions.

With the partial exception of the New Deal, reformers over the past century have pursued the second and third of these strategies to a greater extent than the first, and consequently, the locus of political conflict—and the bargaining and the accommodations that resolve these conflicts—increasingly has moved outside the party system in the United States. Nothing illustrates the extent to which this trend has progressed quite so clearly as Watergate. President Nixon, claiming a mandate from his landslide victory in the 1972 election, sought at the beginning of his second term to centralize his control of the entire administrative apparatus of the federal government, at the expense of the institutions with which his opponents were affiliated—the Congress, the press, and the bureaucracy itself.[106] These institutions and political forces launched a counterattack; they argued that the president's efforts to centralize power violated the Constitution. Assisted, to be sure, by Nixon's having clearly broken a criminal law, they were able to secure his removal from office. A number of aspects of this struggle for power are especially noteworthy: it was conducted almost entirely outside the realm of electoral politics; political parties played at most a secondary role in it; it took the form in large measure of an institutional conflict; and the institutions opposing the president, by driving him from office, proved themselves to be powerful enough to reverse a decision (tainted though it might have been) made earlier in the electoral arena.

Only time will tell whether the Watergate episode signals the emergence of yet another American party system—one in which political parties and elections play a smaller role than ever before.

Part II

ECONOMIC INTERESTS
AND POLITICAL ORGANIZATION
IN THE UNITED STATES

Trade Unions and Political Machines: The Organization and Disorganization of the American Working Class

THE DECADES following the outbreak of the Civil War witnessed the consolidation of the major organizations through which workers were to make demands upon, and reach accommodations with, other elements of American society during much of the twentieth century: trade unions and political machines. It was during this period that many of the practices and institutions of contemporary "labor relations" emerged: carefully planned and highly organized strikes, collective bargaining between employers and representatives of their employees, the oldest surviving national labor unions, and the American Federation of Labor. At the same time the Republicans and Democrats became entrenched as the nation's major parties, and their local organizations carved out a similar position for themselves in cities throughout the country. By the end of the nineteenth century the dominant segment of the nation's trade union movement and the local machines affiliated with the nation's major parties had institutionalized a series of distinctions between the claims workers made upon their employers and the state, the modes of collective action through which they asserted those claims, and the composition of the groups with which workers allied in pursuing their goals in the economic and political arenas.

Trade unions were organized at workplaces—factories, mines, construction sites, railroad yards—and the targets of their organization were employers. The constituency of the trade union movement at the end of the nineteenth century was composed largely of skilled wage laborers. Excluded, on the one hand, were employers and members of the middle class and, on the other hand, most unskilled workers, all Asians and most blacks, and, at various times, members of one or another of the nation's newer European immigrant groups. The major demands made upon employers concerned the terms and conditions under which union members labored. Both the rhetoric and the behavior of trade unions were quite militant: they insisted that a fundamental conflict of interest existed between employers and employees, and the characteristic collective activity in which they engaged was the strike. In the main, however, American trade unionists at the end of the nineteenth century were not revolutionaries: they called strikes to

extract concessions from employers, not to topple the state; they were prepared to concede control over the nation's political institutions to the Democratic and Republican parties; and they were prepared to negotiate national
trade agreements that bound workers at the plant level not to strike. In other
words, by the 1890s a majority of trade unionists in the United States rejected anarchism, socialism, and syndicalism.

Political machines differed from trade unions in each of these respects.
The constituency of political machines tended to be defined along ethnic
lines and to cut across lines of social class—unskilled workers, unionized
skilled workers, and middle-class elements of various ethnic groups were
united with segments of the local business community. The sites of their
grass-roots organizations were the neighborhoods in which workers lived;
the major demands they organized into politics concerned the allocation of
public jobs among the city's various ethnic groups and of public facilities
among its various neighborhoods; and the machine secured these benefits
for its constituents by organizing them for combat in the electoral arena. And
though there were substantial variations among American cities in the relationship between local machines and trade unions, in at least the nation's
largest cities differences between the two institutions enabled them to establish a modus vivendi with one another.

Although many of the organizations and practices of twentieth-century
American labor relations and politics became institutionalized in the postbellum decades, the trade union and the political machine were by no means
the only types of organizations to which workers belonged in these years.
Similarly, demands for higher wages and for political patronage were not the
only claims workers made upon other segments of American society, nor
were voting their approval or disapproval of trade agreements negotiated by
national union leaders and marching to the polls to cast their ballots for the
Democratic or Republican ticket the only forms of collective action in which
workers engaged. The late nineteenth century was a period in which major
changes occurred in the structure of the economy, cities, and political system that profoundly altered the conditions workers faced on their jobs, in
their communities, and in the political realm. In responding to those
changes that affected them adversely, workers exhibited dispositions to engage in numerous modes of collective action and to establish many types of
organizations that to a greater or lesser degree challenged the ethos of acquisitive individualism preached by the upper and middle classes and the
patterns of behavior that factory managers and public officials allied with
those classes were seeking to impose upon workers.

These differences between the interests, values, and behavioral dispositions of workers and employers sparked conflicts during the post–Civil War
years that at times approached full-scale class warfare. The labor union and

the political machine institutionalized an accommodation between these warring forces. By no means did the emergence of these organizations end such conflicts. Nonetheless, this chapter argues, the institutionalization of the trade union and the political machine established the characteristic manner in which class conflicts in the United States could be channeled and thereby contained.

This argument is elaborated below. The first section analyzes the character of and major changes in the realms of production, community life, and politics in the United States between 1861 and 1894, and describes the ways in which these were experienced by members of the working class. The second discusses the numerous ways in which workers responded to these changes—the variety of claims they asserted, modes of collective action in which they engaged, and types of organizations they created or joined; the third analyzes the conditions that influenced the disposition of workers to respond in these different ways. The fourth section seeks to explain how one set of these organizations, the trade union and the political machine, came to be institutionalized. The concluding section briefly analyzes the implications of this process of class formation for the character of the working class in the United States and discusses some of the challenges that confronted trade unions and political machines in the twentieth century, thereby shaping the subsequent evolution of the American working class.

THE ORGANIZATION OF PRODUCTION, COMMUNITY LIFE, AND POLITICS, 1861–1894

The period between the Civil War and the depression of 1894 was one of enormous growth and change in the American economy. In 1860 the manufacturing sector in the United States was by no means insignificant—it generated 12 percent of the nation's private production income and America ranked fourth among the world's industrial powers—but it was dwarfed by the agricultural sector, which produced 31 percent of the nation's income. (The balance was generated by commerce, transportation, and services.) By the eve of the 1894 depression the nation's industrial production, railroad mileage, and gross national product had more than tripled; manufacturing generated more income than agriculture; and the United States had become the world's leading industrial power.[1] The American economy did not, however, grow at a uniform rate over these thirty-five years. The nation suffered a major depression in the years 1873–78 and a somewhat less severe one in the years 1882–85.[2] In the timing and rapidity of its industrialization and the severity of the depressions that punctuated it, American economic development during the late nineteenth century resembled that of Germany.

The United States occupied a distinctive niche in the world economy of this period. Relative to other industrializing nations, natural resources—agricultural land, coal, iron ore, and timber—were abundant in America and labor was scarce, which had important consequences for the nation's pattern of economic development.

Once the extension of the railway network and the invention of the steam-ship made it possible to ship bulk commodities cheaply from the Midwest and Great Plains to the cities of the United States and Europe, American farmers could compete on favorable terms with grain and meat producers anywhere. Except where tariff barriers stood in their way, American farmers fed industrial workers throughout the western world.[3] As farmers special-ized in cash crops, they began to purchase goods they formerly had pro-duced themselves, and this created an enormous internal market for the products of American industry.

At the same time, food exports from the Midwest and Great Plains con-tributed to the decimation of agriculture in the American Northeast and throughout much of Europe. Many displaced American farmers and Euro-pean peasants (as well as many European industrial workers and miners) migrated to American cities, because the scarcity of labor in the United States made industrial wages relatively high. From the 1860s through the mid-1890s, immigration to the United States averaged more than 300,000 persons a year. (An indication of the extent to which there was an integrated international labor market in the late nineteenth century is the fluctuation of emigration from Europe to America with the demand for labor in the United States: emigration rose to 400,000 a year during the peaks of the American business cycle and fell to half that number at the troughs of American de-pressions.) The immigrants who came to the United States during the three decades following the Civil War played a crucial role in the industrialization of America. England, Wales, and to a lesser extent Germany supplied many of the skilled workers in the American textile, mining, and metal industries; Ireland, Scandinavia, and China supplied many of the laborers who con-structed the railroads and worked as common laborers in manufacturing and mining.

Another aspect of the organization of production in this period also had important consequences for the working class. Even in the most advanced sectors of the economy—the iron and steel industries, railroads, coal mining, and textiles—skilled workers "exercised broad discretion in the direction of their own work and that of their helpers," as David Montgomery has noted. He cites the example of iron rollers in a mill in Ohio in the mid-1870s, whose workers

> negotiated a single tonnage rate with the company for specific rolling jobs the
> company undertook. The workers then decided collectively, among them-

selves, what portion of that rate would go to each of them . . . ; how work should be allocated among them; how many rounds of the rolls should be undertaken per day; . . . and how members should be hired and progress through the various ranks of the gang. To put it another way, all the boss did was buy the equipment and raw materials and sell the finished product.[4]

The knowledge of productive techniques monopolized by skilled workers in the late nineteenth century and the key role they played in the organization of production gave them leverage to extract high wages from employers, to enforce work rules, and to establish output quotas that restricted managerial discretion and further increased unit labor costs.

The high wage bill they faced by virtue of both the relative scarcity of labor in the United States and the crucial role of skilled workers provided factory owners with an incentive to reorganize production in ways that reduced their dependence upon this costly input. The creation of a national railway network, and thereby a national market in manufactured goods, turned this incentive into an imperative. With the destruction of local monopolies, any firm that failed to reduce labor costs could be undersold by firms in other cities.[5] By mechanizing production and/or increasing the division of labor, employers sought to increase the output per worker or, better still, substitute lower-wage unskilled labor for higher-wage skilled labor. (A case in point is the McCormick Harvesting Machine Company, which, in the wake of a successful strike by skilled iron molders in 1885, installed pneumatic molding machines, fired all its unionized molders, and replaced them with unskilled and less well paid machine tenders.)[6]

To be sure, Taylorism still lay in the future. The effort by employers to restructure the jobs performed by their workers was not as methodical in the decades immediately following the Civil War as it was to become in the first two decades of the twentieth century. Moreover, the introduction of new technologies created entirely new skilled trades, such as steamfitters and structural iron workers in the construction industry. Consequently the number of skilled workers actually increased from roughly 1 million to 2 million between 1870 and 1890, and the proportion of the urban working class belonging to this aristocracy of labor remained more or less constant during this period, fluctuating between 17 and 20 percent.[7] Nonetheless the possibility that employers would introduce machinery or otherwise reorganize production to reduce the autonomy, dilute the skills, and lower the wages of their employees was a major fear of workers and a central theme in conflicts between labor and capital in the late nineteenth century.[8]

Efforts by employers to increase output per worker and to reduce labor costs by purchasing new machinery, introducing prefabricated parts, tightening supervision of their employees, and changing methods of compensation (for example, paying piecework rates rather than hourly wages or subcontracting out jobs to work crews through competitive bidding) had profound implications for workers. These were particularly great for first-generation factory workers, whether they had previously been farmers, rural outworkers, or artisans in Europe or America. The factory system demanded a new sense of time and, indeed, a new way of life among workers—one that stressed sobriety, industry, and frugality.[9] The owner of a factory whose very functioning (or, at least, whose profitability) depended upon the close integration of specialized tasks performed by different workers would not tolerate half his employees staying home Monday mornings to sleep off hangovers from weekend drinking bouts. The conflicts between workers and employers in the late nineteenth century, however, were not simply the expression of the disjunction between the worldviews of "traditional" workers and the demands of a "modern" economy. Workers who were born and brought up in the economic and moral worlds of industrial capitalism experienced the efforts of employers to extract more output from them as attacks upon their independence.[10]

The Painite vocabulary of antebellum artisans remained available later to both first- and second-generation industrial workers for expressing their opposition to such attacks. Among the key words in this vocabulary were "slavery" and "manliness." Irwin Yellowitz reports that Toledo cigar workers striking against the introduction of the cigar mold in 1871 conceded that such opposition had failed in Europe, but European workers were "only 'a grade above the slave' whereas American workers would assert their rights." Similarly, coopers objecting to the introduction of machinery into their trade in the 1870s argued that "employers were attracted to machinery because it allowed them 'to make money and enslave coopers' by superseding the skilled worker."[11] The term "wage slavery" was also widely used in the years following the Civil War by all segments of the American labor reform movement. One major argument made for the movement's central demand during this period—the eight-hour day—was that if workers were to be subject to the control of their employers while on the job, the length of the working day should be limited so that those subject to the "wages system" at least would have an equal number of waking hours in which they were their own masters, and which they could devote to self-improvement and the exercise of the rights that were theirs as citizens of a republic.[12]

American workers at the time contrasted "slavery" or "slavishness" with "manliness." As David Montgomery notes:

> Few words enjoyed more popularity in the nineteenth century than this honorific, with all its connotations of dignity, respectability, defiant egalitarianism, and patriarchal male supremacy. The worker who merited it refused to cower before the foreman's glares—in fact, often would not work at all when a boss was watching. When confronted with indignities, he was expected to respond

like the machinist in Lowell, who found [restrictive] regulations posted in his shop in 1867. . . . "Not having been brought up under such a system of slavery, . . . I took my things and went out, followed in a few hours by the rest of the men."[13]

This code also demanded manliness in dealing with one's fellow workers. It enjoined them to observe informal restrictions on output in order not to deprive other workers of jobs; even when piece-rate systems promised higher earnings to those who produced more, workers were expected to observe these restrictions as an act of "unselfish brotherhood." In a similar fashion they were enjoined to resist the lure of the profits to be made by becoming subcontractors and exploiting their fellow workers. In these respects, an important segment of the working class rejected the acquisitive individualism of middle-class society.

The late nineteenth century also witnessed major changes in the character of the communities in which American workers lived. The first industrial revolution occurred initially in the towns and small cities of New England's river valleys. Textile mills in the 1830s and 1840s relied on water power to drive their machinery, barges to transport their raw materials and finished products, and the daughters and sons of American farmers as a source of labor. Consequently they were located in places such as Lowell and Lawrence, Massachusetts; Manchester, New Hampshire; and Pawtucket, Rhode Island. Even in the 1860s, when the adoption of steam power and the construction of an extensive railroad network made it possible for factories to locate elsewhere, manufacturing employment grew somewhat more rapidly in small cities than in the nation's great metropolises. After 1870, however, manufacturing began to concentrate more heavily in big cities. Over the next three decades smaller industrial cities scarcely stagnated—manufacturing employment in the cities that were ranked twenty-first through fiftieth in population grew by 158 percent between 1870 and 1900—but industrial growth was even more rapid in the largest cities in the United States. During these thirty years manufacturing employment in New York, Philadelphia, and Chicago increased by 245 percent.[14]

Major changes occurred in the distribution of people not only among cities, but also within them. The days were long past when persons unrelated by ties of blood or matrimony (other than servants) lived in the household of their employers. In addition, the invention of the trolley enabled members of the middle class to move from the sooty and congested neighborhoods downtown and into "streetcar suburbs" miles from the heart of town.[15] Through this process, the population of inner-city neighborhoods became more uniformly working class in composition. It was not until the twentieth century, however, that zoning codes were enacted that sought to separate residential and industrial districts. Before this workers lived in the shadows of the factories, mills, and foundries that employed them, and sweatshops were established in the tenement houses in which poor workers resided.

Ethnicity was as important as social class in shaping the residential patterns of American cities in the late nineteenth century. Because immigrants found housing through relatives or fellow townsmen from the old country or through boarding-house runners (who specialized in recruiting immigrants from a single country), foreign-born workers generally lived in neighborhoods inhabited by other members of their ethnic group. The Boston Tenement House Survey of 1892, conducted by the Massachusetts Bureau of Labor Statistics, gathered very complete data on the birthplaces of tenement dwellers. In 1892 there were 204 electoral precincts in Boston, with an average tenement population of 1,518. Of Boston's 7,905 Russian-born tenement dwellers (the vast majority of whom were Jewish and who comprised Boston's largest foreign-language ethnic group) only 14 percent lived in the 188 precincts inhabited by fewer than 100 other Russian-born Jews (see table 4.1). Almost double this proportion—25 percent—lived in the eight precincts in which there was a significant presence of between 100 and 400 Jews, and fully 61 percent lived in the eight precincts inhabited by more than 400 Jews. Similarly, 82 percent of Boston's Italian tenement residents lived in only ten of the city's 204 precincts, and of these well over half lived in the three most heavily Italian precincts in the city. The Irish, who were Boston's largest immigrant group and whose countrymen had lived in large numbers in Boston for a half-century by 1892, were more evenly dispersed through the city than either the Russian-born Jews or the Italians, but there also was some unevenness in their distribution among the city's precincts. At one extreme, sixty-one precincts (30 percent of the city's 204) had very small Irish tenement populations; at the other, 38 precincts had more than 400 Irish tenement residents, and 43 percent of Boston's Irish population lived in such heavily Irish neighborhoods. It should be noted, moreover, that these figures refer only to the foreign-born. These data do not classify second-generation immigrants, including young children living with their families, in the same category as their parents, and therefore understate the extent to which the members of Boston's major ethnic groups tended to live in clusters.

The neighborhoods inhabited by the great majority of workers in large American cities of the late nineteenth century differed dramatically from the middle-class sections of these cities. In particular, most working-class neighborhoods were characterized by very high population densities, extraordinary rates of population turnover, an absence of many of the public facilities that now are taken for granted—and as a result of all of these, a great deal of congestion, dirt, and disease. These differences between working- and middle-class neighborhoods were chiefly a consequence, in turn, of the distribu-

TABLE 4.1

Residential Concentration among Russian-, Italian-, and Irish-born
Tenement Dwellers in Boston, 1892

Country of Birth	No. of Group in Precinct	No. of Precincts	No. of Persons	% of Group's Population
Russia	0–99	188	1,126	14.2
	100–399	8	1,953	24.7
	400+	8	4,826	61.1
Italy	0–99	194	1,065	17.8
	100–399	7	1,771	29.6
	400+	3	3,148	52.6
Ireland	0–99	61	3,427	7.2
	100–399	105	23,509	49.6
	400+	38	20,478	43.2

Source: Compiled from Massachusetts Bureau of Statistics of Labor, *Twenty-Third Annual Report* (Boston: Wright & Potter Printing Co., 1893), 170–87.

tion of income between and within the social classes and the character and modes of financing of public services in the nineteenth-century city. There were, however, important variations within the working class, and therefore all working-class neighborhoods were not identical.

Approximately 40 percent of the American working class in the late 1880s lived in poverty, earning less than the $500 a year that was minimally necessary for a family of five to afford an adequate diet.[16] One out of every four members of this group was at best a marginal member of the labor force and survived by scavenging, begging, and stealing. The remaining three-fourths were unskilled laborers whose wives and children had to work if their family was to get by. Because the amount they could afford to spend for shelter was sharply limited, they lived in extremely crowded conditions: families in one or two rooms in cheap tenements; single men, as Jacob Riis's photographs indicate, in flophouses or even coal cellars.[17] Moreover, because "public improvements" such as street paving, street lighting, and the installation of sewer and water lines characteristically were financed through assessments on local property owners and the owners of tenements had no incentive to incur these costs, these basic public services often were not provided to neighborhoods inhabited by the poor.[18] (Jane Addams reported that she and some fellow residents of Hull House once decided to see how far down through the compacted garbage on a local street it was necessary to dig to reach the pavement below: the answer was a foot and a half.)[19] The combination of inadequate nutrition, congestion, and poor sanitation led to extremely high morbidity and mortality rates among both adults and children in poor neighborhoods. For example, in 1890 the mortality rate in one of

Boston's poorest wards, the thirteenth, was 3,365.36 per 100,000—more than twice the rate of 1,578.95 in the predominantly middle-class eleventh ward; and the mortality rate in the thirteenth ward from childhood diseases (diptheria, croup, whooping cough, and measles) was 312.85—more than five times the eleventh ward's rate of 55.40.[20] People living in such conditions had few reasons to be attached to their city, and this helps explain why Stephen Thernstrom found that more than 44 percent of the unskilled workers living in Boston in 1880 had moved from the city by 1890.[21]

A slightly larger segment of the working class—45 percent in the late 1880s—lived in better circumstances. Skilled workers earning from $500 to $800 per year did not go hungry as long as they remained employed, could rent an apartment with a separate bedroom for the parents and another for the children, and could afford the dues for a fraternal organization and trolley fare for an occasional outing. Even so, residential densities were high by present-day standards (the boarder was a common figure in working-class households), public services were limited (landlords here too had a limited incentive to pay local assessments for public improvements), and mobility rates were high (37 percent of the skilled workers in Thernstrom's sample moved from Boston between 1880 and 1890). None of these conditions was as extreme as in neighborhoods inhabited by common laborers, however, and if the skilled worker's wife through constant cleaning managed to rid their apartment of the dirt from the streets below and the soot from the factory chimneys above, if the family was able to survive periods of unemployment, and if its members joined with their friends and neighbors to avoid being demoralized by the bleakness of their surroundings, they could lead lives that accorded with the ideals of cleanliness, thrift, temperance (if not total abstinence), and also mutuality.[22]

The top 15 percent of the working class, composed of the most highly skilled workers—such as glass blowers, pattern makers, and railroad engineers—lived in neighborhoods similar to those inhabited by the lower middle class. Indeed, as members of the middle class moved to newly built streetcar suburbs, this upper stratum of the working class purchased their homes. The residential densities in their neighborhoods were relatively low; as homeowners they had an incentive to pay for public improvements; and they had a stronger reason than their fellow workers to remain in their neighborhood and city. Thus, in conjunction with shopkeepers, clerks, and lawyers newly risen from the working class, they often were in a position to be major contenders for the political leadership of their city.[23]

One final point about the relationship between social class and residential communities in post–Civil War America should be made. The distance between working- and middle-class neighborhoods was socially as well as physically greater in large cities than in small ones. The gang was a prominent institution in the working-class neighborhoods of large cities; its mem-

bers regarded themselves as manly and looked with some scorn upon mid-
dle- and upper-class "long hairs"; and they gave a hard time to any such
intruders into their neighborhood, as well as to intruders from other working-class neighborhoods. Members of the middle class relied upon professional police forces to keep undesirables out of their neighborhoods, and
their sense of distance from the working class was expressed in the use of
such terms as "the dangerous classes" to refer to the poor.[24] In small cities
the social distance between such neighborhoods was not so great. Herbert
Gutman argues that the residents of small cities were more likely than their
counterparts in the nation's great metropolises to regard themselves as
members of a common community and that the middle class was more inclined to consider factory owners, rather than workers, as the disruptive
force there.[25] This had important consequences when conflicts between
labor and capital erupted in such settings.

Three characteristics of the nineteenth-century American political system
had important consequences for the formation of the nation's working class.
The first was the early advent of universal suffrage (or, more precisely, white
manhood suffrage) and the concomitant mobilization of the working class
into politics by parties whose leaders already occupied positions of power in
the American regime. The second was the peculiar character of the "output"
institutions of American government. In contrast to the major regimes of
continental Europe, America was not governed by a centralized administrative apparatus. Rather, power was divided among genuinely independent
local, provincial, and national governments and, within each of these governments in turn, authority was shared by legislative, executive, and judicial
officials. During the Federalist and Jeffersonian eras various arrangements
to cope with this fragmentation and give the government some administrative capacity had been tried, but it was only in the 1830s that the one that
was to prevail through the remainder of the nineteenth century emerged—
a "state of courts and parties," as Stephen Skowronek has termed it.[26] Laws
were administered chiefly through the courts, and political parties played
the major role in staffing and achieving a measure of coordination among the
nation's political institutions. The third aspect of American politics that had
important implications for the working class was the pattern of cleavages and
alignments among the political elites of the day. The major event of the
1860s was of course the Civil War, and the major source of contention in
politics after Appomattox was what to do with the institutions that had been
created and the policies that had been enacted during the war. This touched
upon questions of concern to various contenders for the leadership of American workers.

The advent of suffrage was experienced most directly by the working
class. There was an extraordinarily high level of popular involvement in
party politics during the late nineteenth century.[27] Turnout rates in elec-

tions averaged 85 percent or more of the eligible electorate, and because aliens who merely declared their intention of becoming citizens were permitted to vote in a number of states and machine politicians were more than willing to help aliens obtain naturalization papers elsewhere, even recent immigrants were part of that eligible electorate. Moreover, elections for city, county, state, and national offices characteristically were not conducted simultaneously, and therefore electioneering occurred throughout the year: as one contemporary politician observed, "We work through one campaign, take a bath, and start in on the next."[28] These campaigns were a major form of popular entertainment, involving torch-light parades, brawls, and the marching of voters to the polls. This does not, however, mean that politics had no other significance to members of the working class. Voters were prepared to listen to two-hour orations extolling the virtues of American democracy at Fourth of July celebrations and to equally long speeches during election campaigns expounding party principles.[29] The mobilization of the working class into politics through the nation's political institutions, rather than in opposition to them, made its members intensely loyal to the American regime.[30]

The peculiar structure of the American state—its relatively limited domain and its fragmentation—also had implications for working-class daily life. As indicated above, in working-class neighborhoods officials performing public services—or, more precisely, services that now are regarded as public—were more notable for their absence than for their presence, and many public works were constructed only in neighborhoods whose residents could afford to finance them. What little relief was available to the poor at times of distress was provided by private charitable organizations. Moreover, the repeal during the Jacksonian era of licensing requirements to enter many trades, the abolition of imprisonment for debt, and the absence of a system of internal passports left most American workers free to move among jobs as they chose. In a similar fashion, the absence of any laws regulating private associations left workers free to form mutual aid societies and trade unions. Where workers faced restrictions in these areas they were less likely to be imposed by the state than by employers' associations (which maintained blacklists of union members), private security forces (such as the Pinkerton Detective Agency), and that extreme manifestation of the rights of private property, the company town.

The fragmentation of public authority in the United States and the dominance by political parties over public agencies and employees at all levels of the federal system were also experienced quite directly by the working class. The substantial decentralization of government in nineteenth-century America meant that the public officials and employees with whom workers and their families were most frequently in contact—policemen, magistrates, teachers, inspectors—were more likely to be employees of the municipal than of the national government, and they were relatively accessible to the people upon whose lives they impinged. In small cities and towns it often was possible for members of the working class in coalition with groups immediately above them in the social structure to boot out mayors or police chiefs who directed their subordinates to behave in undesirable ways, and such coalitions also found it possible to block the proposals of the city's business elite.[31] In large cities, in which the municipal government was not as immediately accessible, the party organizations that slated and deslated elected officials and hired and fired public employees found it in their interest to direct their functionaries to behave in ways that would serve the party's electoral interests. One need not accept the romanticized picture of the generous ward politician and the friendly neighborhood cop—ignoring the fact that parties had an incentive to respond to pressures from above as well as those from below, and overlooking the coercive aspects of the relationship between machine politicians and citizens—to recognize that at least public officials and employees could be "reached" by the working class. A member of the family could be sprung from jail or given a job on a public works crew by speaking to the ward leader. Workers in the United States, in contrast to their German counterparts—to cite the other extreme—did not find themselves subjugated by an official, and officious, class. This in conjunction with the relatively narrow domain of government in the United States during the late nineteenth century meant that on the whole whatever oppression or exploitation American workers experienced was not oppression by the State.

There were some exceptions to this rule, all of which were to have important implications for patterns of working-class activity and organization. The first of these was that pietistic forces did attempt to use public authority to alter the way of life of the immigrant working classes, most importantly by regulating the sale and consumption of liquor.[32] The targets of this Protestant crusade regarded this as an assault upon their personal liberty. Secondly, although private security forces played a more important role than the U.S. Army in breaking strikes, state militias and municipal police forces, under conditions to be described, were used quite regularly to protect strikebreakers during labor disputes.

Finally, there was the Civil War. In the years 1861–65 a state was constructed that dwarfed anything with which Americans were familiar. President Lincoln was commander-in-chief of an army in which more than 2,000,000 men served, and that, along with its Confederate counterpart, killed 600,000 of the nation's citizens. This army eventually relied upon conscription to fill its ranks, an exercise of state power that ignited the New York Draft Riot of 1863, the bloodiest riot in American history. In large sections of the country martial law was declared, the right of habeas corpus suspended, politicians and editors suspected of being disloyal to the Union cause summarily arrested, and military force used to break strikes in plants producing war matériel. The imperatives of financing the war led to the enactment of a system of national taxation and to the creation of a national debt and a national currency. The burdens of the former and the inflation generated by the latter ate into the real income of the working class. And the Thirteenth Amendment, enacted at the end of the war, released a major fraction of the nation's laborers from bondage, converting them from subjects of their masters into citizens of the United States.[33]

The war was a central event in the lives of most Americans, workers and nonworkers alike. But not everyone—not even all northern whites—experienced it in the same way. If some regarded the measures that were adopted to prosecute the war as oppressive, others experienced them as liberating— providing them with the opportunity to fight on behalf of the noble causes of national unity and free labor, in opposition to a society based upon slave labor. The divisions generated by the war, it should be noted, cut across class lines. Workers and their employers could agree, and millions did, that the taxes and tariffs enacted during the war were onerous, that the efforts by Republicans to extend the rights of blacks threatened the hegemony of the white race, and that the powers exercised by the army during and after the war were tyrannical. It was equally possible for millions of other workers and *their* employers to endorse whatever measures were necessary to ensure that the rebellion was crushed and to guarantee that the principles for which the war was fought would not be lost after it ended.

This brings us to the final major aspect of American politics in the late nineteenth century that had important implications for the working class— the pattern of cleavages and alignments among major political forces. During Reconstruction, issues related to the war continued to dominate political discourse and determine political alignments—in particular, the terms upon which the southern states and their black population should be integrated into the Union and the extent to which the institutions constructed and the policies enacted during the war should be maintained. The cleavages generated by these issues, like those evoked by the war itself, cut across class lines.

The changes in the American economy described above contributed to the emergence of another issue in the 1860s and subsequent decades: What position should the increasingly numerous class of wage laborers occupy in the nation's economic and political life? The very depth of the cleavages generated by the issues of the Civil War and Reconstruction created opportunities for working-class spokesmen to insist forcefully and effectively that the injustices associated with the system of wage slavery cried out for redress as much as did those associated with the system of chattel slavery. The effort to cope with these demands ultimately led political and economic elites to regroup in a new alignment—with major implications for the nation's working class.[34]

THE WORKING-CLASS RESPONSE:
PATTERNS OF BEHAVIOR

Workers responded in a wide variety of ways to the changes they experienced in their daily lives during the 1860s, 1870s, and 1880s. They exhibited dispositions to engage in many different forms of collective action and to create or join many different types of groups and organizations in an effort to cope. These collectivities, groups, and organizations asserted a broad spectrum of claims against the state, employers, and members of the working class itself, for during this period the position workers were to occupy in industrial America was very much an open question. Institutions and values that are widely accepted in the United States today—the wage-labor system, the concept of managerial prerogatives, the division of labor between union leaders and party politicians, the ethos of acquisitive individualism in the realms of both production and consumption—were matters of sharp contention a century ago.

The most characteristic form of collective action by workers in the late nineteenth century was the strike. Strikes were certainly not unknown prior to the Civil War, but in the late 1860s important changes began to occur in the way they were initiated, conducted, and concluded. Previously strikes had taken one of two forms. The first, characteristic of strikes by unskilled laborers, was the unplanned walkout. Generally not in a position to organize unions, these workers walked off their jobs more or less spontaneously and staged marches calling upon other workers to join their walkout. This pattern was exemplified in a strike by miners at the Cooper and Hewitt ironworks in 1867:

> Led by a local political aspirant, they closed eighteen mines within two days by marching in body from pit to pit, stopping teamsters from hauling ore, and, when the owners tried shipping ore by canal boat, filling in large sections of the canals. When state militia arrived to escort the boatmen, the strike was broken. It is noteworthy that even amidst this undisciplined action there was no violence. . . . The miners sought to raise their wages from $1.65 to $2.00 a day, but, said proprietor Abram Hewitt: "They struck first without making any demand."[35]

Strikes by skilled workers, able to organize trade unions, followed a somewhat different pattern. Representatives of unions and employers did not engage in collective bargaining in the present-day sense. Rather, to increase the wages of its members, a trade union would enact a "rule" declaring that after a designated date its members no longer would work for less than a stipulated rate. The union would "banner" any "rat shop" that refused to pay the new rate as a way of warning its members against working in the shop and encouraging consumers to boycott its products. "Rats" who violated the rule and worked for less than the new rate would be expelled from the union. A union would regard a strike as successful once all of its members were employed at the new rate, even if there were some shops in the city that employed nonmembers at a lower wage.

As Montgomery notes, "Union methods based on the unilateral adoption of rules to control the sale of their labor were peculiarly appropriate for the workingmen who had progressed but partway down the path from journeyman artisan to factory wage-laborer."[36] On the one hand, the rise of the factory system made collective action by workers against their employers considerably more feasible than it had been when workers lived in their employer's household. On the other hand, these methods—which are closer to those of present-day trade associations than labor unions—did not limit the independence of individual workingmen to any great degree. It is true that union members bound themselves to observe the rules enacted by a majority of their fellow tradesmen, but this involved no delegation of authority to, or submission to the leadership of, union officials.

These methods, however, had their limitations—in particular, they were extremely rigid. They gave employers no alternative but to capitulate to the union and pay the wages it decreed or to defy the union and insist on the old rate. Conflicts between employers and employees over rates of pay are inherent in the wage-labor relationship, and the potential for conflict was heightened still more by the different views nineteenth-century craftsmen and employers characteristically had of their rights and obligations in this relationship. Consequently employers always had an incentive (which, to be sure, might be outweighed by countervailing considerations in any given case) to pursue the latter course of action if it appeared that they could hold out longer than their striking employees or could find a sufficient number of craftsmen who were prepared to work at less than the union scale.

Beyond this, the changes in the American economy described above gave some employers in the post–Civil War years additional incentives to resist the demands of their workers. The expansion of the nation's railway network made it impossible for manufacturers to pay wages higher than those paid in the lowest-wage city in their market area. At the same time, the easier it became for workers to move among cities, the less likely it was that the great majority of craftsmen seeking employment in any given trade in a given city would belong to the local trade union and regard themselves as bound by its rules. In some cases mechanization also made it easier than it previously had been to replace striking craftsmen because it reduced the skills required to do their jobs.[37]

To overcome the limitations inherent in their older practices and to cope with these changing conditions, unions embarked upon new modes of collective action and adopted new forms of organization. Unable to promulgate and enforce wage rates unilaterally, unions undertook to negotiate wage scales with employers before staging walkouts, and even if no agreement could be reached and a strike was called, they sought to negotiate the terms of a settlement. This procedure—then termed "treating with employers" and striking only as a "dernier resort"—was more likely to yield a mutually acceptable conclusion. Moreover, when unions did strike, they took care to accumulate strike funds beforehand; they called walkouts during those seasons of the year or phases of the business cycle when employers were least willing to see their factories shut down and/or could most afford to accede to the unions' demands; and they sought to ensure that all firms operating within a market area were shut down simultaneously. In the language of the day such careful planning was termed "acting conservatively."[38]

These changes presupposed and further encouraged the strengthening and extension of union organization. Collective bargaining could only take place if workers were prepared to delegate to union leaders the authority to speak for them. Workers in established trades were not all willing to renounce their traditional independence, and strikes were defeated because of the resulting divisions in their ranks. This lesson was not lost upon workers at the time, however, and the 1860s and early 1870s witnessed the emergence of the nation's first professional union leaders, who perfected the organization of their unions and imposed a substantial measure of discipline upon their members. One aspect of this strengthening and extension of union organizations was the formation of national trade unions, which sponsored the creation of new union locals, raised and distributed strike funds, and sought to control the supply of labor and to establish uniform wages for their trade throughout the nation. Another was the emergence of municipal trade assemblies, which, among other things, raised strike funds and organized boycotts of shops that employed nonunion labor.[39]

There were, however, four interrelated differences between the strikes of this period and those of today. First, in the absence of the Wagner Act's provisions defining the legal obligations of workers and employers in the process of collective bargaining and guaranteeing the stability of labor unions, and in the absence of multimillion-dollar strike funds (let alone unemployment compensation for striking workers), strikes required a very strong sense of solidarity among the workers participating in them. Second, workers who did not belong to unions often were caught up in strike movements, and strikes mobilized their participants outside their places of work.

Third, strikes at times were used as a political weapon, and their target could be the state as much as the employers of the participants in the strike. Fourth, both in the content of their demands and the rhetoric with which these were justified, strikes were used to pursue a broader range of goals than is the case today.

The workers who participated in strikes during the post–Civil War years commonly had to be prepared to make substantial sacrifices and take great risks. It was not until the 1880s that unions began to amass permanent strike funds, and therefore workers had to go without any assured income during strikes; they also faced the possibility of not being rehired—and often of being blacklisted—after a strike was terminated. In addition, the benefits strikers sought most notably, higher wages, were "collective goods" that would accrue to workers who did not make these sacrifices as much as to those who did, and unions as yet did not possess the legal authority to levy sanctions against such "free riders."[40] Nonetheless, strikes did occur, and workers at times stayed off their jobs for weeks or months. That they were prepared to do so reflects the strong solidarities linking workers to one another on the job. This is the significance of the ethical code of the craftsman described above and of the rejection of "hoggish" behavior and the praise of "unselfish brotherhood" that was at the heart of that code: many nineteenth-century American workers did not conform to the model of *homo economicus* that generates the free-rider problem in neoclassical economic theory. Or at least, in contrast to their employers, they did not hold up that model as an ideal. As a banner carried by members of the Detroit coopers' union in an 1880 parade asserted:

> Each for himself is the bosses' plea
> Union for all will make you free.[41]

This points to the second distinctive characteristic of strikes in the late nineteenth century: they often drew upon the strong communal and ethnic solidarities in working-class neighborhoods, and wives and/or neighbors of the striking workers often became involved. An episode during a strike by Slavic miners in Wilkes-Barre, Pennsylvania, is indicative of this pattern: "As soon as the [strikebreakers] appeared at the mine head and prepared to leave, violence broke out. 'The strikers assailed their enemies with clubs, stones, and pistols, and beat some of them in a terrible manner.' The assault was definitely a group affair, as women also participated. Their nationality was obvious from a banner held aloft proclaiming in Polish, 'Kill the men who have taken the bread out of our mouths.'"[42] A common feature of large strikes during this period was a march by crowds from factory to factory in working-class neighborhoods, calling upon all employees to walk off their jobs. The railway strike of 1877, the largest of the nineteenth century, precipitated sympathetic walkouts by coal miners and factory workers in dozens of cities and full-scale general strikes in Toledo and St. Louis. The marches and open-air meetings that occurred in the course of these strikes invited the participation of all segments of the population in working-class neighborhoods: unionized workers, nonunionized workers, unemployed men, women, and children.[43] A number of strikes during this period were also associated with riots—most notably, the 1863 draft riot in New York, an 1867 strike on behalf of the eight-hour day in Chicago, and the 1877 railroad strike in Pittsburgh and Baltimore. The participants in these riots extended far beyond the striking workers, and the crowd actions of these episodes were not centered on the workplaces of the rioters.[44]

Another important feature of many strikes during the 1860s and 1870s was their political or quasi-political character. During these years workers struck to "enforce" state laws defining the length of a legal day's work and the procedures to be used in weighing the coal produced by miners who were paid on a per-ton basis—laws that state governments were unable to implement in the face of resistance by employers. These statutes had been enacted initially as a result of electioneering and lobbying efforts by labor reformers, and inasmuch as strikes were the only means to secure the implementation of these laws, they were yet another weapon in the political arsenal of labor.[45] And in some instances the strike was used as a weapon to secure the enactment of legislation. The public meeting that authorized the 1877 general strike in St. Louis resolved

> that, as the condition of an immense number of people now forced in idleness, and the great suffering for the necessaries of life caused by the monopoly in the hands of capitalists, appeals strongly to all industrial classes for prompt action, therefore, to avoid bloodshed or violence, we recommend a general strike of all branches of industry for eight hours as a day's work, and we call on the legislature for the immediate enactment of an eight hour law, and the enforcement of a severe penalty for its violation, and that the employment of all children under fourteen years of age be prohibited.[46]

More generally, as Montgomery notes of the 1877 strikes, "Everywhere the first target of the crowd's fury was the interlocking directorate of railroad executives, military officers, and political officials, which constituted the apex of the country's new power structure."[47] The destination of the largest mass march during the St. Louis general strike was the Four Courts building—the symbol of The Law in that city and, significantly, the major strong point being garrisoned by the militia that the city's political and business elite established in response to the strike.[48] In San Francisco, Denis Kearney, the leader of the Workingmen's party that was created in the aftermath of the 1877 upheaval, not only led marches of his supporters to the Central Pacific Railroad and other major employers, demanding that Chinese workers be fired and white men hired in their stead, but also invaded ward meetings of the major parties. Alexander Saxton observes,

> Kearney's style was that of a declaration of war against the two-party establishment. Not only must the Chinese go. The boodlers, and monopolists and corruptionists of both parties must go with them. To this end Californians would organize a new party of their own. "We propose to elect none but competent workingmen and their friends to any office whatever. The rich have ruled us until they have ruined us. We will take our own affairs into our own hands. The republic must and shall be preserved, and only workingmen will do it."[49]

Related to these political characteristics, the goals workers pursued through strikes extended well beyond wages to the central question of the day: who was to control and benefit from the new economic and political order being constructed in the United States? This was most clear in those strikes that escalated into violent attacks upon the powers that be, but it was true as well of more peaceful strikes on behalf of the central goal of the labor movement during the post–Civil War decades—the eight-hour day. Its proponents argued that the hours of labor should be limited so that workers would have the time not only for relaxation but also for self-improvement and for fulfilling their obligations as citizens of a democracy. At stake in strikes over the eight-hour day was whether workers and their children would, like Chinese coolies or Russian serfs, spend virtually all their waking hours and working lives toiling so that a privileged class could live in luxury, or whether they would be free men, the equal of all others in the American republic. Labor reformers commonly spoke of the "emancipation of the working class" as the goal of their movement, and this term—as well as "wage slavery," also often used in the late nineteenth century—had both political and economic connotations.[50]

Although the strike was the most dramatic form of collective action of the period, it was not the only form. Groups of workers also formed producer cooperatives. For example, to release its members from the grip of the "wages system," the iron molders' union established twelve cooperative foundries in the 1860s, and the coopers' union established seven cooperative barrel factories during that decade. There was another spurt in the formation of producer cooperatives in the early 1880s, with the Cooperative Board of the Knights of Labor serving as the major source of financial assistance and advice.[51]

Workers also engaged in collective actions and constructed cooperative institutions within the realm of consumption—boycotts, union labels, and consumer cooperatives. "Non-intercourse" proclamations had been issued against offending merchants by the Sons of Liberty during the Revolutionary period, by abolitionist societies during the antebellum era, and by municipal trades assemblies as early as 1863, but the term "boycott" itself is of Irish origin, and Michael Gordon argues that it became a major weapon in the hands of workers in the United States through the adaptation of this Irish institution to conditions in large American cities.[52] As practiced by the Land League in Ireland, the boycott involved total social ostracism of landlords, their agents, and others who refused to acknowledge peasant claims. During strikes in the United States, Irish immigrants did ostracize—or, as it was termed, "leave severely alone"—fellow workers who acted as scabs, but this scarcely served as a meaningful sanction against employers who lived in another part of town, with whom workers had no social relations to sever. They could, however, injure an employer by refusing to buy his products and by urging other workers to do the same. To succeed, such a tactic presupposed the existence of a fairly high degree of class consciousness among workers in their capacity as consumers.

The converse of the consumer boycott was the union label, a device for encouraging consumers to purchase products manufactured by union labor. (Probably the earliest manifestation of this device, however, was the "white label," developed in the 1860s in California to distinguish cigars manufactured by shops that hired white men exclusively and would not employ Chinese.)[53] Another institution involving joint efforts among workers in the realm of consumption was the consumer cooperative. During the 1860s municipal labor federations established thirty-seven cooperative stores in cities from Maine to California. In the 1870s the Sovereigns of Industry, a nationwide cooperative society, had ninety-six local branches that sponsored such stores. And in the 1880s the Cooperative Board of the Knights of Labor carried on this tradition.[54]

Workers also banded together for the purposes of fellowship in good times and mutual assistance in times of need. For the most part they joined with other residents of their neighborhood or members of their ethnic group—in neighborhood saloons and in fraternal organizations and mutual aid societies that defined their membership along ethnic or religious lines. But some of these groupings and organizations were created by workers at (or in association with) their places of work. A number of restaurants in the factory district of Lynn, Massachusetts, for example, catered to an exclusively—and self-consciously—working-class clientele: so many unemployed shoe workers spent their days at Hunt's Cafe that it came to be known as "Crispin's Congress," and Mackenzie's Lunch found it useful to advertise itself as a "strictly union house."[55] Some fraternal organizations restricted their membership to persons belonging to the working (or producing) classes—the Supreme Mechanical Order of the Sun was the largest of these in the 1860s—and others were organized along craft lines. A number of craft-based fraternal societies functioned as trade unions, as the names of some of the major labor unions of the 1860s and 1870s indicates: the Knights of St. Crispin, the Brotherhood of the Footboard, and the Sons of Vulcan. The secrecy, the ritual, and the fraternal spirit of such organizations served a number of purposes for labor unions. Secrecy was a way of dealing with blacklists; elaborate rituals, oaths, and titles enabled organizations, which did not enjoy the protection or control the sanctions that the Wagner Act later granted unions, to distribute "solidary inducements" to their members. Most important of all, the fraternalism that characterized such organizations was quite similar to the spirit of mutual assistance among brother workers that labor unions drew upon and sought to strengthen among their members.[56]

Another way in which workers sought to improve the conditions under which they lived and labored was through participation in labor reform associations. These associations were roughly comparable to the abolitionist societies of the 1840s and 1850s and the civil rights organizations of the 1940s and 1950s. They sought through education, agitation, and lobbying to secure the enactment of legislation beneficial to workers. Their membership was open to anyone who shared their principles, workers and nonworkers alike. The most prominent of these organizations were the Eight Hour Leagues, which sought to get state legislatures to enact statutes declaring eight hours to be a "legal day's work."[57]

Labor parties were another component of the labor reform movement during the quarter century following the outbreak of the Civil War. In 1869 the Independent party, organized by the Knights of St. Crispin, elected two dozen state legislators from industrial towns in Massachusetts; in 1878 the Greenback-Labor party elected a number of mayors in industrial and mining towns in Pennsylvania and New York; and in 1886 labor tickets won municipal elections in dozens of communities throughout the country. Labor reformers also organized a succession of national labor or farmer-labor parties during the 1860s, 1870s, and 1880s; none of these, however, managed to win a substantial number of working-class votes.[58]

Many of these disparate goals, modes of collective action, and organizational forms characterized the largest labor reform organization of the late nineteenth century, the Knights of Labor. The organization, whose full name was the Noble and Holy Order of the Knights of Labor, was founded as a fraternal society among Philadelphia garment workers in 1869, and especially during the first decade of its life it shrouded its affairs in secrecy (members were forbidden to mention the organization's name to outsiders, let alone the names of fellow members), and practiced an elaborate ritual of oaths, passwords, and ceremonies.[59] Members of the Knights—sometimes with the sanction of the organization, sometimes without—also participated in strikes, and the organization's leaders engaged in collective bargaining with employers.[60] In connection with these activities the Knights sponsored boycotts and attached an identifying label to goods manufactured by firms that negotiated contracts with the organization.[61] The Cooperative Board of the Knights, as mentioned above, helped set up both producer and consumer cooperatives. The Knights also participated actively in electoral politics. Terrence Powderly, the organization's Grand Master Workman, was elected mayor of Scranton, Pennsylvania, in 1878, and district assemblies of the Knights played a major role in the surge of labor activity in the elections of 1886.[62] A noteworthy feature of most of the organizations established by workers was their extremely amorphous structure. The Knights provide a striking example of this. After the order shed its secrecy in 1879, it was very easy to join it and consequently its total membership fluctuated wildly. The most dramatic fluctuation occurred during the second half of the 1880s: between July 1885 and July 1886 the Knights' membership increased from 104,000 to 703,000; it then reversed direction and declined to its original level by the end of the decade.

Not only was movement into and out of labor organizations easy and frequent, so too were the boundaries between them highly permeable. Many skilled workers belonged to both a trade union and the Knights; Samuel Gompers himself was such a "two-card" man. Similarly, many socialists played an active role in the Knights and in the trade unions of the day. As Alexander Saxton says of the San Francisco labor movement of the early 1880s, "Everything in the house of labor in those days was interpermeable; ideas overlapped; and personnel swapped places. Haskill [a Socialist], editing what had become the official organ of the Trades Assembly, devoted his columns to the service of the Knights with impartial enthusiasm."[63]

It was possible for trade unionists, Knights, socialists, and other labor reformers to work together because to a considerable degree they shared a common vocabulary and set of objections to the dominant institutions and values of the late nineteenth century American economic order. There were differences among them, but the similarities were sufficiently great to make it possible to speak of the existence of a single, albeit amorphous, labor reform movement in the United States during the twenty-five years after the outbreak of the Civil War.[64]

The focus of traditional American labor historiography upon the conflict between bread-and-butter trade unionists (who supposedly shared the materialistic values of American society and simply wanted to secure higher wages for the members of their trade) and impractical reformers (who either wanted to return to a simpler age or who preached doctrines alien to American workers) obscures the rather substantial areas of agreement among trade unionists, Knights, and socialists and the very profound objections they all raised to some of the central practices and values of industrial capitalism.[65] Trade unionists, as much as Knights and socialists, spoke of "the abolition of the wages system" and "the emancipation of the working class" as their ultimate goal.[66] And all segments of the labor movement regarded themselves as engaged in a struggle with "capital" or "wealth" over the very shape of American society. The preamble to the constitution adopted by the Knights of Labor in 1878 declared that, as summarized by Joseph Rayback: "'Wealth' . . . had become so aggressive that 'unless checked' it would lead to the 'pauperization and hopeless degradation of the toiling masses.' If the toilers, therefore, wanted to enjoy the 'blessings of life' they had to organize 'every department of productive industry.' . . . The ultimate aim of the order would be the establishment of 'cooperative institutions productive and distributive.'"[67] The preamble of the constitution adopted by the American Federation of Labor (AFL) in 1886 asserted, in a rather similar vein, that a "struggle is going on in all the civilized world between oppressors and oppressed of all countries, between capitalist and laborer which grows in intensity from year to year. . . . It therefore behooves the Representatives of the Trades and Labor Unions of America . . . to adopt such measures and disseminate such principles among the mechanics and laborers of our country as will permanently unite them."[68]

It is in this context that the rather substantial role socialists played in the American labor movement of the post–Civil War decades can be understood. For reasons to be discussed, socialism was not a significant force in American electoral politics during this period. Socialist doctrines concerning the inevitability of conflict between capital and labor, however, resonated with experiences that many workers had had on their jobs, and when such conflicts were especially intense other elements of the labor reform movement were prepared to associate themselves with socialists. In particular, in 1869, when the campaign for an eight-hour day was sweeping the nation, the National Labor Union announced its intention of affiliating with the International Workingmen's Association (IWA)—the First International.[69] The IWA's successor, the Workingmen's Party of the United States, played an important role in the leadership of the 1877 strike movement in a number of cities, most notably in St. Louis, where a majority of the members of the executive committee that ran the general strike were members of the party.[70] Socialists also gained a major voice in the Knights of Labor and the AFL during the crisis of the 1890s.

In addition, the commitment of Marxian socialists (as opposed to Lassalleans) to the organization of labor unions meant that men who were, or once had been, socialists played a major role in the American trade union movement. In New York City, for example, members of the "Stanton Street group"—a circle of IWA members and their associates, the most prominent of whom were Adolph Strasser, Samuel Gompers, and Peter Maguire—led the drives to organize the city's cigarmakers and carpenters in the 1870s.[71] In San Francisco a similar grouping, which Saxton terms "the socialist academy," played a major role in organizing the Coast Seamen's Union and the city's Trades Assembly in the 1880s.[72] The important role socialists played in the organization of unions laid the groundwork for socialists and nonsocialists in the American labor movement to influence one another.

One final characteristic of the collective endeavors in which workers engaged and the organizations they formed during the post–Civil War years is worth emphasizing again at this point—the often close articulation between the claims that workers made upon their employers and the state, and the activities and organizations through which they asserted these claims. Workers sought both to pressure employers directly and to obtain the support of state governments for their efforts to secure the eight-hour day, to increase mine safety, and to secure relief from the competition of "coolie labor." They pursued these goals by staging strikes, threatening to switch their votes between the major parties, entering labor tickets in elections, and lobbying. It was not uncommon during this period for labor organizations (the Knights were the most important example) to engage in several of these activities; thus workers often made claims upon both their employers and the state through one and the same organization. It is true that most trade unions, for reasons to be discussed below, scrupulously avoided official involvement in electoral politics; it remains the case, however, that the leaders of these "pure and simple" unions played a major role in founding labor reform organizations that were heavily involved in political action.

What all of this means is that the wide array of groups and organizations established by workers in the decades following the Civil War were more the vehicles through which a social movement—the labor movement—operated than a set of interest groups occupying an established and limited niche in the American economic and political order. Their goals were broad—involving nothing less than transforming the position workers occupied in American society—and quite threatening to the nation's upper class and its political leadership. Moreover, these groups and organizations were not highly "institutionalized"; they were not characterized by a high degree of organizational "autonomy," "coherence," and "adaptability," to use Samuel P. Huntington's terminology.[73] This is especially clear in the case of the period's largest labor reform organization, the Knights of Labor. Far from enjoying a substantial measure of autonomy from its social base, the Knights quite accurately reflected the temper of the working class: its membership shot up in the mid-1880s as the number of persons caught up in the spirit of the labor movement increased—the hope that workers could improve their lives through their collective efforts. These new members, sharing the militant mood of the day—that workers should "give no quarter" in the fight for their rights—drew the Knights into the great strike wave of 1886.[74] Correlatively, the leaders of the Knights were able to exercise little control over their members; in particular, they were not in a position to decree when strikes would be called and terminated and, as we shall see, they were unable to shed old goals and methods and to adopt new ones for the sake of preserving their organization.

Although it makes sense to speak of a single, albeit amorphous, labor reform movement in the United States during this period, this is not to say that all elements of that movement had identical goals or that there was unanimity among them on questions of strategy and tactics, any more than speaking of a civil rights movement in the 1960s implies that all blacks who participated in the quest for "freedom now" or "black power" had a common understanding of the meaning of those slogans or agreed on the best means to achieve those ends. One of the most important divergences among participants in the labor reform movement concerned their view of the scope of the movement's constituency—their understanding of the boundaries of the working class. In their words and deeds labor reformers revealed a wide range of views on the boundaries of the collectivity whose interests they sought to advance.

The most comprehensive of these understandings regarded "labor" as including all members of the "producing classes"—common laborers, skilled workers, farmers, members of the middle class, and even manufacturers. This view was especially prevalent during the early part of the period. In the 1860s and early 1870s the term "working classes" always was used in the plural; "labor" was used to refer both to workers and manufacturers; and its antonym, "capital," referred exclusively to financiers and *rentiers*. Those sharing this comprehensive understanding believed that there were no inherent conflicts of interest between employers and employees, and that the labor reform movement need not be one of wage laborers alone.[75] During the 1860s and early 1870s members of the middle class played an important role in the Eight Hour Leagues, in many sections of the International Workingmen's Association, and in the National Labor Union (NLU) and the National Labor Reform Party.[76] Under the constitution adopted by the Knights of Labor in 1878, membership in the order was open to any person "working for wages, or who at any time worked for wages," with the exception of bankers, lawyers, doctors, and liquor dealers—whose very businesses and professions involved the exploitation of productive labor. Significantly, employers were not excluded from the order.[77]

Although the national leaders of the Knights argued that the interests of employers and employees were fundamentally similar and were therefore reluctant to endorse strikes, the members of numerous local assemblies of the order indicated that they had a less inclusive understanding of the boundaries of the working class by walking off their jobs to put pressure on and extract concessions from their employers.[78] Trade unionists, who in word and deed excluded employers from the working class—who used the term "working class" in the singular and did not hesitate to use the strike as a weapon—established the Federation of Organized Trades and Labor Unions (FOTLU) in 1881, the first national labor reform organization composed of wage laborers alone, and the precursor of the American Federation of Labor.[79]

Participants in the labor reform movement—and American workers generally—also displayed a variety of dispositions toward those who differed from them in race and sex. Whites, blacks, and Asians often competed for the same jobs, as did men and women; moreover, employers at times used blacks, Asians, and women as strikebreakers. Labor reformers responded in two different ways to this situation. On the one hand, many local and national crafts unions excluded the members of racial minorities and women from their ranks and sought to drive them from their trades.[80] And all national labor organizations, from the NLU through the AFL, sought to ban all immigration to the United States from China. In California, the Workingmen's party, the Knights, and San Francisco's Federated Trades Council went even further and sought to expel the Chinese. During the 1880s in several small cities and mining camps in the Far West white workers (and small businessmen) took the law into their own hands and drove the Chinese out of their communities by force.[81]

On the other hand, white and black workers and also male and female workers at times united across these lines in strikes, election campaigns, and in labor reform organizations. Black sewer workers in Louisville, Kentucky, and black stevedores in Cairo, Illinois, took part in the strike movement that swept the country in the summer of 1877.[82] In the 1886 municipal elections in Richmond, Virginia, the Knights of Labor and black Republicans endorsed a common slate of candidates, and together they won control of the city council.[83] The NLU and the Knights encouraged the organization of blacks, albeit often in segregated locals; in 1886 the Knights had 60,000 black members.[84] Among labor unions, the United Mine Workers was especially active in recruiting blacks and a black organizer, Richard Davis, served on that union's national executive board in the 1890s.[85] As for women, the NLU seated delegates from Working Women's Protective Unions at its national conventions and advocated equal pay for equal work; many local and district assemblies of the Knights in the shoe and garment industries admitted women to their ranks; and strikes in these industries often mobilized both male and female workers.[86]

Immigrants comprised a much larger proportion of the industrial work force than blacks or women in the late nineteenth century, and thus the relationship between ethnicity and class—the tendency of workers to divide along ethnic lines or to unite across them—is a matter of great importance that will be discussed further below. Suffice it to say here that this relationship was also a multifaceted one. Many strikes were lost because employers brought in gangs of immigrants to serve as strikebreakers.[87] For this reason all national labor organizations in the post–Civil War years sought to ban the importation of immigrant contract labor, and the passage of the Foran Act in 1885, which outlawed this practice, was generally regarded as one of labor's major legislative victories in the nineteenth century.[88] On the local level many trade unions dominated by native-born workers or the members of older immigrant groups refused to admit newer immigrants to their ranks. In Scranton, Welsh miners who dominated the Workingman's Benevolent Association took such a stance toward Irish and Germans; in Milwaukee, the Irish and Germans who dominated that city's labor unions refused to recruit into their ranks members of that city's large Polish community.[89]

Nativism, however, was not a major theme in the labor reform movement during the postbellum years. Immigrants from England, Wales, and Germany played a major role in organizing trade unions (and also consumer cooperatives) during this period. A major reason that the Knights of Labor shed its secrecy in 1878 was to enable Catholic immigrants to join the order without violating the Church's ban on membership in secret societies. And many trade unionists recognized that the only way they could effectively counter the tactic of using immigrants as strikebreakers was to recruit the latter into their ranks.[90]

THE WORKING-CLASS RESPONSE: SOURCES OF VARIATION AND CHANGE

As amorphous in structure as the labor reform movement of the late nineteenth century was and as disparate the views of its members were, by no means did most American workers respond to the changes they were experiencing by participating in that movement. Only a minority of the nation's wage earners ever took part in a strike, belonged to a trade union or other labor reform organization, or voted for a labor ticket. Moreover, significant changes occurred during the period in the relative importance and character of both the various modes of collective action in which workers engaged and the organizations to which they belonged. These variations across groups of workers and through time were a function of the structure of and changes in the patterns of economic, community, and political life within which workers were situated.

Variations and Changes

Although it is impossible to obtain data on the numbers involved, it is probably true that more workers sought to overcome the difficulties they faced through individual endeavors than by joining in a collective effort to improve their lives. As mentioned above, rates of population mobility were extraordinarily high, especially among persons at the bottom of the class structure; those unable to find work in one city would move on to another. The most extreme manifestation of this phenomenon was tramping: thousands of men rode the rails from city to city to eke out an existence. Occasionally these transient laborers would join together under the leadership of a tribune who gave voice to their common grievances: Denis Kearney in the late 1870s and Jacob Coxey in 1894 drew many followers from this source.[91] More commonly, however, they suffered their fates in solitude.

Moreover, though many workers rejected the acquisitive and individualistic values preached by the Henry Ward Beechers and Horatio Algers of the time, many others did not. The ubiquity of small shops in working-class neighborhoods gives testimony to the determination of many workers to scrimp and save so that they and their children could move out of the factories. And the proliferation of subcontracting practices in American industry—the most notorious being the sweatshop system in the garment trades—indicates that there were large numbers of workers who could not resist the temptation of becoming small entrepreneurs and profiting from the exploitation of other workers. The ideal of self-improvement that animated the labor movement was separated by only a narrow line from the impulse to move up the class scale through one's individual efforts. Mutualistic and individualistic manifestations of this ethos could coexist in the late nineteenth century because America in the Gilded Age was a land in which workers both suffered massive exploitation and had genuine opportunities (or at least their children did) to move out of the working class or up within it.[92]

When workers did join with others in an effort to improve their lives, ethnicity was at least as likely as social class per se to be the basis of association. It will not do, however, to speak of ethnicity and class as competing principles of identification and organization—the prevailing fashion in the historiography of the period—as many examples cited below will indicate. Nonetheless it was not uncommon for ethnic subcommunities to unite behind those of its members who broke strikes called by workers belonging to other ethnic groups. For example, during a coal strike in Scranton in 1871, Irish and German mine laborers broke ranks with striking Welsh miners, hoping to take their jobs and provoking violent clashes between the ethnic subcommunities.[93] It is also true that ethnicity and religion were the most common bases of association for mutual aid and fraternal societies that provided members with such benefits as burial insurance, mutual support in abstaining from alcohol, or good fellowship to accompany their liquor.

Also, though labor tickets were entered in hundreds of local and state elections in the postbellum period and the effort to create a national farmer-labor party was a persistent theme, the victories labor reformers won in the electoral arena were at best evanescent and the great majority of American workers cast their ballots for the Democratic and Republican parties. Indeed, the institutions with which the largest number of American workers almost certainly identified were these national parties, the common activity in which they most frequently engaged was voting the Democratic or Republican ticket on election day, and the organizations to which the largest number of them belonged were the local machines affiliated with the major parties. The two major parties and their local machines could not be indifferent to the concerns of their working-class constituents, but the cleavage between them cut across class lines—however broadly or narrowly the boundaries of the nation's social classes might be defined—and this meant that all the hoopla of nineteenth-century electioneering divided the working class and stressed the ties that workers had with their fellow partisans from other social classes.

Not only did substantial differences exist at any given time in the disposition of various segments of the working class to participate in the labor reform movement, significant changes occurred during the late nineteenth century in the activities and organizations comprising that movement. In particular, major changes occurred both in the frequency and the character of strikes during the three decades following the Civil War. The number of workers involved in strikes increased over time, but there were substantial fluctuations within this trend. Equally important, changes occurred in the role unions played in strikes: the proportion of strikes that were called by unions (as opposed to unorganized, spontaneous walkouts) rose during the years 1869–74, fell during the remainder of the 1870s, and then resumed climbing from just under 50 percent in 1881 to over 70 percent in the early 1890s. With increasing organization came changes in the goals of strikers. The proportion of strikes in which wages were the central issue fell from 75 percent in the early 1880s to 50 percent in the early 1890s, and the number dealing with organizational issues—such as strikes to secure union recognition or to defend union members against retaliation—rose steadily. In addition, between 1885 and 1894 the number of sympathy strikes increased dramatically. In one respect, however, both the focus and setting of strikes became narrower during the second half of our period. During the decade and a half following 1877, strikes were not used as a political weapon to the extent they had been during the previous fifteen years and, correspondingly, they were more likely to occur exclusively at workplaces than to take the form of community uprisings.[94]

These variations in participation in the labor reform movement and changes through time in its activities and organizations were a function of the character of and changes in broader economic, community, and political relationships. Workers, after all, did not exist *in vacuo*; as the relationship between any segment of the working class and other social forces varied—and as the relationship among these other groups changed—so too did the behavior of the workers in question.

Relations of Production

The modes of collective action in which different workers engaged and the types of organizations they formed were shaped first by the web of economic relations in which they were enmeshed—their relationship with competitors for their jobs, with other workers on their jobs, and with their employers. The image of a web is particularly appropriate because changes in any one of these relationships could alter the others, and changes in economic relations in which workers were not directly involved, such as the relationship between their employer and his competitors, could alter those that did touch them directly. A number of such changes occurred during the last decades of the nineteenth century.

The relationship between workers and potential competitors for their jobs is the focus of the central law of neoclassical labor economics: the more completely a group of workers can restrict entry into a labor market, the more readily they can form a trade union and compel their employer to bargain with them.[95] The ability to restrict entry into a labor market is, in turn, heavily influenced by the skill required to do the job in question. The oldest and most stable labor unions in the nineteenth century were those organized by highly skilled workers—among them typographers, iron molders, machinists, locomotive engineers, carpenters, and bricklayers—because employers faced with a walkout by such craftsmen could not readily replace the strikers and therefore had an incentive to come to terms with the unions these workers formed. By contrast, unskilled workers who walked off their jobs could easily be replaced, and employers had little reason to enter into stable bargaining relationships with labor unions that unskilled workers might seek to form.

The relationship of skilled workers to their fellow workers on the job was at least equally important, however, in explaining why they were able to organize unions and conduct strikes successfully. As indicated above, skilled workers played a crucial role in the organization of production in the nineteenth-century factory. They often knew better than their employer himself how the production end of his business was conducted, and they exercised more control over the day-to-day operations of his plant than he did. To the extent that this was true, these workers were indispensable and had considerable bargaining leverage.[96] Moreover, the relationship of skilled workers to each other on the job had an ethical dimension that was fundamentally collectivist (as opposed to individualist) in orientation, and the unions these workers organized drew upon these solidarities.[97]

The business cycle also influenced the ability of workers to control labor markets. Strikes could be more successfully conducted and unions more readily organized during periods of prosperity, when the labor market was tight, than during depressions, when firms could easily replace striking workers with the unemployed, including unemployed union men who were driven by necessity to work for less than the union scale. Thus the first great wave of union organization in the late nineteenth century occurred during the flush years of the late 1860s and early 1870s; union membership declined precipitously during the depression of 1873–78; and the Knights of Labor grew in membership during the relatively prosperous 1880s. With some important qualifications to be noted, the number of workers involved in strikes also rose and fell with the business cycle.

The relationship between fluctuations in the business cycle and rates of strike activity and union formation was not perfect, however. As mentioned earlier, there was a secular increase both in the number of workers involved in strikes and in the extent to which strikes were carefully planned and organized. This rising baseline is to be explained in the first place by a number of changes in the structure of the American economy that affected the relationship of business firms to one another, of employers to employees, and ultimately of workers to each other.

Prior to the depression of 1873 most manufacturing firms in the United States were quite small—in 1869 the average factory had only eight employees—and the great majority of such establishments were family firms or partnerships whose owners played an active role in their management.[98] In these circumstances it was possible for employers to maintain something of a personal relationship with their employees, and the concept of the "producing classes" made sense phenomenologically. Samuel Walker says of the workingmen of Scranton during this period:

> Many Scranton workingmen ... had worked side by side with the George Scrantons and Thomas Dicksons [the city's two leading industrialists] in the 1850s and 1860s. George Scranton, for example, wielded hammer and chisel in his initial attempts to manufacture iron. One workingman recalled the time when "Thomas Dickson ... appeared in blue denim trousers and blouse on him. He took the hammer from one man and took his place for about fifteen minutes, then stepped over to the other side and spelled another man for fifteen minutes."[99]

Conflicts between employers and employees existed, to be sure, and workers staged strikes to increase the wages they earned and reduce the hours they labored, but union leaders continued to insist that the interests of the two sides were fundamentally in harmony, and they sought to resolve such disputes by dealing personally with their employers.

Economic developments during the late nineteenth century disrupted such relationships. As noted, the extension of the railroads made it difficult for any employer to treat his employees more decently than his least scrupulous competitors in other cities. Beyond this, the absorption of small firms by stronger ones during the depressions and recessions of the period, the spread of the corporate form of business organization, and the emergence of a class of professional managers destroyed the organizational base upon which personal relations between employers and employees had been grounded. Workers for a time resisted the reduction of all relations to the cash nexus. Walker reports that as late as 1877, well after corporations based in New York City had taken control of Scranton's major industries, delegations of workers sought to settle disputes by traveling to New York to talk personally to the president of the corporation that employed them.[100] Such appeals, of course, fell on deaf ears, and workers in time learned how to organize themselves more effectively to advance their interests in this new economic environment.

Class divisions became more pronounced and strikes became more frequent and more highly organized not simply because manufacturers, driven by the lure of profits and the lash of competition, sought to squeeze more output from their men, but also because workers themselves, in striving to advance their collective interests, took steps that sharpened the line between employers and employees. Work-rules unions enacted that established output quotas and prohibited participation in various subcontracting schemes served the collective interests of the union's members by imposing restraints on the efforts of individual wage laborers to get ahead at the expense of their brothers. These work rules were essentially a codification of the informal norms, described above, that had emerged in the course of earlier struggles between craftsmen and their employers. Unions codified these norms and established formal procedures to enforce them—shop committees to monitor compliance, strikes called against employers who violated the union's rules, and eventually sympathy strikes against employers who violated the work rules of other unions—to better ensure that employers would adhere to the union's standards. These developments in union practice heightened class divisions.[101]

Factory owners, on their part, undertook to reorganize the process of production in their plants—adopting new and improved technologies and new techniques of supervision, reward, and punishment—in order to overcome the limitations that their employees sought to impose upon them. The employers' associations they established and the mergers into which they entered were influenced by this same consideration.[102] This in turn shaped the tone and tenor of relations between employers and employees. There was, then, a dialectical interaction between changes in the organization of production and changes in the character and extent of class conflicts, class consciousness, and working-class organization.

Finally, from time to time during the late nineteenth century there were bursts of strike activity above and beyond what can be explained by this rising trend and fluctuations of the business cycle. In the summer of 1877, during the American economy's worst depression up to that time, the nation was convulsed by a strike wave larger than any it had previously experienced. In 1886 the number of workers involved in strikes shot up to 407,000 from an average of 124,000 in the years between 1881 and 1885. Finally, in 1894, at the trough of the worst depression of the nineteenth century, the number of strikers shot up to its highest level in that century—505,000, a figure roughly double that of the preceding and following years.

The strikes of 1877 and 1886, and to a lesser extent those of 1894, spread in a contagious fashion and involved workers who had not previously participated in the labor reform movement. Each of these strike waves was precipitated by a walkout of railway men. The central role that railroads played in the American economic order of the nineteenth century was well understood at the time, and the spectacle of workers rising up against the nation's key economic institution inspired others to do the same. As each strike wave gathered momentum it appeared that the entire structure of authority, both industrial and political, to which workers were subjected was crumbling. If the sense that workers could indeed change the conditions under which they labored led increasing numbers to join these strike movements, it provoked fear and outrage among the upper and middle classes and led them to stage counterattacks.[103]

The years following the Great Uprising of 1886 witnessed an especially sustained antilabor crusade. The Knights were its first target. As Rayback notes:

> Leaders of the campaign against them were the employers from whom the order had secured concessions. . . . [They] began to organize into associations which openly and deliberately moved to destroy the order by systematic violation of trade agreements, refusal to arbitrate industrial disputes, and resort to lockouts, black listing, and yellow-dog contracts. Such activity led to some fearsome conflicts. Nearly 100,000 Knights were involved in strikes and lockouts in the latter months of the year 1886.[104]

In addition, business firms that competed with the cooperative enterprises sponsored by the Knights induced other firms to refuse to sell equipment and supplies to them, and within two year's time all of these enterprises were destroyed.

During these years many employers also undertook to destroy the trade unions that organized their workers. Their employees responded by striking and by calling upon their brother workers to stage sympathy strikes. These confrontations led to some of the largest and most bitter strikes of the nineteenth century—the strikes at Homestead, at Coeur d'Alene, and on the New Orleans docks in 1892, and the Pullman and bituminous coal strikes in 1894. As will be discussed, employers were able to get the militia, the army, and the courts to intervene on their behalf in many of these conflicts.

This counteroffensive by business and the state threatened the very survival of the labor movement. It also fostered deep divisions within the movement over the question of how, in this increasingly hostile environment, workers could best improve the conditions under which they labored.

Community Life

The size and structure of the communities in which workers lived also shaped the modes of collective action in which they engaged. In small cities and mining towns where a majority of wage earners might work in a single industry or even for a single firm, ties of community and class often reinforced one another: a wage cut or lockout in the town's key industry was an attack upon all or most workers in the town. At the same time, the division between the working and middle classes characteristically was not as pronounced in small cities as in large ones. The neighborhoods in which workers lived were, quite literally, less distant from those inhabited by the middle class, and there were greater opportunities for interaction between individuals across class lines. This made it less likely that the members of the working and the middle classes in small cities would come to view the world in entirely different ways.

These aspects of community life had a number of important consequences. The doctrines of labor reform organizations, such as the Knights of Labor, that sought to unite all "producers"—laborers, skilled workers, shopkeepers, and farmers—in the battle against "monopoly" found their readiest audience in smaller cities, and the mixed assemblies of the Knights—whose membership was not confined to a single craft—was a widely adopted form of organization in these locales. Strikes in smaller cities commonly were community affairs, with the workers involved receiving the support of their fellow townsmen. As one coal miner said of a strike in St. Clair County, Illinois, in 1868, "We had support from the shopkeepers, farmers, and everyone else to stand out against our oppressors."[105] Just as trade unions and unorganized strike movements were able to draw upon the strong solidarities linking workers to one another on the job to sustain themselves in the absence of the sanctions provided by the Wagner Act, so too were they able to draw upon the solidarities linking workers to their neighbors. For example, the coal miners who staged a strike in Tioga County, Pennsylvania, in 1874 were able to hold out for three months until the company capitulated, even though they had no strike fund to draw upon, because local shopkeepers and householders provided them with food and shelter.[106]

These same community solidarities also often ensured that workers did not have to fear that the local government would intervene on behalf of their employers during strikes. During a strike by coal miners in Braidwood,

Illinois—a town of 6,000—in 1874, the mine operators hired Pinkerton agents and sought to have them deputized by the sheriff so that they could arrest striking workers for trespassing on company property. The sheriff, however, refused to do so. Instead he and the mayor appointed as special deputies a dozen members of a committee the strikers had established to prevent violence and property destruction.[107] Labor reformers also enjoyed greater success in small cities than in large ones when they entered the electoral arena. Three years after the miners' strike in Braidwood, for example, the president of the miners' union was elected mayor. More generally, the candidates nominated by the Greenback-Labor party in the mid-and late-1870s won hundreds of councilmanic, state legislative, and congressional elections in small cities, but very few in the nation's great metropolises.

What was true of small towns as a whole was usually true of the ethnic subcommunities within them. The great majority of both Irish-Americans and immigrants from southern and eastern Europe in these towns tended to be laborers and workers, and hence the small number of middle-class members of these groups could scarcely escape identification with the class position of their countrymen: to be a Polish or Hungarian shopkeeper in the mining towns of northeastern Pennsylvania was to belong to an ethnic group whose members were overwhelmingly proletarian. This meant that strikes by such mine workers were actions of the entire ethnic subcommunity. In his account of a strike by East European miners in the Pennsylvania anthracite fields in 1888, appropriately titled "A Slavic Community Strikes," Victor Greene reports that a rally to support the strikers called by a Ukrainian priest was addressed by the editors of the local Lithuanian and Ukrainian newspapers, a Slovak merchant, and a Polish shoemaker.[108] And ethnically based organizations in these communities were more likely to be dominated by working-class militants than by members of the group's middle class. For example, following the destruction of the anthracite miners' union in the "Long Strike" of 1874, the Molly Maguires, a secret society within the Ancient Order of Hibernians, emerged as the vehicle for the miners' struggle against their bosses. At this point homicide—murder and capital punishment—became the chief means through which class conflict was conducted in the coal fields: the Mollys murdered mine superintendents, and the mine operators secured the conviction and execution of twenty alleged members of the order by hiring a Pinkerton agent to infiltrate it, collect evidence, and testify against its members.[109] In the early 1880s, branches of the Land League—at the time the most prominent Irish nationalist organization—in the mining towns of Pennsylvania and the Far West and in the small manufacturing cities of the Northeast and Midwest were dominated by leaders who asserted that the struggle of American workers against their employers was the same as the struggle of Irish tenant farmers against their landlords.

Significantly, many of these League branches were organized at workplaces and even included members of ethnic groups other than the Irish.[110]

In the nation's major metropolises there was more residential and social segregation of the working and middle classes. Especially in large commercial and financial centers, with their armies of clerks, the middle class was numerous enough for its members to establish a full set of institutions enabling them to shop, pray, play, and educate their children without coming into contact with members of the working class. Correspondingly, shopkeepers, preachers, teachers, and newspaper editors could cater exclusively to a middle-class clientele. Beyond this, different segments of the working class—defined along lines of income and/or ethnicity—generally lived in different neighborhoods. Even in the middle-sized city of Scranton, the predominantly Welsh miners, who were the aristocracy of the local working class, lived apart from the Irish and German mine laborers and workers in other trades.[111] These aspects of community life in large cities affected patterns of working-class behavior and organization.

The residents of large cities were less available than their small-town counterparts for mobilization by organizations that sought to unite all producers. If the geographic center of gravity of the mixed assembly of the Knights was small-town America, the center of gravity of the trades assemblies of the Knights and of craft unions was in the nation's larger cities. Moreover, though workers in large cities often united across craft and ethnic lines when conflicts between capital and labor were most intense, when such episodes passed, these cleavages reemerged to divide the working class. During the 1877 general strike in St. Louis, for example, the employed and unemployed and the German- and non-German-speaking members of the city's working class displayed a remarkable degree of unity and discipline. Yet in the elections after the strike, the Workingmen's party, whose members occupied a majority of seats on the executive committee that ran the strike, was able to elect candidates only in the city's German neighborhoods.[112] When Terrence Powderly was elected mayor of Scranton on the Greenback-Labor Party (GLP) ticket immediately following the 1877 strike, which had involved workers in the city's iron mills and coal mines as well as railroads, he won the votes of the traditionally Republican Welsh as well as the traditionally Democratic Irish. Within a year's time, however, the city's Welsh voters had returned to the GOP, and Powderly only won reelection because he received the Democratic as well as the GLP nomination. He won a third term running on the Democratic ticket alone.[113]

In large and medium-sized cities labor reformers not only faced difficulties overcoming ethnic and craft divisions within the working class but also had to contend with sharp cleavages between the working and middle classes. In particular, members of the middle class in large cities were more likely to sympathize with employers than with employees in labor disputes.

This freed municipal governments in large cities to intervene against workers in strikes and labor demonstrations. In Chicago Mayor John Rice mobilized the police and a local militia company to break a strike by unions seeking to enforce the eight-hour day in 1868; the New York City police broke up an entirely peaceful meeting in Tompkins Square in 1874 at which speakers called upon the city to put the unemployed to work on public construction projects; and the "pick handle brigade," upon which the city government of San Francisco relied to restore order during the July 1877 riots against the Chinese and the business firms that employed them, was drawn primarily from the city's middle class.[114]

In large cities the middle-class elements of local ethnic groups were also more likely to assume the leadership of their subcommunity. A major reason they were in a position to do so was that in large cities this segment tended to be both numerically and proportionately larger than in smaller factory and mining towns. The Irish Land League of the 1880s can serve again as a case in point. In Boston and New York City, in particular, the League was controlled by members of each city's large Irish middle class, who craved respectability in the eyes of their city's Protestant upper class.[115]

Employers reacted in a variety of ways to these differences. One response, especially prevalent in industries like mining with no locational flexibility, was to establish company towns that were structured to deprive workers of an autonomous community life. Another was to call upon higher authorities for assistance when local officials refused to intervene on their behalf in labor disputes. Firms that had some locational flexibility reacted to the hostile climate of smaller cities by moving to or initially setting up shop in the nation's great metropolises. This helps explain why manufacturing employment in America's largest cities grew more rapidly in the 1870s, 1880s, and 1890s than in smaller cities—reversing the pattern that had characterized the 1860s.[116]

Politics

The distinctive character of the American political regime and changes in the structure of national politics during the postbellum years also influenced the successes and failures of the various organizations workers joined and the various modes of collective action in which they engaged. This in turn helped determine which of these organizations and patterns of behavior would survive into the twentieth century.

The strong attachments members of the working class developed to the two major parties by virtue of having been mobilized into politics through the nation's political institutions had particularly important consequences for American labor unions. The constitutions and by-laws of unions in the late nineteenth century invariably prohibited them from taking stands on political issues or endorsing candidates for public office, because this would alienate rank-and-file members who had other commitments and might well lead these members to quit the union. The secretary of the Bricklayers International Union expressed this in 1872: "We have excellent trades' unionists, who are warm democrats and zealous republicans . . . and who are ready to point with suspicion to every movement on our part towards the formation of political organizations. . . . The only way we can be successful with our local and national trades unions is by excluding politics from them."[117]

At the same time, union leaders recognized that government actions and policies had important implications for the well-being of both members of their organizations and the working class at large, and they wanted to be able to influence those policies. In an effort to accomplish this without risking splitting their unions, many of them sought to establish the various local and national labor parties mentioned above—parties that were organizationally distinct from unions. The labor leaders who founded these parties were hedging their bets. They hoped that the members of their unions—and of the "producing classes" in general—would cast their ballots for labor's candidates. But if their members' attachment to the Democratic and Republican parties was so strong that they would not vote for a labor ticket, the absence of any official union involvement in these third-party campaigns would ensure that "warm democrats" and "zealous republicans" would have no reason to walk out of the union. It turned out that trade union leaders were wise to take these precautions. The labor reform parties of the period either were totally insignificant electorally (e.g., the National Labor Union and National Labor Reform party) or at most succeeded in winning isolated elections and were unable to repeat their victories (e.g., the Greenback-Labor party).

These labor parties were the victims of a dilemma that ultimately sprang from the openness of the American political system to the participation of working-class voters. On the one hand, that openness compelled unions to detach themselves from partisan activity. On the other, the absence of organizational ties between the labor parties and trade unions of the postbellum decades often enabled middle-class reformers to dominate the parties because they alone could afford to devote their time to party business between annual conventions. Consequently the ideologies and programs of post–Civil War labor parties spoke as much to the concerns of middle-class activists within the labor reform community as to those of working-class trade unionists.[118] The National Labor Union, for example, eventually devoted more attention to the greenback issue than to the eight-hour day. This detached trade union leaders who participated in politics through third parties from rank-and-file union members—who at the same time, however, were becoming increasingly willing to follow these leaders when they called strikes, negotiated contracts, and so forth. Thus the openness of the American political system fostered a division between the organizations through which workers pursued their interests at their workplace, on the one hand, and in the realm of politics, on the other.

This is the converse of the British experience. In an effort to win the elective franchise during the nineteenth century, the leaders of England's skilled workers entered into a political coalition with the class beneath them in the social structure rather than with the one immediately above. During this common struggle to gain the right to vote, artisans transmitted their ideology to laborers, and skilled and unskilled workers came to regard themselves as belonging to a single class, with interests in both the political and economic realms that were distinct from those of other social classes.[119]

The political behavior of the postbellum labor movement was also shaped by the fragmented structure of the American regime. This is indicated by the way labor reformers worked to achieve one of their major goals of the late nineteenth century—the eight-hour day. In the late 1860s and early 1870s the National Labor Union and its state and local affiliates sought to get Congress and the state legislatures to declare eight hours to be a "legal day's work." At the outset, however, they conceded that it was entirely beyond the authority of the national government to regulate the hours of workers in the private sector: all they asked of Washington was that it serve as an exemplary employer by limiting the hours of the workers on its own payroll. The statutes they proposed at the state level did apply in the private sector, but they included no governmental mechanism to compel employers to comply with the law. Labor reformers never proposed—indeed, they never conceived of—the creation of public bureaucracies to serve this function. They simply sought to get the state legislature to declare that the community at large regarded eight hours as an appropriate working day. The actual task of "enforcing" the law, however, would remain in the hands of trade unions, and the means they would use to secure compliance was their usual one—the strike. Nonetheless, labor reformers anticipated that their victories in the political arena would strengthen their hand by bringing the force of public opinion to bear against recalcitrant employers.[120]

As it turned out, labor's legislative victories did not have these effects. Few employers were moved to reduce the hours of their employees simply because the legislature passed what amounted to a nonbinding resolution commending such a course of action. And when unions struck to enforce the eight-hour law, the only ones that succeeded were those that were in a position to secure this concession regardless of the state legislature's action. One result of this experience in the 1860s and early 1870s was that when the

Federation of Organized Trades and Labor Unions decided to embark upon a new eight-hour campaign in 1886, it eschewed legislative action entirely and sought to accomplish its goal entirely through economic action.

Although government institutions in the United States were highly fragmented, the American regime had the capacity to defend the prerogatives of employers against the efforts of workers to circumscribe them. This was accomplished through two mechanisms, each described by Tocqueville in the 1830s and much in evidence later: the extraordinary authority of the American judiciary and the remarkable capacity of Americans—in this case members of the upper and middle classes—to organize private associations to advance their interests.

During the late nineteenth century the American courts developed several doctrines that hindered (though did not entirely block) the efforts of labor reformers to improve the lot of the working class through both political and economic action.[121] One of these, developing from Justice Stephen J. Field's dissenting opinion in the Slaughterhouse cases of 1873, recognized corporations as persons subject to the protection of the due process clause of the Fourteenth Amendment and interpreted that protection as rendering unconstitutional any legislation that limited the right of its owners and managers to do what they pleased with their property. Once this doctrine of "substantive due process" was accepted by a majority of Field's brethren, the Supreme Court began striking down state laws regulating railroad rates, safety conditions in mines and factories, and the like. A parallel development involved judicial interpretations of the constitutional prohibition against laws impairing contracts: the courts cited the contract clause to invalidate legislation regulating the relations between employers and employees. In 1876 the federal eight-hour law became one of the first casualties of this interpretation. And beginning in the 1890s the federal courts refashioned the doctrine of relief in equity so as to enable employers to secure injunctions against strikes.

Members of the American upper and middle classes also displayed a notable ability to organize in their own defense against threats from below. Where regular army troops or militia companies were not available in adequate numbers, local businessmen organized Committees of Public Safety, Citizens Volunteer Companies, or Citizens Alliances to fill in the gap. This occurred during the Draft Riots in New York City in 1863, the anti-Chinese riots in San Francisco in July 1877, and during the Great Railway Strike in Indiana and Missouri in the summer of 1877.[122]

It must be noted that the structure of the American state, the influences to which it was subject, and the uses to which it was put did not remain completely constant during the late nineteenth century; changes occurred as the composition of the nation's governing coalition shifted. Shifting patterns of cleavage and alignment within the nation's political system, in turn, shaped the incentives workers had to channel their energies through the regime's dominant institutions and the availability of allies and prospects for success if they engaged in collective actions outside those institutions.

Broadly speaking, the late nineteenth century witnessed an increasing tendency on the part of the nation's economic and political elites to close ranks in an effort (that largely succeeded) to stave off challenges from below to their prerogatives. This occurred in two phases. The first was the period of Civil War and Radical Reconstruction, whose peak years were 1861–68 but which did not fully end until the compromise of 1876–77; this was a period of intense and violent conflict among elites both across and within the nation's major regions. The second was the classic phase of American competitive party politics, which began in 1868, reached its peak in 1876–86, and collapsed in 1894; during this period the major parties displayed an extraordinary capacity to channel and contain political conflicts, although some conflicts still erupted outside the nation's dominant institutions and ultimately contributed to another realignment in 1896. As this periodization indicates, the boundaries between these phases were not sharply defined; during each one there were subordinate (or contradictory) tendencies that eventually undermined the dominant pattern of elite cleavages and coalitions and set the stage for the succeeding one.

The central events of the 1860s and early 1870s were the Civil War and Reconstruction, and both involved the use of force to settle conflicts between the dominant political groupings in the North and South: the armies of the Union and Confederate governments together killed 600,000 persons, and the U.S. Army occupied the defeated southern states for periods extending from three to twelve years after the war ended. In addition, bitter intrasectional conflicts erupted during the war over the policies the administrations in Washington and Richmond pursued to fight and finance the war, as well as over the terms upon which peace should be sought. And after Appomattox such conflicts raged over the conditions that should be established for admitting the southern states back into the Union, the rights that should be extended to blacks, and the extent to which the policies Washington had enacted during the war—especially protective tariffs and the greenback currency—should be maintained or repealed.

There were two different lessons that the lower classes—both urban and rural—drew from these conflicts. On the one hand, the war strengthened the attachment of the working class to the American regime. It united wage workers and employers in defense of a nation that was the world's only democracy and in opposition to a society based upon the principle of slave labor. Although American labor conflicts were more violent than those of any other industrialized nation, the number of workers killed by the Confederate Army exceeded by a factor of more than one hundred the number killed in conflicts with their employers. The loyalties to the regime forged during this titanic conflict were strong and enduring.[123]

To be sure, the measures the Lincoln administration adopted to prosecute the war were extremely controversial, and the effort of the Radical Republicans to preserve many of the wartime institutions and policies during Reconstruction defined the central political issues and divisions of the immediate postwar years. However, the divisions aroused by the issues of Reconstruction, like those generated by the war itself, cut across class lines. And inasmuch as these issues were the central source of contention between Democratic and Republican parties in the 1860s, the very intensity of the passions they aroused cemented the loyalty of most American workers to the major parties.

On the other hand, Barrington Moore notwithstanding, cleavages among the nation's political and economic elites enabled and even encouraged radical currents to bubble up from below.[124] The violent language Democratic politicians used to denounce the Conscription Act of 1863 both legitimated the indignation the poor felt against a statute that permitted members of the middle and upper classes to purchase an exemption from the draft and almost certainly contributed to the numerous episodes obstructing its implementation by force.[125] The principles the Radical Republicans used to justify confiscating the property of southern slaveholders and depriving them of political power could be extended to justify placing restrictions on the privileges and powers of northern industrialists. Such a conclusion was drawn by the Boston Labor Reform Association, which in 1865 resolved: "So too must our dinner tables be reconstructed . . . [and] our dress, manners, education, morals, dwellings, and the whole Social System."[126] To bring about this reconstruction, workers were prepared to use the strike as a political weapon in the manner already described. In addition, the assault that Democrats launched against the legitimacy of every policy the Republicans had enacted since coming to power in 1861 implied that the entire corpus of public policy was open to question. Such questioning could come from more than one direction; in particular, the rural districts in the Midwest where Democrats were strongest during the war and the early years of Reconstruction became centers of Greenbackism in the late 1860s and the 1870s, and Democratic elites in the South also faced challenges from agrarian radicals.

The eruption of class conflicts in the cities and of agrarian radicalism in the countryside raised the possibility that disaffected workers and farmers might join in an attack upon industrialists, bankers, and railroad barons, and throw out the Republican and Democratic politicians allied with these interests. The effort in the 1870s to deal with this threat led to a reorganization of coalitional patterns at the peak of the American political system.

The lead in fashioning the political settlement that contained the turbulence of the Civil War and Reconstruction eras was taken by a group of professional politicians who moved into a dominant position in the Republican and Democratic parties in the 1870s.[127] These politicians searched for compromises on the issues that had so deeply divided the nation during the previous decade. It is crucial to note, however, that the stands taken by the major parties on the central issues of the 1870s and 1880s were not identical; there were areas of disagreement as well as agreement between them, which had important consequences for the political behavior of the working class.

With regard to the "southern question," the Republican party by 1877 abandoned the effort to use the U.S. Army to protect the rights of blacks in the South and to sustain state governments that depended upon black votes. Nonetheless, Republican candidates in the North regularly denounced "southern outrages" and "waved the bloody shirt" in their campaigns; and as late as 1890 the GOP threatened to reintroduce a federal presence in the South to protect the rights of blacks.[128] The Democrats, in the so-called "New Departure," accepted the legitimacy of the three Reconstruction amendments to the U.S. Constitution and, after gaining control of southern state governments, permitted blacks to vote, hold public offices, serve on juries, and patronize many of the same public accommodations as whites.[129] However, lynching and kindred acts of terror against blacks were not suppressed: northern and southern Democrats in Congress insisted that the doctrine of states rights precluded the federal government from acting to protect the rights of blacks, and they backed this up by drastically reducing the size of the army and outlawing its use as a *posse comitatus* to enforce the law.[130]

On the currency and tariff issues, Republican and Democratic leaders sought to hammer out compromise positions that could keep their respective parties from fracturing along regional lines, though here too differences between the parties remained. Generally, Republican congressional leaders and presidential candidates were more flexible on the currency issue than their Democratic counterparts, whose defense of sound money tended to be more doctrinaire. The GOP was identified with high tariffs, as the party with the closest ties to manufactures; the Democrats were most closely aligned with commercial interests that were advocates of free trade.[131]

The Republican and Democratic parties after Reconstruction also differed in their stands on sumptuary legislation. The GOP was open to influence by prohibitionists, sabbatarians, and nativists. The Democratic party stood squarely for "personal liberty" on these issues.[132]

Finally, and of special relevance here, professional politicians in both parties were prepared to make concessions to labor reformers. In the 1870s six states established bureaus of labor statistics, and Congress created such an agency on the national level in 1884.[133] Between 1883 and 1886 Democratic legislatures in four industrial states and Republican legislatures in two others enacted statutes limiting the use of convict labor.[134] And, as mentioned above, in 1885 Congress passed the Foran Act, prohibiting the importation of immigrant contract labor. Most significantly, the state and federal governments tacitly acknowledged the legitimacy of the institutions and procedures that were emerging for resolving industrial disputes. Strikes, boycotts, and trade unions were not for the most part outlawed, enjoined, and suppressed by legislators, judges, and executive officials.

Public officials were only prepared to tolerate strikes, however, if they were confined to work places and did not turn into community uprisings or attacks upon the regime. This limitation was enforced chiefly by the National Guard. In the wake of the 1877 railroad strike, which did turn into an uprising against the new order by the working class in some cities (and by the entire community in a number of others), every state in the nation reorganized and strengthened its militia.[135] Especially in the industrial states of the Northeast, armories were constructed in major cities to provide facilities for training National Guard units and storing weapons, and garrisons from which the guard could be deployed to put down civil disorders in general and disruptive strikes in particular.

The political settlement that ended Reconstruction had several significant effects on the working class. First, the great majority of workers and working class leaders acquiesced to the limitations it imposed on the modes of political action in which they could engage. After the suppression of the 1877 railroad strike and the local upheavals connected with it, there was talk within the Socialist Labor party—whose members had played a prominent part in some of these disruptions—of forming military clubs and of using strikes as a political weapon, but the closing of ranks by the nation's political and economic elite and the formation of military clubs—otherwise known as the National Guard—by the upper and middle class made it so unlikely that such a strategy could succeed that few workers were prepared to associate themselves with such a great gamble. Moreover, the possibility of using the ballot to influence the conduct of public officials encouraged the great majority of American workers to channel their political energies through the nation's institutions, rather than seeking to overturn them. Under these conditions anarchists who called upon workers to rise up and smash the state were unable to acquire a substantial following.[136]

Second, the issues Democratic and Republican politicians organized into politics in the 1870s and 1880s were deeply meaningful to most workers. Democratic denunciations of "black Republicanism" and the waving of the bloody shirt by GOP politicians drew upon the loyalties and hatreds that Americans, workers and nonworkers alike, had developed during the Civil War and its immediate aftermath. Moreover, the argument by party politicians that employees shared the interests of their employers on the tariff issue was substantially correct. Politicians drove this point home further by arguing that their party's stance on these questions was of a piece with its position on sumptuary legislation. Democrats argued that the Republican impulse to tax (via the tariff) every article the workingman consumed and to elevate blacks to a position of equality with whites was related to its desire to tell him what he could or could not do on his Sundays and that the Democratic party's devotion to Jeffersonian principles and personal liberty provided him with his best defense against this meddling fanaticism. Republicans argued that the Democrats' indifference to the plight of the American workingman facing unemployment as a result of the importation of goods produced by cheap foreign labor was akin to its indifference to the plight of blacks and the morals of American citizens.

Nonetheless there were challenges to the hegemony of Republican and Democratic party politicians during the 1870s and 1880s by spokesmen for political forces who regarded the compromises struck by these politicians as bad bargains. One such challenge came from an influential group of intellectuals and professionals who had close ties to the northeastern financial and commercial elite and who opposed the concessions that professional politicians made to workers, farmers, and manufacturers in seeking to win electoral majorities.[137] Small farmers who were exploited through the credit system—exploitation compounded by the relentless deflation of the period, which kept them in bondage to their creditors—also periodically rose up against the major parties.[138]

In addition, labor reformers were not satisfied with the concessions the major parties made in their efforts to secure working-class votes. Greenbackism, with its promise of expanding the money supply sufficiently for industry to prosper so that workers and employers need no longer be at each other's throats, exerted a persistent appeal to that segment of the labor reform movement devoted to the producer ethic.[139] The legislative program adopted by FOTLU at its founding in 1881 provides a typical statement of the other policies labor reformers wished to see enacted. In addition to eight-hour laws, bureaus of labor statistics, prohibitions on convict labor and immigrant contract labor, and Chinese exclusion, FOTLU called for factory safety legislation, increasing the liability of employers for industrial accidents, prohibitions on child labor, and compulsory education.[140] Rank-and-file workers were willing to abandon the major parties and vote for labor tickets when public officials intervened in industrial disputes on behalf of employers. Such episodes led workers to respond to leaders who argued that if Democratic and Republican officials were using their authority to protect capital at the expense of labor, workers had no choice but to form a party of their own and elect officials sympathetic to their cause.

The intensification of industrial strife and agrarian unrest in the years following 1886 shook the foundations of the political settlement worked out in the 1870s. As the number of workers involved in strikes increased, as employers launched their counterattack upon the Knights and the trade union movement, and as the Farmers Alliance gathered support, Democratic and Republican leaders struggled to keep their political coalitions from fragmenting. In their efforts to maintain the support of workers, legislators in the industrial states enacted many of the measures labor reformers had been advocating for the previous twenty years; major party politicians in the agrarian South and West made concessions on some of the less threatening measures in the program of the Farmers Alliance; and Republicans and Democrats beat the drum on ethnocultural issues—especially liquor legislation—ever more loudly. On the other hand, executives, legislators, and judges rose to the defense of public order and the rights of property. President Benjamin Harrison dispatched the army to break the strike of silver miners at Coeur d'Alene in 1892; President Grover Cleveland used federal troops to break the Pullman strike in 1894; and the National Guard was mobilized by governors with increasing frequency during the period—most notably in the Homestead strike of 1892. And, as Rayback notes, after the Haymarket affair drove the upper and middle classes to new heights of hysteria over the menace of anarchy in the United States, "state legislatures rushed laws curbing the freedom of action of labor organizations onto the statute books. The courts began to convict union members of conspiracy, intimidation, and rioting in wholesale lots."[141] This counteroffensive presented the labor movement with the pressing question of how best to respond.

TRADE UNIONS AND POLITICAL MACHINES:
THE INSTITUTIONAL LEGACY
OF THE LATE NINETEENTH CENTURY

Confronted with this trend toward an increasingly hostile environment, labor reformers could respond in a number of ways. They could organize as many workers as possible into labor unions and pursue a strategy of escalation on the economic front. Alternatively (or at the same time), they could escalate the conflict on the political front by attempting to take control of the state through electoral or other means. Finally, labor reformers could retreat to their strongest redoubt and seek an accommodation with the forces arrayed against them—thus attempting to protect the gains of at least a segment of the working class by narrowing the constituency of labor unions and seeking to placate politicians and public officials by agreeing to stay out of the political arena.

There were advocates of each of these courses of action within the labor reform movement, and the 1890s witnessed sharp conflicts among them

over which of these paths to take. It would be a mistake, however, to regard these conflicts as disputes between completely distinct types of labor
leaders—backward-looking idealists in the Knights, ideologues out of touch
with American realities in the socialist movement, and hardheaded realists
in the AFL. Substantial commonalities in the outlook of these segments of
the labor movement remained into the 1890s.[142] Moreover, though the
choices national labor leaders made were crucial in determining the direction the American labor movement took, these issues were not decided simply through debates and votes at national conventions of the Knights, the
Socialist Labor party, and the AFL. There was constant interaction among
the views of labor activists, the outcomes of conflicts in the economic and
political arenas, and the modes of organization the labor movement adopted.
Ultimately a majority of the nation's trade union leaders opted for the last of
the above-mentioned courses of action. The unions they led emerged as the
dominant force in the American labor movement because (1) efforts to pursue the other strategies met with defeat; (2) "pure and simple" trade unionism proved to be capable of meeting the imperatives of organizational maintenance; and (3) this mode of working-class organization was a mutually
acceptable arrangement to important segments of America's political leadership, economic elite, and the working class itself. The organizational manifestations of this accommodation among these social forces were the trade
unions and political machines that became institutionalized in the 1880s
and 1890s.

The Defeated Alternatives

Organizing unskilled as well as skilled workers into unions and escalating
the conflict with capital on the industrial front enjoyed widespread support
among labor reformers. Indeed, all segments of the labor movement expressed their dedication to this approach in one form or another. Although
Terrence Powderly and his associates in the national leadership of the
Knights did not believe it was possible to achieve the emancipation of the
working classes through strikes alone—"Strike at the boss and hit yourself,"
he had warned Maryland coal miners who walked off their jobs in 1882—
local assemblies that counted unskilled as well as skilled workers among
their members staged numerous strikes throughout the order's history, especially in response to the counterattack employers launched against them
in the late 1880s.[143]

   The late 1880s and early 1890s also witnessed an upsurge of strikes by
trade unions affiliated with the AFL, and these trade unionists also spoke of
the necessity of organizing the unskilled as well as the skilled. The constitution of the AFL provided for the organization of unskilled workers into

"labor" unions (as distinguished from "trade" unions), and in the early 1890s the two most important industrial unions of the nineteenth century—the United Mine Workers and the American Railway Union—were organized.

Finally, the dominant faction within the American socialist movement in the 1890s also advocated pursuing a strategy of mobilization on the economic front. A number of national unions and municipal labor federations were controlled by socialists during this decade—among them the Bakers and Confectioners, the Boot and Shoe Workers, the United Brewery Workers, and the New York and Brooklyn Central Labor Federations—and the leaders of these unions sought to win industrial conflicts by bringing all workers in their industry into their union, drawing upon the energy and solidarity that unskilled workers had displayed during the 1886 strike wave, and, as Martin Dodd says of the Shoe Workers, stressing "class consciousness and locally controlled and financed strikes as organizing tools."[144]

These efforts to pursue a strategy of mobilization in the economic arena encountered serious difficulties. Businessmen fought back furiously: they organized employers' associations, drove unions to strike, and then called upon the government to defend their right to hire strikebreakers. In these confrontations workers found it increasingly difficult to win the support of the middle-class residents of their communities. This was a consequence partly of the anti-union hysteria following the Haymarket affair and partly of changes in the economy. The merger movement of the 1890s and the emergence of multiplant firms made it easier for employers plausibly to threaten to close down any plant whose workers were too obstreperous. This could decimate the economy of the community in question, and such threats therefore frequently led retail merchants and other members of the local middle class to identify their interests with the town's or city's factory owners, rather than its industrial workers.[145]

The Knights as a national organization had no effective answer to these problems. The order never had offered striking local assemblies much financial support and in 1888 it decided to devote even more of its resources to an educational campaign on behalf of its political program. The insistence of the order's national leadership that the interests of employers and employees were fundamentally harmonious—Powderly, for example, insisted that businessmen could be persuaded that it was in their interest to grant workers an eight-hour day—simply did not accord with the experiences of the bulk of their members. This led the great majority of members to abandon the Knights in the late 1880s and early 1890s, and many of the skilled workers among them joined trade unions that accepted class conflict as a fact of life.[146]

The trade unions belonging to the AFL may have accepted the inevitability of class conflict, but the great majority of them sought to cope with the hostile climate they faced at the end of the nineteenth century by reaching a tacit accommodation with employers to be discussed further below. Among its terms was the abandonment by the AFL of its professed intention of organizing unskilled workers and the imposition by national union leaders of very severe restraints on the right of union locals to call strikes.

Such an accommodation, of course, could only be reached if both employers and union leaders were prepared—even if reluctantly—to make a deal. Where employers could count on the local, state, or national government to back them, however intransigent they might be in dealing with their employees, unions found it almost impossible to survive. And though there were some exceptions, unions controlled by socialists or other radicals who proclaimed the impossibility of achieving a satisfactory resolution of class conflicts as long as the capitalist system remained intact generally found that the only alternative to adopting the technique of organizational consolidation advocated by the leadership of the AFL was defeat and destruction.[147]

An equally widespread impulse among labor reformers was to respond to the increasingly hostile environment that confronted them in the years after 1886 by entering the electoral arena at the local, state, and national levels. The prospects for the success of such a strategy seemed especially good because the hegemony of the nation's political elite was then being challenged by millions of farmers in the South and West—first through the Farmers Alliance and then through the Populist party. It thus appeared that the coalition of dissatisfied workers and farmers that the Greenback-Labor party had sought with only limited success to mobilize in the 1870s might sweep the field in the 1890s.

The Knights threw themselves into this endeavor. The order played a leading role in the selection of and campaigning for labor tickets in local and state elections in 1886 and 1887.[148] And in 1888 the national convention of the Knights, at Terrence Powderly's urging, decided to concentrate the resources of the order on promoting a national political program of currency reform, government control of railroads and telegraphs, and government taxation and management of the land. Powderly himself thought that through education and agitation all producers—including employers—could be convinced that their interests would be served by such a program, and that the major parties thus would be compelled to adopt it by 1892. To rally agrarian support, he led a delegation of Knights to the 1889 national convention of the Southern Farmers Alliance. The Knights endorsed the alliance's program, merged its Washington lobby with the one run by the alliance, and agreed to endorse only those candidates who would support the alliance program. In the early 1890s, especially in the South and the West, local assemblies of the Knights cooperated with the electoral activities of the alliance and its political arm, the Populist party.[149]

Many trade unionists also responded to the events of the late 1880s and the 1890s by entering the electoral arena. Municipal labor federations participated along with Knights, socialists, and single-taxers in selecting and campaigning for labor slates in the local elections of 1886. And many local trade unions, chiefly in the South and the West, campaigned for Populist candidates in elections in the 1890s. In 1892 socialists within the AFL introduced a resolution at the federation's national convention that cited the recent defeats of labor—a reference, in particular, to the use of troops to break the strikes at Homestead and Coeur d'Alene—as indicating the "impotency" of pure and simple trade unionism to "cope with the great power of concentrated wealth" and that would commit the AFL to lead an independent political movement. This resolution was defeated, though the convention did endorse some planks in the Populist platform, including one calling for government ownership of the telephone and telegraph systems. Heartened by this, the socialists submitted a political program to the 1893 AFL national convention advocating, among other things, "the collective ownership by the people of all means of production and distribution." This time the convention voted to submit the program to its constituent unions for their consideration. After the great majority endorsed the socialist program and it was presented to the AFL's 1894 national convention for a substantive vote, it only was defeated as a result of parliamentary sleight-of-hand of Gompers and other leaders of the federation.[150] The delegates who supported the program retaliated by defeating Gompers's bid for reelection to the presidency of the AFL (1894 was the only year from the federation's founding in 1886 until Gompers's death in 1924 that he did not serve as president) and part of the compromise that secured his return to the presidency in 1895 involved the AFL's adopting the socialists' political program as its "legislative platform."

The various efforts by labor reformers in the 1890s to secure fundamental changes in government policy through electoral activity ultimately were defeated. Powderly's expectation that the major parties could be compelled through such pressure to adopt the program of the Knights and the Farmers Alliance in the 1892 election proved, of course, to be unfounded. Grover Cleveland and Benjamin Harrison, the Democratic and Republic presidential candidates that year, were scarcely the men to lead a crusade that Powderly envisaged to "control the dollar, curb the power of money, and kill the trusts."[151] In 1893, he was deposed as Grand Master Workman by a coalition of socialists and agrarian radicals within the Knights who sought, in effect, to merge the organization with the Populist party.

The strategy of working through a third party, the Populists, was also defeated, however. The sources of this defeat were somewhat different in the states of the South and the West, on the one hand, where alliances between workers and poor farmers were most easily established, and the states of the Northeast, where such alliances never emerged. In the South the leaders of the Democratic party, who were closely tied to that region's

agrarian, commercial, and financial elites, managed to overcome the threat
of Populism by relying upon a combination of race baiting, force, and fraud
and by exploiting the political incapacity of the poor farmers who provided
the Populists with much of their leadership.[152] The Democrats then attracted many of that party's supporters into its ranks by adopting the free-
silver doctrine—the plank in the Populist platform that least threatened the
interests of regional elites. In the West the lure of controlling the nomination of a major party also eventually led the Populists to fuse with—and
disappear into—the Democratic party. In 1896 a coalition of southern and
western silverites secured the Democratic presidential nomination for William Jennings Bryan.

In the nation's industrial heartland—the belt of states running from Illinois to New England—where the great majority of workers lived in large
cities and had no contact with farmers, it was considerably more difficult to
forge the sort of alliance that the Populists and the national leadership of the
Knights of Labor sought to establish. The greatest impediment the proponents of such an alliance faced was convincing workers, who were subject to
exploitation through the wage-labor system, to identify their interests with
farmers, who were subject to a different mode of exploitation, the credit
system.[153] (An excellent example of the difficulty of doing so is provided by
Samuel Gompers himself, who considered the small farmers who formed the
mass base of the Populist party to be exploiters, rather than victims of exploitation, because many of them employed wage laborers.) For this reason eastern workers were not attracted to the vision of a cooperative commonwealth
of all producers that the Populists put forward. Beyond this, the local machines of the Democratic and Republican parties tended to be stronger in
the Northeast than elsewhere, and the Populists found it difficult to shatter
the ties linking workers to these machines. The Populists also had difficulty
countering the not implausible argument of Republican and Democratic
politicians that protective tariffs and/or sound money, by making it profit-
able for businessmen to invest their capital, would contribute to the prosperity of employers and workers alike.

The Democrats' nomination of Bryan did little to change this situation. In
the Northeast it drove most of the upper, middle, and working classes into
the Republican party: the doctrine of free silver did not speak to their interests; the evangelical Protestant tone of Bryan's campaign was threatening to
the heavily Catholic urban working class; and the Republicans, in contrast,
successfully presented themselves as the party of industrial prosperity and
ethnocultural tolerance. All of this contributed to a landslide victory for the
Republicans and the passing of America's "populist moment."[154]

The economic and ethnocultural cleavages that divided poor farmers in
the South and West from workers in the East were not inherently unbridge-
able: after all, in the 1930s Franklin D. Roosevelt managed to bring together

a coalition that included these groups. Labor unions were to play a major role in the New Deal coalition. At the end of the nineteenth century, however, a number of organizational, economic, and political considerations encouraged the top leaders of America's trade union movement to pursue a different course of action.

"Pure and Simple" Trade Unionism

Despite their flirtation with alternative responses to the crisis confronting the labor movement, a majority of the nation's trade unionists followed a more accommodating strategy, and their unions came to overshadow the organizations that pursued less conciliatory policies. Unions affiliated with the AFL in the main chose this course of action because their leaders concluded from the experiences of the late nineteenth century that "pure and simple" craft unionism was the only viable form of working-class organization in the United States as the twentieth century began: the only form that at once could meet the imperatives of internal organizational maintenance, carve out a niche for itself in the age of corporate capitalism, and accommodate itself to the harsh political climate confronting labor at the time.

The experience of the post–Civil War decades clearly indicated the great difficulties trade unions confronted sustaining themselves in the face of periodic business depressions, bitter employer resistance, and hostile public authorities. To cope with these problems, Gompers and his associates—first in his home union, the Cigar Makers International Union, then in the FOTLU, and finally in the AFL—argued that unions had to "perfect" their organization and establish themselves on a "permanent" basis by providing their members with unemployment benefits, burial insurance, sick pay, and strike benefits. This would give workers an incentive to remain in their union despite the inevitable setbacks to be expected during depressions, strikes, eras of political reaction, and periods of personal distress. A second element of organizational perfection was the centralization of authority in the hands of national union officials. Local unions engaged in strikes or experiencing unusually high levels of unemployment could only afford to provide their members with benefits if they could draw on the resources of union locals in other cities whose members were still working. This, in turn, entailed transferring to the national level the authority "to decide whether a strike is practicable," so that impetuous members of one local would not be in a position to squander the funds collected by their more prudent brothers in other cities.[155]

This mode of organization was far easier to establish with unions that represented skilled rather than unskilled workers. Unions could only provide their members with meaningful benefits and pay the salaries of full-time officers if they levied higher dues than unskilled workers could readily afford. In addition, it was more difficult for union leaders to assert control over unskilled workers, who tended to move from job to job, than over skilled workers, who were more likely to establish enduring ties to the other members of their local and to its leaders. These problems were demonstrated in the enormous difficulty Terrence Powderly had influencing the behavior of the hundreds of thousands of workers who flooded into the Knights in the mid-1880s, called strikes he deemed inadvisable, and then left the organization in droves when these strikes were defeated.

The case of the Boot and Shoe Workers union illustrates quite clearly why a majority of the nation's trade unions came to adopt the organizational forms advocated by the AFL. The union was founded by socialists, who sought to organize skilled and unskilled workers alike. Its dues were low; it provided little in the way of financial benefits to its members; and its national leaders did not seek to restrain local strikes. In the 1890s the union lost a number of strikes because manufacturers organized themselves more effectively than ever before to rid themselves of the "'annoying' intercession of labor agents" and because, for the reasons mentioned above, striking workers no longer could count upon the support of the local middle class in their battles with their employers. As a result of this experience the shoemakers, like workers in many other industries, "learned to mistrust their communities and came to rely instead on . . . craft solidarity." In 1899 the Boot and Shoeworkers Union adopted a new constitution that sharply increased dues, established strike and sick-benefit funds, and placed authority over the dispersal of these funds in the hands of the union's national leadership. Arguing for the new constitution, the union's national secretary drew the following lesson from recent experience: "Numerous examples can be cited where organizations with high dues and benefits have even passed through defeat and still maintained their organization and quickly rallied, ready once more to face the enemy, but all cheap unions go down alike regardless of what their theory or philosophy."[156]

One other aspect of trade union organization is worth noting here. It was a concern for organizational stability in particular that led to the founding of the AFL. In 1886, after the Knights and New York's cigar manufacturers reached an agreement that froze out the New York local of the Cigar Makers International Union, the FOTLU demanded that the Knights disband its trades assemblies in crafts already organized by a union, refuse to enroll anyone who had been expelled from a union or worked for less than the union scale, and not place its own label on any product for which there was a union label. When the Knights refused to accede to these demands, the trade unions organized themselves into the American Federation of Labor and declared war on the order. The founders of the AFL were prepared to wage war over these issues because where they were unable to establish themselves as the exclusive bargaining agent for the members of a trade it was difficult for them to exert discipline over their members and win conflicts with employers. It is significant that it was a concern for mundane questions of organization, exclusive jurisdiction, and discipline, rather than loftier ideological disputes, that led to the formation of the AFL, that ultimately enabled trade unions to survive the crisis of the 1890s better than any other component of the nineteenth-century labor reform movement, and that made it possible for a federation of trade unions, which enrolled only a small fraction of the American working class, to claim to be the representative of labor in the United States.

The second lesson that most trade unionists drew from the events of 1886–94 was that the great industrial combines that were being organized during this period were powerful adversaries indeed. The two largest sympathy strikes of the day—the Homestead and Pullman strikes—were unequivocal victories for, respectively, the Carnegie Steel Corporation and the railroads belonging to the Chicago General Managers' Association. More generally, the counterattack upon labor launched by the upper and middle classes in the 1890s threatened the existence of all trade unions. This threat took its most serious form in the open shop movement of the following decade.

To deal with this threat, a majority of the nation's trade unionists sought to demonstrate to employers that the labor movement was reasonable and responsible. The AFL and many of the national trade unions affiliated with it renounced sympathy strikes, indicated their willingness to cooperate with the efforts of employers to increase labor productivity, insisted that they regarded contracts negotiated through collective bargaining to be binding upon workers as much as on employers and therefore undertook to restrain "wildcat strikes" by union locals or dissident workers, and provided manufacturers who signed such contracts with union labels that helped them sell their products in the working-class market. In addition, the AFL never carried out its professed intention of organizing unskilled workers. The trade unionists who made these concessions hoped that employers in return would accept the unionization of at least the skilled workers in their plants and make wage concessions to them, however they might treat unskilled workers.

A third conclusion drawn by a majority of trade unionists from the events of the late nineteenth century was that workers had to rely chiefly upon economic rather than political action to achieve their goals. In so doing they abandoned the strategy of constructing a political alliance among all "producers," which had been pursued by the two largest labor organizations from 1861 to 1886, the NLU and the Knights.

The leadership of the AFL renounced this strategy for a combination of reasons. First, they feared that such a course of action, like any other foray into the electoral arena, might divide their unions. Second, even the most impressive efforts at forging such a coalition—including those of 1886–87 and those associated with the Populist party in the early and mid-1890s— ultimately had failed. The labor campaigns of 1886–87 had demonstrated once again that workers would rise up in anger against the Democrats and Republicans when public officials elected by the major parties blatantly used their authority to help capital in its conflicts with labor, but this outburst, like earlier ones, subsided after the major parties made some concessions; workers then returned to their former political homes. The labor campaigns of 1886–87 and the Populist campaigns of the early 1890s also demonstrated that a majority of middle-class voters could be whipped into hysteria, and their loyalties to the major parties reinforced, by the charge that these efforts represented nothing less than an attempt to foment class warfare in the United States and involved an assault on the very institution of private property.

Even those members of the middle class who did not swallow this line were regarded by the AFL leadership as more of a burden than a benefit to the labor movement, because they had their own political agenda that was based upon the false premise that employers and employees had harmonious interests and that diverted workers from militantly pursuing their interests where they did conflict with their employers. As Stuart Kaufman notes, Gompers insisted that "the emancipation of the working class had to be achieved by the workers themselves. This at base was the issue between the Federation and the Knights of Labor. From the beginning the greatest danger to the AFL appeared to Gompers to be 'the unnecessary desire of persons thrusting their individual opinions upon organized workers.'"[157]

Gompers also rejected the counsel of socialists, who shared his understanding of the boundaries of the working class but who argued that the only way to secure its emancipation was for the labor movement to enter the political arena with a program calling for the collective ownership of the means of production. In addition to fearing the divisive effects this might have upon the labor movement, Gompers read the evidence of the times as indicating that when the government involved itself in issues of concern to the working class it was less likely to serve the interests of workers than those of capital. He said in a speech in 1891: "Against us we find arrayed a host guarded by special privilege, buttressed by legalized trusts, fed by streams of legalized monopolists, picketed by gangs of legalized Pinkertons, and having in reserve thousands of embryo employers who, under the name militia, are organized, uniformed, and armed for the sole purpose of holding the discontented in subservient bondage to iniquitous conditions."[158] In his autobiography Gompers asserted that the Tompkins Square "riot" of 1874—in which the New York City police brutally attacked a peaceful protest meeting called by the IWA—convinced him that it was self-defeating for labor to identify itself with radical groups and causes because this simply provided labor's enemies with ammunition to discredit the labor movement and to justify the use of force against it. The Haymarket episode reinforced this conclusion.

The eight-hour day was the central demand of the American labor movement during the half-century following the Civil War. The changes in the way labor reformers pursued this goal provide a telling indication of the transformations that occurred during the late part of the century in the labor movement's orientation to politics, in the modes of collective action and organization through which workers sought to accomplish their goals, and in the vocabulary working-class leaders employed to justify their claims. The first nationwide campaign for the eight-hour day was initiated by the National Labor Union in the late 1860s, and the various labor reform organizations affiliated with the NLU directed this demand to both the state and employers: they sought to get state legislatures to declare eight hours to be a "legal day's work," and after succeeding they staged strikes to "enforce" these laws. Moreover, as Jama Lazerow argues, "In the 1860s, the most significant aspect of the eight-hour demand had been its class nature. By establishing a specific part of the day which could not be purchased by an employer, working people challenged the prevalent concept of private property and struck a blow for freedom from wage slavery."[159] It is important to note that the concept of wage slavery had political as well as economic connotations. In arguing for the eight-hour day labor reformers claimed that it would give workers the time to devote themselves both to self-improvement and to exercising the rights and obligations of republican citizenship.

As discussed above, the eight-hour campaign of the late 1860s and early 1870s bore little fruit, and labor reformers initiated new campaigns in 1886 and 1890. Rhetorically there were some similarities between the earlier campaign and these later ones. In Boston, for example, George McNeill—who had participated in the eight-hour movement of the 1860s, was a prominent figure in the Knights, and was a major leader of the 1886 campaign—linked it to the other major struggles for liberty in American history, the Revolutionary War and the Civil War. Speaking at a meeting of the Knights on the anniversary of the Battle of Lexington, he said: "I am glad to welcome you here tonight on this 19th day of April, a day ever dear to the heart of every American . . . and as this is the anniversary of the day when the Christian soil of virgin villages was stained with the blood of our fathers, and as they died to put down that chattel system of slavery, so we stand here remembering that blood shed and that sacrifice."[160] He concluded that "the success or failure of the republican experiment rests with us," implying that if the status quo persisted, the United States would not warrant being called a republic.

Trade unionists used some of the same republican vocabulary. In striking to secure the eight-hour day from the Master Builders Association in 1886, the Carpenters Union denounced their target for the "unrepublican" character of its name: the name "master," they asserted, was "foreign and offensive to our sense of citizenship, as well as offensive to the fundamental principles on which the republic is based." And Frank Foster, a leader of the AFL in Boston, argued in 1890 that "the man whose hours of toil are fixed for him by another is not free."[161]

Nonetheless, there were some important differences between the eight-hour movements of 1886 and 1890 and those of the late 1860s and early 1870s. The later demand for an eight-hour day was directed exclusively against employers, and the strike was labor's weapon of first rather than last resort to secure this goal. By 1890 the campaign for an eight-hour day no longer had the character of a mass movement: not only did the AFL eschew appeals to the state legislature or to the public at large through mass demonstrations, it also drew back from its initial plans for calling a general strike to secure shorter hours for the members of all unionized trades. Rather, it decided that only one union, the Carpenters, which had a great deal of bargaining leverage, would strike, and that the members of other unions would continue working and would provide the Carpenters with financial support during their strike. The major arguments used by trade unionists in 1886 and 1890 on behalf of the eight-hour day were economic, not political, and they implicitly accepted the existence and persistence of the wage-labor system. Boston's Central Labor Union argued in 1886 that by reducing the hours of labor, unemployment would drop and therefore wages would rise: "Overwork and machinery combine to increase the army of the unemployed. Every unemployed man is an obstacle to our common advancement. An army of unemployed men is an army of obstacles. To remove them they must be employed by reducing the hours of labor. Let us act!"[162] And a statement issued by Boston's carpenters during their strike in 1890 implied that they fully accepted that labor was a commodity, to be bought and sold like any other: they demanded "the right to name both the price and length of our day's labor, the same as any other merchant selling his commodity."[163] The culmination of this trend can be seen in a statement issued by striking workers at the Bethlehem Steel Corporation in 1910, whose arguments on behalf of shortening their working day referred exclusively to the private sphere of life: "The overtime feature of employment having been a detriment to our health, our homes, and our families, we ask for its abolition. If it must be a feature of future employment, we ask for an additional compensation in the form of time and 1-half time for overtime, so that we may procure additional nutriment to give strength to our bodies to perform the task."[164]

Although by the end of the nineteenth century the dominant wing of the trade union movement in the United States abandoned efforts to change the character of the American regime fundamentally, this is not to say that its members no longer sought to influence particular public policies. The AFL, state and local labor federations, and individual trade unions lobbied to secure the enactment of laws limiting the working hours of women and children, requiring safety inspections of factories and mines, and providing for the arbitration of industrial disputes; Gompers admonished workers when voting to reward the friends of labor within the Democratic and Republican parties who supported such legislation and to punish their enemies who refused to do so. Of equal significance, local craft unions, especially in the building trades, established ties with the locally dominant political party in an effort to get municipal governments to enact and enforce regulations, such as building codes, that provided additional jobs for their members. In some ways most interestingly of all (because it revealed how the boundaries of the American working class ultimately came to be defined), the AFL campaigned to restrict immigration from China, Japan, and eventually southern and eastern Europe. The precedent for this campaign was the anti-Chinese movement in California of the 1860s and 1870s. The initial social base of anti-coolie sentiment was among unskilled workers facing competition from Chinese laborers who could be hired at very low wages. Skilled workers did not face such competition, but their unions rallied to the anti-coolie cause as a way of mobilizing support among unskilled workers for legislation that was of benefit to skilled workers. Democratic and Republican politicians joined the crusade, because proposing restrictions on Chinese immigration was an easy way of winning votes among skilled and unskilled workers alike. As Saxton argues, this same calculation—and the same arguments that had been used in California against the Chinese—led the AFL beginning in 1897 to call for limitations on immigration of Latin and Slavic Europeans as well as Asians and to acquiesce in efforts to drive blacks from the skilled trades, along with efforts to reverse almost every other gain blacks had made since the Civil War.[165] Thus racism was one of the terms in the accommodation organized labor sought to establish with the powers that be in twentieth-century America.

In sum, the doctrine of "pure and simple" trade unionism advocated by and institutionalized in the AFL asserted that workers—or at least a subset of them—could organize to advance their common interests in the economic arena largely apart from what they or the nation's governing elite did in the political realm. Indeed, it presupposed a distinction between the economic and political realm that was foreign to the thought of those labor reformers who earlier had spoken of "wage slavery" or America's "republican experiment." By enjoining workers to reward labor's friends and punish its enemies within the Democratic and Republican parties—and to restrict their political efforts to the act of voting—the dominant wing of the trade union movement largely renounced efforts to influence the fundamental character of the American regime and the composition of the nation's governing class. They hoped that in return the public officials elected by the Democratic and Republican parties would not interfere with the operation of trade unions within the domain to which they were prepared to confine themselves.

Political Machines

The political and class conflicts of the late nineteenth century also led to the institutionalization of the American party system in its classic form. On the national level the Republicans and Democrats became entrenched as the nation's major parties and professional politicians securely established their leadership over them. On the local level, these politicians increasingly perfected the organizations through which they mobilized the mass electorate—that is, they constructed political machines. At least in the nation's major cities, these machines consolidated their position as the most important vehicle through which the working class participated in politics.

The machine politicians who moved to the fore of American urban politics late in the century established their political hegemony by arranging an accommodation among the major political forces in the city. The precise terms varied from city to city, as did the process through which the locally dominant machine became institutionalized. It is not feasible to describe these variations here; the account below will focus upon a single city, New York. Nonetheless, the events that led to the institutionalization of New York's Tammany machine were basically similar to those that occurred in other large American cities.[166]

Machine politicians in New York, as in other cities, appealed in a number of ways to the working-class voters who provided them with the bulk of their popular support. First, they picked up and enacted many of the legislative proposals advanced by labor reformers. For example, the New York state legislature, with the support of the Tammany delegation, created a board of mediation and arbitration, prohibited employers from coercing union members, and established a ten-hour day for women and children.[167] Second, the machine created an elaborate unofficial welfare system. During the severe winter of 1870–71, for example, Tammany's Boss Tweed spent $50,000 of his "own" money (whose ultimate source, of course, was the city treasury) to buy coal for the poor in his ward. Machine politicians also relied upon ethnic appeals to win the support of working-class voters: they provided public subsidies and grants of public authority to charitable institutions run by members of the city's major ethnic groups;[168] they nominated and appointed a substantial number of immigrants—especially the Irish—to public offices; and they defended the political rights of immigrants. In the "naturalization frauds" of 1868, for example, the machine's functionaries brought hundreds of immigrants at a time before Tammany judges, who turned them en bloc into citizens, voters, and, not least, Tammany Democrats. Over the next twenty-five years, Tammany defended these voters against efforts by the Republicans to disfranchise them.[169] Moreover, in 1870 Boss Tweed secured the enactment of a new city charter abolishing a number of state-appointed metropolitan commissions that controlled policing, fire fighting, public health, and parks in the city; in their stead the new charter created municipal departments whose commissioners were appointed by the mayor. There were a number of impulses behind the creation and abolition of the metropolitan commissions, but the one of greatest relevance here is that Tweed's charter placed control over these important public functions in the hands of officials who ultimately were responsible to the city's heavily immigrant electorate.

It is important to note that the methods the machine used to appeal to foreign-stock voters buttressed the political position of middle-class elements of the city's ethnic groups relative to less respectable or more radical contenders for the leadership of the group in question. The charitable institutions that benefited from this public support were run by the wealthier members of the city's immigrant subcommunities, and the recipients of the most lucrative forms of patronage the machine distributed were not members of the working class, but rather contractors, lawyers, and the owners of firms that sold supplies to the municipal government. It was these same elements of the city's ethnic subcommunities that rose to positions of leadership in the machine. Seymour Mandelbaum has written of Tammany's first Irish leader, John Kelly, who came to power in 1872: "In Kelly, the Irish middle class asserted its claim to a place on the dais."[170]

At the same time, the machine politicians who rose to prominence in the 1870s enjoyed the support of and provided substantial benefits to important segments of the upper class. Considering again the case of New York, John Kelly's candidacy for the leadership of Tammany Hall was backed by, among others, August Belmont, the representative of the House of Rothschild in the United States and the chairman of the Democratic National Committee; Samuel Tilden, one of New York's leading corporation lawyers and the Democratic party's presidential candidate in 1876; and Abram Hewitt, an iron manufacturer and the national Democratic party's leading spokesman for free trade. The Tammany-backed administrations that controlled City Hall in the 1870s pursued extremely tight-fisted financial policies; in particular, they cut the wages of city laborers during that decade's depression. On the affirmative side, the machine sent congressmen to Washington and backed presidential candidates who were staunch advocates of the monetary and tariff policies that were favored by the Democratic party's allies within the business community.[171]

The political parties of the antebellum era also had constructed cross-class coalitions, and the package of policies upon which such coalitions were based was roughly similar to those pursued by Kelly's machine. There was, however, an important difference between Kelly's Tammany Hall and the Tammany of earlier party leaders in New York up to and including Boss Tweed. In the 1850s and 1860s the Democratic machine was quite fragmented and amorphous: Democratic machine politicians were for the most part independent political entrepreneurs and the institutions through which they mobilized votes in working-class neighborhoods—volunteer fire companies, gangs, militia companies—were not fully subject to party control.[172] Indeed, one reason that the Tweed ring engaged in massive corruption was that bribery was the only reliable way in which Tweed could influence the behavior of other politicians.[173] In contrast, Kelly undertook to centralize and strengthen the Tammany organization. Under his leadership, Tammany's Committee on Organization purged members of the party's district committees deemed to be disloyal to the organization; it distributed patronage through these reorganized district committees rather than granting it to individual ward politicians; and it regularly gave instructions to legislators elected with Tammany's support. Finally, under Kelly, and his successor Richard Croker, Tammany extended throughout the city a mode of organization—the district club—that was found to be a more successful means of ensuring voter loyalty to the machine than working through autonomous neighborhood institutions. In short, under Kelly and Croker, the Tammany machine became increasingly institutionalized.[174]

The institutionalization of the Tammany machine was a response to two developments—the mobilization of a mass electorate and the emergence of an increasingly well organized labor movement—that gathered force in the years following the Civil War and that culminated in crises to which party leaders were compelled to respond. The spiral of competitive mobilization that was initiated in the Jacksonian era and reached a crescendo in the naturalization frauds of 1868 presented party leaders with the problem of controlling the thousands of ward politicians who linked these voters to the machine. When Tweed's response to this—widespread and costly corruption—became public knowledge in 1871, it threatened to discredit the Democratic party in New York City and to destroy Tammany Hall. Kelly and the Tilden-Hewitt forces had a stake in preserving the organization that provided them with a political base, and hence they sponsored the centralizing reforms mentioned above, which enabled them to purge politicians implicated in the Tweed scandals and to control local politicians without relying upon Tweed's methods.

The second development that contributed to the institutionalization of the machine was the emergence of an increasingly well organized labor movement. This development, however, did not confront Tammany with a major crisis until a decade and a half after the fall of Tweed. In the late 1860s and early 1870s New York's Workingmen's Union and its German-language counterpart, the Arbeiter-Union, were the strongest municipal trade assemblies in the United States, but nonetheless when they staged a foray into electoral politics in 1869 they were unable to prevent their movement from being captured by regular party politicians. And the depression of the 1870s greatly weakened the city's trade union movement.

In 1882 a new municipal federation of trade unions, the Central Labor Union (CLU), was organized in New York. Leaders of the radical wing of the Irish nationalist organization, the Land League—most prominently, Patrick Ford and Robert Blissert—played a major role in the founding of the CLU. Indeed, the new labor federation grew out of a meeting of 12,000 union members who, like Ford and Blissert, believed that major economic reforms were called for in the United States as well as in Ireland. In 1886 the CLU and the Knights of Labor formed the United Labor Party (ULP) and nominated Henry George for mayor; Ford and many veterans of the Land League's radical wing actively participated in the ULP campaign. George went on to win a substantial portion of the working-class and Irish vote in New York.[175] As Eric Foner notes, the struggle for the leadership of Irish-Americans—a struggle that in New York City culminated in the George campaign—reflected

> the existence of two overlapping but distinct centers of power, or poles of leadership, within the Irish-American community. Those who opposed Ford reflected the views of a nexus composed of the Catholic Church, the Democratic party, and the Irish-American middle class. The social dominance of this triple alliance was challenged in the 1880s by the organized social radicalism articulated and institutionalized in the Land League's radical branches and the Knights of Labor. Here were the only organized alternatives to the Tammany-oriented saloon and local clubhouse, as a focus for working class social life in the Irish-American community. . . . [They] embodied a social ethic that challenged the individualism of the middle class and the cautious social reformism of the Democratic party and Catholic Church.[176]

The ULP's mayoral campaign had some enduring consequences for New York politics. Tammany responded to the labor party's challenge to its political hegemony within New York's Irish-American community—and other ethnic subcommunities as well—by extending a network of district clubs throughout the city. This institutionalization of the party's base strengthened the bonds linking both working- and middle-class foreign-stock voters to the machine, making it that much more difficult for any subsequent competitor for the leadership of these groups to succeed. Moreover, Gompers, who had supported George's mayoral candidacy, concluded from the ULP's defeat that it was pointless for labor to devote its energies to political campaigns. Gompers and the AFL unions that followed his leadership were willing to acquiesce to the Democratic and Republican parties' dominance of both national and local politics. In return they sought above all to ensure that public officials elected by these parties would not intervene in labor disputes. Eventually such a *modus vivendi* between political machines and trade unions was established.

THE AMERICAN WORKING CLASS ON THE EVE OF THE TWENTIETH CENTURY

In sum, the craft unions and political machines that became solidly established at the end of the nineteenth century were the organizational manifestations of an accommodation between one segment of America's wage-labor force and other social forces in the United States. The organizations that embodied this accommodation institutionalized only a limited subset of the numerous dispositions American workers had exhibited in the decades immediately following the Civil War. In so doing they largely defined—and delimited—the shape and character that the American working class was to assume for the next several decades.

Three terms of the accommodation embodied in the craft union and the political machine are particularly noteworthy. First, this accommodation institutionalized a distinction between the organizations through which workers asserted claims upon their employers and upon the state: the former was the province of trade unions, the latter the province of party machines. As indicated above, the labor reform organizations of the post–Civil War years and the strike movements of that period had not always drawn this sharp distinction.

Second, the settlement embodied in the craft union and the political machine institutionalized a multifaceted definition of the collectivities to which workers belonged. In the economic realm the AFL unions officially defined their constituency—"labor" or the "working class"—to include only wage earners, thereby excluding the employers, farmers, shopkeepers, and clerks who formerly had been defined as belonging to the producing or working classes. (In practice, the definition of organized labor's constituency was even narrower, excluding unskilled laborers and frequently the members of racial and ethnic minorities as well.) Along with this narrower understanding of the boundaries of the working class went a militance in fighting for its distinctive interests that was considerably greater than that of those nineteenth-century labor reformers who regarded the interests of workers and employers as harmonious and who endorsed strikes only with the utmost reluctance. The machines that dominated the political arena in America's industrial cities at the end of the nineteenth century emphasized a different set of cleavages. On the whole, they organized cleavages of ethnicity and community into politics, uniting under a common banner skilled workers who belonged to trade unions, unskilled laborers for whom unions refused to accept responsibility, and members of the middle and upper classes. And these machines displayed a militance in their campaigns (as Richard Jensen has noted, both the rhetoric and practice of party warfare in the late nineteenth century was drawn from the military)[177] that was akin to that of contemporary trade unions, though the groups and issues on behalf of which they fought were rather different.

Finally, the accommodations that were embodied in craft unions and political machines institutionalized at least a partial distinction between the claims workers asserted against their employers and those they asserted against the state. The former centered on wages, hours, and, for a time at least, control over the workplace. The latter centered on issues of ethnicity and community—which ethnic groups would be rewarded with jobs on the public payroll and which neighborhoods would benefit from the construction of public works. However, an important qualification to this last point must be noted. Although machine politicians generally sought to emphasize issues that would keep their party from fracturing along class lines, they were prepared to enact measures that had initially been proposed by trade unionists when electoral conditions required them to do so, even if these measures were opposed by some of the business interests with which their party was allied. The willingness of machine politicians to accept conflict—including class conflict—as a fact of life enabled them to stay in tune with the sentiments of their constituents at times of industrial strife and to triumph over that segment of the labor reform movement whose quest for ways to restore harmony between employers and employees—such as currency reform or the single tax—made it lose touch with workers for whom such conflicts were part of their daily lives.[178]

It is important, however, not to overestimate the extent to which the accommodation institutionalized in the craft union and the political machine was accepted by employers, political elites, leaders and would-be leaders of the working class, and workers themselves. This accommodation embodied a number of tensions and was subject to persistent challenges from above, from below, and from without. Employers chafed under the restrictions that unions placed upon their ability to control and deploy their labor force, and many sought to overcome these restrictions by adopting the changes in the organization of production advocated by Frederick W. Taylor and taught in the nation's new schools of engineering and business administration, and/or by joining the open-shop drive of the National Association of Manufacturers. And within the political arena, Progressive reformers argued that the class compromise institutionalized in the machine was a bad deal: businessmen and members of the middle class should not have to bear the financial and moral costs of machine government in order to avoid the dangers of working-class and agrarian radicalism. To eliminate this necessity the Progressives advocated changes in election laws, municipal charters, and procedures for recruiting public employees that, when enacted, contributed to a weakening of political machines, a reduction in voter turnout, and the election of candidates committed to conducting public affairs according to business principles.[179]

The hegemony of machine politicians and "pure and simple" trade unionists also was challenged by other competitors for the leadership of the working class, who at times managed to win a substantial following. During the first two decades of the twentieth century the Socialist party elected thousands of its candidates to local offices in cities and towns across the country, and socialists continued to be a substantial force within the AFL: socialists of various persuasions controlled a number of the national unions affiliated with the AFL, as well as many union locals; at the 1902 AFL national convention the Socialist platform was defeated by the remarkably close vote of 4,171 to 4,897; and at the 1912 AFL convention the Socialist candidate secured one-third of the votes in a bid to unseat Gompers from the federation's presidency.[180]

During this same period there was a considerable amount of strike activity in the United States that was conducted outside the confines of the AFL or without the sanction of its national leadership. Among the miners, lumbermen, migratory farm workers, and casual laborers in the West, strikes were led by the Western Federation of Miners (WFM) and the International Workers of the World (IWW)—organizations that were bitterly opposed to the AFL. During the second decade of the twentieth century there was an enormous surge in wildcat strikes by skilled craftsmen resisting the introduction by their employers of scientific management techniques—especially incentive-pay schemes. And simultaneously there was a wave of strikes by unskilled workers, the majority of whom were immigrants from southern and eastern Europe seeking wage increases that would maintain their standard of living in the face of inflation.[181]

There were three noteworthy characteristics of these strikers and their strikes. First, they involved workers who either were excluded from the set of accommodations embodied in the craft union and the machine or who explicitly rejected those accommodations. The AFL and, for the most part, the major party organizations did not undertake to organize the highly transient unskilled workers in the extractive industries of the West or the factory operatives—who, in the main, were new immigrants from eastern and southern Europe—in the nation's industrial heartland; this left these workers available for mobilization by other leaders. And the skilled crafts-men who struck on behalf of "workers' control" (a term that came into com-mon use after World War I) did not believe that the AFL leadership's will-ingness to concede managerial control over the workplace in exchange for binding trade agreements was a bargain that served their interests. Second, the modes of collective action in which these workers engaged, the forms of organization they adopted, and the ideology their leadership espoused dif-fered substantially from those advocated by the dominant faction in the AFL. These workers relied on direct action (spontaneous walkouts, massive rallies); they established ad hoc workers' councils to coordinate strikes whose jurisdiction crossed craft lines; they sought to decentralize authority to shop committees; and their leaders were revolutionaries.[182] All of this contrasted with the AFL's advocacy of carefully accumulating strike and benefit funds; the negotiation of national contracts that would commit union locals not to strike; and the centralization of authority in the hands of na-tional craft union leaders, who were prepared to make their peace with the nation's captains of industry and political leaders. Third, and finally, the great majority of these strikes failed: they had to contend with the concerted opposition of Citizens' Alliances, local police forces, the judiciary, and not infrequently, the military; and striking workers generally could be replaced with new recruits from the reserve army of the unemployed. In the final analysis, the AFL's assessment of the political and economic constraints within which the American labor movement was compelled to operate dur-ing the early decades of the twentieth century was, in fact, a rather accurate one.[183]

These challenges to the set of institutions and accommodations that linked the American working class to the nation's economic and political order reached a new crescendo during the Great Depression of the 1930s, and was expressed by changes in the behavior of workers (and also farmers and businessmen) in factories, on the streets, and in voting booths. In the heat of this crisis a number of new institutions were forged—among them industrial unions, welfare bureaucracies, and the New Deal wing of the Democratic party. The craft unions and political machines that had been organized in the late nineteenth century found it necessary to adjust to these changes in the dispositions of their members and constituents, and to reach a modus vivendi with these new institutions. Some were incapable of making these adjustments and collapsed; others were more adaptable and survived. The precise nature of these adaptations and their implications for the character of the contemporary American working class is, however, another story.[184]

CHAPTER 5

Regional Receptivity to Reform
in the United States

PATRONAGE PLAYS a larger role in the politics of most cities and states in the northeastern quadrant of the United States than it does in the western half.[1] In this chapter, I attempt to account for this difference in the character of party politics in major regions of the United States.[2] I will argue that these regional differences in American politics are an enduring legacy of the way political order was restored in the United States after the Civil War and Reconstruction. The "third" American party system was the central institution through which political stabilization was achieved after the upheavals of the 1860s and early 1870s, and patronage played a pervasive role in party politics in all regions of the nation at the time.[3] However, the party organizations constructed in the cities and states of the West were, as a result of this process of stabilization, weaker and more narrowly based than their counterparts in the Northeast. Consequently, in the West during the Progressive Era, opponents of the patronage system were in a position to mobilize numerous voters who had never been attached to the norms and practices of the nineteenth century political order, and they were thereby able to overwhelm the regimes that governed the cities and states in that region. By contrast, in the Northeast, where party organizations were stronger and more broadly based, the Progressives were unable to destroy these organizations and reconstitute the electorate. Old-line party organizations in this region have to the present day managed to fight an extended, and partly successful, series of rearguard actions in defense of the patronage system against the successive reform movements that have attacked it during the twentieth century.

THE ENDURING CONSEQUENCES
OF PARTY ORGANIZATIONAL STRENGTH

Before proceeding to explain why strong party organizations emerged in the Northeast but not in the West during the late nineteenth century and how the structure of that period's party system has had such an enduring influence on the character of American politics, it would be useful to present some evidence, shown in Table 5.1, to support these claims.

TABLE 5.1
The Enduring Impact of Party Organizational Strength

% of Urban Population in Cities with Partisan Elections, 1975		Avg. Presidential Vote Turnout, 1876–1892		Volatility of GOP Gubernatorial Vote, 1876–1895	
Ind.	97.9	Ind.	92.7	N.H.	1.24
Conn.	97.9	N.J.	92.2	Ind.	2.05
Penn.	96.8	Ohio	92.1	Ill.	2.08
N.Y.	90.2	Iowa	91.8	Ohio	2.46
Md.	84.4	N.H.	89.7	Del.	2.50
R.I.	76.2	N.Y.	89.0	Conn.	2.83
Vt.	55.2	W. Va.	89.0	N.J.	3.00
Mont.	50.6	Ill.	86.1	Iowa	3.10
N.J.	45.8	Conn.	82.8	Mass.	3.68
Ky.	42.3	Penn.	82.7	Maine	4.18
W. Va.	32.3	Md.	81.4	Mo.	4.28
Ohio	29.4	Wisc.	81.3	Vt.	4.28
N.H.	28.8	Kan.	80.1	Mich.	4.36
Minn.	20.8	Mo.	78.2	Md.	4.98
Ill.	14.8	Mich.	76.8	Ky.	5.46
Maine	14.8	Ky.	76.4	N.Y.	5.50
Kan.	8.6	Del.	76.1	Wisc.	5.77
Iowa	8.0	Mont.	74.2	Kan.	6.12
Mass.	4.7	Nev.	73.9	Colo.	6.31
Mo.	4.2	Vt.	73.4	W. Va.	6.40
Neb.	3.4	Maine	73.3	Penn.	6.46
Mich.	3.2	Calif.	72.4	Minn.	7.16
Ore.	2.7	Mass.	71.8	Mont.	7.80
Wisc.	1.1	S.D.	70.7	Ore.	7.80
Del.	0.0	Minn.	70.3	R.I.	7.88
Nev.	0.0	Wash.	67.3	Nev.	7.88
S.D.	0.0	Neb.	66.1	Neb.	8.92
Calif.	0.0	Ore.	64.9	Wyo.	11.50
Idaho	0.0	Idaho	63.1	Calif.	12.04
Wash.	0.0	N.D.	56.6	N.D.	13.60
N.D.	0.0	Colo.	55.5	S.D.	16.50
Colo.	0.0	R.I.	52.5	Idaho	16.50
Wyo.	0.0	Wyo.	47.7	Wash.	20.70

Sources: *The Municipal Yearbook, 1978* (Washington, D.C.: International City Management Association, 1978), 9–43; *Historical Statistics of the United States: Colonial Times to 1970*, Bicentennial Edition, Part 2 (Washington, D.C.: Bureau of the Census, 1975), 1071–72; *Guide to U.S. Elections* (Washington, D.C.: Congressional Quarterly, 1975), 397–437.

The units of analysis in Table 5.1 are the nonsouthern states that were admitted to the Union prior to the collapse of the third-party system in 1896. The three columns in the table list the states according to their ranking on three indicators. The first is the percentage of the state's urban population living in cities in which local elections were conducted on a partisan rather than on a nonpartisan basis in 1975.[4] This is a crude indication of whether reformers have been able to deprive political parties of the patronage they could obtain from controlling municipal governments.[5]

In the second column, these states are ranked according to the average percentage of the eligible electorate that voted in the five presidential elections (1876–92) prior to the realignment of 1896. This is the period immediately preceding the attack on the patronage system launched by the Progressives, and electoral turnout in this period thus provides a measure of the breadth of support mobilized by the state's parties when there was as yet no impediment to the use of patronage.

The third column ranks the states according to the volatility of the Republican gubernatorial vote between 1876 and the last state election prior to 1896—that is, the average absolute change from one election to the next in the percentage of the total vote won by the Republican candidates.[6] This is a measure of the ability of the Republicans to hold on to their supporters in the face of third party challenges and national surges against it, and hence is an indication of how strong and reliable were the ties between the party and its mass base.[7]

There is a strong relationship between the regional location of states and their ranking on each of these three indicators. Thirteen of the eighteen northeastern states, but only three of the fifteen in the West, rank at or above the median in the column of percentage of urban population living in cities with partisan elections. Thirteen of the eighteen states in the northeast were among the top half of states in voter turnout in presidential elections between 1876 and 1892; the comparable figure for the western states again is three of fifteen. Finally, the Republican vote in gubernatorial elections between 1876 and 1895 was less volatile than the median value in thirteen of the eighteen states in the Northeast; this was true of only three of the fifteen states in the West.

The ranking of states according to the percentage of their urban population living in partisan cities in 1975 is quite similar to their ranking on the two measures of the strength of their party organizations during the late nineteenth century. The method of paired comparisons indicates that in 68 percent of all pairs, the state that ranks higher in the first column of Table 5.1 ranks higher in the second column.[8] The comparable figure for the first and third columns is 64 percent.

The data reported in Table 5.1 indicate that in the northeastern states, where political parties had mobilized the broadest popular following and had constructed the strongest organizations when there was as yet no impediment to the use of patronage, politicians down to the present day have been better able to put up some resistance to successive waves of reformism. By contrast, in the western states, where politicians had failed to construct strong party organizations prior to the reformist challenges of the twentieth century, opponents of the patronage system have enjoyed greater success.

THE POST-RECONSTRUCTION POLITICAL SETTLEMENT AND PARTY ORGANIZATIONAL STRENGTH, 1876–1896

The data in the section above suggest that patterns of politics prevailing today in the United States reflect in significant ways institutions that were established in the aftermath of the Civil War and the period of Reconstruction. This section analyzes some factors that can help explain why the Democratic and Republican parties of the late nineteenth century were better organized and more broadly based in the northeastern quadrant of the country than in the states of the West.

Cities and states do not have autonomous political systems.[9] To explain why in the late nineteenth century strong, broadly based party organizations were constructed in the Northeast but not in the West, one must understand the relationship between, on the one hand, national political cleavages and coalitions, and on the other, the structure of state and local politics in different regions of the country.

Following the Civil War and Reconstruction there occurred a process similar to the one that Charles Maier has described as following World War I in Europe.[10] In Europe at that time there was a great deal of turbulence as a consequence of wartime mobilization and the example of the Russian Revolution. Maier argues that in Europe conservative forces regrouped during the 1920s and restored order by creating corporatist institutions. Similarly, in the United States there was considerable turmoil during the late 1860s and early 1870s—in the South as a consequence of the Radical Republican effort to remake the political and social system of the former Confederate states, and in the North as a consequence of wartime mobilization and the example of Radical Reconstruction. In the United States during the 1870s there was also a regrouping of conservative forces and a similar extrusion of radical elements from the political system. But in contrast to Europe, political stabilization was achieved in the United States not through the creation of corporatist institutions, but rather through the reconstruction and institutionalization of the party system.

The lead in fashioning the political settlement that ended the turbulence of the Civil War and Reconstruction periods was taken by professional politicians from the Northeast who moved into dominant positions in the national parties during the 1870s.[11] A major reason these politicians moved to the fore of both parties was that they developed a formula for uniting their respective parties, minimizing defections to potentially threatening third parties, and attracting the contributions the parties needed to run their campaigns. Elements of each party resisted this settlement, but it ultimately came to define the character of political debate in American politics.

As the nineteenth century progressed, both parties came to give less attention to the "southern question."[12] Republican politicians continued to "wave the bloody shirt" and denounce "southern outrages" in their campaign rhetoric, and as late as 1890 they threatened to introduce a federal presence in the South to protect the franchise of black men. But by the mid-1870s Republicans had basically abandoned the idea of using a military occupation to remake the social system of the former Confederate states. As for the Democrats, they continued to rail against "black Republicanism" and to champion "states' rights," but in the so-called New Departure they accepted the legitimacy of the three Reconstruction amendments to the Constitution. Republican and Democratic politicians came to give less attention to the plight of blacks in the South, in part because this issue lost some of its popular appeal as the Civil War receded in time. But attention also shifted because the emerging labor conflicts and agrarian radicalism in the North and West led businessmen allied with the two parties to regard as potentially disruptive the extreme positions the parties had staked out on racial issues during the period of Radical Reconstruction.[13]

Many influential Democratic and Republican politicians also were prepared to arrange compromises on the issue of currency inflation or deflation—an issue that threatened to split the parties along sectional lines and drive large numbers of voters to third parties, and that had the dangerous potential of serving as a basis for an alliance between poor farmers in the South and West.[14] Both parties also took moderate positions on labor issues—for example, by supporting the creation of a Bureau of Labor Statistics—so as to avoid party splits along class lines.[15] Both parties also supported civil service reforms that satisfied the demands of merchants for increased economy and efficiency in government (particularly in the major customs houses and post offices), without reducing the total amount of patronage available to the parties or turning the bureaucracy into an autonomous center of power.[16]

Finally, the two parties agreed to disagree on the issue of tariffs.[17] By focusing on tariffs, the Republicans could attach manufacturers firmly to their cause, and also appeal to laborers who worked in protected industries. The Democrats found the issue equally useful. Tariff reform appealed to merchants engaged in foreign trade, to the bankers who financed this trade, and to industries interested in cheaper raw materials.[18] To drive home their point that workers and farmers, as well as businessmen, had a strong stake in tariff levels, each party argued that its stance on tariffs was consistent with its stance on ethnocultural and racial issues.[19] The Democrats argued that the efforts of the GOP to place a surcharge on every item the worker consumed were similar to its effort to dictate what he could and could not do on his Sundays and to elevate blacks to a position of equality with whites. Democrats asserted their party's commitment, by contrast, to "personal liberty" and limited government as the best defense against this meddling fanaticism. The Republicans sought to identify the indifference of the Democrats to the plight of American workers who lost their jobs as a result of goods produced by cheap foreign labor with their indifference to public morality and to the plight of blacks who were being deprived of their right to vote in the South.

The fact that the division between the two parties on the national level involved an issue that was more salient to important interests in the Northeast than in the West contributed to the emergence of strong, broadly based party organizations in the Northeast and to the failure of such organizations to be constructed in the western states during the late nineteenth century.

Party Organizations in the Northeast

Democratic and Republican party leaders who sought to secure their control over municipal and state governments in the Northeast during the late nineteenth century had to deal with a number of problems. They had to manage ethnic tensions among their constituents and cope with competition from the labor movement for the loyalty of their working class supporters.[20] They also had to worry about ward leaders who devoted more attention to solidifying their own positions by distributing patronage to their personal followers than they devoted to mobilizing new voting groups that could help the party win elections. Another danger they faced arose from corruption on the part of subordinate politicians, since revelations of corruption—which was rampant in American politics in the years following the Civil War—could provide the other major party with an issue it could use to advantage.

There were two ways in which political actors during this period sought to deal with the problem of corruption: by strengthening public bureaucracies or by strengthening party organizations. The former alternative was the one advocated by Mugwump reformers. By establishing competitive examinations to control the hiring and promotion of public employees and by protecting civil servants against arbitrary dismissal, reformers sought to reduce the range of public benefits over which politicians would be able to exercise control, and thereby to diminish the variety and quantity of patronage that politicians would be in a position to sell.

Corruption also could be reduced by strengthening local party organizations because, as Henry Jones Ford has written, "the weakness of party organization is the opportunity of corruption."[21] A politician who is an independent political operator is more likely to seek quick financial gains in politics and to ignore the problems his rapaciousness creates for the party as a whole than one who is subject to the discipline of a party organization. To cite the most extreme case, it was the very weakness of New York City's Tammany machine that contributed to the massive corruption of the Tweed Ring, because bribing his political associates or providing them with the opportunity to steal from the public treasury were the only ways in which Boss Tweed could exert any influence over other politicians.[22] By strengthening and centralizing the organizations they led, top party officials sought to acquire the capacity to impose a measure of discipline on their members in less politically dangerous ways. Party leaders would then be in a position to compel ward politicians and public officeholders to take the long-run interests of the party into account by moderating (though not completely abandoning) their efforts to make money in office. In particular, they would be compelled to limit themselves to what George Washington Plunkitt termed "honest graft," rather than using any and all means to maximize their income in the short run, regardless of the consequences for the party as a whole.[23]

Strengthening their party organizations would also address the other major problems confronting Democratic and Republican party leaders. By developing a more highly articulated structure at the ward level, the party would be better able to hold on to its followers in the face of competition from the labor movement and from politicians who relied on strident ethnic appeals. In addition, by centralizing control at the city level, party leaders could compel ward bosses to bring new voters into the party's camp and to reward precinct workers on the basis of their contributions to the party's total vote, rather than on their personal fealty to the incumbent ward leadership.

If power within a party organization was to be centralized, its leader needed to acquire control over some resource crucial to the party's success, so that his subordinates needed him more than he needed any one of them. Party leaders accomplished this centralization during the late nineteenth century by entering into alliances with prominent members of the local business community. By forging such alliances, party leaders gained access to a legitimate source of campaign contributions, and, equally important, they acquired a measure of respectability that enabled the candidates they backed to win middle class votes. The Tammany organization in New York City provides a particularly clear example of this strategy of party leadership. John Kelly, who in the words of one contemporary "found Tammany a horde [and] left it a political army," strengthened and centralized the Tammany organization in the 1870s by allying with such wealthy Democrats as Samuel Tilden, New York's leading corporation lawyer, Abram Hewitt and Edward Cooper, iron manufacturers, and Augustus Schell, a director of the New York Central and a half dozen other railroads.[24] Similarly, Pat Maguire, under whose leadership the Democratic City Committee in Boston reached the peak of its power in the 1880s and 1890s, was allied with such Brahmins as Josiah Quincy III and Nathan Matthews.[25] Finally, Boies Penrose, who took control of the Philadelphia Republican machine in the 1880s, was himself a member of a socially prominent local family.[26]

For their part, metropolitan elites were prepared to enter into alliances with state and local party leaders, and to collaborate in their efforts to strengthen the state and local organizations of the Democratic and Republican parties, because the national parties split along lines that mirrored the central cleavage that divided northeastern businessmen. This cleavage was between low-tariff commercial and financial interests, and high-tariff industrial interests. By helping to centralize and to extend the popular base of the Democratic or Republican party, as the case might be, these elites helped strengthen the very institutions that fought their battles in national politics and that worked to exclude from the national political arena issues that might lead to a dangerous alliance between southern and western agrarian radicals. At the same time, strong local party organizations could serve their interests in city politics because they had the capacity to place at least some limits on municipal corruption and expenditures, and to exclude from the local arena potentially threatening forces, such as the labor movement.

The highly organized political machines that were constructed during the late nineteenth century also served the interests of the subordinate politicians who were prepared to accept their discipline. Prior to the emergence of these party organizations, local politics had been a very freewheeling business. The precinct captains and ward leaders who worked for centralized machines, and the public officials who were elected with their support, enjoyed less autonomy than their predecessors; but they received a considerable measure of political security in return. Moreover, the construction of well-organized and broadly based machines enabled these political functionaries, who commonly were recruited from the middle class or the upwardly mobile working class, to drive out competitors for the political leadership of the city's immigrant masses. Such competitors included gang leaders and volunteer fire captains who formerly had played major roles in partisan combat, and the union leaders who in the 1880s staged forays into electoral politics.[27]

In sum, in the states and cities of the Northeast, both politicians and businessmen found it in their interest to strengthen the local organizations of the national political parties during a period when they were in a position to make use of patronage for this purpose without arousing any substantial opposition. As a result, much of the electorate came to be linked to the polity through patronage-oriented party organizations, which had the capacity to induct successive generations of voters into this pattern of political activity.

Party Organizations in the West

In contrast to their counterparts in the Northeast, politicians in the territories and states of the West did not build highly structured and broadly based party organizations during the late nineteenth century. Strong party organizations failed to emerge during these decades partly because the West had only recently been settled, but also because politicians did not find it necessary to construct them in order to gain or retain power. In addition, the most important local political forces did not find that their interests would be served by strengthening the Democratic or Republican party organizations. The reason that politicians and local elites found it neither necessary nor especially advantageous to build strong party organizations ultimately concerned the West's peripheral status in both the economic and political systems of late nineteenth century America.[28]

The most important institutions in the economies of the western states and territories in the late nineteenth century were railroads (and in some states mining corporations) controlled by outsiders. In addition, the national parties, under whose labels politics was conducted, were controlled by politicians from the Northeast and were closely allied with economic interests from that region of the country.

These characteristics of the western states had two important consequences for the structure of party politics in that region. The first was that in efforts to gain office and remain in power, politicians could draw on the resources of "the company"—the railroad or mining corporation that overshadowed all other local institutions.[29] Railroads were particularly powerful because they commanded enormous resources, penetrated throughout the hinterland of the territory or state, and occupied a strategic position in the local economy. As a result, local businessmen and farmers found it was in their interest to promote the interests of the railroad. The railroad could provide the politicians with money to finance campaigns and with a network of agents scattered throughout the state—services that politicians in the Northeast constructed political machines to obtain.[30]

The second reason that politicians and their allies were not driven to engage in competitive party building was that the issue that most clearly divided the national parties up to the late nineteenth century—the protective tariff—was not the most salient one in the West. Westerners were not indifferent to the tariff, but prior to the crisis of the 1890s the issue of railroad regulation was more salient to merchants and farmers in the West. Their own prosperity and the prosperity of their communities was less a function of whether the goods they produced or sold were protected by a tariff than of whether they had access to rail transportation and of the freight rates they were charged. A striking incident illustrating this point with regard to farmers occurred in 1890 after California citrus growers secured an increase in the tariff on lemons. As soon as Congress raised the tariff, the Southern Pacific Railroad boosted the rate it charged for shipping lemons to the East Coast, thus wiping out much of the benefit of the tariff increase.[31] As for western merchants, their chief concern was competition with businessmen in other cities. This competition was unaffected by tariff schedules, and was largely a function of relative transportation costs.

Because the issues of greatest salience to western merchants and farmers were not those that divided the Republican and Democratic parties nationally, cleavages on these issues cut across party lines. The railroads enjoyed allies and exercised influence in both parties, and there were anti-railroad forces in each. Consequently, conflicts between pro- and anti-railroad forces most commonly took the form of factional struggles within each party rather than of battles between the parties. For this reason, political elites in the West, unlike their counterparts in the East, were not driven to strengthen the organizations of the Republican and Democratic parties in the course of struggles over the issues of greatest concern to them.

But why did not the pro- and anti-railroad forces in each party attempt to overwhelm the opposing faction and seize control of the party by outmobilizing and outorganizing the other side? The answer to this question lies in part in the way conflicts over railroad issues divided states during the nineteenth century, and in part in the character of the institutions through which these conflicts were settled. The issue of railroad regulation divided states along geographic lines. For example, communities that were served by a single railroad line had an interest in strong regulatory statutes that would reduce railroad rates. Communities that were served by two or more railroads were less concerned about regulation to the extent that they could count on competition to keep their rates down. Communities not served by any railroad were opposed to rate regulation because railroads financed new construction with bonds whose repayment was financed by the profits made on their existing lines.[32] During the nineteenth century these conflicts between the proponents and opponents of railroad regulation were fought out in state legislatures and in party conventions. In both of these institutions, votes were allocated among communities on a population basis, and hence the pro- and anti-railroad forces would gain no advantage by working to secure large electoral majorities behind the legislators or delegates pledged to their cause. Rather than competing through a process of mobilization and countermobilization, then, the proponents and opponents of railroad regulation sought to gain control of legislatures and party conventions by striking compromises, by making deals, and by seeking to outmaneuver the other side. In this process of factional bargaining and maneuver, the railroad had the advantage of its ability to buy the votes of neutral delegates and even delegates pledged to its opponents. It is little wonder, then, that the western Progressives regarded political parties as tools of "the interests." Accordingly, they sought to destroy parties and return government to "the people" by establishing direct primaries and the initiative, referendum, and recall. In time, they were able to overwhelm the prevailing regimes in the western states by pursuing a strategy of mobilization.

ELECTORAL MOBILIZATION DURING THE
PROGRESSIVE ERA

The different trajectories of party development in the western and northeastern states during the late nineteenth century have had enduring implications for the structure of politics in these regions. Because political parties in the West were so loosely organized and narrowly based, reformers during the Progressive Era were able to deal them a crippling blow by bringing into the electorate voters who had not been mobilized by, or socialized into the values of, the prevailing regime. Reformers in the Northeast, by contrast, were not in a position to attract unaffiliated voters. As a result, locally dominant political machines suffered only temporary losses during the Progressive Era, and were able in large measure to reassert themselves after Progressivism declined. An analysis of the structure of the Progressive vote in California and New York—the largest western and eastern states—indicates the extent to which the electoral foundations of Progressive reform differed in these two regions.

California: Electoral Mobilization and Progressive Victory

The structure of politics in California during the last decades of the nineteenth century and the first of the twentieth century conforms closely to the western pattern outlined above. Politics in California during this period was ridden with patronage, but the state's party organizations were weak. The most powerful force in state politics during this period was not a party organization, but rather the Southern Pacific Railroad. The most influential political figure in California was not a party boss, but rather the head of the railroad's Political Bureau.

It was in this context that the Progressive Movement emerged in California with the announced purpose of securing the "emancipation of the Republican Party in California from domination by the Political Bureau of the Southern Pacific Railroad Company and allied interests," in the words of the leading Progressive organization in the state, the Lincoln-Roosevelt League.[33] It is beyond the scope of this chapter to consider the origins of California Progressivism or to recount its history, but suffice it to say that immediately after its founding in 1907, the Lincoln-Roosevelt League scored a remarkable string of victories. In the first gubernatorial campaign after the League was organized, the Progressives managed to take over the Republican Party and to elect their candidate, Hiram Johnson, as governor. The ease with which they won was a token of both the organizational weakness and the narrow popular base of the regime they overturned. In the 1906 gubernatorial election, the one immediately preceding the Progressive challenge, a majority of the eligible electorate—50.2 percent—failed to vote.[34] For these reasons, the Progressives were able to mobilize new voters into the electorate and put together a political coalition whose composition differed considerably from any that had previously existed in the state.

Table 5.2 indicates the sources from which Hiram Johnson drew his support in his two campaigns for governor.[35] In the case of Johnson's 1910 campaign, everyone eligible to vote that year either had voted for the Republican candidate in the previous gubernatorial election (1906), had voted for the Democratic or some minor party candidate that year, had not been eligible to vote in California in 1906, or had abstained from voting even though eligible to do so. All Johnson voters in 1910 had occupied one of these categories in 1906, and each is listed in Table 5.2.

The column of figures headed "Proportion within Each Category Going to Johnson" indicates the proportion of 1906 Republican voters, Democratic or minor party voters, ineligibles, and abstainers who voted for Hiram Johnson in 1910. The column headed "Proportion of Total Johnson Vote Coming from Each Category" indicates the proportion of 1910 Johnson voters who in 1906 had voted for the Republican gubernatorial candidate, voted for the Democratic (or minor party) candidate, been ineligible to vote, or abstained from voting. The figures in the first column, then, enable one to answer such questions as: What proportion of 1906 abstainers voted for Johnson in 1910? Those in the second column enable one to answer a somewhat different question: What proportion of Johnson's vote in 1910 came from 1906 abstainers?

The estimates reported in the first column of Table 5.2 indicate that the Progressives in 1910 were able to win extensive support among voters who had backed other parties in the previous election. Almost one-quarter of the 1910 voters who had supported the Democrats or a minor party in 1906 cast their ballots for Johnson in 1910. (At the same time, however, one-third of the 1910 voters who had supported the Republicans in 1906 refused to stay with the GOP after Johnson captured its gubernatorial nomination.) The

TABLE 5.2
Sources of the Progressive Vote: California

Gubernatorial Campaigns of Hiram Johnson	Proportion within Each Category Going to Johnson	Proportion of Total Johnson Vote Coming from Each Category
Johnson 1910		
1906 Democrats and Minor Parties	.24	.25
1906 Republicans	.68	.48
1906 Ineligibles	.11	.08
1906 Abstainers	.10	.19
$R^2 = .802$		
Johnson 1914		
1910 Democrats and Minor Parties	.19	.09
1910 Republicans	.46	.18
1910 Ineligibles	.28	.51
1910 Abstainers	.27	.22
$R^2 = .018$		
Johnson 1914 (allowing for intrastate regional differences)		
1910 Democrats and Minor Parties	.25	.10
1910 Republicans	.46	.15
1910 Ineligibles	.28	.44
1910 Abstainers (South and Central Valley)	.06	.01
1910 Abstainers (North) .	.48	.31
$R^2 = .210$		

Sources: Voting data from Interuniversity Consortium for Political Research; size of eligible electorate interpolated from Bureau of the Census, Thirteenth Census of the United States (Washington, D.C.: Government Printing Office, 1913), 2: 169–79; and Bureau of the Census, Fourteenth Census of the United States, vol. III (Washington, D.C.: U.S. Government Printing Office, 1922), 112–17.

Note: For clarity of presentation, standard errors are not reported along with the estimates in Tables 5.2 and 5.3. In no case, however, does one exceed .03, and in all cases the estimates are considerably greater than twice their standard errors.

estimates reported in the second column reveal how substantially the coalition the Progressives constructed in 1910 differed from the one that had elected the Republican gubernatorial candidate in 1906. An estimated 52 percent of those who supported Johnson in 1910 had not voted for the Republican candidate in the previous election. Approximately half of these had not participated at all in the previous election—8 percent of the 1910 Johnson voters had not been eligible to vote in 1906, and 19 percent had abstained from voting in 1906.

In 1914 the Progressives substantially reorganized their coalition, mobilizing yet more voters into the electorate. The 1914 Progressive campaign differed from the 1910 campaign in two ways that must be noted when interpreting the figures reported in Table 5.2. First, between the elections of 1910 and 1914 California granted women the right to vote—thus sharply increasing the number of newly eligible voters. The analysis below must assume that the structure of the female vote was not so completely different from that of the male vote as to render a comparison between the 1910 and 1914 elections meaningless. Second, in contrast to 1910, when he ran for governor as the Republican candidate, Johnson and his associates in 1914 bolted the GOP and organized the Progressive party. Johnson ran for a second term as the nominee of that new party.

Even with these qualifications, the extent to which Johnson remade his electoral coalition in his second gubernatorial campaign remains striking. Only 46 percent of the voters who had supported Johnson in 1910 voted for him again in 1914. And 73 percent of Johnson's votes in 1914 came from persons who had not voted in 1910. To be sure, the enormous drop in support for Johnson among those who had voted for him in his first campaign was influenced by the fact that he ran for reelection as a third party candidate and against a regular Republican. Thus, it is not entirely surprising that slightly more than half of the voters who marked their ballots for Johnson on the GOP line in 1910 refused to vote for him four years later when he ran on the Progressive line. Moreover, the enormous role that persons who had not voted in 1910 played in Johnson's 1914 coalition was substantially (though not entirely) a function of the advent of women's suffrage: 51 percent of those voting for Johnson in 1914 had not been eligible to vote four years earlier. This fact does not, however, provide grounds for dismissing these changes in the structure of the vote for Johnson as a consequence of "mere" changes in legal forms, because the decisions of the Progressives to establish an independent party and to enfranchise women were taken in full cognizance of their political significance: the new party was the mechanism through which the Progressives reorganized their electoral base, and the Progressives expected that they would benefit disproportionately from female suffrage. This expectation proved to be correct. Among those newly eligible voters who did participate in the 1914 election, Johnson won the support of 51 percent, his Republican opponent received the votes of 32 percent, and the Democratic and minor party candidates won 16 percent (46 percent of the newly eligible did not vote).

Two other features of the 1914 election merit mention. First, a remarkable 22 percent of Johnson's 1914 vote came from persons who had abstained from voting in 1910 though eligible to vote that year. These voters evidently were mobilized into the active electorate by events transpiring between the two campaigns. Second, there is scarcely any relationship between Johnson's 1914 vote and the distribution of votes across counties in 1910 (the R^2 of the 1914 Johnson equation is a mere .018).

One possible explanation for this latter finding is that the assumption in the analysis above—that voter transition rates are uniform across all counties in the state—is false.[36] In fact, there are good reasons to believe that voter transition rates between 1910 and 1914 did vary in different regions of the state. In 1910, Johnson focused his campaign exclusively on the railroad issue. This issue had especially strong popular appeal in the agricultural counties of the Central Valley and southern California. During his first term, however, Johnson made a strong bid for labor support, endorsing much (though not all) of the legislative program of the California Federation of Labor.[37] Johnson's stand on labor issues appealed to members of the working class, especially in the San Francisco Bay area, but it infuriated many of the conservative anti-railroad forces that had supported Johnson in 1910.

A second set of figures shown in Table 5.2 was estimated to test this hypothesis concerning changes in support for Johnson in different regions of California, and to find out more about the group of greatest relevance to this analysis—those who abstained in the 1910 election, but voted for Johnson in 1914. Separate transition rates were calculated for abstainers in the Central Valley and southern California, on the one hand, and the remainder of the state, on the other.[38]

Two conclusions emerge from this procedure. First, the variance explained by the second Johnson 1914 equation is significantly higher than by the first, thus indicating that making a distinction between the rate at which abstainers in different regions of California moved into the electorate substantially increases one's ability to ascertain the sources from which Johnson drew his 1914 vote. Second, the figures reported in the second column of Table 5.2 indicate that very few of the 1910 abstainers who voted for Johnson in 1914 lived in the Central Valley or southern California. Rather, they came almost entirely from the remaining counties, the bulk of whose population was concentrated in the San Francisco Bay area. It seems reasonable to infer that many of these new voters were members of the working class who had been unmoved by Johnson's 1910 anti-railroad campaign, but who were mobilized into the electorate by Johnson's strategy during his first term of appealing for working class support by securing the passage of labor legislation. The fact that many members of San Francisco's heavily Catholic working-class population were mobilized into politics through this appeal to their collective interests may help explain why the political orientations of immigrants in that city, and more generally in the West, differ markedly from those of more patronage-oriented working-class voters in the East, though regional differences in the social structure of ethnic subcommunities almost certainly played a role as well.

The estimates reported in Table 5.2 indicate that a substantial proportion of Hiram Johnson's support came from voters who were newly mobilized into the electorate, or at most loosely tied to the previous regime, and who therefore were unlikely to be strongly attached to its norms and practices.[39] These voters provided the Progressives with the popular base from which they launched their frontal attack on the system of party and patronage politics as previously conducted in California.

Because the Progressives in California were able to mobilize an extensive and independent base of support for themselves, they were able to exert a strong influence on the way politics was conducted thereafter in the state. The voters who rallied to the Progressive cause formed the initial mass base for the candidate-centered or issue-oriented style of electoral politics that has been evident in the state since the Progressive Era. These voters enabled the Progressives to gain control of the state legislature as well as the governorship, and thereby to enact legislation that dealt a fatal blow to the state's weak Democratic and Republican party organizations.[40] Some of these "reforms" (such as the provision in the state's election law that enabled an office seeker to run in the primary of more than one party) contributed to a decline in competition in general elections, and consequently to a decline in voter turnout at the end of the Progressive Era. And the destruction of party organizations in the state has meant that elites who have sought to protect the bureaucracy against the raids of patronage-seeking politicians have faced little effective opposition. (The success in the early 1940s of the neo-Progressive crusade launched by Earl Warren and his allies against Governor Culbert Olson's administration, which did attempt to influence the appointment of civil servants, stands as a case in point.)[41] The destruction of party organizations in the state also has left California's political system vulnerable to penetration by outside forces. Some of these (such as the Democratic and Republican club movements of the 1950s and 1960s) helped foster and maintain an issue-oriented style of politics in the state. But California also is the home of the nation's first political public relations firm, and a number of the most successful politicians in California in recent years have been as adept at manipulating political symbols as they are at expounding political ideas.

New York: Party Organization and Progressive Defeat

The pattern of party development in New York during the late nineteenth century differed considerably from that of California. Two strong, centralized, and broadly based party organizations were constructed in New York during the last three decades of the century: the Republican state machine under the leadership of Roscoe Conkling and Thomas Platt; the Democratic organization under the leadership of Dean Richmond and David Hill in Albany, and Tammany bosses John Kelly and Richard Croker in New York City. During the two decades prior to the 1896 realignment, the volatility of the Republican gubernatorial vote in New York was less than half as great as it was in California, and the mean voter turnout in presidential elections was 16.6 percent higher. Moreover, the two major parties were considerably more successful in New York than in California in holding on to their supporters in the face of third party challenges—the mean third party vote in New York gubernatorial elections was 3.6 percent, compared to California's 10.9 percent.

Progressivism in New York, as in California, was a political movement of groups that did not enjoy privileged access to the leadership of the state's parties. But the character and course of Progressivism in New York differed considerably from the California variant because political parties in the two states were so different. Because New York's parties rested on an extremely broad popular base—84.3 percent of the eligible electorate voted in the election immediately preceding the one that elevated a Progressive, Charles Evans Hughes, to the governorship[42]—the Progressives were not in a position to seize control of the parties by mobilizing previously inactive voters behind their cause. Hughes was nominated and elected as governor in 1906 and 1908 not so much because the Progressives overwhelmed the Republican Party's Old Guard leadership in a full scale battle, but because the Old Guard recognized that it would be prudent to acquiesce to Hughes's nomination to placate the party's Progressive wing, thereby preventing their defection and avoiding the consequent danger of a Democratic victory.[43]

The data reported in Table 5.3 indicate how greatly the coalition that elected Hughes in New York in 1906 differed from the one that elected Johnson to his first term as a governor of California in 1910. Approximately three-quarters of Hughes's support came from voters who had cast their ballot for the Republican ticket in 1902. By contrast, less than half of Johnson's 1910 vote came from those who had voted Republican in the previous gubernatorial election. An estimated 15 percent of Hughes's support came from previous Democratic voters; the comparable figures for Johnson is 25 percent. But most significantly of all, Hughes received only 5 percent of his votes from previous abstainers; persons who had failed to vote in the previous election though eligible to do so composed almost four times as large a proportion of the coalition that elected Johnson to his first term in office (19 percent).

The contrast between the coalitions that elected Hughes and Johnson to their second terms is even more striking.[44] In interpreting the figures regarding Hughes's 1908 electoral coalition it must be kept in mind that Hughes's bid for a second term coincided with a presidential campaign. But even acknowledging this fact, the extent to which the vote for Hughes in

TABLE 5.3
Sources of the Progressive Vote: New York

Gubernatorial Campaigns of Charles Evans Hughes	Proportion from Each Category Going to Hughes	Proportion of Total Hughes Vote Coming from Each Category
Hughes 1906		
1902 Democrats	.18	.15
1902 Republicans	.84	.76
1902 Ineligibles	.29	.04
1902 Abstainers	.09	.05
$R^2 = .795$		
Hughes 1908		
1904 Democrats	.00	.00
1904 Republicans	.97	.94
1904 Ineligibles	.49	.06
1904 Abstainers	.00	.00
$R^2 = .931$		

Sources: Voting data from Interuniversity Consortium for Political Research; size of eligible electorate interpolated from Census Office, *Twelfth Census of the United States*, vol. 1, part 1 (Washington, D.C.: U.S. Census Office, 1901), 991–92; and Bureau of the Census, *Thirteenth Census of the United States* (Washington, D.C.: Government Printing Office, 1913), 2: 227–37.

1908 was simply a party vote is extraordinary. The estimates reported in the first column of Table 5.3 indicate that the proportion of 1904 Democrats voting for Hughes in 1908 was too small to be discernible, and that an estimated 97 percent of 1904 Republicans supported Hughes in 1908. The figures reported in the second column indicate that 94 percent of Hughes's support in 1908 came from voters who had cast their ballot for the Republicans in 1904 and none came from 1904 abstainers.

In sum, the Progressives in New York did not disrupt traditional voting patterns to the same extent as their California counterparts. Although other factors played a role as well, the failure of the Progressives in New York to build an independent base of support for themselves contributed to their inability to get the state legislature, which remained in the hands of old-line politicians, to pass the full range of antipartisan reforms enacted by the Progressive-controlled legislature in California. Most importantly, Governor Hughes failed in his efforts to get the legislature to establish a system of primary elections.[45] Consequently, after the Progressive Movement waned, the Republican and Democratic machines in the state were able to reassert themselves. In 1913, for example, Tammany boss Charles Murphy was able to secure the impeachment and removal from office of Governor William

Sulzer, who had refused to follow completely Murphy's orders concerning the distribution of patronage.[46] In the decades following the Progressive Era not only did Tammany reach the zenith of its power in New York, but so too did the political machines in many cities and states in the Northeast.

This is not to say that the Progressives and subsequent reformers had no impact upon the conduct of politics and government in New York. By allying with upstate Republicans who sought to reduce the political weight of overwhelmingly Democratic New York City, they were able to secure the enactment of ballot laws that contributed to a rise in split-ticket voting, and voter registration laws that contributed to a decline in voter turnout by making it more difficult to vote.[47] In addition, the predominantly Irish leadership of New York's Democratic machines, and their predominantly white Anglo-Saxon Protestant counterparts in the Republican party, had little interest in sharing power with the immigrants from southern and eastern Europe, who came to account for an increasing proportion of the population of the city and state during the early decades of the twentieth century. Hence, these party leaders did not make an all-out effort to bring the members of these groups into the electorate. This factor also contributed to a reduction in the popular base of New York's political machines relative to the size of the potential electorate.

The party realignment of 1928–36, however, mobilized hundreds of thousands of new immigrants into the electorate in New York, as in many other states.[48] Because patronage-oriented party organizations survived the Progressive Era in New York, they were available to channel the participation of many of these new voters, as well as to buttress the position of ethnic leaders who sought to live off politics—in the face of stiff competition in the 1930s and 1940s from their more ideologically oriented rivals in the American Labor Party.[49] In addition, these organizations were able to transmit to large numbers of these new voters an understanding of politics—including a view of patronage—whose roots lay in the political conflicts, compromises, and institutions of the nineteenth century. In an attenuated form, a similar process occurred with regard to blacks in New York during the 1960s and early 1970s.[50]

Because reformers in New York and throughout much of the Northeast have enjoyed only episodic success in the electoral arena, they have concentrated their efforts on creating public agencies insulated from the influence of electoral politics—professionalized police and welfare departments, independent authorities, financial control boards, and the like. Politicians in the Northeast often have been willing to avoid intervening in these agencies in order to prevent the business community from financing, and the press from supporting, reform campaigns that may not prove to be fatal in the party organizations they lead, but nonetheless would prove costly and fraught with uncertainties.[51] In this way, city and state governments in New York and elsewhere have been carved up along functional lines, chunks of which have been distributed to various contenders for power. Patronage-oriented party organizations have thereby purchased from potential opponents acquiescence to their control of lower-level elective offices, portions of the judiciary, and some public works and regulatory functions of municipal governments.[52] As a result of this process (and related ones, such as the unionization of public employees), the scope of the patronage system has contracted and old-line party organizations have become considerably weaker in New York and elsewhere in the Northeast than they were three-quarters of a century ago. Nonetheless, machine politicians have been able to defend vestiges of the patronage system. Though they may no longer dominate the input and output arenas of government, in New York, and many other Northeastern cities and states, machine politicians remain forces with which other political actors must contend.

POLITICAL PARTIES AS MECHANISMS OF POLITICAL CONTROL

In the current political science literature, parties are viewed chiefly as institutions of representation. The analysis in this chapter suggests, however, that in addition to serving as institutions through which elites can be influenced by citizens, political parties can serve as mechanisms for political stabilization that enable elites to exercise control over citizens.[53] The "third" party system was the major institution through which political order was restored in the United States under conservative leadership after the enormous upheavals of the Civil War and Reconstruction. The national party system of the late nineteenth century organized into the political process issues that were highly salient to northeastern industrial, commercial, and financial interests, and organized out of politics issues that might have led to a coalition between southern and western agrarian radicals. The creation of such a national party system, moreover, had important implications for the ways in which political conflicts were expressed and resolved in different regions of the country.

In the Northeast, politicians and the elites with whom they were allied had an incentive to respond to the various threats they faced—including threats from each other—by using the resources of the national, state, and municipal governments to strengthen and expand the popular base of the local organizations of the Republican and Democratic parties. In this way, centralized party organizations enjoying widespread popular support were constructed in the Northeast when there was as yet no substantial bar to the use of patronage for the purposes of party building and political mobilization. As a consequence of this process, the ethnic working classes in the Northeast were brought into the political system under a patronage-oriented political leadership. This enduringly influenced their political outlook and helped "immunize" them to the appeals of more radical political movements.[54]

The party organizations constructed in the Northeast during the late nineteenth century eventually achieved a considerable measure of autonomy from the businessmen who had earlier supported their construction. This development led many of these elites to attack political machines during the Progressive Era. The strong party organizations of the Northeast have generally been able to withstand such attacks—though not without costly struggles. As a result of this stalemate, old-line party organizations, and the elites who had joined in the attack on them, have found it useful to come to terms with one another. A major result of this pattern of party development in the nineteenth century and the subsequent accommodations between machine politicians and their erstwhile opponents in this century is that old-line party organizations have been strong enough to withstand the efforts of a succession of ideological movements to penetrate the political arena. This, in turn, has helped reduce polarization and lower the intensity of political conflicts.

Cities and states in the West followed a very different trajectory of party development by virtue of that region's peripheral position in the political system and economic order of late nineteenth century America. Because the national parties did not divide on issues of primary concern to the West and because railroads played such an important role in the political and economic life of that region, politicians and their elite allies did not have an incentive to respond to the challenges they faced by seeking to strengthen the organization or the popular base of the Democratic and Republican parties. Therefore the Progressives were able to overwhelm the railroad machines, uproot the patronage system, and destroy whatever semblance of party organization had existed in the West by mobilizing into the electorate voters who had not previously participated in politics and who therefore had no attachments to the institutions and practices of the nineteenth century political order.

A major consequence of the weakness of party organizations in the West in the late nineteenth century, and their even greater weakness during the twentieth century, is that the intensity of political conflict has often been higher in that region than in the East. Thus, during the late nineteenth and early twentieth centuries, western farmers and laborers were considerably more prone than their eastern counterparts to desert to politically oriented—and often quite radical—farmer and labor movements. In particular, the Farmers Alliance, the Populist Party, and the Socialist Party were substantially stronger in the West than in the East. And in more recent years, the relatively weak party organizations of the West have been far more vulnerable than those in the East to being taken over by political movements or the supporters of candidates on the left of the political spectrum, in the case of the Democrats, and on the right, in the case of the Republicans.[55] Consequently the level of polarization between the parties characteristically is higher in the western than in the eastern states.

The conclusion I would draw from these contrasting regional patterns is that strong, broadly based, patronage-fueled party organizations—such as those constructed in the Northeast as a consequence of the post-Reconstruction political settlement—can create a stable political order that is routinely amenable to the influence of elites, more reliably than a regime that does not encourage the great mass of citizens to direct their political energies through established party channels and into electoral politics. This is because the very process of channelling political participation through established institutions and into the electoral arena contains participation and limits its disruptive effects.[56]

Methodological Appendix

THE HYPOTHESES in this chapter can be tested by using ecological regression to estimate with county level data the cell entries in an inter-election transition matrix of the form illustrated in Table 5.A.[57] Before explaining the procedures that were employed to determine the sources from which the Progressives in the largest western and eastern states drew their votes, it would be useful to explain the notation and define the variables that will be used in this analysis. Let:

t and $t-1$	respectively represent an election and the one immediately preceding it;
E^t	represent the number of persons eligible to vote in election t;
A^t and A^{t-1}	respectively represent the number of abstainers in elections t and $t-1$, that is, the number of persons eligible to vote in the election in question who fail to do so;
N^{t-1}	represent the number of persons eligible to vote in election t, but not eligible to vote in election $t-1$;
J and I	respectively represent the number of parties presenting candidates in elections t and $t-1$;
$j = 1, \ldots, J, A^t$	index the alternatives available to persons eligible to vote in election t;
$i = 1, \ldots, I,$ A^{t-1}, N^{t-1}	index the positions these same persons could have occupied in election $t-1$;
V_j^t and V_i^{t-1}	respectively represent the (raw) vote cast for party j in election t, and for party i in election $t-1$;
b_{ij}	represents the proportion of those occupying position i in election $t-1$ who then moved to alternative j in election t.

It is important to note that because this analysis seeks to determine the role the electoral mobilization, participation, and abstention played in the victories of Progressive candidates, the population of concern to it is the total _eligible electorate_ in the year the Progressives came to power, not merely those persons who actually did vote. The column headings in Figure 5.A represent all the alternatives open to eligible voters in that election, election t: they could vote for any of the parties presenting candidates that year, or they could abstain. The column marginals indicate the total vote

TABLE 5.A
Inter-Election Transition Matrix

| | Election t | | | |
	Party$_1$ ...	Party$_J$	Abstainers	Row Marginals
Election t − 1				
Party$_1$	b_{11}	b_{1J}	b_{1A}	V_1^{t-1}
Party$_2$	b_{21}	b_{2J}	b_{2A}	V_2^{t-1}
.				
.				
.				
Party$_1$	b_{I1}	b_{IJ}	b_{IA}	V_I^{t-1}
Abstainers	b_{A1}	b_{AJ}	b_{AA}	A^{t-1}
Not Yet Eligible	b_{N1}	b_{NJ}	b_{NA}	N^{t-1}
Column Marginals	V_1^t	V_J^t	A^t	E^t

received by each of these parties $(V_1^t, \ldots, V_J^t)$ and by the Party of Abstainers (A^t). Because these exhaust the alternatives open to persons eligible to vote in that election, the sum of the column marginals equals the size of the eligible electorate that year (E^t).

The rows of the matrix indicate all the sources from which the parties in election t could possibly have obtained their votes. Phrased differently, the rows provide an exhaustive listing of all the positions the members of E^t might have occupied during the previous election, t − 1: in that election they either had voted for one of the parties presenting candidates that year $(V_1^{t-1}, V_2^{t-1}, \ldots, V_I^{t-1})$; they failed to vote though eligible to do so (A^{t-1}); or they were by virtue of age, residence, citizenship, or sex, not eligible to vote in election t − 1 (N^{t-1}), though they were to become eligible in election t. The row marginals indicate the total number of persons in each of these categories, and their sum is equal to the sum of the column marginals (E^t).[58]

The cell entries (b_{ij}) in the matrix represent the transition probabilities or proportions moving from each row position to each column position. For example, b_{11} denotes the proportion of those who had voted for party$_1$ in election t − 1 who again voted for party$_1$ in election t: b_{21} denoted the proportion of those voting for party$_2$ in election t − 1 who then voted for party$_1$ in election t, and so forth.

The total number of votes received by any party in election t is equal to the sum of the number of persons who moved from each of the row positions into that party's column. And each of these subquantities is equal in turn to the following product: (a) the transition rate from that row position to the column position in question; multiplied by (b) the total number of persons occupying that row position. Proceeding in this way down a column, it is evident that

$$V_j^t = \sum_{i=1}^{I} b_{ij} V_i^{t-1} + b_{aj}A^{t-1} + b_{nj}N^{t-1} + e$$

where e denotes an error term.

The coefficients in this equation can be estimated by least-squares regression with counties as the unit of analysis. The data can be normalized by dividing all the variables by the number of persons in the county eligible to vote in election t—not, it should be emphasized, by the number of persons who actually did vote in either election or election t − 1.

There is one further complication. Because every member of E^t necessarily occupies one of the row positions in the matrix above, the full set of independent variables in the regression equation are linearly dependent (that is, if each row marginal is divided by E^t and the resulting quantities are summed, that sum necessarily is 1.0). Consequently, one of these explanatory variables must be omitted if the equation is to be estimated. Consideration of substantive meaning as well as technical considerations (namely, minimizing multicollinearity among the independent variables) point to the omission of A^{t-1}. This yields the following regression equation:

$$\frac{V_j^t}{E^t} = a_j + \sum_{i=1}^{I} b_{ij}\frac{V_i^{t-1}}{E^t} + b_{nj}\frac{N_i^{t-1}}{E^t} + e$$

The omission of A^{t-1} from the above equation entails no loss of information, because its coefficient is estimated by the constant term a_j. This procedure does however, alter the meaning of the regression coefficients. It transforms b_{21}, for example, into an estimate of the *difference* between the proportion of those voting for party$_2$ and those abstaining in election t − 1 who then vote for party$_1$ in election t. An estimate of the proportion of those voting for party$_2$ in election t − 1 and for party$_1$ in election t can be obtained simply by adding the constant term a_j to b_{21}. In the general case, if p_{ij} denotes the transition rate from party$_i$ in election t − 1 to party$_j$ in election t, then

$$p_{ij} = a_j + b_{ij}$$

In addition to these transition rates, it is useful to know what proportion of the total vote received by the various parties in election t comes from persons who had occupied each of the row positions in election t − 1. This is obtained by multiplying the transition rates p_{ij} by the raw votes received by each "party" in election t − 1 (including, as usual, the Party of Abstainers and Party of Not-Yet-Eligibles) to arrive at an estimate of the number of voters who moved from each row position to each column in election t. The proportion of party$_j$'s support in election t coming from row position i in election t − 1 can be denoted q_{ij}, and is calculated by dividing the product $p_{ij}V_i^{t-1}$ by the total vote party$_j$ received in election t:

$$q_{ij} = \frac{p_{ij}V_i^{t-1}}{V_j^t}$$

_____ **Part III** _____

POLITICAL PARTIES AND
POLITICAL CONTROL

CHAPTER 6

Political Incorporation and Political Extrusion:
Party Politics and Social Forces in
Postwar New York

THE MOVEMENT of new social forces into the political system is one of the central themes in the study of American political development on both the national and local levels. For example, Samuel P. Huntington has characterized the realignment of 1800 as marking "the ascendancy of the agrarian Republicans over the mercantile Federalists, 1860 the ascendancy of the industrializing North over the plantation South, and 1932 the ascendancy of the urban working class over the previously dominant business groups."[1] And the process of ethnic succession—the coming to power of Irish and German immigrants, followed by the Italians and Jews, and then by blacks and Hispanics—is a major focus of most analyses of the development of American urban politics.

Most accounts of political incorporation, however, are based on an analysis of only one face of a two-sided process. The process through which new social forces gain a secure position in American politics is simultaneously a process of political exclusion. This process involves not simply a conflict between the new group and established forces over whether or not the newcomers will gain representation, but also a struggle over precisely who will assume leadership of the previously excluded group. Established political forces are not indifferent to the outcome of these leadership struggles, and the defeat of potential leaders who are regarded as unacceptable by established forces is the price that emergent groups must pay to gain access to power.

After discussing the linkages among political incorporation, political realignments, and political exclusion, the sections below provide evidence for this argument by analyzing the process through which—and the terms upon which—Jews, Italians, and blacks gained a secure position for themselves in New York City politics in the 1940s and 1950s. To be sure, the incorporation of these groups occurred under conditions—a Cold War abroad and McCarthyism at home—that scarcely were typical in the history of American urban politics. The extrusion of ideologically unacceptable contenders for the leadership of previously excluded groups, however, is a characteristic aspect of the process of political incorporation in American cities.[2] It is instructive that in the nation's largest city during the McCarthy era this extrusion was accomplished in the main not through legislative hearings and blacklists but rather through the normal institutions of party politics. The experience of New York during the postwar period thus reveals how these institutions are able to maintain themselves in the face of major social changes and political turmoil.

POLITICAL INCORPORATION, CRITICAL REALIGNMENTS, AND POLITICAL EXTRUSION

The phenomenon of political incorporation is more complex than is commonly recognized. In the first place, social forces are never entirely homogeneous, and a group may be incorporated into the political system on terms that are of greater advantage to some of its members than others. For example, the agrarian interests represented by the Republican party of the 1790s were comprised of both subsistence and commercial farmers. Broadly speaking, the radical or Old Republican wing of the party spoke for subsistence farmers, who generally opposed the commercialization of American society and who were radically democratic in their politics. The Republican party's moderate wing, on the other hand, spoke for commercial farmers who favored the building of a commercial society in the United States and the creation of a government that, in Richard Ellis's words, would be "responsible to but not directly and immediately controlled by the people." It was under the leadership of the moderate Republicans—most importantly, Jefferson and Madison—that agrarian interests were incorporated into American politics in 1800. In office, the Republicans did not undertake to democratize the Constitution or dismantle the national government (as the party's radicals wanted), and they embarked upon an ambitious program of commercial development—rechartering the Bank of the United States, proposing an extensive program of internal improvements, and ultimately enacting a protective tariff. Indeed, by favoring commercial over subsistence elements of the agrarian sector, the Jeffersonian Republicans laid the groundwork for the Jacksonian Revolution of the 1820s.[3]

In addition, there is a wide variety of ways in which a social group—even a relatively homogeneous group—can gain representation in politics. Hanna Pitkin, for one, has distinguished among four forms or modes of representation: formal, descriptive, symbolic, and substantive.[4] For example, blacks have been represented at various times and places by gaining the right to vote, the appointment and/or election of black representatives to public office, public recognition of the contributions blacks have made to the nation's life, and the enactment of policies that serve the interests of racial minorities. But even Pitkin's fourfold schema understates the full range of possibilities, because there are various ways in which the substantive interests of a group can be understood and advanced. Thus at different times and places, serving the interests of blacks in local politics has been understood to mean the protection of civil rights, the provision of social welfare benefits, and both less intrusive and more aggressive patrolling by the police in black neighborhoods.

Finally, a previously excluded group may—or may not—be able to achieve a secure claim on the political benefits its members receive. Again, blacks provide the clearest example. Although freedmen in the South gained a number of civil and political rights during Reconstruction, the political coalitions of which they were a part fell from power on both the national and state levels in the 1870s. In subsequent decades, blacks were driven from politics and deprived of many of the rights they formerly had been granted. This suggests that it is useful to distinguish between a group's gaining *representation* and its achieving full *incorporation* into politics, according to whether the group's newly won position in the political system is secure or insecure.

Not only is the phenomenon of political incorporation more complex than is often recognized, so too is the process through which it occurs. Bringing a new group into the political system has the potential of disrupting established patterns of political precedence and public policy. Consequently, the politicians who benefit most from those patterns are not likely to sponsor the incorporation of new groups. Political outsiders, on the other hand— counterelites, insurgents, reformers—have less to lose by bringing new groups into politics.

Such counterelites are most likely to encourage the entry of new groups into politics during periods of political crisis, because their entry at such a time can contribute to the toppling of the existing regime. Moreover, it is at times of crisis that the members of excluded groups are most likely to mobilize politically, because during such periods the incumbent regime no longer appears beyond challenge or change. For these reasons the process of incorporating new groups into American politics has been closely linked to the nation's periodic episodes of political upheaval and realignment.

Political mobilization that occurs at times of crisis, and often outside established institutional channels, is not readily controlled.[5] It provides numerous contenders for the leadership of the excluded group—party politicians, social movement leaders, radical ideologues, religious and communal leaders—with the opportunity to seek dominance. These contenders may have substantially different views of where the true interests of the group lie.

Actors in the broader political system who seek to put together a majority coalition are not indifferent to the outcome of such leadership struggles within the previously excluded group. They have an interest in the defeat of those contenders whose behavior or views are inconsistent with the principles around which they are seeking to forge a majority coalition, and in the triumph of those contenders whom they and their allies would find most acceptable as coalition partners. To help bring this about, they may join with "responsible" contenders for the leadership of the new social force in a campaign to expel from the political system contenders whom they regard as irresponsible, demagogic, or un-American.

In other words, the process of political incorporation is at one and the same time a process of political exclusion. Just as the Old Republicans were defeated and the Democratic-Republican societies disbanded after 1800, so too were the Workingmen's parties and the Radical Republicans after the realignments of the 1820s and the 1860s, the Populists after 1896, and the Henry Wallace Progressives after the realignment of the 1930s.

Similar processes occur in American local politics. Although the urban machine has been depicted as a marvelously efficient engine for bringing successive waves of immigrants into city politics, it is not a mechanism that functions automatically or smoothly. In cities, as on the national level, only major crises can convince established politicians to sponsor the entry of new ethnic groups into politics. And in the local as well as the national arena, the process of political incorporation has been closely linked to a process of political extrusion. The experience of Jews, Italians, and blacks in New York City in the 1930s, 1940s, and 1950s stands as a case in point.

TAMMANY HALL AND THE NEW IMMIGRANTS

During the first third of the twentieth century, New York's Democratic county machines were the most powerful political organizations in the city.[6] Candidates backed by the Democratic county organizations won eight of the ten elections for mayor between 1900 and 1932, as well as the overwhelming majority of other elective offices in the city—comptroller, president of the board of aldermen, members of the city's delegation to the state legislature, and so forth.

The power of the machine contributed, in turn, to the political strength of the Irish, who were the dominant group within Tammany and its sister Democratic organizations.[7] In 1929 at least twenty-five of Tammany's thirty-four district leaders were Irish.[8] The Irish also occupied a disproportionate number of public offices. During the 1920s, Irishmen occupied at least one, and usually two, of the three municipal offices with citywide constituencies (mayor, comptroller, and president of the board of aldermen), and between 35 and 50 percent of the seats on the board of aldermen and the city's delegation to the state assembly.[9] Yet during this period the Irish comprised no more than 15 percent of the city's population.

Conversely, prior to 1933 the Italians, and to a lesser extent the Jews, did not receive their proportionate share of the benefits of New York City politics. During the 1920s these groups constituted respectively 14 percent and 29 percent of New York's population, yet in 1921 only 3 percent of the city's aldermen and assemblymen were Italian and only 15 percent were Jewish. Italians and Jews were also underrepresented in top appointive and party offices. During the 1920s fewer than 10 percent of the city's cabinet-level appointees were Jews and fewer than 3 percent were Italian. And in 1929 only four of Tammany's thirty-four district leaders were Jewish and only one was Italian.[10]

In the domain of political ideology and public policy Tammany in particular also failed to represent important segments of Jewish and Italian opinion in New York. When Al Smith was governor in the 1920s liberals enjoyed access to the machine through him. But after a faction at odds with Smith took control of Tammany in 1929, this source of access closed. In the early 1930s, the dominant faction in Tammany—and also in the Brooklyn machine—strongly opposed Franklin Roosevelt and the New Deal, despite his enormous popularity among Jewish and Italian, as well as many other, New Yorkers. (However, the Democratic leader of the Bronx, Ed Flynn, was a close ally of Roosevelt.)

Prior to 1933 the Republicans made only limited efforts to exploit the potential for mobilizing support against the machine that this underrepresentation created. In 1913 the Republicans did join forces with reformers and nominate a Jew for the borough presidency of Manhattan. Also, in 1919, when it appeared that many ethnic voters might abandon the Democrats because of unhappiness with the peace treaties negotiated by Woodrow Wilson, the Republicans nominated the city's most prominent Italian-American politician, Congressman Fiorello La Guardia, for president of the board of aldermen. And in 1929 the Republicans nominated La Guardia for mayor, although this was of limited significance because there was absolutely no chance that the enormously popular incumbent, Jimmy Walker, could be defeated at the time. Even so, the city's three leading Republican newspapers, which regarded La Guardia's record in Congress as too radical, refused to endorse the GOP mayoral candidate until a few days before the election. (The city's leading reform organization, the Citizens Union, also refused to endorse La Guardia.) A series of scandals compelled Walker to resign in 1932, and in the special election that year to replace him, the GOP returned to its practice of nominating white Anglo-Saxon Protestants for mayor.

REFORM AND MOBILIZATION

The year 1933 witnessed efforts to organize another of New York's periodic coalitions—or "fusion" movements—among Republicans, reformers, and other opponents of the Tammany machine. La Guardia announced his interest in receiving the fusion mayoral nomination that year, as well as his intention of running as an independent if he was not designated as the candidate of the fusion forces. The question confronting the machine's opponents was whether to select a candidate from among the groups that traditionally provided fusion movements with the bulk of their support—business interests and middle-class WASPs—or to bring new voters into politics under the banner of reform. For a variety of reasons, in 1933 many of Tammany's opponents were prepared to strike out in new directions and thus to consider nominating a candidate such as La Guardia.

In the first place, with Franklin Roosevelt's accession to the presidency in 1933, the Republicans were deprived of access to government at the federal, state, and local levels. Moreover, Roosevelt's extraordinary popularity suggested that the GOP might remain politically isolated for years to come. Consequently, the leaders of the GOP were prepared to go to unusual lengths to reverse their party's fortunes in New York City. In addition, with Roosevelt safely in the White House, many of his political allies in New York were willing to break openly with Tammany and support a mayoral candidate friendly to the president. Some of these New Dealers—chiefly, liberal intellectuals—advocated the nomination and election of La Guardia. Others refused to endorse a Republican, and backed the candidacy of Joseph McKee, a member of Ed Flynn's Bronx Democratic organization. McKee's candidacy divided the Democratic vote and facilitated the election of a fusion mayor.[11] Finally, many reform elites also were prepared to take a leap in the dark in 1933 and back a mayoral candidate whom the Citizens Union had labeled a demagogue only four years earlier. A major reason for this was their fear of disorder as the city slid deeper into the Depression. Reformers argued that corruption by public officials led ordinary citizens to lose respect for the law, and as lawlessness increased in the 1930s they were prepared to go to unusual lengths, and appeal for new sources of support, in an effort to drive corrupt machine politicians from power.[12]

In an effort to win new votes for their cause, the fusion forces in 1933 selected the first ethnically balanced ticket in the city's history. It included not only La Guardia but also the first Jew to be nominated for citywide office by a major party in Greater New York. In addition, La Guardia appealed for Jewish votes by addressing Jewish audiences in Yiddish and by charging that a magazine article written fifteen years earlier by McKee was anti-Semitic.

The estimates of ethnic voting behavior reported in Table 6.1 indicate that fusion efforts to win the support of Italian and Jewish voters in 1933 were fairly successful.[13] Relative to the mayoral election of 1925, the vote for the Republican candidate in neighborhoods inhabited by foreign-born Italians jumped from 24.6 percent to 69.4 percent. In neighborhoods inhabited by foreign-born Jews, the effect of the La Guardia candidacy was more modest,

TABLE 6.1
Ethnic Voting for New York City Republican Mayoral
Candidates, 1925 and 1933

	Waterman	La Guardia
Native-born of native parentage	66.4%	54.7%
Native-born of foreign parentage	30.2	42.6
Foreign-born		
Italian	24.6	69.4
Jewish	36.6	41.6
Irish	3.5	6.7
German	42.6	27.1
Other	64.1	56.2

Sources: New York City Board of Elections, Annual Report, 1925,
1933; U.S. Bureau of the Census, Fourteenth Census of the United
States, vol. 3 (Washington, D.C.; Government Printing Office, 1922),
679.

but nonetheless significant—increasing the vote for the GOP candidate
from 36.6 to 41.6 percent. Along with increases in the Republican vote in
neighborhoods inhabited by second-generation Americans, this more than
compensated for Republican losses among the native-born of native parentage, the Germans, and a residual category of foreign-born (a majority of
whom were from northern Europe).

After entering City Hall, La Guardia undertook to solidify his base of
support within the city's Jewish and Italian communities. He expanded social programs, encouraged union organization, and doubled the number of
Jews and Italians occupying major appointive offices in city government.[14]
La Guardia's efforts were extremely successful, and they provided one of the
motives for the organization of the American Labor Party (ALP).

The ALP was organized in 1936 by leaders of the Congress of Industrial
Organizations (CIO)—especially in the heavily Jewish garment trades—to
provide a mechanism for supporting Franklin Roosevelt and Fiorello La
Guardia while keeping distance from Tammany and the city's other Democratic machines.[15] It sought to play balance-of-power politics. For the most
part, the ALP endorsed candidates nominated by the major parties (rather
than nominating candidates of its own), thereby compelling the Republicans
and Democrats, as they selected their own candidates, to take account of the
Labor party's likely reaction. In the late 1930s and early 1940s the party was
very successful. The ALP provided La Guardia with more than one-third of
his votes—and his margins of victory—in his campaigns for a second and
third term in 1937 and 1941.

Confronted with such a successful challenge, the Democrats were compelled to respond. The party sought to regain majority status by, first of all,

nominating an increasing number of Jews and Italians for public office—
a trend that culminated in its first ethnically balanced ticket (including an
Irishman, Italian, and Jew for three top citywide offices) in 1945. In addition, Democratic machine politicians made peace with the New Deal. In
1937 Tammany did back an anti-Roosevelt candidate in the Democratic
mayoral primary, but in 1941 and 1945 it joined with the other county Democratic organizations in support of a New Deal liberal, William O'Dwyer, for
mayor. The Democrats also nominated candidates jointly with the ALP. Indeed, they continued to do so for a period even after the ALP's left-wing
faction (in which Communists and fellow travelers were influential) gained
control of the party in 1944, and the ALP's moderates bolted and organized
the Liberal party. In particular, during the 1945 municipal elections the
Democrats and the ALP united behind the slate headed by William
O'Dwyer, while the Republicans united with the Liberals behind a competing ticket. The Democratic/ALP slate then scored a solid victory.

After regaining control of City Hall in 1945, the Democrats sought to put
an end to the political uncertainty and upheaval of the 1930s and early 1940s
and to stabilize their rule. There were four interrelated aspects to this endeavor. First, the leaders of the Democratic party entered into a series of
collusive relationships with their GOP counterparts. Second, as the Cold
War intensified and the costs of tolerating Communists and fellow travelers
increased, the Democrats and Republicans undertook to isolate politically
and destroy the city's Communist party and the ALP. Third, top Democrats
in the city undertook to purge from the system machine politicians who
were closely allied with gangsters and who had gained influence within
Tammany in the 1930s and 1940s. Fourth, the Democrats during the 1940s
and 1950s sought to work out a relationship with the city's growing black
population that would win the votes of racial minorities without alienating
whites in the process.

MAJOR PARTY COLLUSION

During the late 1940s and the early 1950s the leaders of New York's regular
Democratic and Republican party organizations established a modus vivendi with one another. This major party détente took a number of forms.
First, the Democrats and Republicans sponsored changes in the rules of
electoral combat that were beneficial to the leadership of the two major
parties. Second, the Democrats provided the Republicans with patronage—
in exchange, essentially, for agreeing not to contest seriously Democratic
control of the municipal government. Third, and finally, as Figure 6.1 indicates, a remarkable pattern of joint nominations by the Democrats and Re-

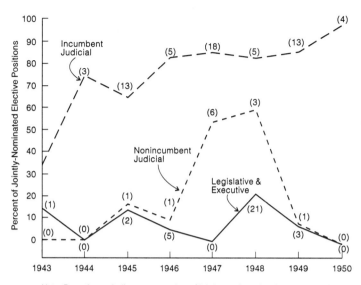

Note: Parentheses indicate raw number of jointly-nominated major party candidates

FIGURE 6.1 Major Party Collusion in New York City: Elective Positions for Which Democrats and Republicans Nominated a Common Candidate, 1943–1950 (*Source*: New York City Board of Elections, *Annual Report*, 1943–50)

publicans developed in the 1940s. The major parties jointly nominated a common candidate in an ever-increasing proportion of elections involving incumbent judges in the 1940s. In judicial elections involving nonincumbents, and in elections for legislative and executive positions, joint nominations increased significantly in the mid-1940s, and then declined.

Why did the Republicans and Democrats forgo opportunities to compete, and instead come to terms with one another in these ways? In answering this question it is useful to discuss first the purposes or ends the major parties achieved through collusion, and then to consider why they pursued these goals through collusion more in the period following the Democratic recapture of City Hall in 1945 than they had during the previous dozen years.

The first goal that the Democrats and Republicans sought to achieve through bipartisan collusion was to isolate and destroy the ALP and the city's Communist party. The most important changes in election law they sponsored in the late 1940s were the Wilson-Pakula law, which, as will be described below, worked to the disadvantage of the ALP, and the repeal of proportional representation (PR) in elections for the New York city council, which was justified as a way of eliminating Communist representation on the council. (One Communist had been elected to the twenty-three-member city council in 1941 and a second was elected in 1945.) In addition, many of the bipartisan nominations of the Democrats and Republicans were directed against candidates of the ALP or the Communist party.

A second reason why the leaders of New York City's major parties colluded with one another was to enhance organizational control over the nominating process and over the behavior of public officials. Although the election of Communists to the city council was the major argument used by Democratic and Republican leaders in the successful 1947 campaign against PR, this was not their only motive in opposing it. They had fought against PR since it had been proposed in 1936, five years before a Communist was first elected to the council. Their strongest objection to PR was that it weakened their ability to dominate the nomination and election of councilmen: candidates who established an independent name for themselves had a clear electoral advantage over other members of their party; such candidates had a great deal of leverage in seeking a major party nomination, and to the extent that they were not beholden to the organization for their nomination or election, they did not have to pay heed to its leaders once they were in office. An indication of the lengths to which the Republican leadership was prepared to go to reassert organizational control over city councilmen is that they supported a return to plurality elections in single-member constituencies even though this drastically (and predictably) reduced Republican representation on the council from four of the twenty-three seats in 1945 to one of twenty-five in 1949. Evidently, Republican leaders attached limited value to the election of councilmen who, though nominal members of the party, were not beholden to them.

The desire of the leaders of the major party organizations to preserve their control of the nominating process was also one of the motives behind many of the joint Democratic-Republican nominations of the post-war era. It is significant that the most comprehensive of these bipartisan cartels—a joint Democratic-Republican ticket in the 1948 state legislative elections in the Bronx—was arranged by Ed Flynn, who ran the most tightly centralized county party organization in New York City. Flynn wanted to destroy the ALP not solely—or even primarily—for ideological reasons but because it presented a threat to discipline within his machine. In districts where the ALP held the balance of power, a candidate who might secure that party's endorsement had a great advantage in obtaining a major party nomination, and if he could bring Labor party votes to a joint ticket he was in that measure not beholden to the regular party organization for his victory. Moreover, once in office such a legislator had to pay heed to the wishes of the ALP's leaders if he wanted to obtain the Labor party's nomination again. To Flynn such divided loyalties were intolerable, and therefore he arranged a bipartisan cartel with his Republican counterpart in 1948. This purge of all Bronx assemblymen and senators with ALP connections was successful, and once it was completed Flynn thereafter presented the voters of his borough with straight Democratic tickets, eschewing alliances even with the pro–Fair Deal Liberal party. In a slightly different vein, the major parties in Brooklyn united behind a common candidate for borough president in 1953 because the Liberals fielded a candidate that year who appeared to be strong enough to win a plurality in a divided field. The Democrats and Republicans joined forces not so much to preserve internal discipline as to protect major party dominance of the electoral arena in their borough.

The final incentive for bipartisan collusion was that it enabled the leaders of the regular Republican organization to buttress their position within the GOP, and it was a means by which the Democrats could ensure that the nominal opposition party in the city would be controlled by leaders more interested in reconciling themselves to the Democratic party's hegemony than challenging it. Generally speaking, within the Republican party collusion with the Democrats was supported most strongly by the leaders of the county organization and opposed most vigorously by the rank-and-file (especially in districts where the GOP was strongest), who regarded it as collaborating with the enemy. By cooperating with the Democrats, Republican county leaders could gain control of patronage that could be used to reward subordinate politicians who were loyal to them, thereby solidifying their leadership positions.[16] The Democrats, for their part, had every incentive to strengthen the position within the GOP of leaders who were prepared to collaborate with them. The Bronx, whose party organization was the strongest in the city, provides the most striking example. John Knewitz, who was elected Bronx Republican leader in 1913, was appointed as commissioner of records in the Surrogate's Court by the Democrats in 1918 and retained this appointment throughout Ed Flynn's tenure (1922–53) as Bronx Democratic leader. Flynn and his successor, Charles Buckley, also took care of lesser members of the Bronx Republican organization, and this enabled Knewitz to hold on to his county leadership until his death in 1957—a period of forty-four years. In return Knewitz cooperated closely with Flynn and Buckley.[17]

In a similar fashion, Manhattan Republican leader Tom Curran found cooperation with the Democrats useful for maintaining control over his organization. Curran became county leader in 1941, and in that year he agreed to the first of what was to become nine consecutive multiparty endorsements of Frank Hogan, a nominal Democrat, for district attorney. Two years later he negotiated the first in a series of bipartisan nominations for nonincumbent judges. In 1945 Curran refused to back La Guardia for the Republican mayoral nomination, and even went so far as to propose that the Republicans and Democrats join behind a common candidate to defeat any bid La Guardia might make for a fourth term or any candidate La Guardia might designate as his successor. That year Curran endorsed Jonah Goldstein, a Tammany Democrat, as the Republican nominee for mayor in the hope that the

Democrats might join forces with the Republicans if the joint ticket was headed by a member of their party. Manhattan Republicans got a reasonable amount of patronage from the Democrats in return for this cooperation, and this contributed to Curran's being able to retain his position until his death in 1959, twenty-eight years after becoming county leader.

Although the leaders of the regular Republican and Democratic party organizations in New York found bipartisan collusion advantageous for these reasons, they had not pursued this course of action as extensively in the 1930s and early 1940s as they did in the mid-1940s and early 1950s. What accounts for this change?

There are two conditions under which party leaders are especially likely to collude with one another, and both increasingly came to characterize New York politics during the postwar years.[18] The first obtains when joint action will enable the leaders of the major parties to stave off a common threat or achieve a common gain. The various steps the Democrats and Republicans took to crush the ALP and the Communists fall in this category. These splinter parties were no stronger when the Democrats and Republicans began a concerted drive to isolate and destroy them than they had been a few years earlier, but the onset of the Cold War increased the costs of cooperating with them and provided the major parties with a pretext for taking steps (for example, the abolition of proportional representation) to tighten their control over nominations and elections.

The second condition under which major parties are likely to collude obtains when each is in a position to impose costs or confer benefits upon the other. Such a state of affairs exists most clearly when the different levels of government are controlled by different parties, because each party then commands authority that can be used for bargaining purposes. This situation prevailed in New York beginning in 1945.[19] The Republicans had gained control of the governorship and the state legislature in 1943—a hammerlock on the state government they retained for all but four of the next twenty-two years—and in 1945 the Democrats gained control of the mayoralty and Board of Estimate, and they held on to them for the next twenty years.

This set the stage for many of the collusive arrangements discussed above. Control over the state government made it possible for the Republicans to pass or kill bills of vital interest to Democratic politicians and public officials in New York—in particular, legislation establishing the boundaries of congressional and state senatorial districts, amending the election law, and creating new judgeships. It also enabled the Republicans to conduct investigations of the city government. In a similar vein, control of the White House in the 1950s gave Republicans the opportunity to appoint U.S. Attorneys who could investigate corruption in New York City. Control over the mayoralty and the other institutions of municipal government gave Democrats, in turn, the power to grant patronage and favors to the Republicans.

Neither party, however, exploited these powers as much as it could have to injure the other; rather, divided control of the institutions of government became the basis for mutually beneficial transactions between the Republicans and Democrats. For example, in 1954 the legislature reapportioned state senatorial districts on Manhattan's West Side in a way that suited the Democrats, in return for the city council's redrawing assembly district lines so as to provide the Republicans with two reasonably secure seats on the East Side. Two years later the legislature created several new Supreme Court judgeships in New York City in exchange for a promise of Democratic endorsement of Republican candidates for some of these positions.

One other form of bipartisan comity following the Republican accession to power in Albany is worth mentioning at this point. Although in 1943 a wiretap on the telephone of New York's leading gangster, Frank Costello, indicated that Costello exercised considerable influence in Tammany, an investigation of ties between gangsters and politicians in New York was not initiated until 1951, the year that a committee of the U.S. Senate chaired by Estes Kefauver conducted televised hearings that gave sensational publicity to this state of affairs. The investigating committee appointed by Governor Dewey, the Proskauer Commission, did hold one set of hearings in 1952 to look into the matter, but then it turned its attention to other issues, in particular, labor racketeering on the New York waterfront.

To account for these various forms of bipartisan collusion and comity it is not necessary to suppose that they were all part of some grand concordat arranged through explicit negotiations between the two parties. Some of the agreements described above were arrived at through such negotiations, and in these cases Republican control of the state government and Democratic dominance in the municipal arena provided each party with bargaining counters. But in other instances the following process appears to have been at work: as the Democrats consolidated their hold over New York City's government in the 1940s, GOP politicians reconciled themselves to Democratic control of City Hall. The Democrats had every incentive to encourage the Republicans to accept this state of affairs by giving them some patronage, and the Republicans, so as not to upset this modus vivendi, were disinclined to make use of their control of the state government in Albany to threaten the Democratic hegemony in city politics.

MINOR PARTIES

During the late 1940s and the 1950s Democratic machine politicians in New York undertook to establish a mutually beneficial relationship not only with their Republican counterparts but also with the Liberal party. By establishing such a relationship they sought to win the support of left-of-center Jewish voters. In appealing for this support, however, Democratic leaders did not want to alienate other elements of their party's constituency. Consequently, as the Cold War intensified, they undertook to isolate and destroy the American Labor party as well as the city's Communist party (CP).

This endeavor was remarkably successful.[20] In the 1945 mayoral election 122,316 votes had been cast on the Liberal line and the party had been allied with the Republicans. By the 1953 mayoral election the Liberal vote almost quadrupled (to 467,104) and the party was on the verge of a standing alliance with the Democrats in city politics. On the other hand, the ALP went from 257,929 votes and an alliance with the Democrats in 1945 to fewer than one-fourth as many votes (53,045) and political isolation in 1953—and to extinction before the next municipal election. The Labor party suffered this fate, moreover, even though in the 1930s and 1940s it had commanded the loyalty of thousands of dedicated and hardworking activists, many of whom engaged in union and community organizing as well as electoral canvassing.

Despite this extensive support and the dedication of its cadres, the ALP was destroyed with a combination of the stick and the carrot.[21] The major parties made it increasingly difficult for New Yorkers to participate effectively in city politics through the Labor party. At the same time, the members of ethnic groups that had supported the ALP were encouraged to participate through channels (such as the Liberal party) and in ways (primarily voting) more acceptable to established forces in the city.

The Liberal Party and the American Labor Party

There were three differences between the Liberal party and the ALP that made the major parties far more willing to tolerate the former than the latter. The first of these was ideological. The ideology of the Liberal party was what its name indicated, and the best way to understand what it meant to call oneself "liberal" (as opposed to "progressive") when the party was founded in 1944 is to note that the issue that led it to split off from the ALP was anti-Communism. David Dubinsky, president of the International Ladies Garment Workers Union (ILGWU), and Alex Rose, president of the Hat, Cap, and Milliners Union, walked out of the ALP when the primary elections to select members of its state committee were won by the party's left-wing faction. The faction was composed of Communists, fellow travelers, and supporters of the New Deal who were not so implacably hostile to the Communist party that they were unwilling to cooperate with it for the sake of helping Roosevelt to win a fourth term and his supporters to win elections to other offices.[22] Though they comprised but a minority of the ALP's members, Communists and their closest sympathizers exercised substantial influence over party policy, especially after the death in 1946 of

Sidney Hillman (the one major garment trades union leader who remained in the ALP when Dubinsky and Rose bolted) and the departure of Hillman's union, the Amalgamated Clothing Workers, from the party in 1948.[23]

Another important difference between the Liberals and the ALP was organizational: the Liberals commanded a less extensive and less highly articulated organization than the Labor party. There were several components of the ALP's organization. First, the party had a network of local clubs through which it was able to mobilize thousands of enthusiastic party militants to work on neighborhood issues, as well as in primary and general election campaigns.[24] For example, in a congressional by-election in the Bronx in 1948, two thousand party workers canvassed on election day for the ALP candidate, Louis Isaacson, enabling him to win without a major party nomination in a district that normally gave overwhelming margins to the Democrats.[25] Second, the ALP had close ties to the unions affiliated with the CIO's Greater New York Industrial Council. By virtue of these ties the party was able to involve the shop stewards of CIO unions in its campaigns.[26] The third component of the ALP organization was the following that was brought into the party by Fiorello La Guardia's protégé, East Harlem congressman Vito Marcantonio.[27] Marcantonio's organization was bound together by a peculiar blend of machine politics and programmatic radicalism whose closest analogue in American history was probably the following assembled by Huey Long in Louisiana in the 1920s and 1930s.

In contrast to the ALP, the Liberals did not command a very extensive organization. True, the Liberal party had close ties with the ILGWU and the millinery union, but these unions supplied the party with money more than manpower. It is also true that the Jewish fraternal organization the Workmen's Circle was affiliated with the party and that New York's leading Yiddish newspaper, the *Jewish Daily Forward*, consistently supported it, but in the final analysis by far the most valuable resource controlled by the Liberal party was its line on the ballot. In bargaining with the major parties, the Liberals offered their candidates slots on its ballot line, not campaign workers.

Finally, there were significant differences between the ethnic composition of the two parties. The Liberal party was overwhelmingly Jewish. A number of WASP intellectuals and the president of an Italian local in the ILGWU occupied high offices in the Liberal state organization, but otherwise Jews dominated all levels of the party. The party was effectively controlled by David Dubinsky and Alex Rose, and the weight of Jews among those who voted for it is suggested by an extremely high correlation of .88 between the Liberal vote in the 1945 mayoral election and the Jewish population of the city's neighborhoods.[28]

The ALP was more ethnically heterogeneous than the Liberals. To be sure, there were more Jews at all levels of the party than members of any other ethnic group, but the ALP (and its close ally, the CP) did establish some beachheads within the city's Italian-American and black communities, and it even won a modicum of support among the New York Irish. As for the first of these ethnic groups, the two most prominent politicians who were members of the ALP, Mayor La Guardia and Congressman Vito Marcantonio, were Italian-Americans, and of the four Italians who served on the city council during the period (1937–49) when it was elected by proportional representation, one was a member of the ALP and the other, Peter V. Cacchione, was a member of the Communist party (the other two were Democrats). Maurice Isserman describes the ethnically heterogeneous character of Cacchione's political base as follows: "Jewish neighborhoods in Brooklyn were the strongest center of Communist popular support in the United States. Coney Island, Brighton Beach, Flatbush, Brownsville, East New York, Williamsburgh, as well as some Italian neighborhoods in Williamsburgh, Red Hook, Bay Ridge, and the Brooklyn waterfront, and pockets of strength in black and Irish areas formed a kind of Red belt that turned out, election after election, to back Cacchione."[29]

The extensive organizations commanded by the ALP and the CP help account for the ability of radical candidates to win the support of such an ethnically heterogeneous coalition. Marcantonio was able to turn out the members of his following in Democratic and Republican primaries, as well as in general elections, by relying in part upon the personal organization he constructed in his district and in part on an army of canvassers sent into his district by ALP clubs, the CIO Industrial Union Council, and the Communist party.[30] Similarly, the campaigns of Communist city councilman Peter Cacchione were models of electoral organization—so much so, indeed, that when the Board of Elections discovered a flaw in his election petitions in 1939 and denied him a place on the ballot, the Brooklyn branch of the Communist party organized an extraordinary write-in campaign on his behalf. Even discounting the hyperbole in the description of this campaign by his official biographer, it was quite impressive:

> Pete went on a whirlwind drive, speaking at 226 meetings, countless homes, and on at least a dozen radio stations. Meanwhile, he and his committee conducted an educational crusade on two points: where on the paper ballot to write in Pete's name, and—this was crucial—how to spell it. No method was overlooked. Youth supporters wore white jerseys with the boldly stencilled legend: PETER V. CACCHIONE.
>
> Two baseball teams toured park diamonds showing fans how to write in Peter's name. Shopping bags with Pete's name were distributed near supermarkets and literally hundreds of group sessions were held where spelling Pete's name was practiced. . . . [A supporter] wrote a special campaign song, which, amplified from sound-trucks, helped many a voter get the correct spelling. . . .

Outside the polls they distributed to the voters a last reminder in the form of instruction cards and pencils. Each pencil was inscribed in bold letters: PETER V. CACCHIONE.[31]

This effort did not quite suffice to overcome the handicap of his name not appearing on the ballot, but in the next three elections, when it did, Cacchione won a seat on the city council. In the last of these, the election of 1945, he won more votes than any other candidate from Brooklyn.

The extensive organizations commanded by the ALP and CP also provided them with links to New York's racial minorities. Marcantonio's personal organization linked the ALP to the Puerto Ricans and blacks in his district. And just as the two radical parties provided Marcantonio with campaign workers from elsewhere in the city to help him mobilize voters in East Harlem, so too did they provide such assistance to the politicians with whom they were allied in the black community of Central Harlem. The most prominent of these black politicians was Adam Clayton Powell, who constructed a personal following for himself that was akin to Marcantonio's, but who also found allying with the ALP and CP helpful in securing election to the city council and then the United States Congress. The other major figure in the politics of New York's black community who was supported by the city's radical parties was Benjamin Davis. Davis was a member of the national executive committee of the Communist party, and the support of the CP and ALP enabled him to secure election to the city council in 1943 (succeeding Powell, who left to run for Congress) and to win reelection in 1945.[32]

Finally, labor unions affiliated with the ALP and subject to the influence of the CP provided these radical parties with some links to Irish voters in the 1930s and 1940s. The two most important such unions were Mike Quill's Transport Workers Union and Joseph Curran's National Maritime Union. To be sure, the ALP and CP by no means threatened to displace the machine as the dominant political force in New York's Irish neighborhoods, but they were able to elect Quill to the city council from the Bronx three times between 1937 and 1945.[33]

These differences between the ALP and Liberals provided the city's highest elected officials and the top leaders of the Democratic and Republican parties with strong motives to destroy the Labor party. The campaign against the ALP was initiated by these citywide leaders and it often encountered resistance from candidates running for offices elected by neighborhood constituencies and from subordinate party functionaries. Such resistance arose in districts where the number of votes candidates gained by receiving the endorsement of the ALP exceeded the number lost by virtue of their association with a left-wing party. By contrast, top Democratic and Republican leaders and public officials elected from citywide constituencies had to worry about the possible adverse reaction of voters elsewhere in the city (and even the state and nation) to the alliances their subordinates cultivated in such districts with a party that was so closely tied to the Communists; they also had to be concerned with the reaction to such alliances on the part of elites with whom their party was allied. For example, in 1947 Mayor O'Dwyer moved to overthrow the leader of Tammany because he had often collaborated with Vito Marcantonio, and Francis Cardinal Spellman had indicated that this association with someone so close to the Communists was unacceptable to the Church.[34] In addition, William Randolph Hearst's tabloid the *Daily Mirror*, which had the second highest circulation of any newspaper in the city, conducted a scurrilous campaign against Marcantonio, and, at the other end of the scale, the *Times* and the *Herald Tribune* asserted in their editorials that Marcantonio's representation of a New York City district in Congress was a blot on the city's good name. The voters in East Harlem may have been indifferent to all of this, but the mayor could scarcely be.[35]

The ALP's ethnic heterogeneity, as well as its radicalism, contributed to the desire of the leaders of the Democratic and Republican county organizations to destroy the Labor party. To the extent that the ALP succeeded in mobilizing Jewish, Italian, black, and Irish voters under leaders, in the name of doctrines, and through techniques that differed from those of the regular party organizations, it presented a threat to the effort of machine politicians to assert their leadership over the groups in question. This is not to say that the ALP threatened to win majority support among New York's Italian, black, Irish, or even Jewish voters, but in districts where it simply held the balance of power it posed a threat to discipline within the major parties. Public officials who depended upon ALP votes for their victory margin had to pay heed to the views of the leaders of that party as well as their own if they were to win reelection.

The Tammany Hall of the mid-1940s, however, was the exception that proves the rule. The top leaders of the Democratic organization in Manhattan maintained their alliance with Marcantonio and the ALP even after both elite and public opinion in the city, state, and nation had turned sharply against the Soviet Union. That the leaders of Tammany were prepared to trade votes with the ALP in its strongholds, even though this alienated important groups elsewhere in the city and beyond, is a token of the narrowness of their political perspective. (Indeed, for the sake of helping the Tammany ticket in Harlem, the organization in 1945 even endorsed Benjamin Davis for the city council, despite the severe embarrassment this caused the citywide ticket; Tammany's endorsement of Davis was only withdrawn when O'Dwyer and Flynn threatened to deprive the organization of all patronage unless it did so.) Significantly, it was only after Carmine De Sapio, whose perspectives extended beyond the Lower East Side and Harlem districts where the ALP was strong, consolidated his control over the organization that a Tammany leader was able to enforce a prohibition against alliances with the ALP. Nor was it fortuitous that this ban was established by the same leader who attempted to sever the close ties between Tammany and the underworld (see below).

The Liberal party, by contrast, did not raise severe problems for top party leaders and public officials, and hence they were prepared to tolerate it, even though, as will be noted below, it was within their power to destroy it. Most importantly, the vehemently anti-Communist ideology of the Liberals meant that allying with it in neighborhoods where it was strong was not likely to cost the major parties votes elsewhere in the city or the support of the Catholic Church and the city's newspapers. In addition, the shallow organizational structure of the Liberal party, and its concomitant ethnic homogeneity, meant that it did not pose a threat to the political hegemony of machine politicians among the city's Italian, black, and Irish voters. It is true that the Liberal party threatened their position in the city's Jewish community. New York's mayors and the leaders of the Democratic and Republican parties in the city and state were prepared to pay this cost, however, because there were some compensating benefits. Alliances with the Liberals gave the Republicans their only chance of winning citywide elections and it gave the Democrats their only chance of winning statewide elections, for the very reason that such coalitions provided each with the best means of winning a substantial share of the volatile Jewish vote in the arena where it needed this support to secure a majority. In addition, alliances with the Liberals played an important role in the campaign to destroy the ALP, because the Liberals could bring to this effort the support of Jewish voters who were not prepared to vote the Tammany line.

Destroying the ALP

Mayor O'Dwyer, Governor Dewey, and the leaders of the Democratic and Republican parties in the city and state pursued a number of strategies in their campaign to destroy the Labor party. One of the most important of these involved *isolating the ALP*: Republicans and Democratic leaders sought to prevent their party's subordinate officials and candidates from striking deals with the Labor party and its candidates. The first target of this campaign was Congressman Vito Marcantonio, who, despite being the most prominent member of the ALP's left-wing faction, had won the Republican congressional primary in 1938 and 1940 with the support of local GOP committeemen. In 1942 and 1944 Tom Curran, the Manhattan Republican leader, told party workers in East Harlem to support the congressman's opponent in the Republican nomination. Few heeded Curran, however, and

Marcantonio won the Republican nomination. The tide turned when Governor Dewey joined the campaign to disassociate the GOP from Marcantonio and to isolate the ALP. Threatened with a loss of patronage, Republican committeemen worked for Marcantonio's opponent in the 1946 primary and deprived him of the GOP nomination. Ten state legislative candidates were jointly nominated by Republicans and the ALP in 1946, roughly the same number as in earlier years, but thereafter joint Republican-ALP nominations fell to zero.

The leaders of the Democratic party lagged behind their Republican counterparts in their efforts to defeat Marcantonio and to isolate the ALP. The top leadership of Tammany covertly supported the East Harlem congressman in 1942 and 1944 and openly endorsed him in 1946. The five Democratic county leaders selected a slate of candidates for citywide offices acceptable to the ALP in the 1945 municipal elections, and, with one important exception, they raised no objection in 1946 to Democratic legislative candidates' seeking the endorsement of the ALP, as twenty-nine of them successfully did. The exception was Bronx boss Ed Flynn. In 1945, despite the Democratic-ALP alliance for citywide offices, Flynn had refused to permit any of his organization's candidates to seek or accept ALP designations, a ban he continued in 1946 and subsequent years. Mayor O'Dwyer and then the other Democratic leaders came around to Flynn's view, so that in the 1949 municipal election the Democrats did not join forces with the ALP and in the 1950 state legislative elections not a single Democratic candidate ran with ALP support.

A second strategy the major parties pursued in their effort to destroy the ALP involved *allying with the Liberal party* in its stead. During the late 1940s the pattern of alliances between the major parties and the Liberals recapitulated the one that had characterized their relations with the ALP during the La Guardia years. The Republicans joined with the Liberals and reformers in municipal elections, entering fusion slates in both 1945 and 1949. In elections for state offices the characteristic alliance involved the Liberals and the Democrats, but this alliance did not appear until the late 1940s. In the 1944 state legislative elections the Democrats joined with the Liberals (and not the ALP) to run a common candidate against the Republicans in only 8 percent of New York City's state legislative districts, and in 1946 they did so in only 14 percent of the districts. But in 1948 the proportion of joint Democratic-Liberal nominations in state assembly and senate races in New York City districts shot up to 40 percent, and it remained at or above this level thereafter.

Another strategy in the major party campaign to destroy the ALP involved *changing the rules* under which elections were conducted in New York. The most important of these changes were brought about by the Wilson-Pakula law of 1947, a truly remarkable piece of legislation. The chief (though not the only) target of Wilson-Pakula was Vito Marcantonio, and to this extent it was a bill of political attainder.

As indicated, Marcantonio failed to win the Republican nomination in the 1946 primary, and his Republican challenger was endorsed in the general election by the Liberal party. Marcantonio won the Democratic primary that year, however, and the votes he received on the Democratic line enabled him to triumph in the general election. The Wilson-Pakula law was designed to prevent a recurrence of this unfortunate outcome, that is, to deprive Marcantonio of the Democratic nomination despite his evident ability to defeat challengers in that party's primary. It provided that a candidate belonging to one party (that is, the ALP) could not enter the primary of another party (that is, the Democrats) without receiving the permission of that party's county committeemen in the district in question. In other words, to gain the Democratic nomination Marcantonio would have to win the support not only of a majority of the Democratic voters in his congressional district, but also of the Democratic party workers. To meet this requirement, Marcantonio entered slates of friendly candidates for county committeemen in the 1947 Democratic primary in his district. Messrs. Wilson and Pakula anticipated this maneuver, however, and another section in their bill was designed to counter it. It provided that the county committee as a whole could deprive the committeemen in the district of the authority to grant the required permission; the county committee could transfer that authority to any other duly constituted organ of the party. The Democratic county committee did just this; it transferred this authority to the Tammany executive committee—composed of district leaders from all of Manhattan, not just Marcantonio's bailiwick—and the executive committee refused to grant the East Harlem congressman permission to enter the 1948 Democratic primary.

Marcantonio was not the only target of Wilson-Pakula, however; it was directed against the ALP as a whole, as other provisions of the law indicate. A major source of the ALP's strength was its ability to mobilize thousands of devoted party workers to perform the dreary tasks of electoral politics. To prevent these workers from helping friendly Democratic or Republican candidates win their own party's nomination, the law provided that the petitions necessary to enter the primary election of one party could not be circulated by members of other parties.

The Wilson-Pakula law was designed specifically to weaken the ALP; it did not prevent the Liberal party from playing balance-of-power politics. (This could easily have been done simply by forbidding candidates to appear on more than one ballot line, a provision in the election law of every other state but Vermont at the time.) The Democrats and Republicans were prepared to tolerate the Liberal party because it was not tainted by Communism and because each calculated that the Liberals could be a useful electoral ally.

In the campaign to destroy the ALP—and also the Communist party—the major parties sponsored one other important change in the laws governing elections in New York City: the repeal of proportional representation in city council elections. Whereas the Wilson-Pakula law made it extremely difficult for the ALP to gain influence by allying with elements of the Democratic and Republican parties, the repeal of PR eliminated the one mechanism through which the Labor party could gain representation without entering into such alliances. Beyond this, the repeal of PR had the advantage of eliminating the only way in which the Communist party could gain direct representation in the councils of government.

A fourth line of attack against the ALP and Marcantonio was initiated by Mayor O'Dwyer: *purging the bureaucracy*. Although O'Dwyer had been elected with ALP support in 1945, within a year of taking office he decided it would be politically advantageous to break with the Labor party—or at least to give the appearance of doing so by announcing his intention of using his powers as chief executive against the ALP. In December 1946 he announced that he was shaking up the police department in Harlem—transferring out officers with whom Marcantonio, over the years, had established close ties. This would adversely affect the congressman's political strength because his ability to offer protection from the law was a major reason the Tammany leaders who had ties to the underworld allied with him. A few months later O'Dwyer toppled the leader of Tammany and installed a replacement who was not so publicly identified with Marcantonio by announcing that he would withhold patronage from the organization until his candidate was elected leader.

These maneuvers loosened the ties between Tammany, on the one side, and Marcantonio and the ALP, on the other, but they did not completely sever them. The congressman's underworld allies were still powerful in Tammany, and hence the organization entered a weak candidate against Marcantonio in the 1948 general election, one whom he was able to defeat, and sixteen of its candidates for the state legislature arranged to be endorsed by the ALP. The next year, however, with his reelection campaign approaching, O'Dwyer again found it useful to take a staunch anti-Communist line, and he announced he was purging the municipal bureaucracy of Communists. This contributed to the ALP's decline by convincing many of its cadres—a significant number of whom were city employees—that working for a party generally considered to be a Communist front could cost them their jobs.

Finally, in a repetition of the strategy that had defeated Socialist officeholders after World War I—*arranging bipartisan nominations*—the Democrats and the Republicans (and at times the Liberals) jointly endorsed candidates in their efforts to destroy the ALP following World War II. The most extensive of these bipartisan cartels was arranged by the leaders of the two major parties in the Bronx in 1948. That year in every one of the borough's thirteen assembly districts, and in all of its five state senate districts, the Democrats and Republicans endorsed a common candidate; in addition, in four of the Bronx's five congressional districts the two major parties united with the Liberals behind the same candidate. It required just such a tripartisan deal to deliver the coup de grace to Vito Marcantonio: unable to enter the Democratic primary, deprived of the assistance of as many ALP cadres as in his previous campaigns, and faced with an opponent running simultaneously on the Democratic, Republican, and Liberal lines, Marcantonio at long last was defeated in 1950. A similar tripartisan coalition defeated Benjamin Davis's bid for reelection to the city council in 1949.

———

The collapse of the ALP and the incorporation of the Liberal party into New York's postwar regime was significant because it had major implications for the way in which the members of the city's various ethnic groups were integrated into the local political system. The most evident of these implications concerned the city's Jewish community. Jews acquired a substantial measure of influence and representation in New York politics during the postwar decades, and the Liberal party played an important role in making these gains. Most directly, in choosing candidates Democratic leaders would enter into negotiations with the Liberals and select nominees they found ideologically acceptable, in order to ensure that the Liberals would not enter a separate slate or ally with the Republicans, thereby depriving the Democratic ticket of the support of the thousands of Jews who voted on the Liberal line. A pattern-setting example of this occurred in 1949 when Carmine De Sapio, the new leader of Tammany, selected Robert F. Wagner, Jr., as his candidate for borough president, after Alex Rose had indicated in private discussions with him that the Liberals were prepared to give Wagner their nomination.

In addition to this way of gaining influence, Jews rose to public and party office during the postwar period through regular party channels in numbers fully equal to their proportion in the city's population. Even in the absence of explicit bargaining between Democratic and Liberal leaders, however, their ability to make these gains was assisted by the presence of that minor party. The incumbent leaders of the Democratic organization accommodated themselves to the rise of the Jews, not because they feared that if they failed to do so Jews would desert to the Republicans—Jews were too strongly committed to the New Deal to make this a major threat—but rather because they knew that nominating conservative Irish machine stalwarts in predominantly Jewish districts would lead the Liberals to field a candidate, either on their own or in conjunction with the Republicans, who would draw Jewish votes away form the Democratic line. In other words, the Liberal party was the shotgun behind the door that made the process of ethnic succession work for the Jews. To make these gains, it should be noted, Jews had to reject the efforts of the ALP to assume their political leadership, for, as indicated above, a balance-of-power strategy such as the Liberals pursued can only succeed if the major parties are willing to tolerate the minor party that engages in it.

The collapse of the ALP and the institutionalization of the Liberal party also had significant implications for the politics of New York's black, Irish-American, and Italian-American communities. The case of the blacks will be discussed in a separate section below, and of the Irish-Americans it need only be said that the withdrawal of labor leaders such as Mike Quill and Joseph Curran from the ALP removed a thorn from the side of the regular Democratic party organization, because it ended a small but not insignificant challenge to the political hegemony of machine politicians among the New York Irish.

The implications of the ALP's collapse for the politics of the city's Italian-American community warrants fuller discussion here. As mentioned above, New York's two most prominent Italian-American politicians of the 1930s and 1940s—Fiorello La Guardia and Vito Marcantonio—joined the ALP when it was organized in 1936 or shortly thereafter, and in the wake of the factional struggles of 1944 that led the right wing to secede and form the Liberal party, both remained with the ALP, now dominated by the left. Beyond this, Marcantonio's voting record in Congress on questions of both domestic and foreign policy adhered quite closely to the Communist party line, and despite pressure from various quarters to do so, La Guardia never disowned his protégé, nor did he undertake to purge Communists from the municipal bureaucracy. A striking example of the working relationship between La Guardia, Marcantonio, and the Communists occurred in 1944 when the mayor needed the support of the party's two city councilmen to enact a municipal sales tax. The two—Peter Cacchione and Benjamin Davis—insisted that they would never vote for the measure on the grounds that it was regressive. During a council recess La Guardia got them to switch their votes, however, by calling Marcantonio and having him intercede with Earl Browder, the party's national leader, who in turn directed the councilmen to support the mayor.[36]

Of course, the support that Marcantonio, La Guardia, and even Cacchione received from their constituents should not necessarily be attributed to their radicalism. Marcantonio and La Guardia relied upon appeals to ethnic pride to rally their fellow Italians, and the East Harlem congressman, with resources provided by La Guardia, was able to distribute patronage to his closest supporters and to perform favors for individual constituents. As for Peter Cacchione, it is likely that many Italian-Americans voted for him because he was a member of their ethnic group, not because he was a member of the Communist party; he took every available occasion to call attention to his being an avid fan of the Brooklyn Dodgers, and one suspects that he did this in an effort to show his constituents that despite his Communist affiliation, he really was one of them. Finally, however much La Guardia was prepared to tolerate or even cooperate with the Communists, he publicly disavowed their endorsement, and his alliances with the New Deal and the municipal reform movement were infinitely more important sources of his political success.

However, even if Italian-American voters supported La Guardia, Marcantonio, and Cacchione chiefly for ethnic reasons, it remains significant that they were willing to vote for public officials who were radicals or who cooperated with radicals. After the ALP and the Communist party collapsed, there no longer was any organized support for radicalism in the Italian-American community. Indeed, because the Liberal party was far less ethnically heterogeneous than the ALP, there was limited institutional support among New York's Italian-Americans during the postwar decades for liberalism—for candidates such as Charles Poletti and Ferdinand Pecora, who had been among the most prominent Italian-American politicians during the 1930s and 1940s. Rather, political leadership in the Italian-American community was assumed by machine politicians, be they Republicans or Democrats, whose ties were not to the radical or liberal political activists and trade unionists among their fellow ethnics, but rather to lower middle class homeowners and small businessmen, on the one hand, or to unions in the building trades as well as to contractors, realtors, insurance brokers, and lawyers seeking to use their political connections to advance their fortunes, on the other hand.

To be sure, machine politicians had played a prominent role in the Italian-American community prior to the postwar period, but after La Guardia's involuntary retirement in 1945, the repeal of PR in 1947, and the three-party gang-up on Marcantonio in 1950, their claims to the leadership of New York's Italian population no longer were subject to challenge. The tradition of Italian-American liberalism and radicalism institutionalized in the ALP lay largely dormant after the Labor party's destruction, until Mario Cuomo revived it in campaigning for governor of New York more than thirty years later.

In sum, the collapse of the ALP and the incorporation of the Liberal party into New York's postwar regime involved the defeat of would-be leaders of the city's Jewish and Italian communities who were radical in ideology and who relied upon the support of an extensive party organization staffed by left-wing political activists and trade unionists. In their stead, the political leadership of the Jewish community was assumed by the more moderate trade unionists, intellectuals, and lawyers of the Liberal party, and by regular Democratic politicians whose bargaining power was enhanced by the very existence of the Liberals. The political leadership of the city's Italian-Americans was assumed by machine politicians. In other words, the price that the members of both of these ethnic groups had to pay for retaining power in New York politics was rejecting the claims to leadership of politicians who were unacceptable to other powerful groups in the city by virtue of their ideology.

THE DEMOCRATIC PARTY ORGANIZATION

New York's Democratic party organizations served as another channel through which Italians and Jews gained entry into the city's postwar regime. This process of incorporation was bound up with the extrusion of politicians from these ethnic groups who were unacceptable to other participants in the political system not because of their ideology, but rather because of their criminal ties.

The Irish leaders who dominated New York's Democratic county machines (especially the Tammany organization in Manhattan) had done little prior to the 1930s to encourage the members of the city's newer immigrant groups to participate in party affairs. Rather than pursuing a strategy of mobilization, many Irish leaders in Tammany retained power during the 1930s in districts that no longer were predominantly Irish by allying with Italian and Jewish gangsters—such as Lucky Luciano, Frank Costello, Louis Lepke, and Dutch Schultz—or with politicians from these groups who in turn had ties to the mob. These alliances were mutually beneficial. On the one side, district leaders could provide criminals with protection from the law (Tammany retained considerable influence within the judiciary in New York County throughout the 1930s and 1940s); on the other side, gangsters could provide district leaders with manpower to deal with challenges in primary elections and with money they could use both for campaigning and for lining their own pockets.

Such alliances between district leaders and criminals were by no means novel in the 1930s. They form a repetitive theme in Tammany's history because the structure of incentives confronting party leaders in many districts encouraged their formation. The first concern of a local politician was carrying his own district in general elections and, even more importantly, in party primaries. In heavily Democratic districts, where the outcome of general

POLITICAL INCORPORATION AND EXTRUSION 223

elections was not in doubt, the job of winning primaries was all the easier the smaller the number of politically active Democrats; and in districts where a majority of the potential electorate was of a different ethnic background than the incumbent party leaders, the incentive to keep electoral participation low was all the stronger because, if mobilized, these voters might well support politicians from their own group who sought to displace the incumbent leaders. In such districts incumbent leaders could most easily maintain their control by cultivating alliances and establishing clients among gang leaders and politicians from the numerically predominant ethnic group who were prepared to cast their lot with the powers-that-be rather than take the riskier course of challenging them, and who in return for personal rewards were willing to help the incumbent leadership maintain its control over their fellow ethnics.

The leader of the party organization as a whole, on the other hand, had to be concerned with maximizing the party's vote—especially in solidly Democratic districts—so that it could defeat its opposition in citywide and state elections. He also had reason to oppose the involvement of district leaders with disreputable characters, because such relationships, if exposed, could cost the party votes in these elections. If the concerns of the central party leadership were to prevail over those of the district leaders, the former had to be strong enough to compel the latter to act in ways that furthered the collective and long-run interests of the organization, rather than their personal and short-run interests. During the 1930s, however, Tammany's central leadership was weak: Tammany was hostile to the Roosevelt administration in Washington much longer than the Democratic organizations in the city's other boroughs, and with its political opponents also controlling City Hall, the central leadership of Tammany commanded relatively little patronage it could distribute to compliant district leaders and withhold from recalcitrant ones. Given this freedom, Irish district leaders in the heavily Italian and Jewish neighborhoods of Manhattan sought to maintain control of their districts by doing business with gangsters.

The most important of these gangsters was Frank Costello. During the 1930s Costello established close ties with a number of Tammany district leaders, providing them with the manpower and money they needed to hold on to their positions.[37] In the early 1940s, however, according to Warren Moscow, who at the time was the chief political correspondent of the *New York Times*, Costello decided that rather than buying protection in this way, it would be cheaper and more reliable to install his own associates in district leaderships.[38] Costello was able to do this because the district leaders against whom he moved had relied upon his troops to maintain themselves in power and therefore could not survive once he withdrew his support. Had they (or someone else) established a broad following among the Italians and/or Jews in their districts they might have been able to withstand Costello's opposition.

Costello was an equal opportunity employer. The district leaders whom later investigations identified as being closely associated with him included a few Irishmen (the most important of whom were Clarence Neal and Edward Loughlin), but the largest number came from the ethnic groups that previously had been underrepresented on the Tammany executive committee—the Italians and the Jews. Among the former were John De Salvio, Carmine De Sapio, Francis X. Mancuso, and Paul Sarubbi. Among the latter were Harry Brickman, Samuel Kantor, Sidney Moses, Abraham Rosenthal, William Solomon, Bert Stand, and Alfred Toplitz. It was through Costello's sponsorship in the 1940s that Italians and Jews first moved into Tammany leadership positions in substantial numbers.

During the 1940s Costello and the politicians associated with him became a major force in Tammany not only on the district level, but also at the very peak of the organization. In 1942 the executive committee voted to depose Tammany leader Christopher Sullivan, but the organization was so factionalized that no candidate to succeed him was able to round up a majority of votes on the committee. This factionalism placed Costello in the position to be a kingmaker, for he controlled at least three and perhaps six of the twelve votes needed to elect a new leader.[39] Costello later testified that Michael Kennedy, one of the candidates to succeed Sullivan, came to him and asked for his support in the leadership fight, a request to which Costello acceded after it became clear that the candidate he initially supported could not round up the necessary votes. Costello's switch put Kennedy over the top. Two years later Costello withdrew his support from Kennedy and threw it behind Edward Loughlin, a maneuver that toppled the former and elected the latter as Tammany leader. During Loughlin's tenure as leader, which ran from 1944 through 1947, Tammany actually was run by two politicians who served as liaisons between the organization and the mob—Clarence Neal, chairman of the organization's elections committee, and Bert Stand, secretary of Tammany Hall.[40]

Although Costello was the most influential figure in Tammany in the 1940s, he did not command a solid majority on the organization's executive committee. Consequently, the tenure of Manhattan Democratic leaders was brief and their turnover rate high: the leadership of Tammany changed five times between 1942 and 1947. Contributing to this instability was the independent role William O'Dwyer played in these factional struggles after he became mayor in 1946. Whenever accusations about the criminal associations of Tammany politicians threatened to embarrass him politically, O'Dwyer would withhold patronage from the incumbent Tammany leader, thereby inducing the executive committee to oust him and install a leader the mayor was prepared to support. This game of musical chairs led in 1949

to the elevation of Carmine De Sapio to the leadership of Tammany Hall—
the first Italian ever to hold that position.

Carmine De Sapio had been elected Tammany leader with the support of
Frank Costello, but he recognized that the influence gangsters exercised
within the organization could create potentially serious political problems.
It gave Tammany's opponents in election campaigns ammunition to discredit the machine's candidates; this was precisely the strategy that Edward
Corsi, the Republican candidate, and Vincent Impellitteri, the independent,
used in the 1950 mayoral election.[41] The losers in struggles for power within
Tammany also had an incentive to point out the role that criminals had
played in the victory of their opponents. In 1950, for example, someone
tipped off District Attorney Frank Hogan that two gunmen had been present at a meeting of county committeemen in one Manhattan assembly district at which a resolution was passed deposing the incumbent district
leader; this revelation was embarrassing to De Sapio personally, as well as to
Tammany institutionally, for De Sapio was present at the meeting and his
political allies were the beneficiaries of the gunmen's intervention.[42] This
accumulation of charges made for a great deal of dramatic televised testimony by major figures in organized crime and by important public officials
and politicians from New York before the Kefauver committee and led to the
creation of the Proskauer Commission by New York State.[43] The damage
these revelations could cause the machine was indicated when the counsel
for the Kefauver committee, Rudolph Halley, won a special election for
president of the city council in 1951 running on the Liberal line alone.

To avoid such dangers, De Sapio proceeded to purge district leaders who
had criminal ties. By 1953 these efforts were largely successful. After the
primary election and the reorganization of the Tammany executive committee that year, only one district leader remained among those whom investigating committees identified as having criminal ties.[44]

Significantly, many of the targets of De Sapio's attack were Italian and
Jewish, because through their ties to the underworld large numbers of Italian and Jewish politicians had moved into leadership positions in Tammany. But De Sapio's purge did not reduce total Italian and Jewish representation on the Tammany executive committee. The Italian and Jewish
district leaders of the 1950s, however, were politicians of a different stamp
than many of their predecessors; indeed five were endorsed by the Citizens
Union, the first time that good-government organization ever endorsed candidates for party (as distinguished from public) office. In other words, the
upshot of De Sapio's campaign was to bring Italians and Jews into the Tammany organization under the leadership of politicians who were acceptable
to other members of the regime that came to rule New York in the 1950s.
The purge from Tammany of Italian and Jewish district leaders having underworld connections, and their replacement by other Italian and Jewish

politicians more acceptable to established interests in the city, was similar in its sponsorship, motivation, and consequences to the simultaneous displacement of Jewish and Italian radicals in the ALP by Jewish politicians and trade unionists allied with New York's Liberal party.

RACIAL MINORITIES

During the 1940s and 1950s blacks, like Jews and Italians, gained influence in New York politics, and their incorporation into the city's postwar regime involved reaching accommodations with more established groups. During the postwar decades, however, the political power of blacks was considerably less than that of New York's major white ethnic groups.

During the early decades of the twentieth century, the entrenched Irish leadership of Tammany had no more desire to share the spoils of office with blacks than with Jews or Italians. As had been true in the case of Jews and Italians, Tammany leaders found that they could deal with blacks at lowest cost by working with elements of the subordinate group belonging to the demimonde, because such politicians, in return for protection, would undertake to control the current black electorate rather than seek to expand it. For example, the most influential black politician in Harlem's nineteenth and twenty-first assembly districts in the mid-1930s—Kid Banks and Herbert Bruce—were both cabaret owners.[45]

Blacks eventually rose to district leaderships in Tammany in the 1930s and 1940s, but largely as a consequence of the factional divisions within the machine analyzed in the previous section.[46] Such cleavages broke the united front of whites and provided black politicians with important support. Although in their efforts to win district leaderships a number of black politicians did engage in old-fashioned, door-to-door canvassing, their ability to gain support through factional maneuvering enabled blacks to win seats on the Tammany executive committee without mobilizing as broad a following as otherwise would have been necessary.[47]

The Democrats and Republicans were not only hesitant about admitting blacks into leadership positions in the regular party organizations but also were cautious about raising issues of concern to blacks and nominating them for public office. But just as party factionalism made it difficult to exclude blacks entirely form district leadership positions, so too did factional cleavages and party competition prevent the Democrats and Republicans from ignoring blacks in general elections, for in this arena, as much as in party primaries, divisions among whites at times enabled blacks (and liberal whites allied with them) to hold the balance of power. The Democrats and Republicans adopted a number of strategies, however, to minimize the risk of losing white votes in the course of appealing for the support of blacks and their allies.

One such strategy was for the two parties jointly to sponsor civil right measures. For example, in 1957 the city council enacted the Sharkey-Brown-Isaacs bill, outlawing racial discrimination in the sale and rental of housing. The sponsors of this bill were the Democratic majority leader of the council (Sharkey), the Republican minority leader (Isaacs), and a black city councilman (Brown). In a similar fashion, the bill outlawing housing discrimination introduced in the state legislature was sponsored by a black Democrat (Bertram Baker) and a white Republican (George Metcalf).

Another way in which the major parties sought to minimize the loss of white votes while appealing for those of blacks was to nominate blacks with impeccable credentials for offices that had biracial constituencies. This enabled party leaders, public officials, and the press to argue that the candidate in question, though black, was "fully qualified" for the office he sought. In point of fact, however, such candidates were often ridiculously overqualified. A case in point is Francis Rivers, who earned his Phi Beta Kappa key at Yale and his LL.B. from Columbia Law School; he was the first black assistant district attorney in Manhattan. In 1943, after holding an interim appointment, Rivers was nominated and elected by the Republicans and the ALP to a full term on the City Court, becoming the first black to be elected to a public office in a constituency that was less than 50 percent black. The jurisdiction of the City Court, it should be noted, is limited to minor civil cases. Similarly, the first black to serve on the Magistrates Court was a graduate of Columbia Law School; the first black on the Court of Domestic Relations received an LL.B. at Yale; and the candidate the major parties nominated in 1949 to oppose Benjamin Davis in a biracial city council district was a Harvard graduate, as was the Republican candidate for Manhattan borough president in 1953, and the first black to hold a cabinet-level appointment in city government. The nomination or appointment of blacks with degrees from Ivy League institutions for these positions is noteworthy because most whites serving in these positions, if they had graduated from college at all, were most likely to have attended institutions at the other end of the academic hierarchy.

To avoid being in an exposed position—too far out in front or behind its opponent—the two parties also frequently acted in tandem in extending nominations to blacks. The most striking example of this involved the nominees for Manhattan borough president in 1953. The Republicans, the Liberals, the Democratic faction backing mayoral candidate Vincent Impellitteri, and the Democratic faction backing mayoral candidate Robert Wagner all nominated blacks for this position. Thereafter, the Manhattan borough presidency came to be recognized as the black seat on the Board of Estimate.

More generally, during the entire period from 1945 to 1960 the major parties nominated almost identical percentages of blacks for elective offices in Manhattan—12 percent for the Democrats, 13 percent for the Republicans.[48]

Finally, during the postwar period major party candidates and elected officials sought as much as possible to avoid raising racially contentious issues. The most striking example of this policy of silence involved the potentially explosive issue of school integration. The New York City Board of Education established a commission on integration in 1954, and over the next decade agitation on this issue by both proponents and opponents of integration steadily gathered force. Nonetheless, both Democratic and Republican elected officials left the matter completely in the hands of the Board.[49] The avoidance of the issue by the major parties caused an upsurge of electoral activity outside regular party channels in the 1960s, not only among proponents of school integration (through that decade's fusion movement), but also among the opponents of school busing (through the Conservative party).

The circumspection with which the major parties approached issues of potential concern to blacks, their caution in nominating black candidates, and their reluctance to mobilize large numbers of blacks into the electorate (for so doing would only compound their dilemma) left New York's black population open for mobilization by leaders who did not have ties to the regular party organizations and who relied upon racial and/or radical appeals. The most important of these politicians was Adam Clayton Powell.

Powell rose to prominence entirely outside party channels. He was assistant minister and then minister of Harlem's largest church; he first made a name for himself in the 1930s by leading protest movements calling for the reinstatement of five black doctors who had been discharged from Harlem Hospital and demanding that shops and public utilities in Harlem hire blacks. Powell also wrote a column for the *Amsterdam News*, appropriately called "The Soapbox," and in 1942 he and an associate began publishing their own newspaper, the *People's Voice*. Powell cashed in on his growing visibility by successfully campaigning in 1941 to become the first black elected by proportional representation to the city council, and in 1944 to be elected as the first black congressman from New York City.

In many ways Adam Clayton Powell occupied a place in New York's black community in the 1930s, 1940s, and 1950s rather similar to the one Fiorello La Guardia had occupied during the years 1918–33. Both rose to their preeminent positions outside party channels (though prior to 1920 La Guardia was more a party man than Powell had been in the early phase of his political career); moreover, both sought election to Congress, published newspapers, adopted a pugnacious style, and presented themselves as spokesmen for their entire ethnic community.[50] (One indication of Powell's success at establishing his claim to be a spokesman for the entire black community is that in his first congressional campaign he entered and won the Democratic, Republican, and ALP primaries.) Moreover, in the 1930s and 1940s, Powell, like La Guardia before him, stood at the left end of the city's political spectrum. His campaigns for the city council and Congress were supported by the American Labor party and the Communist party, he appeared at rallies with leaders of the CP, and his newspaper, the *People's Voice*, moved ever closer to the Communist party line.[51] Despite this radicalism, Powell drew support from the black middle class—a majority of his parishioners/campaign workers were members of the black bourgeoisie— just as the members of the Fiorello H. La Guardia political club were drawn from the middle stratum of New York's Italian-American community. Finally, with blacks as with the Italians a decade or two earlier, it was the absence of a significant cadre of elected officials who could serve as *representatives* of the group that enabled their highest elected official to serve as the group's *spokesman*.

The second most prominent radical politician in New York's black community was Benjamin Davis. Davis, a member of the national executive committee of the Communist party, was elected to the city council in 1943 after Powell, who intended to run for Congress the next year, declined to stand for a second term. Davis drew support from all segments of the black community. As Edwin Lewison notes, "When he announced his candidacy for the city council, the New York *Age* listed his Communist Party activities in the same sentence that it told its readers of his membership in the exclusive black college fraternity Alpha Phi Alpha and the Negro Elks."[52] Powell served as co-chairman of Davis's 1945 election campaign; Davis was endorsed by all the Democratic district leaders in Harlem; and the New York *Age* suggested he should also be supported by the Republican party.

Benjamin Davis was a canker in New York's postwar body politic, just as was Vito Marcantonio, so Mayor O'Dwyer and Carmine De Sapio undertook to remove him. In 1945 O'Dwyer insisted that Tammany withdraw its endorsement of Davis. Davis won election to the city council nonetheless, and in 1949 De Sapio insisted that Powell renounce ALP support in 1950 or face a Tammany-backed opponent in the Democratic primary that year.[53] This was an adjustment to the constraints of postwar New York politics that Powell was willing to make.

Six years later, however, Powell violated another of De Sapio's cardinal principles—party regularity. Claiming that the Democratic party's position on civil rights was too weak, Powell endorsed President Eisenhower's bid for a second term in 1956. Outraged, De Sapio recruited a candidate to oppose Powell in the Democratic primary. Powell's opponent, Earl Brown (who had defeated Benjamin Davis in the 1949 city council election), was endorsed by five of the six black district leaders in Harlem and by the black

Manhattan borough president, Hulan Jack. To ensure that he would have a place on the November ballot whatever the results of the Democratic primary, Powell sought to enter the Republican primary. Over the objections of Manhattan Republican leader Tom Curran, the Republican county committeemen in Powell's district granted him permission to do so. This insurance proved to be unnecessary. Powell overwhelmed Brown three-to-one in the Democratic primary.

Several aspects of De Sapio's effort to purge Powell are noteworthy. It is striking that the identification of Harlem's Democratic district leaders with the party organization was so strong and/or their dependence upon De Sapio was so great that all but one of them were prepared to oppose the city's most prominent black politician. It is equally striking that the popular base of the Democratic party organization in Harlem was so narrow that the candidate the district leaders supported was trounced by Powell, who was able to depict party discipline as a form of racial subordination. Finally, it is noteworthy that the Manhattan Republican organization had such little interest in competing with the Democrats for the support of blacks that the county leader did not leap at the opportunity to lure Powell into the GOP.

More generally, the purge of Benjamin Davis in 1949, De Sapio's insistence that Powell renounce ALP support in 1950, and the failure of De Sapio's effort to purge Powell in 1958 are significant because they defined the terms upon which, and the leadership under which, blacks would be integrated into the city's postwar regime. Based on the position of blacks in the 1930s, four alternatives appeared possible. First, blacks might have been almost completely excluded from the city's political system, with the help of a *comprador* leadership dependent upon white politicians. Second, blacks could have been integrated into the political system through the Democratic party organization, under the leadership of politicians with a solid base of support within the racial subcommunity, and have received as many benefits from the municipal government as white ethnic groups of comparable size. Third, the political leadership of the black community might have been seized by politicians—such as Benjamin Davis, Vito Marcantonio (many of whose constituents were black), and one face of Adam Clayton Powell in the 1930s and 1940s—who preached working-class unity across racial lines. Finally, blacks might have been led by politicians who relied primarily upon racial appeals.

It turned out that white machine politicians in New York were not unified enough in the 1930s and 1940s to exclude blacks from district leaderships in the party organization. In the late 1940s, however, whites came to be sufficiently united on the unacceptability of the radical class-politics alternative to defeat blacks (as well as whites) identified with it, and to convince Powell that it was prudent to abandon it. Finally, in 1958 it became clear that the volume of resources white political leaders were willing or able to channel to black machine politicians was not great enough to enable these politicians to defeat Powell-the-racial-agitator in a head-to-head confrontation. Through the processes discussed in this section, the terms upon which blacks came to be integrated into New York's political system in the 1940s and 1950s were a consequence not only of the attitudes and opinions of blacks but also of the political dynamics of the city's postwar regime.[54]

The failure of New York's regular Democratic party organization to establish a broad base of support for itself among the city's black population was to have deleterious consequences for the stability of the postwar regime. It left blacks open to mobilization in the 1960s not only by "race men," such as Powell, who operated through the electoral system, but also by those who engaged in nonelectoral forms of political combat.

CONCLUSION

I have argued in this chapter that most analyses of the insertion of new social forces into politics fail to recognize that this process involves conflicts not simply over *whether* or not a previously excluded group will be brought into the political system but also over the *terms* upon which it will be included. At issue is the identity of the leadership under which the group will gain representation and the character of the ties that will bind it to the political system.

If a group is to gain a position in the regime that is secure, it must be integrated into the system in a manner consistent with the interests of other members of the regime's dominant political coalition. Political parties are the institutions that seek to construct such coalitions, and major party leaders cannot be indifferent to the character of the appeals that are used to mobilize new social forces politically because other elements of their party's constituency are not indifferent. Moreover, as the example of New York City illustrates, party leaders may be prepared to engage in collusion with their counterparts in the other major party to help the advocates of acceptable ideologies or modes of political conduct defeat contenders for the leadership of the previously excluded group whom the members of established groups regard as unacceptable. Thus the process of political incorporation is simultaneously a process of political exclusion.

The experience of New York during the postwar period demonstrates that the process of political incorporation as conducted by parties can be as effective as witch-hunts in destroying radicalism. In this respect, as in others,[55] the organization of consent by parties is a two-edged sword: political parties at one and the same time facilitate governance by the people and governance of the people. By so doing, parties enable representative political systems to reproduce and perpetuate themselves.

Methodological Appendix

THE VOTING behavior of ethnic groups reported in Table 6.1 was estimated with logit analysis. The following equation was estimated:

$$\ln (p/(1 - p)) = B_0 + \sum_{i=1}^{6} B_i X_i + U$$

where ln is the natural logarithm, p is the proportion of each district's vote cast for the Republican mayoral candidate, X_1 is the proportion of the district's population that is native-born of foreign parentage, X_2 is the proportion born in Italy, X_3 is foreign-born Jewish, X_4 is foreign-born Irish, X_5 is foreign-born German, X_6 is all other foreign-born, and U is an error term. With the equation specified in this way, the intercept, B_0, provides an estimate of voting behavior of a hypothetical district with no foreign-stock voters—that is, a district inhabited entirely by the native-born of native parentage. B_1 estimates the behavior of second-generation Americans, and the other regression coefficients (B_2–B_6), the vote of districts populated by the various foreign-born groups. The equation was estimated by generalized least-squares (GLS).

CHAPTER 7

New York City's Fiscal Crisis:
Countering the Politics of Mass Mobilization

THE 1975 New York City fiscal crisis was above all a political crisis. Its origins lay in a set of political changes the city experienced in the 1960s, which led municipal expenditures and indebtedness to grow at an explosive pace. And the eruption of the crisis produced a further transformation in the structure of the city's politics.

This is not to deny that changes in the city's demographic and economic base contributed to the problems the municipal government faced. The migration of more than a million poor blacks and Puerto Ricans to New York after World War II placed pressures on the municipal budget at the same time that the movement of business firms and middle-class whites to the suburbs reduced the city's capacity to finance new expenditures. But these developments, which are commonly cited to explain the city's difficulties, cannot in themselves account for the crisis; unemployed men and fatherless children do not, after all, have the authority to appropriate public monies or float municipal bonds. To account for the rapid growth of the municipal budget and debt, one must explain why public officials responded as they did to these changes in the city's demographic and economic base—an explanation to be found in the transformation of New York City politics in the 1960s.

During that decade, the regime that had formerly governed New York City collapsed, and a new coalition of political forces attempted to seize control. This initiated a pattern of political activity that characteristically led to rising public expenditures and indebtedness, financial collapse, and ultimately budgetary retrenchment and a reorganization of politics, shifting the balance of power to the owners of the public debt. This pattern of political and fiscal change was not unique to New York City in the 1960s and 1970s; it has appeared both in other places and in earlier periods of the city's history.

TWO ROUTES TO RETRENCHMENT

The political conditions that lead city governments to increase municipal expenditures at a rapid rate and accumulate large deficits are similar to those that encourage national governments to pursue highly inflationary fiscal and monetary policies. Such policies are likely to be adopted in the following combination of circumstances: (1) a social group that has recently gained political power begins to assert claims upon the government for greater public benefits or a larger slice of the national income; (2) the government responds to these claims either because it is allied with the group in question or because it cannot withstand its opposition; and (3) the government is too weak politically to finance these new claims by reducing the flow of benefits to other groups or by raising taxes. To cover the difference between expenditures and revenues, both municipal and national governments can borrow money. In addition, national governments can print money—in large quantities, if necessary—to finance their deficits, and hence deficit financing on the national level can generate rampant price inflation.

These political conditions have prevailed, as the historian Charles Maier has noted, during the major episodes of national inflation in this century. The hyperinflation in central Europe in the years 1919–22, for example, followed the creation of democratic regimes in Germany and Austria, which for the first time granted representation in the government to working-class parties. These regimes, however, were threatened by antidemocratic forces on the Right and dared not alienate the nation's industrialists. The only economic policies compatible with the maintenance of a tacit coalition between labor and industry were highly inflationary: the industrialists would not tolerate any new taxes on corporate or personal incomes, and the government thus increasingly financed its operations by resorting to the printing presses. Similarly, in Latin America, periods of severe inflation characteristically occur after the rise of regimes that speak for the urban or rural lower classes, but—because of political weakness, administrative incapacity, or corruption—cannot collect taxes from the middle and upper classes, or prevent the wealthy from sending their money abroad, or foster economic development. The Perónist regime in Argentina, for example, sponsored the organization and political incorporation of labor, but failed to industrialize the nation and generate the wealth necessary to pay for the benefits provided its supporters. Consequently, claims to the national income that the government granted exceeded the national income, and inflation followed.

The European nations experiencing the highest levels of inflation recently—Portugal and Italy—were characterized by politics approximating the pattern outlined above. The Italian case is too complex to describe here, but the Portuguese situation is quite straightforward. Following the revolution of 1974, which granted the Portuguese political rights they had been unable to exercise freely for fifty years, a succession of weak governments (six in two years) either encouraged, or found it impossible to resist, the demands of the army for an immediate withdrawal from Portugal's colonies, of agricultural laborers for land, of workers and civil servants for wage increases, and of unions for greater control over factories and offices. The result was a rise in the nation's wage bill, a decline of labor and military discipline, the influx of more than half a million refugees from Angola who had to be housed and fed by the government, a rise in government deficits, and consequently an inflation rate in 1975 of 46 percent.

The conditions fostering very high levels of inflation are inherently unstable. Double- or triple-digit inflation can lead to a credit or liquidity crisis, to balance-of-payments difficulties, and ultimately to a recession. When this occurs, industrialists become less willing to accept inflationary policies. Middle-class *rentiers*, who generally are the most seriously injured by inflation, and who find it difficult under normal circumstances to assert themselves politically against better-organized groups, can erupt into an angry political force when inflation threatens to wipe out the fruits of a lifetime of thrift. And banks, which are in a position to extend the necessary loans for stabilizing the nation's currency and refinancing its international debt, gain enormous political leverage by their ability to attach conditions to their aid. If all these interests coalesce, they can overturn the government that fostered inflation, and install a government that will implement a program of retrenchment.

Retrenchment involves eliminating nonessential public expenditures. What this commonly means in practice is that those groups that only recently gained a measure of power will be deprived of whatever benefits they won by being incorporated into the political system. For the purposes of retrenchment, these groups must either be driven off the political stage, or compelled to accept a more modest role.

Historically, the first of these alternatives is probably the more common: retrenchment often occurs at the expense of democracy. In 1922, for example, the Austrian government received a stabilization loan from the League of Nations by agreeing in the Geneva Protocols to abrogate parliamentary authority over all financial matters for a period of two years. And the agreements that brought stability to Weimar Germany involved the overthrow of the last coalition government in which a working-class party had representation. In Latin America, typically only military governments can carry out the retrenchment policies that international lending agencies insist upon. The post-Perón military regimen in Argentina, as well as Pinochet's Chile, provide stark examples of what the implementation of a retrenchment program can entail.

The alternative route to retrenchment involves a system of discipline imposed upon the new political group not by an alliance of domestic conservatives and foreign bankers, but rather by the leadership of the group in question. And this can lead to harsh measures. The halt of the leftward drift of Portugal's revolution overthrowing the Salazar dictatorship and the rise to power of the moderate Socialist government of Mario Soares came only after many offices of the Portuguese Communist party were firebombed, leftist groups in the military were smashed, the army was purged by a stern disciplinarian, General Ramilho Eanes, and the Socialists allied themselves with the two most conservative parties behind his presidential candidacy. And the success of Italy's retrenchment program in the 1970s ironically depended upon the ability of a Leninist party—the Italian Communist party—to impose its new line (the "historic compromise") upon restive party militants and compel unions affiliated with the Communist labor federation to limit their wage demands.

BOSS TWEED AND TAMMANY HALL

New York City's budget rises and falls in response to a political logic similar to the one outlined above. Periods of increased public expenditures and indebtedness follow upon the rise to power of new but loosely organized political coalitions, and periods of retrenchment are associated with the expulsion of these new forces from the political arena, or their subjugation to tighter political discipline.

In New York City, these new political forces have generally been coalitions of elements of the city's business community and members of ethnic groups that had previously been politically weak. Such political coalitions have traditionally been pieced together by machine politicians, who placed new ethnic groups on the public payroll to win their votes, and at the same time sponsored the public projects favored by their allies in the business community. This method of purchasing political support can be costly. On three occasions in the city's history—in 1871, 1933, and 1975—it led to a fiscal crisis that enabled the banks owning the city's debt to insist that municipal expenditures be drastically reduced as part of a bail-out plan. The politicians in office when the city amassed its debt were discredited by their responsibility for the city's difficulties, and weakened by the retrenchment program; this in turn permitted the political agents of the bankers to call themselves reformers and win the next election. This experience chastened the defeated political forces, and enabled a more sober leadership to emerge among them. It also gave the new leaders an incentive to organize their followers more tightly, and upon returning to power they could be less generous in dealing with their rank-and-file supporters, and more accommodating in dealing with their erstwhile opponents.

The rise and fall of the Tweed Ring illustrates this process quite clearly. Boss Tweed was allied with businessmen who operated chiefly in local markets—building contractors, real-estate men, street-railway promoters, savings bank owners, and manufacturers, who benefited from Tweed's ambitious program of opening up new streets and transit lines in the northern sections of the city. Uptown development had previously proceeded slowly;

city officials had been more responsive to the elite merchants and bankers operating in national and international markets—interests that were oriented to the downtown district and the port, and that regarded as utterly profligate uptown development on the scale proposed by Tweed.

Tweed also sponsored the political incorporation of the immigrant Irish. In the three weeks prior to the election of 1868, the judges allied with the Tweed Ring naturalized several thousand new citizens, and expanded the number of registered voters in the city by more than 30 percent. The attachment of these new voters to the Tammany organization was reinforced by placing many on the public payroll, and with a public welfare program that bore some marked similarities to the poverty programs of the 1960s. (The 1960s poverty programs funneled public monies to community groups and Baptist churches in black neighborhoods; Boss Tweed's public welfare program channeled public funds to charitable institutions and Catholic churches in Irish neighborhoods.)

The cost of bringing the local businesses and the immigrants into the political system was high. The budget of the Streets Department, for example, quadrupled in Tweed's first years as Deputy Commissioner. It was especially high because the Ring was structurally weak. Tweed was unable to command the obedience of other politicians; instead, he was compelled to purchase with cash bribes the support of state legislators, county supervisors, and even his immediate associates. To finance its operations, the Ring levied a surcharge on all city contracts. And because the Ring was weak, Tweed hesitated to raise taxes sufficiently to meet the city's current expenses, let alone to cover the costs of the capital improvements he sponsored. Just as Mayors Lindsay and Beame were to do a century later, Tweed funded short-term revenue notes into long-term bonds. In the last four years of Ring rule in New York, the city's outstanding indebtedness tripled.

The Ring was brought down by the city's creditors, who were driven to act by two events that destroyed their tolerance for a regime based upon the groups from which Tweed drew his support. The first was the Orange Riot of July 1871, sparked by a parade of Irish Protestants celebrating the Catholic defeat at the Battle of the Boyne. Catholic spectators threw stones at the troops protecting the marchers, and the troops responded with a volley of gunfire that killed thirty-seven spectators. The press blamed the city government for provoking the disturbance, and respectable elements in New York concluded from the incident that a municipal government dependent upon the political support of the Irish could not preserve public order. The second event that led the city's financial elite to move against the Ring was the suspension of trading in New York City bonds on the Berlin Stock Exchange, and the refusal of bankers in London, Paris, and Frankfurt to extend any more loans to the city, after a series of exposés in the press revealed the extent of municipal corruption and the size of the city's debt. The collapse of the city's credit threatened the solvency of all the New York banks owning municipal securities. To protect itself, the city's financial community felt it imperative that the Ring be overthrown. This was accomplished, in the words of a contemporary pamphlet, through an "insurrection of the capitalists": a group of the city's most prominent businessmen, the Committee of 70, organized a tax strike, and a thousand property owners refused to pay their municipal taxes until the city's accounts were audited. In addition, the city's bankers refused to lend the municipal government the money needed to meet the city payroll and cover debt-service payments until a reformer, Andrew Haswell Green, was appointed Deputy Comptroller with full authority over the city's finances. The coup de grace was given the Tweed Ring when the Committee of 70 entered a slate of candidates in the 1871 municipal elections and won control of the city government.

The collapse of the Tweed Ring enabled "Honest John" Kelly, in alliance with a group of wealthy, nationally oriented Democrats, to seize control of Tammany Hall. Kelly concluded from the Tweed episode that Tammany could not survive if all elements of the business community united against it, and that to avoid such opposition it must shed its reputation for corruption and profligacy. He accomplished this by purging Tammany of its more disreputable elements and by centralizing and strengthening the party organization. (It has been said that Kelly "found Tammany a horde and left it an army.") Kelly then used this organization to elect a succession of respectable merchants to the mayoralty, discipline lower-level Tammany officials engaged in the grosser forms of corruption, and make himself Comptroller, in which position he pursued an extremely tightfisted policy of retrenchment.

By creating the modern Tammany machine, Kelly and his successors, Richard Croker and Charles Murphy, established a mechanism for incorporating immigrants into the city's political system in a way that was tolerable to, if not entirely to the liking of, the city's propertied elite. This involved extruding from the political system competing contenders for control over the city's immigrant masses. Kelly's victory represented the triumph of a respectable middle-class leadership group among the Irish (Kelly himself was married to a niece of Cardinal McCloskey), and the maintenance of this group's control entailed the defeat of both the lower-class gangs that had formerly played an important role within Tammany, and the trade-union and socialist movements that at various times (most notably in the 1880s and the 1910s) attempted to assume political leadership of the working classes.

The preservation of Tammany's hegemony, however, required that the machine's subordinate functionaries be tightly disciplined, and that new ethnic groups be given a share of the spoils. When the hold of the machine's central leadership weakened, as it increasingly did after Boss Charles Murphy's death in 1925, Tammany officials were free to enrich themselves without limit, and to freeze out newcomers. The bacchanalia of corruption during the administration of Jimmy Walker, and the inability of Tammany's fragmented leadership to face up to, or impose upon their subordinates, the stringencies that the Depression required, set the stage for the New York fiscal crisis of 1933, and the triumph in the municipal election that year of a coalition of reformers, businessmen, Italians, and Jews, under the leadership of Fiorello La Guardia.

FROM ACCOMMODATION TO COMMUNITY PARTICIPATION

The last political leaders in New York to successfully pursue John Kelly's strategy were Carmine De Sapio, Alex Rose, and Robert Wagner. These leaders won a secure position for Italians and Jews in New York politics by helping to expel from the political system those elements of their ethnic constituency who were least acceptable to other groups in the city. De Sapio consolidated his hold over the Democratic Party by purging Tammany of its gangster element, which was primarily Italian, but included Jewish district leaders such as Sidney Moses and Harry Brickman. Rose established the influence of the Liberal Party by destroying the Communist-dominated American Labor Party, which was heavily Jewish, although its most prominent member was the Italian-American Congressman Vito Marcantonio. Both De Sapio and Rose created tightly centralized party organizations, and when they united behind the same candidates, municipal elections involved as little competition as they had during the heyday of machine rule in the 1920s. In the mayoral race of 1957, Robert Wagner, who had the support of both organizations, won 72 percent of the vote and defeated his Republican opponent by almost one million votes.

The politicians who governed New York City during the 1950s defused opposition by accommodating its major organized interests. The downtown business community was satisfied because control over the development programs that were of prime interest to them was placed in the hands of Robert Moses and/or various public authorities responsible only to their bondholders. Municipal civil servants and elite civic associations were granted substantial influence over the city's major service-delivery agencies. And in making revenue and expenditure decisions, elected officials paid special heed to the views of the city's tax-conscious lower middle class homeowners. Consequently, during Mayor Wagner's first two terms, the city government did little that aroused controversy, and its expense budget increased at an average annual rate of only 6.6 percent between 1953 and 1960.

This political calm was shattered in the late 1950s and early 1960s by the emergence of three political movements in New York—the Democratic reform movement, the school-integration movement, and the movement to unionize city employees. The effort of politicians to gain power in the city by allying with these movements destroyed the regime constructed by De Sapio, Rose, and Wagner, and initiated an era of budgetary inflation.

The first of these political movements to emerge was the reform movement in the Democratic Party. In the face of its threat, Mayor Wagner undertook to salvage his career in 1961 by turning on his political mentor, Carmine De Sapio, and seeking renomination with the support of the reformers and the municipal civil service. The steps Wagner took to win their backing—especially his sponsorship of a new city charter—weakened the regular party organizations, loosened some of the restraints upon budgetary inflation in New York, and made him more dependent politically upon groups demanding services. Consequently, municipal expenditures increased during Wagner's third term at an average annual rate of 8.9 percent. Significantly, in 1961 the city's expense budget fell into deficit for the first time since the Depression, and it continued to do so during each year of Wagner's third term.

In 1965, the reformers and liberals abandoned their former allies in the municipal labor movement, and supported the mayoral candidacy of John Lindsay. The political forces backing Lindsay sought to drive the civil service unions from power and seize control of the municipal bureaucracy themselves. Lindsay centered his 1965 campaign around an attack upon the "power brokers" (i.e., civil service union leaders); he undertook to reorganize the municipal bureaucracy into ten super-agencies, which would be responsive to his leadership; and he regularly contracted with outside institutions (such as the RAND Corporation, the Ford Foundation, and various universities) to perform tasks formerly conducted by municipal civil servants. To gain political support, the Lindsay administration allied itself with the third new political movement of the 1960s, the black civil rights movement. Blacks were useful allies because they could be used to legitimize the administration's efforts to seize control of the bureaucracy, which was criticized for its failure to adopt "innovative" programs that were "responsive" to the needs of the black community. And the alliance Lindsay cultivated with blacks provided the administration with shock troops to attack the bureaucracy from below, a function served by the mechanisms of community participation established by the administration.

New York City's budget during the late 1960s reflected the political strategy and political constituency of the Lindsay administration. The three major municipal programs on which expenditures rose the most rapidly during the years 1966–71 were higher education (251 percent), welfare (225 percent), and hospitals (123 percent). The clientele of two of these programs (welfare and public hospitals) was predominantly black, and the explosion in expenditures for the third (higher education) occurred after the enactment of an open-admissions program that tripled black enrollments at the City University. Moreover, the staff providing services in each of these programs (whose salaries account for much of the increase in expenditures) was composed of large numbers of highly educated and well-paid professionals. To be sure, federal and state assistance under Aid to Families with Dependent Children and Medicaid helped the city pay for some of these new expenditures. But so far as the city's own funds (so-called tax-levy expenditures) were concerned, welfare and higher education were the fastest-growing budgetary categories during the first five years of the Lindsay administration.

The Lindsay administration was not in a position to finance the benefits it provided to its constituency by reducing or even holding the line on expenditures for other municipal programs, because Lindsay's victory in the mayoral election of 1965 did not destroy the influence of the unions that represented the employees of the more traditional municipal agencies. After Lindsay's election, the city-employee unions might no longer have had an ally in the mayor's office, but they retained their capacity to strike, to lobby before the state legislature, and to support or oppose candidates in future municipal elections. By the end of his first term, the mayor discovered how vulnerable he was to each of these maneuvers. He initially attempted to break the power of the unions by refusing to enter into the give-and-take of labor negotiations, inviting strikes, and then seeking to mobilize public opinion (and, in one instance, the National Guard) against the unions. These efforts repeatedly failed, and Lindsay eventually learned that he could not govern the city without the cooperation of the unions. In addition to the wages they obtained by striking, the unions were able to secure very lucrative retirement benefits from the state legislature during the Lindsay years, because as the regular party organizations in New York grew weaker, many state assemblymen and senators from the city found the civil service unions to be their most effective source of campaign assistance.

Finally, Lindsay himself was desperately in need of such assistance in his campaign for reelection in 1969. To win union support, he gave the unions everything they demanded during the 1969–70 round of contract negotiations. In these ways, the civil service unions were able to secure substantial salary and benefit increases for city employees during his tenure, thereby compelling the mayor to increase expenditures for the agencies employing their members. During the period 1966–71, the budgets of the traditional municipal departments—Police, Fire, Sanitation, the Board of Education—did not double or triple, as expenditures did for welfare, hospitals, and higher education, but they nonetheless did increase on the average by 66 percent.

SETTING THE STAGE FOR FINANCIAL RUIN

The Lindsay administration did not find it politically possible to obtain either enough additional state aid or enough additional taxing authority to finance all these expenditure increases. Although state aid payments to the city did rise substantially during the Lindsay years, there were limits to the willingness of upstate and suburban legislators to tax their constituents for the benefit of New York City. And the state legislature, when it considered New York City financial legislation, followed a set of informal procedures that enabled political forces unfriendly to Lindsay to block some of his proposals for tax increases and that favored the passage of legislation authorizing the city to borrow money to close its annual budget gap.

The Republican and Democratic leaders in the assembly and senate would round up the votes necessary to pass New York City financial legislation only if every single assemblyman and senator from the city voted in favor of the bills in question. In practice, this informal requirement for unanimous consent meant that these bills had to meet with the approval of each of the major interests enjoying access to the city's legislative delegation, the legislative leaders, and the governor. One such group was lower middle income homeowners, who were unable to defeat Lindsay in mayoral elections, but did send Republican assemblymen and senators to Albany to defend their interests. These legislators found it politically difficult to vote for tax increases, and to avoid losing their votes, the mayor and governor found it necessary to substitute bond and note issues for taxes. The city's major banks, whose views were represented in such deliberations by the governor, were quite happy to endorse deficit financing, because bond and note issues provided them with healthy commissions and good investment opportunities. Moreover, so long as the office boom of the 1960s continued—assisted by capital projects the city and state constructed with borrowed funds—it appeared that rising municipal tax receipts would enable the city to cover its debt-service payments.

The Lindsay administration was ultimately compelled to abandon its efforts to break the power of the public-employee unions, seize control of the municipal bureaucracy, and use the authority of the city government for new purposes. These efforts suffered a number of serious setbacks at the end of the mayor's first term and the beginning of his second. Lindsay's efforts to decentralize the city school system precipitated a bitter controversy and a teachers' strike—the Ocean Hill strike of 1968—and the settlement of the controversy was something of a defeat for the most militant advocates of community control. The upper middle class liberals and blacks who comprised the core of the Lindsay coalition were unable on their own to provide him with the votes he needed to win reelection in 1969, and Lindsay was consequently compelled to come to terms with the civil service unions. And the administration's plans to place a large, low-income housing project in the middle-class neighborhood of Forest Hills in 1971 generated intense local opposition and had to be drastically scaled down.

The defeat at Forest Hills chastened Lindsay, and the growth rate of the city's budget slowed considerably. From 1966 through 1971, operating expenditures had increased at an average annual rate of 16.5 percent. In 1972, the growth rate of the city's budget declined to 8.6 percent; in 1973 it was 9.3 percent. Moreover, much of this budgetary growth resulted from price inflation, and the deceleration of the city's budget after the Lindsay administration had received its political chastening is thus particularly dramatic when measured in constant dollars: annual expenditure increases in constant dollars averaged 11.5 percent from 1966 through 1971; they averaged 3.7 percent in the next two years. Abe Beame's election as mayor in 1973 simply confirmed that a new political and fiscal plateau had been reached. Mayor Beame's budgets, again measured in constant dollars, grew at an average annual rate of only 2.8 percent.

This new political and fiscal plateau did not involve a return to the status quo ante of the pre-Lindsay years. The new players in the political game, whom Lindsay had ushered onto the field, were not expelled—apart from a few unruly ones who had attempted to drive out some of the older players. And the claims of these new players to a share of the gate were recognized. Consequently, as Mayor Lindsay left office and Mayor Beame came in, the city's budget was more than three times as large as it had been at the close of the Wagner administration.

In the mid-1970s, however, it was far more difficult than it had been in the late 1960s for New York City to honor the claims upon its budget granted by the Lindsay administration. Inflation drove up the cost of providing a fixed bundle of municipal services, and the failure of the city's economy to recover from the recession of the early 1970s made it increasingly difficult for New York to cover these rising costs. Moreover, by the mid-1970s there was an explosion in the costs of the retirement benefits that the municipal government and the state legislature had granted to city employees during the previous decade. In 1965, the city's retirement costs had been $364 million; by 1974, they had risen to $1.121 billion, and in 1976 they were $1.48 billion. In 1965, the city's annual debt-service payments had been $470 million; by 1974, they had risen to $1.269 billion, and in two more years they reached $2.304 billion. In order to close the gap between current expenditures and current revenues, and refinance the short-term debt as it fell due, the city resorted ever more heavily to borrowing. By 1975, the city's cumulative short-term debt had risen to $5.3 billion. The budget Mayor Beame initially presented to the state legislature for fiscal year 1976 anticipated a further deficit of $460 million, and had the city been able to borrow all that it wanted in 1975, its short-term debt might have amounted to 33 percent of the entire outstanding short-term municipal debt in the United States! The city's request for huge grants and additional taxing authority from the state legislature, and its enormous demands upon the municipal-securities market for additional loans, set the stage for the New York fiscal crisis of 1975.

THE RISE OF THE BANKS

The fiscal crisis of 1975 was precipitated by a combination of events resembling the taxpayers' strike and bondholders' coup that had brought down Tweed a century earlier. The Republican state senators from New York City banded together in May 1975, and agreed to present a common front against the pressure from their party leaders and colleagues to vote for legislation granting additional taxing authority to the city. The refusal of these spokesmen for the city's taxpayers to consent to any new taxes increased the city's demand for credit, and thereby weakened the market for New York City securities. Later that month, the major New York banks refused to underwrite or purchase any more New York City notes and bonds, thereby driving the city to the verge of bankruptcy.

There is little reason to believe that the Republican legislators and the New York bankers foresaw the enormous consequences their actions would have, or that in precipitating the crisis they were motivated by anything beyond the desire to protect the short-run economic interests of the groups they represented and their own short-run political and institutional interests. As for the Republican state legislators, they were heavily dependent upon the support of small property owners, who were being squeezed by the combination of inflation, recession, high levels of taxation, and rent control in New York, and were increasingly voting on the Conservative party line. Moreover, in 1975 the governor's office was occupied by a Democrat for the first time in sixteen years and hence Republican legislators no longer had a compelling reason to support a tax package hammered out in negotiations between the governor and the mayor.

As for the major New York banks, there were a number of strictly economic reasons why they were becoming increasingly reluctant to purchase the city's securities. Other more lucrative investment opportunities (foreign loans, leasing, consumer financing) had recently been developed by the banks, or had been made available to them by amendments to the Bank Holding Company Act, and the failure of the real estate investment trusts had created liquidity problems for many of them. But most importantly, as the city's short-term debt began to skyrocket, it was becoming increasingly clear to outsiders as well as insiders that the city was engaged in a great Ponzi game: it was financing current expenditures by borrowing, and paying off old debt by issuing new debt. So long as dealing in New York municipal securities had been a high-profit, low-risk venture for the city's banks, they had been quite happy to participate without asking too many embarrassing questions of city officials. But when the eleven major New York banks realized in the spring of 1975 that the outside world would shortly be able to figure out what the municipal government had been doing, they unloaded $2.7 billion in New York City securities that they owned. With the banks flooding the market with old New York bonds at the same time the city was seeking to sell additional hundreds of millions in new municipal notes and bonds, the market in the city's securities collapsed.

This collapse confronted the banks with immediate and grave dangers. Unless the city could borrow additional money, it could not redeem its old notes and bonds as they fell due, and if the city defaulted on these obligations, the value of New York securities remaining in the banks' portfolios would plummet. If this occurred, not only would the banks suffer a direct loss, they also could be sued by the clients whose money they had invested in New York municipal securities. Thus the major New York banks sought desperately to keep the city from defaulting: they pleaded with out-of-town banks to purchase New York securities; when that failed, they pleaded with the federal government to guarantee the city's bonds. Indeed, the very desperation of the banks made it possible for the architects of the plan that bailed out New York to squeeze additional loans out of the banks to shore up the city's finances.

In addition to these short-run economic dangers, the fiscal crisis presented the banks with long-run political opportunities. It enabled the banks (and, more generally, the city's corporate elite) to gain a dominant voice in municipal affairs. Some of this influence rested upon the ability of the banks to extract concessions from the city government in return for lending it money. But the banks actually lent the city less money than either the municipal-employee pension funds or the federal government. The major reason the banks became so influential lies instead in the following combination of circumstances. First, the city had to be able to regain access to the municipal credit market, unless some other means of managing its cash flow, financing capital projects, and discharging its outstanding debts became available. Second, the city had no chance whatever of regaining access unless its most prominent bankers and business leaders were prepared to assert that they were satisfied it was managing its affairs in a prudent and economical fashion. Third, public officials at the municipal, state, and national levels accepted the banks' claim that if the business community's retrenchment program was adopted, the market would reopen to the city—in other words, that enactment of the retrenchment program was sufficient, as well as necessary, for the city to regain access to the market. This claim was, to say the least, highly conjectural.

In the name of making New York bonds marketable, the banks managed to extract enormous concessions from the city. In the process, the local business elite came to play a larger and larger role in governing the city, and the conduct of public policy in New York increasingly came to reflect the priorities of the business community. The state initially created a Stabilization Reserve Corporation (SRC) to market a new series of bonds for the city, and it specifically set aside the proceeds of certain city taxes to cover the debt-service payments on these bonds. When these bonds failed to sell, a new state-appointed board, the Municipal Assistance Corporation (MAC), was created to replace SRC. In addition to being granted the authority to issue bonds and use municipal tax revenues for debt service on these securities, MAC was given the power to revamp New York City's accounting system. When the MAC bonds also failed to sell, the state, at the urging of the banks, passed a statute requiring the city to balance its budget within three years and limit its annual expenditure increases to not more than 2 percent during that period, and creating an Emergency Financial Control Board (EFCB) empowered to freeze the wages of city employees, approve all city contracts, and supervise city finances.

The EFCB was composed of two state officials (the governor and state comptroller), two city officials (the mayor and city comptroller), and three private citizens appointed by the governor. The governor resisted pressure to appoint a labor and a minority representative, and selected instead the top executives of the New York Telephone Company, American Airlines, and Colt Industries. In addition, the mayor—at the urging of the business community—established the Mayor's Committee on Management Survey, chaired by the president of the Metropolitan Life Insurance Company, to reorganize the municipal bureaucracy along business lines. And in response to pressure from the banks, the mayor fired one of his oldest associates as First Deputy Mayor, and appointed prominent business executives to three of the most important financial and managerial positions in the city government: Deputy Mayor for City Finances, Budget Director, and Director of Operations. Just as the New York banks in 1871 were able to install their man, Andrew H. Green, as Deputy Comptroller, thereby gaining control of the city's finances, the leaders of the New York financial and business community were able to install their representatives in key positions, thereby gaining effective control over the city government after its 1975 fiscal crisis.

These spokesmen for the city's business community argued, with considerable justification, that New York had little alternative but to close the gap between expenditures and revenues by reducing expenditures. Tax increases would encourage more employers and taxpayers to leave the city, thus exacerbating New York's economic and fiscal problems. Among the city's expenditures, however, two categories were the particular targets of New York's fiscal overseers. The first were labor costs. In response to pressure from MAC and the EFCB, the city instituted a wage freeze and eliminated 56,000 employees from its payroll. This represents a nineteen percent reduction in the city's labor force. The second were programs with predominantly black clienteles—youth services, addiction services, compensatory higher education—which suffered disproportionately severe budget and personnel cutbacks. Moreover, personnel were fired in disproportionate numbers from job categories—clerical, paraprofessional, and maintenance—heavily staffed by blacks and Puerto Ricans. Consequently, between July 1974 and February 1976, the number of Latinos employed by mayoral agencies declined by 51 percent, and the number of black males declined by 40 percent. What retrenchment meant in practice is that the city curtailed the benefits it provided to two of the groups—civil servants and blacks—that had gained a measure of political power in the 1960s.

THE FALL OF THE BLACKS AND THE UNIONS

Squeezing out the blacks was a rather simple matter. Black leaders had mobilized their constituency in the 1960s by relying upon the resources provided by federal and local agencies, and by drawing upon the publicity and support of the press, national foundations, and universities. In the early 1970s, however, the Nixon administration turned sharply to the right, and federal expenditures for community organization were cut drastically. At about the same time, the Lindsay administration abandoned its mobilization strategy, and the various institutions in the not-for-profit sector that were committed wholeheartedly to social activism in the 1960s felt the pinch of a declining stock market and reduced federal social expenditures, and became far less aggressive politically. Finally, upper middle class youths, who had provided much of the manpower for community organization drives in the 1960s, turned to other causes in the following decade, such as environmentalism, consumerism, feminism, or simply careerism. The 1975 New York fiscal crisis represented the culmination of this trend: blacks were simply abandoned by their erstwhile supporters. It appears that the upper middle classes, who in the flush 1960s saw blacks as useful allies in the drive to extend their influence over municipal government, concluded in the harsher climate of the 1970s that their political interests could better be served by entering into an alliance with the banks. The *New York Times*, for example, uncritically accepted the most questionable assumption underlying the retrenchment program advocated by the city's business leadership—the notion that retrenchment would restore the city's access to the capital market—and it began attacking the civil service not in the name of responsiveness and innovation, but rather in the name of economy and productivity.

It was a far more troublesome problem to deprive the city employees of
the gains they achieved in the late 1960s and early 1970s, because city employees were far better organized than blacks, and their power was less dependent upon the steadfastness of their allies. Nonetheless, the civil service
unions were compelled to accept a wage freeze, layoffs, longer hours, and
heavier workloads. In addition, they were induced to invest (or to commit
themselves to invest) some $3.7 billion of their pension-fund assets in New
York City and MAC bonds. Indeed, after the onset of the fiscal crisis, the
tables were entirely turned in municipal labor relations. No longer did
the unions and the city bargain to determine which of the unions' demands the city would accede to; the question became which of the city's
demands the unions would accede to. How was this accomplished?

In an immediate sense, the tables were turned by the state's Financial
Emergency Act, which granted the EFCB the power to review—and to
reject—municipal labor contracts. But one must ask why the unions agreed
to play by these new rules, instead of striking to obtain higher wages. The
most direct explanation for the unions' meekness was that strikes would
almost certainly fail. New York City's creditors and potential creditors regarded the wage freeze as the acid test of whether public officials in New
York were prepared to mend their ways. Were city and state officials to bow
to the demands of a striking union, the city's sources of credit would dry up.
If the unions were to strike nonetheless—in an effort to compel the mayor
and governor to choose between losing access to credit once the city's current cash balance was depleted, and an immediate and total disruption of
municipal services—the mayor and governor would probably take the latter.
The success of a strike ultimately depends upon public tolerance—or more
concretely, whether the public will countenance the use of the National
Guard to perform the functions of striking workers. Mayor Lindsay floated
the idea of using the National Guard during the 1968 sanitation strike, and
quickly discovered that it was totally outside the realm of political possibility
at that time. It was a measure of how dramatically New York politics were
transformed that the municipal unions dared not tempt the mayor to consider such a proposal after the fiscal crisis.

Another reason for the remarkable restraint of the unions during the crisis
was that they had an enormous stake in the city's fiscal viability. Bankruptcy
would cause the value of the New York City and MAC bonds owned by the
union pension funds to plummet. More importantly still, bankruptcy would
throw the city into the hands of a receiver with the unilateral authority to
abrogate union contracts, slash wages, order wholesale firings, and reduce
pension benefits. This would mean the end of collective bargaining and
would threaten the very existence of the unions. To avoid these dangers,
municipal union leaders undertook the task of selling the retrenchment pro-

gram to their members, convincing them that they had no alternative but to bear with it. And by doing this, they made it unnecessary for the bankers and business leaders to rely upon harsher measures to implement the program. In this respect, the municipal labor leaders played a role in New York politics after the 1975 fiscal crisis similar to that played by John Kelly after the overthrow of Tweed: they assumed the job of disciplining the municipal labor force, just as Kelly imposed a system of discipline upon the ward heelers in Tammany. In praising city union leaders for being "responsible" for urging their members to bear with the wage freeze, the editorial writers of the *New York Times* were saying in 1975 precisely what the editor of the *Commercial Advertiser* said a century previously of Honest John Kelly, in more forthright terms: "Kelly has ruled the fierce Democracy in such a manner that life and property are comparatively safe. . . . It requires a great man to stand between the City Treasury and this most dangerous mass. . . . Dethrone Kelly and where is the man to succeed him?"

ELECTORAL TRANSFORMATION

There were, then, some striking similarities between the financial and political developments in New York following the fiscal crisis of 1975, and those in the aftermath of Tweed's downfall a century before. In each case, municipal expenditures exceeded municipal revenues, and the city was compelled to bring the two into line by reducing its expenditures. Retrenchment involved a reduction in the flow of benefits to groups that had recently acquired political power, which in turn meant that the members of these groups had to endure a new and more stringent fiscal and political order. This process of financial and political contraction was accomplished, in part at least, with the cooperation of leaders from the very groups that were being compelled to lower their sights and accept the harsher discipline of the new order.

The parallel is not perfect, however. The most obvious difference was that blacks and Puerto Ricans had less success defending their economic and political gains after the 1975 fiscal crisis than had the Irish, who defended their political claims through the Tammany Hall of John Kelly. Another difference was that the regime governing the city after 1975 was grounded upon a less organized and disciplined electoral base than the Tammany of Bosses Kelly, Croker, and Murphy. Ed Koch, who trounced Abe Beame in the 1977 mayoral primary, constructed a coalition of political forces strongly committed to municipal retrenchment. But Koch was defeated in the 1989 mayoral primary by David Dinkins. Dinkins drew political support from the racial minorities and municipal employees whose claims had been adamantly resisted by Koch. This helps explain why the Dinkins administration accumulated a deficit and New York City approached bankruptcy in 1991–92, only a decade and a half after its fiscal crisis of 1975.

In his 1977 campaign for mayor, Ed Koch vehemently denounced the political forces—liberal ideologues, black "poverty pimps," and municipal labor unions—that he claimed had driven the city to ruin during the Lindsay and Beame years.[1] After entering City Hall, Koch continued to attack these targets, and his harsh rhetoric made the mayor enormously popular, especially among middle-class Jewish and Catholic voters. But his personal popularity was not enough to enable Koch to govern the city. Therefore he allied with a number of established political forces—among them, the city's regular Democratic party organizations.

Mayor Koch found alliances with Democratic machine politicians useful because he was a political loner. In contrast to the mayors serving in the wake of New York's previous fiscal crises, who had been elected as leaders of reform slates, Ed Koch had run for the city's highest office entirely on his own. Consequently, members of the Board of Estimate and the city council had no political ties, let alone obligations, to the mayor. In the absence of such ties, the most convenient way for the mayor to secure enactment of his budget and legislative program—and thereby build a record on which to run for reelection—was to grant patronage to the party organizations with which a majority of members of the Board and the council were affiliated.

Koch also found it in his interest to establish close relations with a number of other political forces. By attending to the concerns of New York's financial and business leadership, his administration regained the confidence of the municipal capital markets, encouraged corporations to remain and expand in New York, and attracted new business to the city. By cultivating newspaper publishers, the mayor received strong support from the city's press for his administration's policy initiatives. And by supporting Republican candidates for state and national office, the mayor gained a receptive hearing in Albany and Washington for his projects and legislative proposals.

Koch's alliance strategy produced another important benefit for the mayor: it led to an almost total collapse of the opposition in his first two campaigns for reelection. Because the mayor had preempted most of the available sources of political support, the only Democratic official prepared to run against him in 1981 was an obscure state assemblyman, Frank Barbaro, and his leading opponent in the 1985 Democratic primary—City Council President Carol Bellamy—found it impossible to mount a serious challenge to him. Consequently, the press treated Bellamy as a carping critic rather than as a credible alternative to the incumbent.

The Republicans joined the Democrats in nominating Koch for a second term in 1981. In 1985 the GOP nominated a candidate for mayor, Diane McGrath, who had never previously run for elective office and whose cam-

TABLE 7.1

Race and Voting in the 1985 New York City Democratic Mayoral
Primary Election

	Whites	Blacks	Latinos	All Voters
Koch	75%	38%	70%	64%
Bellamy	22	22	20	19
Farrell	3	40	10	13

Source: NBC News exit poll.
Note: This table omits three minor candidates who together received
4 percent of the total vote.

paign ended in disarray: both the most powerful Republican public official
from the city, John Marchi, chairman of the Finance Committee of the New
York State Senate, and even McGrath's running mate for city council president, Eva Guardarramas, endorsed Koch for mayor.

The collapse of the opposition enabled Koch to win landslide reelection
victories in both 1981 and 1985. In the 1985 Democratic mayoral primary,
as Table 7.1 indicates, he trounced Bellamy by better than three-to-one
among both white and Latino voters. Koch won the general election that
year with 78 percent of the total vote. Significantly, however, only 38 percent of the city's registered voters went to the polls in the 1985 general
election, in contrast to the 75 to 80 percent turnout rates that had characterized New York City elections twenty years previously.

BLACK POWERLESSNESS IN NEW YORK CITY

More notable than the failure of New York's Republicans to challenge Koch
effectively in 1985 was the failure of the city's black leadership to do so—
even though many blacks considered the mayor's rhetoric to be racially
biased and his approval ratings in opinion surveys were consistently lower
among racial minorities than among whites. The political ineffectuality of
the mayor's nonwhite opponents during his first two terms was all the more
surprising in light of New York's traditional role as a center of liberalism. In
the year Koch was elected overwhelmingly to a third term, all but one of the
nation's next five largest cities had a black mayor.

Prior to the 1985 election, a majority of New York's most prominent black
politicians did establish the Coalition for a Just New York (CJNY) as a mechanism for selecting a candidate to run against Koch. This effort, however,
was marred by extraordinary factionalism, pitting Manhattan politicians
against Brooklyn politicians, African-Americans against Latinos, and black
clergymen against black elected officials and party leaders. Moreover, the

CJNY made no effort to ally with whites who opposed Koch's reelection. This fragmentation persisted even after the CJNY had selected its mayoral candidate, Herman Farrell, a black assemblyman and Democratic party leader from Manhattan. The Coalition's chairman, Albert Vann, had tried to get the CJNY to endorse a Puerto Rican candidate for mayor, in an effort to win Latino support in his own race for the borough presidency of Brooklyn. The Harlem political establishment was loathe to follow the lead of politicians from Brooklyn, however, and secured the CJNY's endorsement of Farrell. Vann retaliated by refusing to circulate Farrell's nominating petitions along with his own, and as a result the black mayoral candidate was almost denied a place on the ballot. Moreover, nonwhite politicians from other boroughs failed to give Farrell meaningful support. Thus the black mayoral candidate only carried one black assembly district outside his Manhattan bailiwick.

Although factionalism sapped the political strength of New York's racial minorities, it was more a symptom than the ultimate cause of their weakness. Such factionalism characterizes politics under conditions of low electoral mobilization: politicians who do not undertake to outmobilize their opponents seek to prevail by outmaneuvering them. The electoral turnout rates of nonwhites in New York were among the lowest of any major city in the United States. These low mobilization rates were related to one aspect of New York's heritage as the nation's most liberal city—its unusually extensive network of social service agencies.

A large number of nonwhite politicians in New York built their political bases upon community groups that received municipal subsidies for providing social services to neighborhood residents. Because the subsidies they received were not dependent upon their mobilizing an extensive electoral following, New York's black and Puerto Rican politicians were not compelled to undertake such mobilization. By contrast, in cities with a less extensive array of social services, the benefits that nonwhite politicians are able to obtain for their constituents are more likely to be proportional to their electoral clout, which provides these leaders with a strong motive to bring new voters into the electorate.

Koch criticized these linkages between antipoverty agencies and nonwhite politicians when he ran for mayor in 1977, then largely reestablished them after reorganizing the city's poverty program during his first term.[2] This won Koch the support of most black and Puerto Rican city council members in his bids for reelection. Significantly, the nonwhite politicians who opposed Koch in 1981 and 1985 were chiefly members of the state assembly and state senate, whose political organizations were financed by Albany.

The political demobilization of New York's black and Latino communities crippled Farrell's candidacy in 1985. Although half the city's population was nonwhite, only 32 percent of the voters who participated in that year's Democratic primary were black or Puerto Rican. Moreover, Farrell won only 40 percent support among blacks who did vote in the 1985 Democratic primary (barely more than the 38 percent voting for Koch), a mere 10 percent of the Puerto Rican vote, and a minuscule 3 percent of the white vote. Consequently, the black candidate ended up with only 13 percent of the total vote in the 1985 Democratic mayoral primary.

RECONCILING FISCAL AND POLITICAL VIABILITY

Ed Koch was not the first American politician to have won landslide victories within a constricted electoral universe by combining fiscal retrenchment with strident rhetoric. Politicians are most likely to rely upon such a strategy when they appeal for the support of middle-income voters or small property owners who regard themselves as pressured from above and below, but whose concrete grievances they cannot do much to alleviate. Members of the middle class are most likely to regard themselves as subject to such a squeeze during (or immediately after) periods of political turmoil and economic stress. Where the political institutions of a city are also weak, or the economic limits under which they operate are stringent, elected officials are not able to win support by implementing policies that address the substantive problems that these voters face. Therefore, voter participation rates drop and elections are won by politicians who play upon the fears and resentments of their constituents.

For example, following the fiscal crisis and the labor and racial strife that Detroit experienced in the 1930s and 1940s, Albert Cobo won the mayoralty by denouncing his opponents for being soft on communism and crime, and by promising to protect homeowners against the threat of tax increases and racially mixed public housing. Similarly, following its racial and fiscal crises of the 1960s and 1970s, New York was compelled to operate under a set of stringent constraints in order to obtain the loans it needed to stay afloat and to regain access to the public credit markets. These restrictions made it difficult for the mayor to provide his constituents with the municipal services to which they had become accustomed and encouraged Ed Koch to rely upon rhetoric and showmanship to win and retain the loyalty of his supporters.

No matter how successful their campaigns, politicians elected under these circumstances may find it difficult to govern and to secure reelection unless they can institutionalize their rule. The most difficult way to accomplish this is by attempting to organize voters into a new political party or permanent faction; it is considerably easier to ally with the local powers-that-be. (Mayor Dennis Kucinich of Cleveland provides a striking example of the consequence of refusing to reach such accommodations: he found himself completely unable to govern his city and was defeated after a single term in office.)[3] For this reason, though they commonly rely upon a populist or anti-elitist rhetoric, such politicians often come to terms with the local political establishment. Koch's alliances with New York's business leadership and its Democratic party organizations were particular instances of this general pattern.

The accommodation between politicians and the local establishment can be seen as the final phase in the restoration of political order after an episode of turmoil. In the case of New York, the first phase was the effort of Mayors Lindsay and Beame to purchase social harmony during and after the racial turmoil of the 1960s by accelerating the pace of municipal spending. This governing strategy was financially unsustainable, however, and the refusal of the city's creditors to tolerate it any longer enabled Ed Koch to come to power by denouncing the political forces that he claimed had undermined both public order and municipal finances. Though it won him a large popular following, this rhetoric did not guarantee that Koch would be able to govern the city, so he allied with a number of other political forces, including the city's Democratic party organizations. By extending his base of support, these alliances enabled Koch to construct an administration that, in contrast to the Lindsay and Beame mayoralties, was both fiscally and politically viable.

MUNICIPAL SCANDALS, FISCAL RETRENCHMENT, AND THE STRUGGLE FOR POWER IN AMERICAN CITIES

Just as Ed Koch's rise to power and his alliance with machine politicians were not unusual, neither was the crusade against corruption that erupted during his third term. Scandals are commonplace in American urban and national politics. They should not, however, be taken at face value.[4] Rather, scandals should be recognized as political events—an important technique in the struggle for power in American politics.[5]

Historically, allegations of corruption were used by civic notables, chambers of commerce, and newspapers to discredit mass-based party organizations that they were unable to defeat in electoral combat. This technique was imported into national politics by liberal political forces following the trouncing they received in the 1972 presidential election, and was used to drive Spiro Agnew and Richard Nixon from office. In the 1980s, the Reagan administration reexported it to the urban arena in an effort to discredit the Democrats in their strongholds. It was an investigation of municipal corruption by the Republican-controlled U.S. Attorney's office in Chicago that turned up the first evidence of bribery in New York City's Parking Violations Bureau (PVB).

After the U.S. Attorney in Manhattan, Rudolph Giuliani, revealed that he was investigating the PVB, other institutions whose power is enhanced by municipal scandals joined in the quest for corruption in New York: more than a dozen investigating agencies and the city's major newspapers began to search for, publicize, and express indignation over evidence of official misconduct in the city. In their crusade, these defenders of public morality exhibited a certain ruthlessness: threatening draconian prison sentences to induce defendants to turn against one another, prosecuting defendants in both state and federal courts for precisely the same acts, and publicizing unsubstantiated allegations. Even though there never was a suggestion that Koch himself was corrupt, the preoccupation of the press with the scandal was politically costly to him. During his first two terms, the mayor had depended upon the image he projected through the mass media to retain the support of voters, so his inability to dominate the news on his own terms presented him with a serious political problem and contributed to David Dinkins's victory in the 1989 Democratic mayoral primary.

MASS MOBILIZATION AND URBAN FISCAL CRISIS

In the early 1990s New York City approached another fiscal crisis—less than two decades after the 1975 fiscal crisis analyzed earlier in this chapter. New York's most recent financial difficulties were related to the election of David Dinkins to succeed Ed Koch as mayor in 1989 and to a sharp downturn in the city's economy in 1991–92.[6]

A major reason that Koch was defeated when he ran for a fourth term in 1989 was that many voters held him partly responsible for a sharp increase in racial tensions in the city—tensions expressed in, and heightened by, episodes in which mobs of whites attacked blacks and blacks assaulted whites. They believed that a Mayor Dinkins would be better able than Mayor Koch to restore a measure of racial harmony in the streets and parks of New York City.

David Dinkins's election as the city's first black mayor was greatly aided by Jesse Jackson's campaign in New York's 1988 Democratic presidential primary. Jackson had mobilized large numbers of black voters, and 94 percent of the city's expanded black electorate supported Dinkins in the 1989 mayoral primary.[7] In addition, Dinkins was backed by more than 60 percent of Latino voters (many of whom had voted for Koch in previous elections) and his candidacy was endorsed by several major municipal employee unions.

During his campaign for mayor, Dinkins promised to deal more equitably with racial minorities than his predecessor and he also promised to improve relations between City Hall and municipal employee unions. The municipal bond market was appalled by the likely implications of these campaign commitments for the city's finances. Within a month of Dinkins's election, the interest rate on New York City bonds rose from only 0.25 percent above the average interest rate paid by twenty representative issuers of municipal bonds (the Bond Buyers Index) to as much as 1.25 percent higher.

Early in his administration, Mayor Dinkins approved a 5.5 percent wage increase for municipal employees. Since labor costs account for roughly half the city's budget, any decision to increase the pay of municipal employees imposes a major financial burden on the city. This pay increase was negotiated by Edward Schmertz, Dinkins's director of labor relations. Schmertz had served on the city's Board of Collective Bargaining under Mayor Lindsay but had been removed from this position by Mayor Koch, who regarded him as too close to the unions.

The case of Koch indicates that the decline of the machine does not lead all mayors to cultivate the same alliances and pursue similar fiscal policies. Far from allying with municipal labor, Koch presented himself as an opponent of vested interests and the ordinary citizen's friend in City Hall. His administration was marked by some bruising fights between the mayor and city employee unions and by the administration's holding the real wages of municipal employees steady throughout Koch's twelve years in office. But Koch increased the size of the city's work force to counter the claim of critics that there had been a decline in city services during his mayoralty. Though he kept the city's budget balanced during his years in office, Mayor Koch left the municipal government with a work force whose salary might be difficult to meet when the city's economy and tax revenues declined, and when the mayor's office was occupied by a politician less able than Koch to balance the city's budget by slashing expenditures.

In addition to raising the wages of municipal employees, the Dinkins administration increased spending on social services. Between Koch's last year in office and Dinkins's first year, the city's total expenditures increased by $1.5 billion, of which higher municipal labor costs accounted for $1 billion and increased spending for social services comprised $500 million. Under Dinkins, the municipal government picked up a number of social service programs that the Reagan and Bush administrations had cut. If the city's increased labor expenditures can be regarded as a payoff to Dinkins's supporters in the municipal labor movement, its increased spending for social services can be seen as a reward to his administration's supporters in the liberal community.

New York City's revenues increased sufficiently between 1989 and 1990 to cover these higher costs and balance the budget during Mayor Dinkins's first year in office. However, municipal tax revenues slowed in 1991, while the commitments Dinkins had made at the outset of his administration continued to exert pressure on municipal spending. Thus the city faced deficits in the early 1990s.

Dinkins proposed a number of expenditure reductions, tax increases, and labor concessions to cope with the prospect of budget deficits. However, with the decline of the Tammany machine, power in the city had become so fragmented that Dinkins found it difficult to secure the cooperation of even his own department heads, let alone the city council, in implementing these proposals, and the leaders of the municipal employee unions adamantly refused even to discuss labor givebacks with the mayor.

These political developments help to explain New York's recent financial problems. The close relationship between Dinkins's election and the unraveling of New York's finances reflects some of the themes of this chapter and book. Municipal financial problems are related to the politics of mass mobilization, especially mobilization in the absence of a party organization sufficiently well-organized to subject politicians to internally imposed discipline. The claim by the city's creditors that the city's finances are in a state of crisis—their declaration of a "municipal fiscal crisis"—is a way of discrediting the politics of mass mobilization.

Bankruptcy would put an end to local self-government, as the city's creditors take charge of municipal finances. Hence the threat of bankruptcy utterly discredits the politicians the electorate deems to be responsible for this danger. The prospect of a fiscal crisis thus weakens urban politicians associated with expenditure-demanding political forces: it undermines their claim to represent democracy. Political forces associated with taxpayers, who are identified with spending discipline, have their legitimacy enhanced by a fiscal crisis and are able to charge their opponents with representing "special interests," rather than democratic forces and the public interest.

Notes

Preface

1. Theda Skocpol, "Bringing the State Back In: Strategies of Analysis in Current Research," in *Bringing the State Back In*, ed. Peter B. Evans, Dietrich Rueschemeyer, and Theda Skocpol (New York: Cambridge University Press, 1985), 24.

2. See, Ira Katznelson, "Working-Class Formation: Constructing Cases and Comparisons," in *Working-Class Formation: Nineteenth Century Patterns in Western Europe and the United States*, eds. Ira Katznelson and Aristide Zolberg (Princeton, N.J.: Princeton University Press, 1986), chap. 1.

3. Benjamin Ginsberg, *The Consequences of Consent* (Reading, Mass.: Addison-Wesley, 1982).

Chapter 1

1. See James March and Johan Olsen, "The New Institutionalism: Organizational Factors in Political Life," *American Political Science Review* 78 (1984): 734–49; Theda Skocpol, "Bringing the State Back In: Strategies of Analysis in Current Research," in *Bringing the State Back In*, ed. Peter B. Evans, Dietrich Rueschemeyer, and Theda Skocpol (Cambridge: Cambridge University Press, 1985); Skocpol, *Protecting Soldiers and Mothers: The Politics of Social Provision in the United States, 1870s–1920s* (Cambridge: Harvard University Press, 1993), chap. 1; also excellent is Stephen Krasner, "Approaches to the State: Alternative Conceptions and Historical Dynamics," *Comparative Politics* 16 (January 1984): 223–46.

2. For another effort by political scientists in the institutionalist camp to transcend the tension between the "new institutionalism" and the analysis of "public choice," see Karen Orren and Stephen Skowronek, "Beyond the Iconography of Order: Notes for a 'New Institutionalism,'" in *The Dynamics of American Politics: Approaches and Interpretations*, ed. Lawrence Dodd and Calvin Jillson (Boulder, Colo.: Westview Press, 1993).

3. Theodor Adorno, Else Frenkel Brunswick, Daniel J. Levinson, and R. Nevitt Sanford, *The Authoritarian Personality* (New York: Harper, 1950).

4. See the criticisms of the "neoclassical theory of patronage" in Chapter 2.

5. See, e.g., Skocpol, "Bringing the State Back In."

6. Mancur Olson, *The Logic of Collective Action* (Cambridge: Harvard University Press, 1965).

7. See, e.g., Richard Valelly, "Party, Coercion, and Inclusion: The Two Reconstructions of the South's Electoral Politics," *Politics and Society* 21 (March 1993), 37–57.

8. This section and the next three draw on my "Political Parties, Political Mobilization, and Political Demobilization," in *The Political Economy*, ed. Thomas Ferguson and Joel Rogers (Armonk, N.Y.: M. E. Sharpe, 1984), 140–48.

9. Maurice Duverger, *Political Parties* (London: Methuen, 1959), xxiii–xxxviii;

Samuel P. Huntington, *Political Order in Changing Societies* (New Haven: Yale University Press, 1968), 417–19.

10. Duverger, *Political Parties*, xxvii.

11. James Q. Wilson, *Political Organizations* (Princeton: Princeton University Press, forthcoming), chap. 9.

12. This formulation was developed in the course of discussions with my colleague, Benjamin Ginsberg.

13. Walter Dean Burnham, "The System of 1896: An Analysis," in *The Evolution of American Electoral Systems*, ed. Paul Kleppner, (Westport, Conn.: Greenwood Press, 1981); Michael McGerr, *The Decline of Popular Politics: The American North, 1865–1928* (New York: Oxford University Press, 1986).

14. See, e.g., Raymond Carr, *Spain 1808–1939* (Oxford: Oxford University Press, 1966), 394; Denis Mack Smith, *Italy: A Modern History* (Ann Arbor: University of Michigan Press, 1959), chap. 15.

15. James Kurth, "Industrial Change and Political Change: A European Perspective," in *The New Authoritarianism in Latin America*, ed. David Collier (Princeton: Princeton University Press, 1979), 335–37.

16. Gerald Brenan, *The Spanish Labyrinth* (Cambridge: Cambridge University Press, 1960), 5.

17. Richard Hofstadter, *The Idea of a Party System: The Rise of Legitimate Opposition in the United States, 1780–1840* (Berkeley and Los Angeles: University of California Press, 1969), 109.

18. Theda Skocpol, "A Critical Review of Barrington Moore's *Social Origins of Dictatorship and Democracy*," *Politics and Society* 4 (Fall 1973): 1–34.

19. For a general discussion of the influence of the international system on domestic politics, see Peter Gourevitch, "The Second Image Reversed," *International Organization* 32 (1978): 881–912; and Martin Shefter, "International Influences on American Politics," in *New Perspectives on American Politics*, ed. Lawrence Dodd and Calvin Jillson (Washington, D.C.: Congressional Quarterly Press, 1993).

20. Benjamin Ginsberg, *The Consequences of Consent* (Reading, Mass.: Addison-Wesley, 1982), 16.

21. Seymour Martin Lipset and Stein Rokkan, "Cleavage Structures, Party Systems, and Voter Alignments: An Introduction," in *Party Systems and Voter Alignments* (New York: Free Press, 1967), 1–64; Peter Gourevitch, "International Trade, Domestic Coalitions, and Liberty: Comparative Responses to the Crisis of 1873–1896," *Journal of Interdisciplinary History* 8 (1977): 281–313. See also Ronald Rogowski, *Commerce and Coalitions* (Princeton: Princeton University Press, 1989), chap. 2.

22. See Chapter 2.

23. Eric Foner, *Politics and Ideology in the Age of the Civil War* (New York: Oxford University Press, 1980), chap. 3.

24. James R. Kurth, "The Political Consequences of the Product Cycle: Industrial History and Political Outcomes," *International Organization* 33 (Winter 1979): 1–34.

25. Adam Przeworski, "Institutionalization of Voting Patterns, or Is Mobilization the Source of Decay?" *American Political Science Review* 69 (March 1975): 49–67.

26. See, e.g., Paul Johnson, *A Shopkeeper's Millennium: Society and Revivals in*

Rochester, New York, 1815–1837 (New York: Hill and Wang, 1978); Samuel P. Huntington, *American Politics: The Promise of Disharmony* (Cambridge: Harvard University Press, 1981); Charles Maier, *Recasting Bourgeois Europe* (Princeton: Princeton University Press, 1975), part I.

27. See David Collier, *The New Authoritarianism in Latin America* (Princeton: Princeton University Press, 1979), passim.

28. Benjamin Ginsberg, "Electoral Politics and the Redistribution of Political Power," paper delivered at the 1983 Annual Meeting of the American Political Science Association, Chicago, Illinois, September, 1983.

29. See Chapter 2.

30. See Chapter 3.

31. See Chapter 4. Cf. Edward C. Banfield and James Q. Wilson, *City Politics* (Cambridge: Harvard University Press, 1963).

32. See Chapter 5.

33. See Chapter 6.

34. See Chapter 7.

35. Samuel Huntington, *Political Order in Changing Societies*, chap. 7.

36. Benjamin Ginsberg and Martin Shefter, *Politics by Other Means: The Declining Importance of Elections in America* (New York: Basic Books, 1990), chap. 1.

Chapter 2

This is a revised version of a paper that was delivered at the Conference on the Scope and Practice of Social Science History, April 23, 1976, at the University of Wisconsin, and that appeared in the occasional paper series of the Western Societies Program, Center for International Studies, Cornell University. For their helpful comments I would like to thank Douglas Ashford, Peter Gourevitch, Davydd Greenwood, Peter Katzenstein, James Kurth, Peter Lange, Charles Maier, and Sidney Tarrow.

1. James C. Scott, *Comparative Political Corruption* (Englewood Cliffs, N.J.: Prentice-Hall, 1972), 110.

2. Ibid., chap. 6; Carl Landé, "Networks and Groups in Southeast Asia: Some Observations on the Group Theory of Politics," *American Political Science Review* 67 (March 1973): 119; Edward C. Banfield and James Q. Wilson, *City Politics* (Cambridge: Harvard University Press, 1963), 40–41, 122–23, and "Political Ethos Revisited," *American Political Science Review* 65 (December 1971): 1048–62; Elmer Cornwell, "Bosses, Machines and Ethnic Groups," *The Annals of the American Academy of Political and Social Sciences* 353 (May 1964): 27–39; Samuel P. Hays, "Political Parties and the Community-Society Continuum," in *The American Party Systems*, ed. William Nisbet Chambers and Walter Dean Burnham (New York: Oxford University Press, 1967), 173–81.

3. Scott, *Comparative Political Corruption*, 93, 118; Banfield and Wilson, *City Politics*, chap. 9. See also James Q. Wilson, *Political Organizations* (Princeton: Princeton University Press, forthcoming), chap. 6; Leon Epstein, *Political Parties in Western Democracies* (New York: Praeger, 1967), 27–31.

4. R. H. Evans, *Coexistence: Communism and Its Practice in Bologna, 1945–1965* (South Bend, Ind.: University of Notre Dame Press, 1967).

5. Michael Paul Rogin, *The Intellectuals and McCarthy: The Radical Spectre* (Cambridge: MIT Press, 1967), 187; Sidney Tarrow, *Power in Movement* (New York: Cambridge University Press, 1994), chap. 6.

6. Gerald Brenan, *The Spanish Labyrinth* (Cambridge: Cambridge University Press, 1943), pt. 2.

7. David Mayhew, *Placing Parties in American Politics* (Princeton: Princeton University Press, 1986), chaps. 2, 5.

8. Peter J. Larmour, *The French Radical Party in the 1930s* (Stanford: Stanford University Press, 1964).

9. On patronage and party management in the United States in the mid-nineteenth century, see Harry J. Carmen and Reinhard H. Luthin, *Lincoln and the Patronage* (New York: Columbia University Press, 1943). On regional variations in the significance of patronage in present-day American politics, see Raymond Wolfinger, "Why Political Machines Have Not Withered Away and Other Revisionist Thoughts," *Journal of Politics* 34 (May 1972): 397–98. Also, see Chapter 5.

10. Luigi Graziano, "Center-Periphery Relations and the Italian Crisis: The Problem of Clientelism," in *Territorial Politics in Industrial Nations*, ed. Sidney Tarrow, Peter J. Katzenstein, and Luigi Graziano (New York: Praeger, 1978), 312; and Alessandro Pizzorno, "I ceti medi nei meccanismi del consenso," in *Il Caso Italiano*, ed. F. L. Cavazza and S. R. Graubard (Milan: Garzanti, 1974), cited in ibid., 326 n. 59.

11. James Duesenberry, *Income, Saving and the Theory of Consumer Behavior* (Cambridge: Harvard University Press, 1949); Robin Marris, *The Economic Theory of Managerial Capitalism* (New York: Free Press, 1964), chap. 4.

12. Richard M. Cyert and James G. March, *A Behavioral Theory of the Firm* (Englewood Cliffs, N.J.: Prentice-Hall, 1963), chaps. 3–5.

13. Emma Rothschild, *Paradise Lost: The Decline of the Auto-Industrial Age* (New York: Random House, 1973), chaps. 2–3.

14. If a party is to pursue a patronage strategy it must be able to offer to its supporters indulgences that exceed in value the benefits they can obtain from alternative sources. That is, whether a group will respond to a patronage appeal depends in the first instance not upon the characteristics of its members per se—every man, as Hobbes observed, has his price—but rather upon the relationship between the value of the benefits produced by the government, on one hand, and the opportunities available to individuals whose support the party is seeking, on the other. This condition for the existence of a patronage party is not very restrictive. Regimes as weak as those of Jacksonian America and Hanoverian England were capable of generating indulgences that could sustain patronage parties, because even these regimes, through the granting of offices and charters, were in a position to affect the important interests of a considerable portion of the political class. It is only when the jurisdiction of a regime is not commensurate in *scope* with the major interests of its inhabitants that the party controlling the regime would not be in a position to pursue a patronage strategy. The major example of such a setting is the upper income suburb. The regulations from which a suburban politician can exempt a business firm, and the purchases that a suburban government makes, are of insignificant value to businessmen whose firms operate in metropolitan, national, or even international markets. And the jobs such politicians control pay salaries far lower than the ones that the upper-income residents of these communities can obtain from the private

market. A classic fallacy of ecological reasoning thus is involved in the effort to draw inferences concerning the behavior of upper- and middle-class *individuals* from the character of politics in upper- and middle-income *communities* such as Winnetka, Illinois, or Scarsdale, New York. See Banfield and Wilson, *City Politics*, 140.

15. Epstein, *Political Parties*, 110–11.

16. Landé, *Networks and Groups*, 118.

17. Philip Selznick, *Leadership in Administration* (Evanston, Ill.: Row, Peterson and Co., 1957), chap. 2; Ira Katznelson, *Black Men, White Cities* (London: Oxford University Press, 1973), 24.

18. Samuel P. Huntington, *Political Order in Changing Societies* (New Haven: Yale University Press, 1968), 415.

19. Maurice Duverger, *Political Parties* (London: Methuen, 1959), xxiv–xxxvii; Huntington, *Political Order*, 412–20.

20. Cf. Wolfram Fischer and Peter Lundgreen, "The Recruitment and Training of Administration and Technical Personnel," in *The Formation of National States in Western Europe*, ed. Charles Tilly (Princeton: Princeton University Press, 1975), 456–561; and John A. Armstrong, *The European Administrative Elite* (Princeton: Princeton University Press, 1973).

21. H. R. Trevor-Roper, "The General Crisis of the Seventeenth Century," in *Crisis in Europe, 1560–1660*, ed. Trevor Aston (Garden City, N.Y.: Anchor Books, 1967), 87; Isaac Kramnick, *The Rage of Edmund Burke* (New York: Basic Books, 1977), chap. 2; Reinhard Bendix, *Nation Building and Citizenship* (Garden City, N.Y.: Anchor Books, 1969), 86–89; Brenan, *Spanish Labyrinth*, 195, 201.

22. Seymour Martin Lipset and Stein Rokkan, *Party Systems and Voter Alignments* (New York: Free Press, 1967), 50–52.

23. As Carl Landé notes, the leaders of weak regimes are unable to prevent subordinate officials from using their authority to generate patronage and to build personal followings for themselves, because such leaders are dependent upon the support of these officials and their followings to keep the regime in power. This phenomenon can explain why the Christian Democratic party in Italy has become increasingly factionalized and patronage-ridden the longer it is in office. See Landé, *Networks and Groups*, 126–27; Raphael Zariski, "Intra-Party Conflict in a Dominant Party: The Experience of Italian Christian Democracy," *Journal of Politics* 27 (February 1965): 3–34.

24. See, e.g., the account of the development of the CPP machine in Scott, *Comparative Political Corruption*, 124–31.

25. Clement Henry Moore, *Tunisia since Independence* (Berkeley and Los Angeles: University of California Press, 1965).

26. Immanuel Wallerstein, *The Modern World-System* (New York: Academic Press, 1974), chap. 5.

27. For an analysis of variations in the role patronage plays in party politics among the different regions of the United States, see Chapter 5.

28. F. L. Carsten, *The Origins of Prussia* (Oxford: Clarendon Press, 1954), pt. 3.

29. Cf. Fisher and Lundgreen, "Recruitment and Training," 457ff.

30. Hans-Eberhard Mueller, "Bureaucracy and Education: Civil Service Reform in Prussia and England as Strategies of Monopolization" (Ph.D. diss., University of California at Berkeley, 1974), 138.

31. Hans Rosenberg, *Bureaucracy, Aristocracy and Autocracy* (Cambridge: Harvard University Press, 1958), 43ff.

32. Ibid., 66, 68ff.; Mueller, "Bureaucracy and Education," 103, 230.

33. John R. Gillis, *The Prussian Bureaucracy in Crisis* (Stanford: Stanford University Press, 1971), 29ff.

34. Rosenberg, *Bureaucracy, Aristocracy and Autocracy*, chap. 9. The social function of the gymnasiums and universities in Germany and of the ideology of *Bildung* is discussed in Armstrong, *European Administrative Elite*, 135ff., 165ff.

35. Theodore Hamerow, *The Social Foundations of German Unification, 1858–1871: Struggles and Accomplishments* (Princeton: Princeton University Press, 1972), chaps. 4, 7, 9; Arthur Rosenberg, *Imperial Germany: The Birth of the German Republic, 1871–1918* (Boston: Beacon Press, 1964), chap. 1.

36. Karl Hochswender, "The Politics of Civil Service Reform in West Germany" (Ph.D. diss., Yale University, 1962), 63–65.

37. Otto Kircheimer, "Germany: The Vanishing Opposition," in *Political Oppositions in Western Democracies*, ed. Robert Dahl (New Haven: Yale University Press, 1966), 237.

38. Lewis Hertzman, *DNVP: Right Wing Opposition in the Weimar Republic, 1918–1924* (Lincoln: University of Nebraska Press, 1963), 17.

39. Herman Finer, *The Theory and Practice of Modern Government* (London: Methuen, 1932), 2: 1389.

40. The continuities between the civil service of Imperial and Weimar Germany are stressed by Fritz Morstein Marx, "Civil Service in Germany," in *Civil Service Abroad*, ed. Leonard White (New York: McGraw-Hill, 1935), 161–274.

41. Ralf Dahrendorf, *Society and Democracy in Germany* (New York: Doubleday, 1967), 252.

42. Erich Eyck, *A History of the Weimar Republic* (Cambridge: Harvard University Press, 1962), 297.

43. Hertzman, *DNVP*, chap. 5; Charles Frye, "Parties and Interest Groups in Weimar and Bonn," *World Politics* 17 (July 1965): 641.

44. Brian Chapman, *The Profession of Government* (London: Urwin University Books), 284f.

45. Herman Finer, *Governments of the Greater European Powers* (New York: Holt, 1965), 628.

46. Morstein Marx, "Civil Service in Germany," 256.

47. Fritz Morstein Marx, *Government of the Third Reich* (New York: McGraw-Hill, 1937); Hochswender, "Politics of Civil Service Reform," 61.

48. Finer, *Theory and Practice*, 480; James Pollock, "The German Party System," *American Political Science Review* 23 (November 1929): 885.

49. David Schoenbaum, *Hitler's Social Revolution* (Garden City, N.Y.: Doubleday, 1966), chap. 7.

50. Ibid., 221.

51. Hochswender, "Politics of Civil Service Reform," 39.

52. Lewis Edinger, "Post-Totalitarian Leadership," *American Political Science Review* 54 (March 1960): 66.

53. Dahrendorf, *Society and Democracy*, chap. 14.

54. John Herz, *The Government of Germany* (New York: Harcourt, Brace, Jovanovich, 1972), 130.

55. Taylor Cole, "The Democratization of the German Civil Service," *Journal of Politics* 14 (February 1952): 17.

56. Edinger, "Post-Totalitarian Leadership," 80.

57. Herz, *Government of Germany*, 128.

58. Dahrendorf, *Society and Democracy*, chap. 15.

59. Hochswender, "Politics of Civil Service Reform," 193.

60. Ibid., 154.

61. Ibid., 157–59, citing Theodor Eschenburg, *Aemterpatronage* (Stuttgart: C. E. Schwab, 1961).

62. Anderson, *Lineages of the Absolutist State*, pt. 1, chap. 5.

63. Barrington Moore, *Social Origins of Dictatorship and Democracy* (Boston: Beacon Press, 1966), chap. 1.

64. Louis Namier, *The Structure of Politics at the Accession of George III* (London: Macmillan, 1961).

65. This is not true of extraparliamentary groupings such as the Yorkshire Association in the late eighteenth century or the Chartists in the early nineteenth. These formations were the prototypes of what I have termed "externally mobilized parties." On the former, see Ian R. Christie, "The Yorkshire Association, 1780–1784: A Study in Political Organization," *The Historical Journal* 3 (1960): 144–61. On the latter, see Asa Briggs, *Chartist Studies* (New York: St. Martin's Press, 1959).

66. Mueller, "Bureaucracy and Education," 281.

67. The phrase is taken from Theodore Lowi's *End of Liberalism* (New York: W. W. Norton, 1969), 243.

68. Olive Anderson, "The Janus Face of Mid-Nineteenth Century English Radicalism: The Administrative Reform Association of 1855," *Victorian Studies* 8 (March 1965): 231–42.

69. Mueller, "Bureaucracy and Education," 324–30, 344.

70. I owe this insight to a discussion with Martin Bernal.

71. I.e., the redistribution of seats that was part and parcel of parliamentary reform in 1867 and 1884 and the Corrupt Practices Act of 1883. On the latter see Cornelius O'Leary, *The Elimination of Corrupt Practices in British Elections, 1868–1911* (Oxford: Clarendon Press, 1962), chap. 6.

72. James Cornford, "The Transformation of Conservatism in the Late Nineteenth Century," *Victorian Studies* 7 (September 1963): 41f.

73. E. J. Feuchtwanger, *Disraeli, Democracy and the Tory Power* (Oxford: Clarendon Press, 1968), 106–13.

74. E. J. Feuchtwanger, "J. E. Gorst and the Central Organization of the Conservative Party, 1870–1882," *Bulletin of the Institute of Historical Research* 32 (1959): 192–208.

75. Cornford, "Transformation of Conservatism," 49.

76. H. J. Hanham, *Elections and Party Management* (London: Longmans, Green, 1959), 362.

77. Cornford, "Transformation of Conservatism," 44.

78. Feuchtwanger, *Tory Party*, 87.

79. James Cornford, "The Adoption of Mass Organization by the British Conservative Party," in *Cleavages, Ideologies and Party Systems,* ed. Erik Allardt and Yrjo Littunen (Turku: Publications of the Westermarck Society), 411.

80. W. L. Guttsman, *The British Political Elite* (New York: Basic Books, 1963), 78ff. See also James Cornford, "The Parliamentary Foundations of the Hotel Cecil," in *Ideas and Institutions of Victorian Britain,* ed. Robert Robson (London: G. Bell and Sons, 1967), 268–311.

81. R. T. McKenzie, *British Political Parties* (New York: St. Martin's Press, 1963), 180; Samuel Beer, *British Politics in the Collectivist Age* (New York: Alfred A. Knopf, 1967), 98.

82. Cornford, "Transformation of Conservatism," 50ff.

83. H. J. Hanham, "Political Patronage at the Treasury, 1870–1912," *Historical Journal* 3 (1960): 77ff. See also Maurice Wright, *Treasury Control of the Civil Service* (Oxford: Clarendon Press, 1969), 75.

84. John Vincent, *The Formation of the Liberal Party* (London: Constable, 1966), 126–38.

85. H. J. Hanham, "The Sale of Honours in Late Victorian England," *Victorian Studies* 3 (March 1960): 227.

86. McKenzie, *British Political Parties,* 179.

87. Denis Mack Smith, *Italy: A Modern History* (Ann Arbor: University of Michigan Press, 1959), chap. 6.

88. Alexander Gerschenkron, *Bread and Democracy in Germany* (New York: H. Fertig, 1966).

89. See P. A. Allum, *Italy: Republic without Government?* (New York: W. W. Norton, 1973), 4, 22.

90. Mack Smith, *Italy,* chap. 15.

91. Robert Fried, *The Italian Prefects* (New Haven: Yale University Press, 1963), 297.

92. With the signing of the Lateran Pacts in 1929, of course, Mussolini reached an accommodation with the Church. This presaged and made possible the political configuration that was to emerge after World War II. See Richard A. Webster, *The Cross and the Fasces* (Stanford: Stanford University Press, 1960), chap. 7.

93. Norman Kogan, *A Political History of Postwar Italy* (New York: Frederick A. Praeger, 1966), 30.

94. On Christian Democracy in Italy, see Webster, *Cross and the Fasces,* and Mario Einaudi and Francois Goguel, *Christian Democracy in Italy and France* (Notre Dame, Ind.: University of Notre Dame Press, 1952), pt.1.

95. Giorgio Galli and Alfonso Prandi, *Patterns of Political Participation in Italy* (New Haven: Yale University Press, 1970), chap. 5.

96. Graziano, "Italian Crisis," Table 7.

97. Pizzorno, "I ceti medi nel meccanismi del consenso."

98. Sidney Tarrow, *Peasant Communism in Southern Italy* (New Haven: Yale University Press, 1967), 341.

99. P. A. Allum, *Italy,* 25–29.

100. Ibid., 29–32.

101. Luigi Graziano, "Clientelism and the Political System: The Sources of the Italian Crisis" (mimeo, 1975), 5–7 and sources cited therein.

102. Raphael Zariski, "Intra-Party Conflict in a Dominant Party: The Experience of Italian Christian Democracy," *Journal of Politics* 27 (February 1965): 3–34.

103. Sidney Tarrow, "The Italian Party System between Crisis and Transition," *American Journal of Political Science* 21 (May 1977): 217.

104. Ezra Suleiman, *Politics, Power, and Bureaucracy in France* (Princeton: Princeton University Press, 1974), 308ff.

105. See Sidney Tarrow, *Integration at the Periphery: The Grassroots Politics in Italy and France* (New Haven: Yale University Press, 1977), for a striking picture of differences between present-day France and Italy on this score.

106. Alexis de Tocqueville, *The Old Regime and the French Revolution* (New York: Anchor Books, 1955), pt. 2, chap. 2.

107. Nicholas J. Richardson, *The French Prefectoral Corps, 1814–1830* (Cambridge: Cambridge University Press, 1966), 204–6.

108. Theodore Zeldin, *France, 1848–1945* (Oxford: Clarendon Press, 1973), 1:576–79; Larmour, *French Radical Party*, 24.

109. Zeldin, *France, 1848–1945*, 1:603ff., chap. 20.

110. David Thompson, *Democracy in France since 1870*, 4th ed. (New York: Oxford University Press, 1964), 59–63.

111. Suleiman, *Bureaucracy in France*, 46f.

112. David Mayhew, *Placing Parties in American Politics* (Princeton: Princeton University Press, 1986), 234–37; Wolfinger, "Political Machines."

113. Ari Hoogenboom, *Outlawing the Spoils: A History of the Civil Service Reform Movement* (Urbana: University of Illinois Press, 1961); Gerald W. McFarland, *Mugwumps, Morals and Politics, 1884–1920* (Amherst: University of Massachusetts Press, 1975).

114. To be sure, the political cliques that dominated southern politics prior to the Progressive era were even more narrowly based than their counterparts in the western states, and yet patronage still plays a significant role in state politics in the South. The survival of patronage in the South is to be explained more by the weakness of progressivism in that overwhelmingly rural region than by the breadth of support enjoyed by their opponents. In the urban enclaves of the South progressivism was quite successful. See C. Vann Woodward, *Origins of the New South, 1877–1913* (Baton Rouge: Louisiana State University Press, 1951), 388ff.

115. Cf. Mowry, *California Progressives*, chap. 1; and Martin Shefter, "The Electoral Foundations of the Political Machine: New York City, 1884–1897," in *American Electoral History: Quantitative Studies of Popular Voting Behavior*, ed. Joel Silbey, Alan Bogue, and William Flanigan (Princeton: Princeton University Press, 1978), 263–98.

116. Glazer and Moynihan phrase it this way:

> The Catholic ascendary in New York had been based first on numbers, but second on a reasonably well grounded assumption that they normally, as Democrats, would best look after the interests of ordinary people, and would be especially concerned with the least well off, being themselves only recently emerged from that condition. The Protestant elite of the city had always challenged that assumption, asserting instead that the Tammany bosses were boodlers, pure and simple, or in a slightly different formulation such as that of Lincoln Steffens,

were merely paid lackeys of the really Big Boodlers. Either way the charge was that they did not truly represent the people as they claimed to do. In three elections out of four the masses would choose to believe Charlie Murphy's version rather than that of the *New York Times*.

Nathan Glazer and Daniel P. Moynihan, *Beyond the Melting Pot*, 2d ed. (Cambridge: MIT Press, 1971), lxiii.

Chapter 3

1. Walter Dean Burnham, *Critical Elections and the Mainsprings of American Politics* (New York: W. W. Norton, 1970); idem., *The Current Crisis in American Politics* (New York: Oxford University Press, 1982), chap. 3.

2. See Chapter 2.

3. Martin Tolchin and Susan Tolchin, *To the Victor . . . Political Patronage from the Clubhouse to the White House* (New York: Random House, 1971).

4. On the "gentlemen freeholders" of Virginia, see C. S. Sydnor, *Gentlemen Freeholders: Political Practices in Washington's Virginia* (Chapel Hill: University of North Carolina Press, 1952). On the "patriciate" of New Haven, see Robert A. Dahl, *Who Governs?* (New Haven: Yale University Press, 1961), chap. 2. New York and Pennsylvania were to some extent exceptions to this pattern: party organizations were somewhat stronger and a partisan spoils system was more fully developed in these states than elsewhere in the country. See Richard Hofstadter, *The Idea of a Party System: The Rise of Legitimate Opposition in the United States* (Berkeley: University of California Press, 1969), 213; and C. Russell Fish, *The Civil Service and the Patronage* (New York: Longmans, Green, 1905), chap. 1.

5. Richard E. Ellis, *The Jeffersonian Crisis: Courts and Politics in the Young Republic* (New York: W. W. Norton, 1971), chap. 17.

6. Ibid., 279; cf. David Hackett Fischer, *The Revolution of American Conservatism: The Federalist Party in the Era of Jeffersonian Democracy* (New York: Harper and Row, 1965).

7. Vernon Dibble, "The Organization of Traditional Authority: English Country Government, 1558–1640," *Handbook of Organizations*, ed. James G. March (Chicago: Rand McNally, 1965), 884f, cited in Matthew Crenson, *The Federal Machine: Beginnings of Bureaucracy in Jacksonian America* (Baltimore: Johns Hopkins University Press, 1975), 171. Dibble is speaking here of the Justices of the Peace in Elizabethan England, but the same can be said of the notables appointed to office by Washington.

8. Paul Van Riper, *History of the United States Civil Service* (Evanston, Ill: Row, Peterson, 1958).

9. Noble Cunningham, *The Jeffersonian Republicans: The Formation of Party Organization, 1789–1801* (Chapel Hill: University of North Carolina Press, 1957).

10. Hofstadter, *Idea of a Party System*, chap. 5.

11. Noble Cunningham, *The Jeffersonian Republicans in Power, 1801–1809* (Chapel Hill: University of North Carolina Press, 1963), chaps. 2–3; Leonard D. White, *The Jeffersonians: A Study in Administrative History, 1801–1829* (New York: Macmillan, 1951), chap. 24.

12. William N. Chambers, *Political Parties in a New Nation* (New York: Oxford University Press, 1963).

13. Presidents James Monroe and John Quincy Adams even reappointed civil servants who were politically hostile to their administrations, although they could have been replaced under the Tenure of Office Act of 1820. See White, *The Jeffersonians*, chap. 26.

14. Sidney Aronson, *Status and Kinship in the Higher Civil Service* (Cambridge: Harvard University Press, 1964).

15. Luigi Graziano, "Center-Periphery Relations and the Italian Crisis: The Problem of Clientelism," in *Territorial Politics in Industrial Nations*, ed. Sidney Tarrow, Peter J. Katzenstein, and Luigi Graziano (New York: Praeger, 1978).

16. Michael A. Lebowitz, "The Jacksonians: Paradox Lost?" in *Towards a New Past*, ed. Barton Bernstein (New York: Vintage, 1966), 65–89.

17. Lynn Marshall, "The Strange Stillbirth of the Whig Party," *American Historical Review* 72 (January 1967): 445–68.

18. Richard P. McCormick, "Political Development and the Second Party System," in *The American Party Systems*, ed. Walter Dean Burnham and William N. Chambers (New York: Oxford University Press, 1975), 90–116.

19. Crenson, *The Federal Machine*.

20. Crenson's explanation for "the rise of bureaucracy in Jacksonian America" is similar to the explanation for the contemporaneous "discovery of the asylum" proposed by David Rothman, *The Discovery of the Asylum: Social Order and Disorder in the New Republic* (Boston: Little, Brown, 1971). Rothman's analysis has been criticized tellingly by Christopher Lasch, *The World of Nations* (New York: Vintage, 1974), 316, and I draw upon Lasch's argument in my remarks.

21. Richard Hofstadter, *The Age of Reform: From Bryan to F.D.R.* (New York: Knopf, 1955) 240–42; cf. Max Weber, "Politics as a Vocation," *From Max Weber*, ed. Hans Gerth and C. Wright Mills (New York: Oxford University Press, 1958), 77–128.

22. Carl N. Degler, "The Locofocus: Urban 'Agrarians,'" *Journal of Economic History* 16 (September 1956): 216.

23. Amy Bridges, *A City in the Republic: Antebellum New York and the Origins of Machine Politics* (Ithaca: Cornell University Press, 1987), chap. 6.

24. F. O. Gatell, "Money and Party in Jacksonian America: A Quantitative Look at New York City's Men of Quality," *Political Science Quarterly* 82 (June 1967): 235–52.

25. David Montgomery, "The Shuttle and the Cross: Weavers and Artisans in the Kensington Riots of 1844," *Journal of Social History* 5 (Summer 1972): 411–46.

26. Ira Katznelson, "Community, Capitalist Development, and the Emergence of Class," *Politics and Society* 9 (1979): 203–37.

27. Ward heelers, gang leaders, and saloon keepers were "natural leaders" within the city's immigrant and working-class districts and their rise to positions of power during the Jacksonian Era thus has been attributed by many scholars to the parochial and ethnic loyalties of the city's lower classes. They were not, however, the only leaders: the city's patriciate long had claimed that title, and in the 1820s and 1830s trade union leaders and even some radical intellectuals (e.g., Robert Dale Owen and George Henry Evans) sought to assert such a claim. Why did the former set of leaders prevail and the latter lose? To say that this occurred because ethnic loyalties were

more salient to voters than class identifications, or that the American political culture was becoming less "deferential" and more "participant" during this Age of Egalitarianism (as do Lee Benson [1974] and other scholars of the "ethnocultural" school) is simply to describe the phenomenon that requires explanation rather than to offer an explanation for it. A genuine explanation would have to consider the way in which changes in formal electoral arrangements, the availability of organizational resources, the behavior of elites, and the structure of social relations worked to the advantage of one set of leaders and to the disadvantage of others. The excellent studies by David Montgomery ("The Shuttle and the Cross: Weavers and Artisans in the Kensingston Riots of 1844") and Amy Bridges (*A City in the Republic: Antebellum New York and the Origins of Machine Politics*) are exemplary in this respect. I am suggesting that the availability of patronage and public subsides helped sustain the organizations led by one type of working-class political leader, while at the same time changes in the economy and social structure were undermining the organizations led by competing leaders, as Montgomery and Bridges indicate.

28. Marshall, "Strange Stillbirth of the Whig Party."

29. As Leonard D. White, in *The Jacksonians: A Study in Administrative History, 1829–1860* (New York: Macmillan, 1954), chap. 16, points out, the spoils system became increasingly extensive during the years of the second party system regardless of the party in power.

30. Hofstadter, *Idea of a Party System*, 249.

31. Even at its height, the spoils system did not extend to the more technical branches of the civil service, and a system of examinations was instituted to fill some of these positions. See White, *The Jacksonians*, chap. 19.

32. Eric Foner, *Free Soil, Free Labor, Free Men: The Ideology of the Republican Party before the Civil War* (New York: Oxford University Press, 1970).

33. Henry J. Carman and Reinhard H. Luthin, *Lincoln and the Patronage* (New York: Columbia University Press, 1943).

34. Morton Keller, *Affairs of State: Public Life in Late Nineteenth-Century America* (Cambridge: Harvard University Press, Belknap Press, 1977).

35. John G. Sproat, *The "Best Men": Liberal Reformers in the Gilded Age* (New York: Oxford University Press, 1968).

36. David Montgomery, *Beyond Equality: Labor and the Radical Republicans, 1862–1872* (New York: Knopf, 1967).

37. My argument in this paragraph and the ones following concerning the politics of civil service reform in the late nineteenth century draws upon Stephen Skowronek, *Building a New American State* (New York: Cambridge University Press, 1982).

38. Richard Jensen, *The Winning of the Midwest* (Chicago: University of Chicago Press, 1971).

39. See the statement of George William Curtis, the president of the National Civil Service Reform League, quoted in Lawrence D. White, *The Republicans: A Study in Administrative History, 1869–1901* (New York: Macmillan, 1958), 300.

40. Two other conditions contributed to the willingness of the major parties to enact civil service reforms the Mugwumps advocated. First, the parties were coming to rely more heavily for campaign finance upon contributions from businessmen,

rather than political assessments levied on the salaries of civil servants. Second, the Pendleton Act received the support of merchants who wished to increase the efficiency of the largest post offices and customs houses. Significantly, the only positions outside Washington mandated for inclusion in the classified service by the Act were those in post offices and customs houses employing more than fifty persons.

41. A. B. Sageser, *The First Two Decades of the Pendleton Act* (Lincoln: University of Nebraska Press, 1935).

42. Ari Hoogenboom, *Outlawing the Spoils: A History of the Civil Service Reform Movement* (Urbana: University of Illinois Press, 1961).

43. In cities where centralized one-party regimes existed, opposition to the locally dominant political machines took the form of an anti-party or nonpartisan reform movement prior to 1896. On the emergence of the nonpartisan reform movement in New York City following the critical municipal election of 1888, see Martin Shefter, "The Emergence of the Political Machine: An Alternative View," in *Theoretical Perspectives in Urban Politics*, ed. Willis Hawley and Michael Lipsky (Englewood Cliffs, N.J.: Prentice-Hall, 1976), 14–44; and Shefter, "The Electoral Foundations of the Political Machine: New York City, 1884–1897," in *The History of American Electoral Behavior*, ed. Joel Silbey, Allen G. Bogue, and William Flanigan (Princeton: Princeton University Press, 1978).

44. George E. Mowry, *The California Progressives* (Berkeley: University of California Press, 1951).

45. David P. Thelen, *Robert M. LaFollette and the Insurgent Spirit* (Boston: Little, Brown, 1976).

46. Scholars who have attempted to provide a sociological rather than a political analysis of Progressivism assume a priori (and incorrectly) that the same social groups rallied behind the movement in all areas of the country. Because the Progressives generally drew their support from among groups that did *not* enjoy privileged access to the locally dominant regime, it has been possible for historians studying different cities, states, and levels of government to find data supporting divergent conclusions such as that Progressivism was fundamentally a movement of a declining upper class, a rising business and professional elite, or of the working class. See, e.g., Hofstadter, *Age of Reform*, Hays, "The Politics of Reform in Municipal Governments in the Progressive Era," *Pacific Northwest Quarterly* 55 (October 1965): 157–69; and Michael Paul Rogin and James Shover, *Political Change in California* (Westport, Conn.: Greenwood, 1970).

47. Robert H. Wiebe, *The Search for Order, 1877–1920* (New York: Hill and Wang, 1967), chap. 7.

48. Samuel Haber, *Efficiency and Uplift: Scientific Management in the Progressive Era, 1890–1920* (Chicago: University of Chicago Press, 1964).

49. Burnham, *Critical Elections*.

50. P. Van Riper, *History of the United States Civil Service*.

51. Oscar Kraines, "The President versus Congress: The Keep Commission, 1905–1909—The First Comprehensive Presidential Inquiry into Administration," *Western Political Quarterly* 23 (March 1970): 5–54.

52. Herbert Emmerich, "The Johnson System," in *Readings on Congress*, ed. Raymond E. Wolfinger (Englewood Cliffs, N.J.: Prentice-Hall, 1971), 225–41.

53. Van Riper, *History of the United States Civil Service*, 219–23.

54. Martin J. Schiesl, *The Politics of Efficiency: Municipal Administration and Reform in America: 1880–1920* (Berkeley: University of California Press, 1977).

55. Cf. Charles Maier, *Recasting Bourgeois Europe* (Princeton: Princeton University Press, 1975).

56. Grant McConnell, *Private Power and American Democracy* (New York: Knopf, 1966).

57. Van Riper, *History of the United States Civil Service*.

58. Samuel P. Huntington, "Congressional Responses to the Twentieth Century," in *Congress and America's Future*, 2d ed., ed. David Truman (Englewood Cliffs, N.J.: Prentice-Hall, 1973), 6–38.

59. In this respect, the administrative reforms of the Progessives were parallel to the managerial reforms that the Taylorites were advocating in private industry. See Christopher Lasch, *The World of Nations* (New York: Vintage, 1974), chap. 7. These new managerial techniques enabled the directors and executives of corporations to extend their control over the organization of production and the pacing of work, an effort that entailed the destruction of older craft modes of organization and the defeat of the union efforts to assume these prerogatives. Moreover, the very groups that sponsored this effort in the private sector—an emerging national upper class and an increasingly self-confident professional class—advocated, and would benefit from, administrative reforms in the public sector. To this extent, the administrative reforms of the Progressives can be understood as an effort by a would-be governing class to assume control of the means of administration as well as the means of production, divesting in the process the groups that formerly had exercised this control. In the private sector, those who were squeezed out through this process attempted to protect themselves through strikes, an effort that generally failed. In the public sector, they sought to protect themselves by appealing to the Congress or to old-line party organizations, an effort that met with far greater success. (Congress, for example, refused to establish a Bureau of Efficiency under the control of the president, as the Taft Commission had requested, and it did not pass the Classification Acts until the White House was occupied by a conservative Republican.) Through this process, Congress came to represent the interests of "parochial" elites and social groups, and social conflicts came to be expressed as institutional conflicts. It is in this context that the "institutionalization" of the House of Representatives occurred. Cf. Polsby "The Institutionalization of the U.S. House of Representatives," *American Political Science Review* 62 (March 1963): 144–68.

60. Robert P. Sharkey, *Money, Class, and Party: An Economic Study of Civil War and Reconstruction* (Baltimore: John Hopkins University, 1959).

61. Samuel P. Hays, *Conservation and the Gospel of Efficiency* (Cambridge: Harvard University Press, 1958).

62. See Chapter 5.

63. James Sundquist, *Dynamics of the Party System* (Washington, D.C.: Brookings Institution, 1975), chap. 11.

64. The contrast between the number of states adopting the merit system in 1933–49 and in 1917–33 cannot be attributed to the various social changes that supposedly render the patronage system obsolete and reduce its popular appeal (i.e., the increasing complexity of government in the modern era, the assimilation of immi-

grants), because more states adopted the merit system during the still earlier period, 1900–1916, than during 1917–33.

65. Van Riper, *History of the United States Civil Service.*

66. Richard Polenberg, *Reorganizing Roosevelt's Government: The Controversy over Executive Reorganization, 1936–1939* (Cambridge: Harvard University Press, 1966).

67. Barry Karl, *Executive Reorganization and Reform in the New Deal: The Genesis of Administrative Management, 1900–1939* (Chicago: University of Chicago Press, 1963).

68. Polenberg, *Reorganizing Roosevelt's Government.*

69. Robert Merton, *Social Theory and Social Structure* (New York: Free Press, 1957), 71–81.

70. David Greenstone, *Labor in American Politics* (New York: Alfred A. Knopf, 1969).

71. Civil Service Assembly, *Civil Service Agencies in the United States: A 1940 Census*, Pamphlet No. 16 (Washington, D.C.: U.S. Government Printing Office, 1940).

72. Emmerich, "The Johnson System."

73. Sundquist, *Dynamics of the Party System*, chaps. 11–12.

74. Bruce Stave, *The New Deal and the Last Hurrah: Pittsburgh Machine Politics* (Pittsburgh: University of Pittsburgh Press, 1970).

75. James Q. Wilson, *The Amateur Democrat: Club Politics in Three Cities* (Chicago: University of Chicago Press, 1962).

76. James Fenton, *Midwest Politics* (New York: Holt, Rinehart and Winston, 1966).

77. Robert Lee Sawyer, *The Democratic State Central Committee in Michigan, 1949–1959: The Rise of the New Politics and the New Political Leadership* (Ann Arbor: University of Michigan Institute of Public Administration, 1960).

78. Theodore Lowi, "Machine Politics—Old and New," *Public Interest* 9 (Fall 1967): 83–92; Lowi, *The Politics of Disorder* (New York: Basic Books, 1967).

79. Dahl, *Who Governs?*

80. Edward C. Banfield, *Political Influence* (New York: Free Press, 1961).

81. Wallace Sayre and Herbert Kaufman, *Governing New York City* (New York: Russell Sage, 1960).

82. In speaking of the New Politics movement, I am referring to the congeries of groups that took the liberal position on social issue and foreign policy questions from the 1960s through the 1980s, in particular, the antiwar, civil rights, environmental, consumer, and women's movements—as well as organizations, such as Common Cause, concerned more narrowly speaking with questions of electoral and administrative reform. The New Politics movement was extremely heterogeneous and did not speak with a single voice. (The same can be said, of course, of the Jacksonian movement or the Progressive movement, for this is one of the characteristics that distinguishes a political movement from a political organization.) Nonetheless, most of its members supported each of the reforms I discuss in this section. On "movement politics," see Lowi, *The Politics of Disorder*, chaps. 1–2; Sidney Tarrow, *Power in Movement: Collective Action, Social Movements and Politics in the Modern State* (New York: Cambridge University Press, 1994).

83. Robert Axelrod, "Where the Votes Come From: An Analysis of Electoral Co-alitions, 1952–1968," *American Political Science Review* 66 (March 1972): 11–20.

84. Peter Marris and Martin Rein, *Dilemmas of Social Reform: Poverty and Community Action in the United States* (London: Routledge and Kegan Paul, 1975).

85. Daniel Patrick Moynihan, *Maximum Feasible Misunderstanding* (New York: Free Press, 1969).

86. Robert Salisbury, "Urban Politics: The New Convergence of Power," *Journal of Politics* 26 (November 1964): 775–97.

87. Sayre and Kaufman, *Governing New York City*.

88. My argument here is consistent with that offered by Piven and Cloward, *Regulating the Poor: The Functions of Public Welfare* (New York: Pantheon, 1971), chap. 9. My interpretation of the Great Society differs from theirs, however, in two respects: they speak of the national administration as a unitary force; and they assume that the payoff which the proponents of the Great Society expected to reap from its programs was electoral support in national elections. But as Marris and Rein, *Dilemmas of Social Reform*, 246 n.7, observe, they offer no evidence to support their supposition that votes were central in the minds of those who planned these programs. I am suggesting, rather, that at least after 1965 the grant-in-aid programs of the Great Society were pet projects not of the administration (the president increasingly found them an embarrassment) but rather of the administration's liberal wing. These programs were a sincere effort on the part of upper middle class liberals to assist the poorest city dwellers, namely blacks. What this entailed, in their understanding, was getting city bureaucracies to adopt the latest and best ideas, that is, their own ideas. And what this meant in practice was extending their own influence and the influence of their local political allies over municipal agencies and governments.

89. Although there are many insightful observations on the "new class" in the social science literature, to my knowledge there has yet to be published a scholarly analysis of the social bases of the New Politics movement. I would hypothesize that at the core of the movement stood upper middle class professionals and young people who were affiliated with institutions in the "grants economy" universities, government agencies, foundations, consulting firms, churches, charitable institutions, and so forth. This collection of individuals became self-conscious in the course of fighting against the domestic and foreign policies that tied together the coalition of producer interests (including labor) which, as I will note below, played a central role in American politics in the post–New Deal era. The New Politics movement's efforts to "reorder national priorities" (e.g., by reducing the size of the military establishment, enacting a "Marshall Plan for the cities," protecting the environment even at the cost of industrial growth) would reallocate political power, public benefits, and the use of the public domain to the disadvantage of the industrial sector and to the advantage of the institutions with which the members of the new class were affiliated. These policies could also be supported by members of the upper middle class who worked for profit making institutions (e.g., newspapers, law firms, financial institutions, advertising agencies) but whose livelihood was not tied in immediate and obvious ways to the prosperity of the industrial sector and to public policies (e.g., weapons procurement, highway construction, the licensing of power plants) contributing to that prosperity. For a compelling general statement on the role of political conflict in the

process of class formation, see Lasch, "Toward a Theory of Post-Industrial Society," in *Politics in the Post-Welfare State*, ed. M. Donald Hancock and Gideon Sjoberg (New York: Columbia University Press, 1972), 48 n.1. For analyses of the "new class" and its politics, see David Apter, "Ideology and Discontent," *Ideology and Discontent* (Glencoe, Ill.: Free Press, 1964, 15–43; David Vogel, *Fluctuating Fortunes* (New York: Basic Books, 1989), chap. 5.

90. Austin Ranney, *Curing the Mischief of Faction: Party Reform in America* (Berkeley: University of California Press, 1975).

91. James Q. Wilson, "The Bureaucracy Problem," *The Public Interest* 6 (Winter 1967): 3–9.

92. Ira Katznelson, "Was the Great Society a Lost Opportunity?" in *The Rise and Fall of the New Deal Order, 1930–1980*, ed. Steve Fraser and Gary Gerstle (Princeton: Princeton University Press, 1989), 185–211.

93. Edwin Amenta and Theda Skocpol, "Redefining the New Deal: World War II and the Development of Social Provision in the United States," in *The Politics of Social Policy in the United States*, ed. Margaret Weir, Ann Shola Orloff, and Theda Skocpol (Princeton: Princeton University Press, 1988), 81–122.

94. Lewis Anthony Dexter, "Congressmen and the Making of Military Policy," in *New Perspectives on the House of Representatives*, ed. Richard L. Peabody and Nelson W. Polsby (Chicago: Rand McNally, 1963), 305–24.

95. A major scholarly debate has arisen concerning the politics and diplomacy behind American policy in the early years of the Cold War. For a review of the controversy, see Smith, "'Harry, We Hardly Know You': Revisionism, Politics and Diplomacy, 1945–1954, A Review Essay," *American Political Science Review* 70 (June 1967): 560–83.

96. Kenneth Boulding and Martin Pfaff, *Redistribution to the Rich and the Poor* (Belmont, Cal.: Wadsworth, 1972).

97. David Mayhew, *Party Loyalty among Congressmen* (New Haven: Yale University Press, 1966).

98. Ibid.

99. Nathan Glazer, "Towards an Imperial Judiciary?" *Public Interest* 4 (Fall 1975): 104–23; Rexford Tugwell and Thomas Cronin, *The Presidency Reappraised* (New York: Praeger, 1974).

100. Paul A. Weaver, "The New Journalism and the Old: Thoughts after Watergate," *Public Interest* 35 (Spring 1974): 67–88.

101. Karen Orren, "Standing to Sue: Interest Group Conflict in the Federal Courts," *American Political Science Review* 70 (September 1976): 723–41.

102. Morris Fiorina, *Congress: Keystone of the Washington Establishment* (New Haven: Yale University Press, 1977).

103. David Stockman, "The Social Pork Barrel," *Public Interest* 39 (Spring 1975): 3–30.

104. Walter Dean Burnham, "Party Systems and the Political Process," in *The American Party Systems*, ed. Burnham and Chambers, 277–307.

105. Geoffrey Hodgson, "The Establishment," *Foreign Policy* 10 (Spring 1973): 3–40.

106. Richard P. Nathan, *The Plot That Failed: Nixon and the Administrative Pres-*

idency (New York: John Wiley, 1975); Joel Aberbach and Bert Rockman, "Clashing Beliefs within the Executive Branch: The Nixon Administration Bureaucracy," *American Political Science Review* 70 (June 1979): 456–68.

Chapter 4

1. Gilbert Fite and Jim Reece, *An Economic History of the United States* (Boston: Houghton Mifflin, 1973), chap. 16.

2. Edward Kirkland, *Industry Comes of Age: Business, Labor, and Public Policy, 1860–1897* (New York: Holt, Rinehart and Winston, 1961), chap. 1.

3. Peter Gourevitch, "International Trade, Domestic Coalitions, and Liberty: Comparative Responses to the Crisis of 1873–1896," *Journal of Interdisciplinary History* 8 (1977): 281–313.

4. David Montgomery, *Workers' Control in America* (Cambridge: Cambridge University Press, 1979), 11f.

5. See, e.g., Alexander Saxton, *The Indispensable Enemy: Labor and the Anti-Chinese Movement in California* (Berkeley: University of California Press, 1971), 68–78.

6. Robert Ozanne, "Union-Management Relations: McCormick Harvesting Machine Company, 1862–1886," *Labor History* 4 (1963): 149.

7. Andrew Dawson, "The Paradox of Dynamic Technological Change and the Labor Aristocracy in the United States, 1880–1914," *Labor History* 20 (1979): 330–31.

8. Irwin Yellowitz, *Industrialization and the American Labor Movement* (Port Washington, N.Y.: Kennikat Press, 1977).

9. Herbert Gutman, *Work, Culture, and Society in Industrializing America* (New York: Alfred A. Knopf, 1976), chap. 1; and Alan Dawley and Paul Faler, "Working Class Culture and Politics in the Industrial Revolution: Sources of Loyalism and Rebellion," *Journal of Social History* 9 (1975): 466–80.

10. David Montgomery, "Gutman's Nineteenth-Century America," *Labor History* 19 (1978): 416–29.

11. Yellowitz, *Industrialization*, 65, 72.

12. David Montgomery, *Beyond Equality: Labor and the Radical Republicans, 1862–1872* (New York: Alfred A. Knopf, 1967), 238.

13. Montgomery, *Workers Control*, 13f.

14. David Gordon, "Capitalist Development and the History of American Cities," in *Marxism and the Metropolis*, ed. William Tabb and Larry Sawers (New York: Oxford University Press, 1978), 39.

15. Sam Bass Warner, *Streetcar Suburbs: The Process of Growth in Boston, 1870–1900* (Cambridge: Harvard University Press, 1962).

16. The estimates of the income of various strata of the working class in this and the following two paragraphs are drawn from David Montgomery, "Labor in the Industrial Era," in *The U.S. Department of Labor Bicentennial History of the American Worker*, ed. Richard B. Morris (Washington, D.C.: U.S. Government Printing Office, 1976), 117–18.

17. Jacob Riis, *How the Other Half Lives: Studies among the Tenements of New York* (New York: Dover, 1971).

18. Victor Rosewater, *Special Assessments* (New York: Columbia College, 1893).

19. Jane Addams, *Twenty Years at Hull-House* (New York: Macmillan, 1938), 286.

20. U.S. Department of Interior, Census Office, *Report on Vital and Social Statistics in the United States at the Eleventh Census, 1890. Part II: Vital Statistics of Cities of 100,000 Population and Upward* (Washington, D.C.: U.S. Government Printing Office, 1896), 392.

21. Stephen Thernstrom, *The Other Bostonians: Poverty and Progress in the American Metropolis, 1880–1970* (Cambridge: Harvard University Press, 1973), 40.

22. Susan J. Kleinberg, "Technology and Women's Work: The Lives of Working Class Women in Pittsburgh, 1870–1900," *Labor History* 17 (1976): 58–72.

23. Estelle Feinstein, *Stamford in the Gilded Age* (Stamford, Conn.: Stamford Historical Society, 1973).

24. Charles Loring Brace, *The Dangerous Classes of New York* (New York: Wynkoop and Hallenbeck, 1880).

25. Herbert Gutman, "The Workers Search for Power: Labor in the Gilded Age," in *The Gilded Age: A Reappraisal*, ed. H. Wayne Morgan (Syracuse: Syracuse University Press, 1963).

26. Stephen Skowronek, *Building a New American State: The Expansion of National Administrative Capacities, 1877–1920* (Cambridge: Cambridge University Press, 1982), chap. 2.

27. Walter Dean Burnham, "The Changing Shape of the American Political Universe," *American Political Science Review* 59 (1965): 7–28.

28. Morton Keller, *Affairs of State: Public Life in Late Nineteenth Century America* (Cambridge: Harvard University Press, Belknap Press, 1977), 241.

29. Walter Dean Burnham, "Theory and Voting Research: Some Reflections on Converse's Change in the American Electorate," *American Political Science Review* 68 (1974): 1002–23.

30. Dawley and Faler, "Working Class Culture," 474–75.

31. Gutman, *Work, Culture, and Society*, chap. 5.

32. Richard Jensen, *The Winning of the Midwest: Social and Political Conflict, 1886–1896* (Chicago: University of Chicago Press, 1971), chap. 3.

33. Keller, *Affairs of State*, chap. 1; Montgomery, *Beyond Equality*, chap. 3.

34. C. Vann Woodward, *Reunion and Reaction: The Compromise of 1877 and the End of Reconstruction* (Boston: Little, Brown, 1951).

35. Montgomery, *Beyond Equality*, 144; see also Henry Leonard, "Ethnic Cleavage and Industrial Conflict in Late Nineteenth Century America: The Cleveland Rolling Mill Company Strikes of 1882 and 1885," *Labor History* 20 (1979): 536.

36. Montgomery, *Beyond Equality*, 143.

37. See Alan Dawley, *Class and Community: The Industrial Revolution in Lynn* (Cambridge: Harvard University Press, 1976), 143–48, 175–84; John R. Commons, "American Shoemakers, 1648–1895," in his *Labor and Administration* (New York: Macmillan, 1913), 219–66.

38. David Montgomery, "Strikes in Nineteenth-Century America," *Social Science History* 4 (1980): 89.

39. Lloyd Ullman, *The Rise of the National Trade Union* (Cambridge: Harvard University Press, 1955); Montgomery, *Beyond Equality*, 151–76.

40. To be sure, strikers in the late nineteenth century could and often did rely upon extralegal sanctions to deal with free riders—that is, they used threats of ostracism and violence to intimidate strikebreakers. Union leaders, however, recognized that the use of violence was a very risky strategy for workers, because it enabled employers to call upon local authorities to intervene on their behalf to protect law and order. Thus, for example, the leaders of the Amalgamated Iron and Steel Workers during their strike against the Cleveland Rolling Mill Company in 1882 appointed marshals to patrol the streets near the mills to prevent such violence and urged their members to use only "honorable means" against strikebreakers and to "respectfully talk to them and convert them" (Leonard, "Ethnic Cleavage," 529).

41. Quoted in David Montgomery, "To Study the People: The American Working Class," *Labor History* 21 (1980): 502; Dawson, "Paradox of Dynamic Change," 345–48; James Q. Wilson, *Political Organizations* (Princeton: Princeton University Press, forthcoming).

42. Victor Greene, *The Slavic Community on Strike: Immigrant Labor in Pennsylvania Anthracite* (Notre Dame, Ind.: University of Notre Dame Press, 1968), 99.

43. David T. Burbank, *Reign of the Rabble: The St. Louis General Strike of 1877* (New York: Augustus M. Kelley, 1966), passim.

44. Adrian Cook, *The Armies of the Streets: The New York City Draft Riots of 1863* (Lexington: University Press of Kentucky, 1974), 56; Montgomery, *Beyond Equality*, 309–10; David Bruce, *1877: Year of Violence* (Indianapolis: Bobbs-Merrill, 1959), chaps. 6, 8.

45. Montgomery, *Beyond Equality*, chap. 8.

46. Burbank, *Reign of the Rabble*, frontispiece.

47. Montgomery, "Strikes," 95.

48. Burbank, *Reign of the Rabble*, 103.

49. Saxton, *Indispensable Enemy*, 118.

50. Montgomery, "Strikes," 96.

51. Joseph Rayback, *A History of American Labor* (New York: Free Press, 1966), 114, 160.

52. Michael Gordon, "The Labor Boycott in New York City, 1880–1886," *Labor History* 16 (1975): 184–229.

53. Saxton, *Indispensable Enemy*, 74.

54. Rayback, *History of American Labor*, 112; Montgomery, "Labor in the Industrial Era," 121f.

55. John Cumbler, "Labor, Capital, and Community: The Struggle for Power," *Labor History* 15 (1974): 401.

56. See, e.g., P. M. Arthur, "The Rise of Railroad Organization," in *The Labor Movement: The Problem of Today*, ed. George McNeill, quoted in Philip Taft, *Organized Labor in American History* (New York: Harper and Row, 1964), 58.

57. Montgomery, *Beyond Equality*, 135–39.

58. Rayback, *History of American Labor*, 125–26, 136–39, 169–73.

59. See, e.g., John R. Commons et al., eds., *A Documentary History of American Industrial Society* (Cleveland: Arthur H. Clark Co., 1910–1911), 10: 19–32.

60. See, e.g., Katherine Harvey, "The Knights of Labor in the Maryland Coal Fields, 1878–1882," *Labor History* 10 (1969): 555–83; James M. Morris, "The Cincinnati Shoemakers' Lockout of 1888," *Labor History* 13 (1972): 505–19.

61. Gordon, "Labor Boycott," 211–18.

62. Leon Fink, *Workingmen's Democracy: The Knights of Labor and American Politics* (Urbana: University of Illinois Press, 1983).

63. Saxton, *Indispensable Enemy*, 165. See also Richard Oestreicher, "Socialism and the Knights of Labor in Detroit, 1877–1886," *Labor History* 22 (1981): 5–30.

64. I used the term "labor reform movement," which I borrow from David Montgomery, rather than "working-class movement," because the latter term would prejudge the central question this chapter addresses—how America's distinctive working class came to be formed. The character and boundaries of the American working class were very much a matter of contention in the period 1861–86, and by no means can all the dispositions toward collective action exhibited by American workers or all the organizations they formed be classified as part of a common working-class movement.

65. Cf. Gerald Grob, *Workers and Utopia* (Evanston, Ill.: Northwestern University Press, 1961).

66. Stuart Kaufman, *Samuel Gompers and the Origins of the American Federation of Labor, 1848–1896* (Westport, Conn.: Greenwood Press, 1973), 168, 199.

67. Rayback, *History of American Labor*, 145.

68. Quoted in Taft, *Organized Labor*, 115.

69. Montgomery, *Beyond Equality*, 327–28.

70. Philip Foner, *The Great Labor Uprising of 1877* (New York: Monad Press, 1977), chap. 9.

71. Kaufman, *Samuel Gompers*, 58.

72. Saxton, *Indispensable Enemy*, chap. 8.

73. Samuel P. Huntington, *Political Order in Changing Societies* (New Haven: Yale University Press, 1968), 12–24.

74. Rayback, *History of American Labor*, 165.

75. Samuel Walker, "Varieties of Workingclass Experience: The Workingmen of Scranton, Pennsylvania, 1855–1885," in *American Workingclass Culture: Explorations in American Labor and Social History*, ed. Milton Cantor (Westport, Conn.: Greenwood Press, 1979), 366.

76. Montgomery, *Beyond Equality*, chap. 10.

77. Fink, "'Irrespective of Party,'" 329.

78. See, e.g., Harvey, "Knights of Labor," Morris, "Cincinnati Shoemakers' Lockout."

79. Kaufman, *Samuel Gompers*, chap. 6.

80. Gutman, *Work, Culture, and Society*, 193.

81. Saxton, *Indispensable Enemy*, chap. 10.

82. Rayback, *History of American Labor*, 136.

83. Fink, "'Irrespective of Party,'" 333.

84. Montgomery, "Labor in the Industrial Era," 128; Kenneth Kann, "The Knights of Labor and the Southern Black Worker," *Labor History* 18 (1977): 49–70.

85. Gutman; *Work, Culture, and Society*, chap. 3.

86. See, e.g., Mary Blewitt, "The Union of Sex and Craft in the Haverhill Shoe Strike of 1895," *Labor History* 20 (1979): 352–75.

87. Charlotte Erickson, *American Industry and the European Immigrant, 1860–1885* (Cambridge: Harvard University Press, 1957), chap. 6.

88. Ibid., chap. 9.

89. Walker, "Workingclass Experience," 368–69; Gerd Korman, *Industrialization, Immigrants, and Americanizers: The View from Milwaukee* (Madison: State Historical Society of Wisconsin, 1967), 51–53.

90. See, e.g., Greene, *Slavic Community*, chap. 5.

91. Saxton, *Indispensable Enemy*, 143–47; Donald L. McMurry, *Coxey's Army: A Study of the Industrial Army Movement of 1894* (Seattle: University of Washington Press, 1968).

92. Gutman, *Work, Culture, and Society*, chaps. 2, 4.

93. Walker, "Workingclass Experience" 369.

94. Montgomery, "Strikes," 89–100.

95. Ullman, *Rise of the National Trade Union*, chap. 2.

96. Benson Soffer, "A Theory of Trade Union Development: The Role of the 'Autonomous' Workman," *Labor History* 1 (1960): 141–63.

97. Dawson, "Paradox of Dynamic Change," 344–48.

98. Montgomery, *Beyond Equality*, 3–15.

99. Walker, "Workingclass Experience" 364.

100. Ibid., 366.

101. Montgomery, *Workers' Control*, chap. 1.

102. The classic example was the effort of Franklin B. Gowen to unite the railroads that owned the coal fields of eastern Pennsylvania against the anthracite miners' union, the Workingmen's Benevolent Association. See, e.g., Marvin W. Schlegel, *Ruler of the Reading: The Life of Franklin B. Gowen* (Harrisburg: Archives Publishing Company of Pennsylvania, 1947).

103. Montgomery, "Strikes," 94–98; for a discussion of such "moments of madness" in France, see Aristide Zolberg, "Moments of Madness," *Politics and Society* 2 (1972): 183–207.

104. Rayback, *History of American Labor*, 174.

105. Montgomery, *Beyond Equality*, 145.

106. Gutman, *Work, Culture, and Society*, 341.

107. Gutman, "The Workers' Search for Power," 40.

108. Greene, *Slavic Community*, chap. 5.

109. Wayne G. Broehl, *The Molly Maguires* (Cambridge: Harvard University Press, 1964).

110. Eric Foner, "Class, Ethnicity, and Radicalism in the Gilded Age: The Land League and Irish America," *Marxist Perspectives* 2 (1978): 6–55.

111. Walker, "Workingclass Experience" 368.

112. Burbank, *Reign of the Rabble*, 189.

113. Walker, "Workingclass Experience" 372–73.

114. Montgomery, *Beyond Equality*, 310; Herbert Gutman, "The Tompkins Square 'Riot' in New York City on January 13, 1874: A Re-examination of Its Causes and Its Aftermath," *Labor History* 6 (1965): 44–70; Saxton, *Indispensable Enemy*, 114–16. It is revealing that the railroad strike of 1877 involved uprisings of entire communities—including members of the middle class—in many small cities, whereas it precipitated sharp class divisions in larger cities. Contrast Rayback, *History*, 136, and Burbank, *Reign of the Rabble*, passim.

115. Foner, "Class, Ethnicity, and Radicalism," 22.

116. Gordon, "Capitalist Development," 39.

117. Quoted in Montgomery, *Beyond Equality*, 195.

118. Ibid., 421f.

119. Amy Bridges, "Becoming American: The Working Classes in the United States before the Civil War," in *Working-Class Formation*, ed. Ira Katznelson and Aristide Zolberg (Princeton: Princeton University Press, 1986), 157–96.

120. Montgomery, *Beyond Equality*, chap. 8.

121. Victoria Hattam, *Labor Visions and State Power: The Origins of Business Unionism in the United States* (Princeton: Princeton University Press, 1993).

122. Cook, *Armies of the Streets*, 108; Saxton, *Indispensable Enemy*, 115–16; Skowronek, *Building a New American State*, chap. 4.

123. Dawley and Faler, "Working Class Culture," 475–76.

124. Cf. Barrington Moore, *Social Origins of Dictatorship and Democracy* (Boston: Beacon Press, 1966), chap. 3.

125. Iver Bernstein, *The New York City Draft Riots* (New York: Oxford University Press, 1990).

126. Montgomery, *Beyond Equality*, ix.

127. Keller, *Affairs of State*, 561.

128. J. Morgan Kousser, *The Shaping of Southern Politics* (New Haven: Yale University Press, 1974), chap. 1.

129. C. Vann Woodward, *The Strange Career of Jim Crow* (New York: Oxford University Press, 1974), chaps. 1–2.

130. Skowronek, *Building a New American State*, chap. 4.

131. Robert Sharkey, *Money, Class, and Party: An Economic Study of Civil War and Reconstruction* (Baltimore: Johns Hopkins University Press, 1959).

132. See, e.g., Samuel McSeveney, *The Politics of Depression* (New York: Oxford University Press, 1972), chap. 1.

133. Burbank, *Reign of the Rabble*, 191.

134. Rayback, *History of American Labor*, 163.

135. Skowronek, *Building a New American State*, chap. 4.

136. Burbank, *Reign of the Rabble*, 190–91; Montgomery, "Strikes," 96–100.

137. Skowronek, *Building a New American State*, chap. 3.

138. Lawrence Goodwyn, *Democratic Promise: The Populist Moment in America* (New York: Oxford University Press, 1976).

139. Montgomery, *Beyond Equality*, chap. 11.

140. Rayback, *History of American Labor*, 157–58.

141. Ibid., 168.

142. Dawson, "Paradox of Dynamic Change," 245–46.

143. Harvey, "Knights of Labor," 570.

144. Martin H. Dodd, "Marlboro, Massachusetts, and the Shoeworkers' Strike of 1898–1899," *Labor History* 20 (1979): 376–97.

145. Ibid., 391.

146. See, e.g., Morris, "Cincinnati Shoemakers' Lockout," 505.

147. John Laslett, "Reflections on the Failure of Socialism in the American Federation of Labor," *Mississippi Valley Historical Review* 50 (1964): 634–51.

148. Fink, *Workingmens' Democracy*.

149. Kaufman, *Samuel Gompers*, 185–86.

150. Rayback, *History of American Labor*, 198.

151. Kaufman, *Samuel Gompers*, 181.

152. C. Vann Woodward, *Origins of the New South, 1877–1913* (Baton Rouge: Louisiana State University Press, 1951), chaps. 9–10.

153. Lawrence Goodwyn, "The Cooperative Commonwealth and Other Abstractions: In Search of a Democratic Premise," *Marxist Perspectives* (Summer 1980): 8–42.

154. Jensen, *Winning of the Midwest*, chap. 10; Goodwyn, *Democratic Promise*, chap. 9.

155. Kaufman, *Samuel Gompers*, 93–95, 98–99, 117–18.

156. Dodd, "Marlboro, Massachusetts," 377, 395.

157. Kaufman, *Samuel Gompers*, 175.

158. Ibid., 201.

159. Jama Lazerow, "'The Workingman's Hour': The 1886 Labor Uprising in Boston," *Labor History* 21 (1980): 212.

160. Quoted in ibid., 209.

161. Ibid., 209, 213.

162. Ibid., 212–13.

163. Ibid., 213.

164. Robert Hessen, "The Bethlehem Steel Strike of 1910," *Labor History* 15 (1974): 8.

165. Saxton, *Indispensable Enemy*, 270–78.

166. See, e.g., Geoffrey Blodgett, *The Gentle Reformers: Massachusetts Democrats in the Cleveland Era* (Cambridge: Harvard University Press, 1966), chap. 6; William A. Bullough, *The Blind Boss and His City: Christopher Augustine Buckley and Nineteenth-Century San Francisco* (Berkeley: University of California Press, 1979), chap. 4.

167. Rayback, *History of American Labor*, 170.

168. John W. Pratt, "Boss Tweed's Public Welfare Program," *New York Historical Society Quarterly* 45 (1961): 396–411; Erickson, *American Industry*, 95.

169. John I. Davenport, *The Election and Naturalization Frauds in New York City, 1860–1870* (New York: n.p., 1894); Richard Franklin Bensel, *Sectionalism and American Political Development, 1880–1980* (Madison: University of Wisconsin Press, 1984), 83.

170. Seymour Mandelbaum, *Boss Tweed's New York* (New York: John Wiley and Sons, 1965), 93.

171. Ibid., 92, 126; David Hammack, *Power and Society: Greater New York at the Turn of the Century* (New York: Russell Sage Foundation, 1982), chap. 5; Martin Shefter, *Political Crisis/Fiscal Crisis: The Collapse and Revival of New York City* (New York: Columbia University Press, 1992), 16–21.

172. Amy Bridges, *A City in the Republic: Antebellum New York and the Origins of Machine Politics* (Ithaca: Cornell University Press, 1987), chaps. 4, 7–8.

173. Mandelbaum, *Boss Tweed's New York*, chap. 7.

174. Martin Shefter, "The Emergence of the Political Machine: An Alternative View," in *Theoretical Perspectives in Urban Politics*, ed. Willis Hawley and Michael Lipsky (Englewood Cliffs, N.J.: Prentice-Hall, 1976).

175. Martin Shefter, "The Electoral Foundations of the Political Machine: New York City, 1884–1897," in *The History of American Electoral Behavior*, ed. Joel

Silbey, Allan G. Bogue, and William H. Flanigan (Princeton: Princeton University Press, 1978).

176. Foner, "Class, Ethnicity, and Radicalism," 54.

177. Jensen, *Winning of the Midwest*, chap. 6.

178. Montgomery, *Beyond Equality*, 447.

179. Walter Dean Burnham, *Critical Elections and the Mainsprings of American Politics* (New York: W. W. Norton, 1970), chap. 4.

180. Rayback, *History of American Labor*, 232, 240.

181. Montgomery, *Workers' Control*, 100–104; Graham Adams, *Age of Industrial Violence, 1910–1915* (New York: Columbia University Press, 1966), chaps. 4–8.

182. Montgomery, *Workers' Control*, chaps. 4–5.

183. For a comparative assessment of these constraints, see James Holt, "Trade Unionism in the British and U.S. Steel Industries, 1888–1912: A Comparative Study," *Labor History* 18 (1977): 5–35.

184. See, e.g., Montgomery, *Workers' Control*, chap. 7; Theda Skocpol and John Ikenberry, "The Political Formation of the American Welfare State in Historical and Comparative Perspective," *Comparative Social Research* 6 (1983): 87–148.

Chapter 5

1. See David Mayhew, *Placing Parties in American Politics* (Princeton: Princeton University Press, 1986), chaps. 2–6; Raymond Wolfinger, *The Politics of Progress* (Englewood Cliffs, N.J.: Prentice-Hall), 127–29.

2. In this chapter the "Northeast quadrant" (or simply the "Northeast") refers to the states east of the Mississippi River apart from those that joined the Confederacy, and the "West" refers to the states west of the Mississippi with the same exception. The structure of Southern politics is sufficiently distinctive that it will not be discussed.

3. It would be helpful to indicate how some terms that are central to my analysis will be used in this chapter. "Patronage" is a divisible benefit that politicians distribute to individual voters, campaign workers, or contributors in exchange for political support. An electoral strategy that relies on the distribution of patronage to individuals is to be distinguished from one that elicits support by promising to provide collective benefits to, or by appealing to the collective values of, some or all segments of the electorate in question. See James C. Scott, *Comparative Political Corruption* (Englewood Cliffs, N.J.: Prentice-Hall, 1972), 110. Parties that pursue a patronage strategy may or may not be extensively organized and highly centralized. In the analysis below, parties that rely heavily upon the distribution of patronage to mobilize support will be called "political machines" whether or not they command an elaborate and highly centralized electoral apparatus. See Wolfinger, *The Politics of Progress*, 99. Parties that command a broadly based and tightly centralized electoral apparatus will be referred to as "strong party organizations," however they go about amassing support. See Samuel P. Huntington, *Political Order in Changing Societies* (New Haven: Yale University Press, 1968), 408. Finally, it is useful to distinguish between "corruption" and "patronage": a corrupt politician exchanges public benefits for private monetary gain (that is, for cash that goes into the politician's own pocket). Patronage, by contrast, involves the exchange of public benefits for political support or

party advantage. See Huntington, *Political Order*, 70. Therefore it is possible for a city or state governed by a machine to have relatively moderate levels of corruption, and for a regime characterized by little patronage to be quite corrupt.

4. More precisely, the denominator used in calculating the percentages reported in the first column of Table 5.1 is the total population of all cities in the state with more than 10,000 inhabitants, and the numerator is the total population of all cities of this size that have nonpartisan local elections.

5. The most obvious alternative indicator for the extent to which the political parties in a state are patronage-oriented is the proportion of public employees in the state formally covered by a merit system. Numerous ways and means exist, however, for circumventing formal civil service rules, and consequently there are states (such as New Jersey) whose public employees are fully covered by a merit system and yet whose political parties are highly patronage-oriented, as well as states (such as Utah) without a formal merit system whose party politics are not especially patronage-oriented. I selected the proxy used in Table 5.1 because it yields a ranking of the states that better conforms to that provided by more qualitative assessments of the role patronage plays in party politics. See, for example, David Mayhew, *Placing Parties in American Politics*.

6. The mathematical statement of this is:

$$\text{Volatility} = \frac{\sum_{i=2}^{n} |X_i - X_{i-1}|}{n-1}$$

where X_i is the Republican percentage of the gubernatorial vote in election, i, X_{i-1} is the Republican vote in the preceding election, and n is the number of gubernatorial elections between 1876 and 1895.

7. The volatility of a state's Democratic vote is largely a function of the volatility of its Republican vote, and therefore the ranking of the states according to the former is similar to their ranking according to the latter. Thus, the volatility of the Democratic vote is not displayed in Table 5.1.

8. The methodology is based on E. Wood Kelley, "The Methodology of Hypothesis Testing" (unpublished manuscript, Cornell University, Department of Government).

9. Paul Peterson, *City Limits* (Chicago: University of Chicago Press, 1981).

10. Charles Maier, *Recasting Bourgeois Europe* (Princeton: Princeton University Press, 1975).

11. Morton Keller, *Affairs of State: Public Life in Late Nineteenth Century America* (Cambridge: Harvard University Press, Belknap Press, 1977), 561; David Montgomery, *Beyond Equality* (New York: Alfred A. Knopf, 1967), 386.

12. Stanley Hirshon, *Farewell to the Bloody Shirt: Northern Republicans and the Southern Negro* (Gloucester, Mass.: P. Smith, 1968).

13. C. Vann Woodward, *Reunion and Reaction* (Boston: Little, Brown, 1951).

14. Robert Sharkey, *Money, Class, and Party: An Economic Study of Civil War and Reconstruction* (Baltimore: Johns Hopkins University Press, 1959); Irwin Unger, *The Greenback Era* (Princeton: Princeton University Press, 1964).

15. David T. Burbank, *Reign of the Rabble: The St. Louis General Strike of 1877* (New York: Augustus M. Kelley, 1966), 191.

16. Stephen Skowronek, *Building a New American State: The Expansion of Na-*

tional Administrative Capacities, 1877–1920 (New York: Cambridge University Press, 1982), chap. 3.

17. H. Wayne Morgan, "The Republican Party, 1876–1896," in *History of U.S. Political Parties*, ed. Arthur M. Schlesinger, Jr. (New York: Chelsea House, 1970).

18. R. Hal Williams, "Dry Bones and Dead Language: The Democratic Party," in *The Gilded Age: A Reappraisal*, ed. H. Wayne Morgan (New York: Alfred A. Knopf, 1970).

19. Keller, *Affairs of State*, 252.

20. Richard Jensen, *The Winning of the Midwest* (Chicago: University of Chicago Press, 1971), chap. 3; Joseph Rayback, *A History of American Labor* (New York: Free Press, 1966), 125–26, 136–39, 169–73.

21. Quoted in Huntington, *Political Order*, 71.

22. Seymour Mandelbaum, *Boss Tweed's New York* (New York: John Wiley and Sons, 1965), chap. 6.

23. "Honest graft," as Plunkitt termed it, is the use by politicians of inside information and personal contacts to make money—as opposed to embezzlement and other forms of outright theft. See William Riordon, *Plunkitt of Tammany Hall* (New York: E. P. Dutton, 1963), 3–6.

24. M. R. Werner, *Tammany Hall* (Garden City, N.Y.: Doubleday, Doran, 1928), 276; Mandlebaum, *Boss Tweed's New York*, 92; David Hammack, *Power and Society: Greater New York at the Turn of the Century* (New York: Russell Sage Foundation, 1982), chap. 5.

25. Geoffrey Blodgett, *The Gentle Reformers: Massachusetts Democrats in the Cleveland Era* (Cambridge: Harvard University Press, 1966), chap. 6.

26. Walter Davenport, *Power and Glory: The Life of Boies Penrose* (New York: G. P. Putnam's Sons, 1931).

27. In contrast to youth gangs of recent decades, nineteenth century gangs were composed of adults, and they participated in some of the rougher forms of partisan combat in the antebellum city. See Amy Bridges, *A City in the Republic: New York and the Origins of Machine Politics* (Ithaca: Cornell University Press, 1987), chap. 4. On the labor movement's entry into city politics in the mid-1880s, see Eric Foner, *Politics and Ideology in the Age of the Civil War* (New York: Oxford University Press, 1980), chap. 8, and Martin Shefter, "The Electoral Foundations of the Political Machine: New York City, 1884–1897," in *The History of American Electoral Behavior*, ed. Joel Silbey, Allen G. Bogue, and William Flanigan (Princeton: Princeton University Press, 1978).

28. See Walter Dean Burnham, "The System of 1896: An Analysis," in *The Evolution of American Electoral Systems*, ed. Paul Kleppner (Westport, Conn.: Greenwood Press, 1981), 152–53, 168–69.

29. Gerald Nash, *The American West in the Twentieth Century* (Englewood Cliffs, N.J.: Prentice-Hall, 1973), 44–45.

30. Kenneth Owens, "Pattern and Structure in Western Territorial Politics," *Journal of Western History* 1 (1970): 373–90.

31. George Mowry, *The California Progressives* (Berkeley: University of California Press, 1951), 17.

32. Ward McAfee, "Local Interests and Railroad Regulations in California during the Granger Decade, " *Pacific Historical Review* 37 (1968): 51–66.

33. Mowry, *The California Progressives*, 70.

34. Michael Paul Rogin and John Shover, *Political Change in California* (Westport, Conn.: Greenwood Press, 1970), chap. 2.

35. The estimates reported in the first column of Tables 5.2 and 5.3, of the movement of eligible voters between parties and into the active electorate in successive elections, were derived from county-level election and census data by using weighted least squares regression to estimate the cell entries of an inter-election transition matrix. See this chapter's Methodological Appendix.

William Robinson questions the legitimacy of drawing inferences about the behavior of individuals from correlations of aggregate data, for example, reaching conclusions about the criminal behavior of Italian-Americans by correlating demographic data reported by census tracts with information on criminal offenses compiled by police precincts. See idem., "Ecological Correlations and the Behavior of Individuals," *American Sociological Review* 15 (June 1950): 351–57. But for a demonstration that with a well-specified model it is appropriate to use multiple regression analysis to draw inferences concerning individual behavior from aggregate data, see Leo A. Goodman, "Ecological Regression and the Behavior of Individuals," *American Sociological Review* 18 (December 1953): 663–64; and Eric Hanushek, John Jackson, and John Kain, "Model Specification, Use of Aggregate Data, and the Ecological Correlation Fallacy," *Political Methodology* 1 (1974): 89–107.

The proportion of a group's members voting for a particular candidate cannot be less than 0 or greater than 1.00, whereas the coefficients of linear regression equations can exceed these boundaries. Logit analysis enables one to avoid inadmissible estimates. See Eric A. Hanushek and John E. Jackson, *Statistical Methods for Social Scientists* (New York: Academic Press, 1977), 190–200.

36. The low R^2 of the 1914 Johnson equation cannot be attributed solely to the doubling of the eligible electorate with the enfranchisement of women. The coefficient of determination of an equation estimating the sources from which the Democratic gubernatorial candidate in 1914 drew his votes is fairly high: $R^2 = .656$.

37. Rogin and Shover, *Political Change in California*, chap. 2–3; Alexander Saxton, "San Francisco Labor and the Populist and Progressive Insurgencies," *Pacific Historical Review* 34 (1965): 421–38.

38. This was accomplished by estimating a separate slope dummy for the 1910 Abstainer variable in the counties of the Central Valley and the South. See Eric Hanushek and John E. Jackson, *Statistical Methods for Social Scientists* (New York: Academic Press, 1977) 106–8.

39. It should be noted that the procedures used in this chapter enable one to determine how much support a candidate received among abstainers in the election *immediately* prior to the one being analyzed. It is, of course, possible that some of these abstainers might have participated in yet earlier elections. One may reasonably assume, however, that such "in-and-outers" were less strongly attached to the norms and practices of the earlier regime than voters who consistently participated in elections. Such an assumption certainly is consistent with the findings of contemporary survey research.

40. John Owens, Edmond Costantini, and Louis Wechsler, *California Politics and Parties* (New York: Macmillan, 1970), 36.

41. Robert Burke, *Olson's New Deal for California* (Berkeley: University of California Press, 1953).

42. The 1904 gubernatorial election in New York coincided with a presidential

election, and hence is not perfectly comparable to the California gubernatorial election of 1906, which occurred in an off-year. The turnout in the off-year 1902 New York gubernatorial election, however, was 74.0 percent—still considerably higher than California's 1906 turnout of 49.8 percent. To eliminate the confounding effect of turnout fluctuations between presidential and nonpresidential years, the equations estimating the coefficients reported in Table 5.3 regressed elections upon one another in four-year intervals.

43. Richard L. McCormick, *From Realignment to Reform: Political Change in New York State, 1893–1910* (Ithaca: Cornell University Press, 1981), 221.

44. It should be noted that the coefficients of determination of the 1906 and 1908 Hughes equations are very high, and that the estimates of the regression coefficients are quite precise. That is, the equations reported in Table 5.3 explain from 80 to 93 percent of the variation of the Hughes vote across counties, and the standard errors of the regression coefficients estimating the sources from which Hughes drew his votes are in the range of 1 to 2 percent.

45. McCormick, *From Realignment to Reform*, chap. 8.

46. Jacob Friedman, *The Impeachment of Governor William Sulzer* (New York: Columbia University Press, 1939).

47. McCormick, *From Realignment to Reform*, chap. 9. On the other hand, the sharp conflicts and the roughly equal balance between upstate Republicans and downstate Democrats may have provided politicians in New York with a greater incentive to maintain the strength of the party organizations they had constructed in the nineteenth century than was the case in states whose politics were much less competitive after the realignment of 1896. I am grateful to Walter Dean Burnham for this observation.

48. Kristi Anderson, *The Creation of a Democratic Majority, 1928–1936* (Chicago: University of Chicago Press, 1979).

49. See Chapter 6.

50. Ira Katznelson, *City Trenches: Urban Politics and the Patterning of Class in the United States* (New York: Pantheon, 1981).

51. For an analysis of the factors that influenced the relationship between businessmen and politicians in cities, see Edward C. Banfield and James Q. Wilson, *City Politics* (Cambridge: Harvard University Press, 1963), chap. 18.

52. Theodore Lowi, *At the Pleasure of the Mayor* (New York: Free Press of Glencoe, 1964).

53. Benjamin Ginsberg, *The Consequences of Consent: Elections, Citizen Control, and Popular Acquiescence* (Reading, Mass.: Addison-Wesley, 1982).

54. See Walter Dean Burnham, "Political Immunization and Political Confessionalism: The United States and Weimar Germany," *Journal of Interdisciplinary History* 3 (1972): 1–30; Seymour Martin Lipset and Stein Rokkan, *Party Systems and Voter Alignments* (New York: Free Press, 1967), 50–52.

55. See, for example, James I. Lengle and Byron Shafer, "Primary Rules, Political Power, and Social Change," *American Political Science Review* 70 (March 1976): 37.

56. Adam Przeworski, "Institutionalization of Voting Patterns, or Is Mobilization the Source of Decay?" *American Political Science Review* 69 (1975): 49–67.

57. See Irwin Galen and Duane Meeter, "Building Voter Transition Models from Aggregate Data," *Midwest Journal of Political Science* 13 (1969): 545–56; A. G. Hawkes, "An Approach to the Analysis of Electoral Swing," *Journal of the Royal*

Statistical Society, Series A, 132 (1969): Part 1, 68–79; J. Morgan Kousser, "Ecological Regression and the Analysis of Past Politics," *Journal of Interdisciplinary History* 4 (1973): 237–62, W. L. Miller, "Measures of Electoral Change Using Aggregate Data," *Journal of the Royal Statistical Society*, Series A135 (1972): Part 1, 122–42.

58. At this point it should be evident that a simplifying assumption must be made if the analysis is to proceed. One must assume that everyone eligible to vote in election $t - 1$ is a member of E^t. Or more precisely—and more narrowly—one must assume that movements out of the electorate between elections $t - 1$ and t are unrelated to the variables in the regression equations below. This assumption is not unreasonable. The total number of voters who die or move away from a state in a four-year period is small relative to the total size of the electorate, and there is no reason to believe that there are significant differences in death rates or out-of-state movement rates among persons who vote for different parties or abstain from voting.

Chapter 6

I would like to thank the Jonathan Meigs Fund and Project Ezra of Cornell University, which provided financial support for this project. Timothy Byrnes, Michael Peck, Frank Rusciano, Helene Silverberg, and Lynne Wozniak were able research assistants. Karen Orren's and Stephen Skowronek's extensive comments on a draft of this chapter were invaluable.

1. Samuel P. Huntington, *American Politics: The Promise of Disharmony* (Cambridge: Harvard University Press, 1981), 123.

2. For example, with regard to the Irish during the Jacksonian and antebellum periods, see David Montgomery, "The Shuttle and the Cross: Weavers and Artisans in the Kensington Riots of 1844," *Journal of Social History* 5 (1972): 411–46; Amy Bridges, *A City in the Republic: Antebellum New York and the Origins of Machine Politics* (New York: Cambridge University Press, 1984), chap. 6.

3. Richard Ellis, *The Jeffersonian Crisis: Courts and Politics in the Young Republic* (New York: Oxford University Press, 1971), 278.

4. Hanna F. Pitkin, *The Concept of Representation* (Berkeley: University of California Press, 1967).

5. Samuel P. Huntington, *Political Order in Changing Societies* (New Haven: Yale University Press, 1968), chap. 1.

6. Each of the five counties comprising Greater New York has a separate Democratic party organization. For most of the period 1900–1932, the leader of the Manhattan Democratic organization (Tammany Hall) was recognized as *primus inter pares* among Democratic machine politicians in the city. See, for example, *New York Times*, October 7, 1932, p. 4.

7. Thomas McLean Henderson, *Tammany Hall and the New Immigrants: The Progressive Years* (New York: Arno Press, 1976), chap. 1.

8. *New York Times*, April 24, 1929, p. 1.

9. Joseph McGoldrick, "The Board of Estimate and Apportionment of New York City," *National Municipal Review*, supplement 18 (May 1932): 5; Norman Adler, "Ethnics in Politics: Access to Office in New York City" (Ph.D. diss., University of Wisconsin, 1971), table 7.5.

10. Adler, "Ethnics in Politics," table 7.5; Theodore Lowi, *At the Pleasure of the Mayor* (New York: Free Press of Glencoe, 1964), fig. 8.2; *New York Times*, April 24, 1929, p. 1.

11. Arthur Mann, *La Guardia Comes to Power, 1933* (Philadelphia: J. B. Lippincott Co., 1965), chap. 3.

12. Martin Shefter, "Economic Crises, Social Coalitions, and Political Institutions: New York City's Little New Deal" (paper delivered at the Annual Meeting of the American Political Science Association, New York City, September 1981), 9–13.

13. Table 6.1 compares the mayoral elections of 1925 and 1933 because both were held independently of presidential elections, and in 1925 the Republican mayoral candidate was WASP businessman.

An accessible survey of some of the statistical techniques employed in this chapter can be found in the methodological appendix of Kenneth Finegold's study of municipal reform politics during the Progressive Era. See Kenneth Finegold, *Experts and Politicians: Progressive Reform Politics in New York, Cleveland, and Chicago* (Princeton: Princeton University Press, forthcoming), Appendix. For a more technical discussion, which requires some knowledge of mathematics, see Christopher H. Achen and W. Phillips Shively, *Cross-Level Inference* (Chicago: University of Chicago Press, 1994), chap. 2.

The analysis of historical election data with ecological regression is discussed in Gudmund I. Iverson, "Group Data and Individual Behavior," in *Analyzing Electoral History*, ed. Jerome M. Clubb, William H. Flanigan, and Nancy H. Zingale (Beverly Hills, Calif.: Sage Publishers, 1981).

For an exposition of how log-linear regression equations can be used to analyze historical electoral demographic data, see the extremely lucid discussion of J. Morgan Kousser, "Making Separate Equal: Integration of Black and White School Funds in Kentucky," *Journal of Interdisciplinary History* 10 (Winter 1980): 399–428. In compiling ethnicity data, I equated the foreign-born Jewish population with persons born in Russia, Poland, Austria, and Romania. On the preponderance of Yiddish-speakers among New Yorkers born in these countries, see Walter Laidlaw, ed., *Statistical Sources for Demographic Studies of New York, 1920* (New York: New York City 1920 Census Committee, 1922), xxiv–xxv.

14. Charles Garrett, *The La Guardia Years: Machine and Reform Politics in New York City* (New Brunswick, N.J.: Rutgers University Press, 1961), chap. 11; Lowi, *At the Pleasure of the Mayor*, fig. 8.2.

15. Kenneth Waltzer, "The American Labor Party: Third-Party Politics in New Deal—Cold War New York, 1936–1954" (Ph.D. diss., Harvard University, 1977), 81–161.

16. Marvin Weinbaum, "A Minority's Survival: The Republican Party of New York County, 1897–1960" (Ph.D. diss., Columbia University, 1965), 234.

17. New York State Crime Commission, *Public Hearing No. 4*, 1952, vol. 1, 114.

18. See pp. 7–9 above for a general analysis of the conditions encouraging political parties to collude with one another.

19. It is true that during the period 1934–42 the state government and City Hall nominally had been under the control of different parties: Governor Herbert Lehman was a Democrat and Mayor La Guardia was a Republican. La Guardia, however, had at most an arm's-length relationship with the Republican party, and hence the

GOP was not able to take advantage of his presence in City Hall to enter into a bargaining relationship with the Democrats.

20. To be sure, external developments also contributed to the ALP's demise. The electorate's growing hostility to the Soviet Union during the late 1940s and early 1950s could not but take its toll on a party that regularly defended Soviet foreign policy. However, changes in voter sentiment were not sufficient to destroy the ALP in all districts in the city, and therefore Democratic and Republican leaders implemented the extraordinary measures discussed in this section to ensure its destruction.

21. Though committed and hardworking, the ALP's leaders and cadres were doctrinaire, and this made it difficult for them to respond effectively to the efforts of the Democrats and Republicans to destroy their party. For example, when confronted with the charge of being subservient to Moscow, the ALP accused its opponents of red-baiting, while staunchly continuing to defend Soviet foreign policy. (A more institution-serving response would probably have been to ignore foreign policy and focus the party's attention on domestic issues.) The ALP's behavior reflected the increasingly influential role that members of the Communist party came to play in the ALP during the 1940s, as well as the principled stance of the party's noncommunist members, who evidently attached a higher priority to proclaiming their programmatic commitments than to the party's survival. For a general analysis of the maintenance problems of ideological parties, see James Q. Wilson, *Political Organizations* (Princeton: Princeton University Press, forthcoming), chap. 6.

22. Maurice Isserman, *Which Side Were You On? The American Communist Party during the Second World War* (Middletown, Conn.: Wesleyan University Press, 1982), 210.

23. Robert Carter, "Pressure from the Left: The American Labor Party, 1936–1954" (Ph.D. diss., Syracuse University, 1965), 423–24.

24. Kenneth Waltzer, "The Party and the Polling Place: American Communism and the American Labor Party in the 1930s," *Radical History Review* 23 (Spring 1980): 119.

25. David Shannon, *The Decline of American Communism: A History of the Communist Party of the United States since 1945* (New York: Harcourt, Brace, 1959), 157–58.

26. *New York Times*, September 23, 1946, p. 12, Harvey Klehr, *The Heyday of American Communism: The Depression Decade* (New York: Basic Books, 1984), 268.

27. Alan Schaffer, *Vito Marcantonio: Radical in Congress* (Syracuse: Syracuse University Press, 1966), 191–98.

28. William Spinrad, "New Yorkers Cast Their Ballots" (Ph.D. diss., Columbia University, 1955), 109.

29. Isserman, *Which Side Were You On?*, 120.

30. Bella Dodd, *School of Darkness* (New York: P. J. Kennedy, 1954), 143–44.

31. Simon Gerson, *Pete* (New York: International Publishers, 1976), 100ff.

32. Mark Naison, *Communists in Harlem during the Depression* (Urbana: University of Illinois Press, 1983), 312–13.

33. L. H. Whittenmore, *The Man Who Ran the Subways* (New York: Holt, Rinehart and Winston, 1968).

34. Warren Moscow, *The Last of the Big-Time Bosses* (New York: Stein and Day, 1971), 69.

35. Schaffer, *Vito Marcantonio*, 189, 196, 208.

36. Gerson, *Pete*, 168.

37. Charles Van Devander, *The Big Bosses* (n.p.: Howell, Soskin, 1944), chap. 1.

38. Moscow, *Last of the Big-Time Bosses*, 54.

39. The smaller figure was given in public testimony by Costello himself; the larger figure is given by Warren Moscow, citing as his source Bert Stand, who at the time was secretary of Tammany Hall. See *New York Times*, October 26, 1943, p. 1; Moscow, *Last of the Big-Time Bosses*, 56.

40. Moscow, *Last of the Big-Time Bosses*, 58.

41. *New York Times*, October 30, 1950, p. 1.

42. *New York Times*, November 26, 1950, sect. 4, p. 2.

43. *New York Times*, May 6, 1951, sect. 4, p. 2; New York State Crime Commission, *Report to the Governor, the Attorney General, and the Legislature of the State of New York*, 1953, p. 5.

44. *New York Times*, September 12, 1953, p. 10, October 1, 1953, p. 26.

45. Edwin Lewison, *Black Politics in New York City* (New York: Twayne Publishers, 1974), 64, 68.

46. Lewison, *Black Politics in New York City*, 69, 89.

47. George Furniss, "The Political Assimilation of Negroes in New York City" (Ph.D. diss., Columbia University, 1969), chap. 9.

48. Weinbaum, "A Minority's Survival," 142.

49. Diane Ravitch, *The Great School Wars: New York City, 1805–1973* (New York: Basic Books, 1974), 256.

50. Charles V. Hamilton, *Adam Clayton Powell, Jr.: The Political Biography of an American Dilemma* (New York: Atheneum, 1991).

51. Naison, *Communists in Harlem*, 267–68.

52. Lewison, *Black Politics in New York City*, 77–78.

53. Carter, "American Labor Party," 407.

54. Cf. James Q. Wilson, *Negro Politics: The Search for Leadership* (New York: Free Press, 1960).

55. See, e.g., Benjamin Ginsberg, *The Consequences of Consent* (Reading, Mass.: Addison-Wesley, 1982); Huntington, *Political Order in Changing Societies*, chap. 7; Adam Przeworski, "Institutionalization of Voting Patterns, or Is Mobilization the Source of Decay?" *American Political Science Review* 69 (March 1975): 49–67; see also Chapter 5.

Chapter 7

1. This and the next three sections of this chapter draw heavily on Martin Shefter, "New York's Fiscal Crisis, Municipal Corruption, and the Koch Phenomenon," in *Political Crisis/Fiscal Crisis: The Collapse and Revival of New York City* (New York: Columbia University Press, 1992), xix–xxv.

2. John Hull Mollenkopf, *A Phoenix in the Ashes: The Rise and Fall of the Koch Coalition in New York City Politics* (Princeton: Princeton University Press, 1992), 160.

3. Todd Swanstrom, *The Crisis of Growth Politics: Cleveland, Kucinich, and the Challenge of Urban Populism* (Philadelphia: Temple University Press, 1985).

4. As serious as the crimes attributed to various New York machine politicians in

the 1980s may have been, it is worth putting the sums they are charged with having stolen into perspective. During the years 1978–85, these politicians allegedly collected some $3 million in bribes. Over this same period, New York City and New York State limited public spending by permitting the growth of welfare grants to lag behind increases in the cost of living, resulting in a collective loss of approximately $2 billion in purchasing power by close to one million of the city's poorest residents. It can be argued in defense of these cuts that when the fiscal crisis erupted New York's welfare grants were out of line with those of other cities, and the municipal government had few alternatives to reducing these expenditures. But this issue received scant attention in the press relative to the scandal, despite the vastly larger number of people and sums of money involved.

5. Benjamin Ginsberg, Walter Mebane, and Martin Shefter, "The Disjunction between Political Conflict and Electoral Mobilization in the Contemporary United States," paper delivered at the Annual Meeting of the American Political Science Association, Washington, D.C., September 1993.

6. This section draws on Shefter, *Political Crisis/Fiscal Crisis*, xi–xv.

7. Mollenkopf, *Phoenix in the Ashes*, 178–79.

Author Index

DATE DUE

DEMCO 38-297